Market Dynamics and Strategies in a Post-Crisis World

Navigating a World in Flux

World Scientific Series on New Paradigms in Sustainable Business Economics in Emerging Markets

Series Editor: Aviral Kumar Tiwari
(Indian Institute of Management Bodh Gaya, India)

Published

Vol. 1 *Market Dynamics and Strategies in a Post-Crisis World: Navigating a World in Flux*
edited by Vinita S Sahay, Chandan Parsad, Raveesh Krishnankutty and Aviral Kumar Tiwari

Market Dynamics and Strategies in a Post-Crisis World
Navigating a World in Flux

editors

Vinita S Sahay
Chandan Parsad
Raveesh Krishnankutty
Aviral Kumar Tiwari

Indian Institute of Management Bodh Gaya, India

NEW JERSEY · LONDON · SINGAPORE · BEIJING · SHANGHAI · HONG KONG · TAIPEI · CHENNAI · TOKYO

Published by

World Scientific Publishing Co. Pte. Ltd.
5 Toh Tuck Link, Singapore 596224
USA office: 27 Warren Street, Suite 401-402, Hackensack, NJ 07601
UK office: 57 Shelton Street, Covent Garden, London WC2H 9HE

Library of Congress Cataloging-in-Publication Data
Names: Sahay, Vinita S, editor. | Parsad, Chandan, editor. |
  Krishnankutty, Raveesh, editor. | Tiwari, Aviral Kumar, editor.
Title: Market dynamics and strategies in a post-crisis world : navigating a world in flux /
  editors, Vinita S Sahay, Chandan Parsad, Raveesh Krishnankutty,
  Aviral Kumar Tiwari, Indian Institute of Management Bodh Gaya, India.
Description: Hackensack, NJ : World Scientific, [2025] | Series: World Scientific series on
  new paradigms in sustainable business economics in emerging markets ; volume 1 |
  Includes bibliographical references and index.
Identifiers: LCCN 2024018806 | ISBN 9789811292095 (hardcover) |
  ISBN 9789811292101 (ebook for institutions) | ISBN 9789811292118 (ebook for individuals)
Subjects: LCSH: Organizational effectiveness. | Industrial management.
Classification: LCC HD58.9 .M3743 2025 | DDC 658.4/012--dc23/eng/20240514
LC record available at https://lccn.loc.gov/2024018806

British Library Cataloguing-in-Publication Data
A catalogue record for this book is available from the British Library.

Copyright © 2025 by World Scientific Publishing Co. Pte. Ltd.

All rights reserved. This book, or parts thereof, may not be reproduced in any form or by any means, electronic or mechanical, including photocopying, recording or any information storage and retrieval system now known or to be invented, without written permission from the publisher.

For photocopying of material in this volume, please pay a copying fee through the Copyright Clearance Center, Inc., 222 Rosewood Drive, Danvers, MA 01923, USA. In this case permission to photocopy is not required from the publisher.

For any available supplementary material, please visit
https://www.worldscientific.com/worldscibooks/10.1142/13811#t=suppl

Desk Editors: Aanand Jayaraman/Nicole Ong

Typeset by Stallion Press
Email: enquiries@stallionpress.com

© 2025 World Scientific Publishing Company
https://doi.org/10.1142/9789811292101_fmatter

Preface

In the wake of the unprecedented global upheaval caused by the COVID-19 pandemic, the dynamics of global markets have undergone a profound transformation. Understanding these shifts and crafting strategic responses have become not only pertinent but also imperative.

Market Dynamics and Strategies in a Post-Crisis World serves as a beacon, illuminating the intricate interplay of consumer behaviour, digital migration, and sectoral resilience across diverse global contexts in the aftermath of the pandemic.

This volume presents a comprehensive exploration of the impacts of COVID-19 on market dynamics. The chapters within this compendium delve into various facets of this transformative period. For instance, empirical analyses scrutinize how consumer behaviours in the fast-moving consumer goods sector have evolved amidst uncertainties and changing priorities. Insights into digital transformation in healthcare highlight its pivotal role in enhancing accessibility and resilience during times of crisis. Similarly, studies on the hospitality and tourism sectors underscore the adaptive strategies needed to recover and thrive in a post-pandemic landscape.

Furthermore, the book explores the profound shifts in online shopping behaviours, reflecting a broader digital migration accelerated by the crisis. It also examines the role of digital marketing and social media in shaping consumer perceptions and preferences during and after the pandemic. Chapters dedicated to green marketing and sustainable development underscore the growing importance of environmental considerations in shaping post-crisis market strategies.

We extend our sincere gratitude to World Scientific Publishing Co Pte Ltd for their meticulous attention to detail and unwavering support throughout the production of this book. Their commitment has been instrumental in bringing this scholarly endeavour to fruition.

As you delve into the following pages, may this volume serve as a guiding compass for scholars, practitioners, and policymakers navigating a world forever changed by crisis. Together, let us utilize these insights to forge resilient strategies and pave the way towards a sustainable and prosperous future.

About the Editors

Vinita Sahay is a professor and the director at the Indian Institute of Management Bodh Gaya (IIM Bodh Gaya), India, in the area of marketing management. Prior to joining IIM Bodh Gaya, she was associated with the Indian Institute of Management Raipur and the Institute of Management Technology (IMT), Ghaziabad, as a professor in the area of marketing management. Her areas of interest are service marketing, retail management, customer value & satisfaction, and trust & relationship in supply chain. She has published research papers in various journals published by Emerald Group Publishing Limited, IGI Global Publishing, and MacMillan India.

She has worked on many projects in collaboration with various governments and governmental bodies, including the Government of Chhattisgarh on the Sahakari Dugdh Utpadak Mahasang project, the Chhattisgarh State Cooperative Marketing Federation Ltd., the Airport Authority of India, the Ministry of Human Resource Development on TEQIP, and the Ministry of Tourism of the Government of Bihar. She has also served as the chairperson of conference sessions and as the facilitator of corporate training and faculty development programmes.

Moreover, she was honoured with the Business School Affair Award and the Dewang Mehta B-School Award for the Best Teacher in Selling Management.

Chandan Parsad is an assistant professor in the Marketing Department of IIM Bodh Gaya, India. Dr. Parsad received his title of fellow (doctorate) from the Indian Institute of Management Raipur. Prior to this, he worked as a faculty member at the Rajagiri Business School in Kochi, Kerala. He holds an MBA in the area of software enterprise management from C-DAC (Ministry of IT), Noida, and a bachelors in instrumentation engineering from Maharishi Dayanand University, Rohtak. Prior to completing his PhD, he worked as an engineer in the steel manufacturing industry. During his doctoral work, he investigated how different personalities of consumers impact their impulsive buying nature. He has published more than 50 research papers and case studies.

He has worked on projects for the World Bank and the Ministry of Tourism of the Government of Bihar. He has also chaired conference sessions and conducted corporate training as well as faculty development programs. The major interest areas of his current teaching, research, and practice include marketing, business research, mindful marketing, marketing analytics, and sales and distribution.

Raveesh Krishnankutty is an assistant professor in the Finance and Accounting Department of IIM Bodh Gaya, India. He received his PhD and MPhil from ICFAI University in Tripura. Before joining IIM Bodh Gaya, he worked as an assistant professor at ICFAI Business School Hyderabad and Rajagiri Business School. His research interests lie in corporate finance and financial economics banking. He has published several research papers in national and international journals and has also presented his research at national and international conferences.

Aviral Kumar Tiwari is an associate professor and chairperson, research and publications, at the IIM Bodh Gaya, India. He also serves as a CEENRG research fellow at the Department of Land Economy, University of Cambridge, UK, and as a research fellow at the Laboratoire d'Economie d'Orléans (LEO — CNRS), University of Orleans, France, and at the University of Economics Ho Chi Minh City, Vietnam. Prior to joining IIM Bodh Gaya, he worked as an associate professor at Rajagiri Business School (RBS), India, and at Montpellier Business School (MBS), Montpellier, France, from where he received his postdoc as well. He has published widely in peer-reviewed international journals and contributed more than 100 ABDC-A and A* research papers so far. He is the only economist from India included in the career ranking of the world's top 2% scientists list of 2021 published by Stanford University. He is ranked in the first position in India as a researcher by IDEAS. He is one of the most highly cited researchers in 2020, according to Clarivate™ of the Web of

Science™. He is one of the recipients of the M. J. Manohar Rao Award (for young econometrician) for 2014 from the Indian Econometric Society. He is a life member of the Indian Economic Association, India, and a member of several other international associations, such as the International Association for Energy Economics (IAEE), USA, the Association for Comparative Economic Studies, USA, and the Western Economic Association International, USA. He holds different editorial positions in more than 10 journals of international repute (including *ABDC*-, *Scopus*-, and *ABS*-indexed journals).

Contents

Preface		v
About the Editors		vii
Chapter 1	COVID-19 Panic Buying Behaviour: Individual Differences among Consumers *Nimmy Lovely George and M. Rakesh Krishnan*	1
Chapter 2	Purchase Intention and Satisfaction of FMCG Shoppers: Empirical Analysis from a Post-COVID-19 Outlook *Shaply Abdul Kareem, D. Yuvaraj, S. Aswini Priya, Pulidindi Venugopal, and S. Anjani Devi*	23
Chapter 3	Predicting Visit Intention after COVID-19 Using Theory of Planned Behaviour *N. Muhammed Sajid, Meera Peethambaran, and K. Jiyas*	41
Chapter 4	A Study on Consumer Behaviour towards Digital Food App Services in India *Kritika Mahensaria and Supriyo Patra*	55
Chapter 5	Consumers' Online Shopping Behaviour: A Post-COVID-19 Analysis in India *Mallika Srivastava, Mudita Sinha, and Biranchi Narayan Swar*	67

Chapter 6	Substantial Changes in Consumer Buying Behaviour in the Post-COVID-19 World *Tania Chauhan*	73
Chapter 7	A Study of Disruptions in Consumer Behaviour and Marketing Strategies in Response to the Pandemic in India *Reetika Jain*	79
Chapter 8	A Narrative of Needs Assessment through Psychobiography of COVID-19 Patient by Observing Moment of Truth *Jyoti and Sarvesh Kumar*	87
Chapter 9	Digital Migration and Survival of Fashion Industry Post New Normal *Jahanvi and Meenakshi Sharma*	97
Chapter 10	Rural Healthcare: Recovery and Resilience through Digital Health Entrepreneurial Foresight in Developing Countries Post-COVID-19 *Rahul Khandelwal*	113
Chapter 11	Impact of Social Media during COVID-19 Using Binary Logistic Model *Rachna Bansal, Prabhat Mittal, and Priti Verma*	129
Chapter 12	Digital Transformation for Recovery, Resilience, and Adaptation Post-COVID-19 in India *G. V. Sobha and P. Sridevi*	139
Chapter 13	COVID-19: A Blessing in Disguise for Social Commerce in India *Dawn Jose and E. Sulaiman Ebrahimkunju*	163
Chapter 14	Purchasing Criteria of Wealthy Single Urbanites with Respect to Mobile Phone Accessories: A Post-COVID-19 Study *Harshvardhan N. Bhavsar*	173

Chapter 15	Indian Teens' Buying Behaviour towards E-Commerce *Ruchika Dawar, Sonika Siwach, and Sapna Sehrawat*	183
Chapter 16	Revamping Hospitality and Tourism: A Review of Service Quality Perceptions Post-COVID-19 *Chahat Jain, Pallavi (Joshi) Kapooria, and Saurabh Singh*	201
Chapter 17	Sustainable Development through Green Marketing: Application and Its Environmental Importance *Pavnesh Kumar and Ravindra Kumar*	213
Chapter 18	Effect of Subjective and Objective Knowledge on Consumers' Willingness to Purchase Health Insurance during COVID-19 Pandemic *Tanuj Mathur*	227
Chapter 19	Modelling Challenges Faced by the Retail Sector in the COVID-19 Outbreak *Subhodeep Mukherjee, Chittipaka Venkataiah, Manish Mohan Baral, and Sharad Chandra Srivastava*	239
Chapter 20	Pioneering Digital Marketing: How Service Sector Companies in Bangladesh are Re-redesigning Their Marketing Strengths *Preeti Mehra and Tanvirul Islam Mahim*	259
Chapter 21	Enhancing Resilience in Times of COVID-19 Crisis: Evidence from Indian Hotel Industry *Sukhpreet Kaur, Deepa Guleria, and Gurvinder Kaur*	275
Chapter 22	Clustering and Topic Modelling of Business Research Trends during COVID-19 *Rohit Bhuvaneshwar Mishra and Hongbing Jiang*	287

Chapter 23	Resilience of Street Food Vendors of Lucknow during COVID-19 Pandemic *Shatrughna Ojha, Vandana Dubey, and Claire Buisson*	315
Chapter 24	Exploring the Impact of Organizational Culture on Employee Performance *Saloni Devi and Garima Kohli*	331
Chapter 25	Mindfulness Practices and Their Essentiality for Teachers *Pooja Deshmukh*	353
Chapter 26	Women Faculty and Increased Working Hours due to COVID-19 in Higher Educational Institutions: An Empirical Analysis *Rizwana Rafiq and Mir Insha Farooq*	361
Chapter 27	Analyzing Business and Functional Areas of 'Didi Ki Rasoi': A JEEViKA Initiative *Mrinal Keshri and Yash Kumar*	369
Chapter 28	A Digital Transformation Toolkit to Formulate CXO Office Strategy Overcoming Disruptions, Including the COVID-19 Pandemic *Ashutosh Dubey and Arif Khan*	411
Chapter 29	Impact of Online Reputation on Neobank Adoption during COVID-19 *Puneett Bhatnagr, Anupama Rajesh, and Richa Misra*	425
Chapter 30	Technological Developments and Innovations to Drive the Post-COVID-19 World Economy *Shyam Sundar Panigrahi*	451
Chapter 31	Agri-Tech Start-ups in India: Present Status and Future Scope in Reference to COVID-19 *Supriya Singh and Alka Lalhall*	461

Index 479

Chapter 1

COVID-19 Panic Buying Behaviour: Individual Differences among Consumers

Nimmy Lovely George[*,‡] and M. Rakesh Krishnan[†,§]

[*]*Department of Management Studies, Rajagiri College of Social Sciences, Kochi, Kerala, India*

[†]*School of Management, Cochin University of Science and Technology, Kochi, Kerala, India*

[‡]*nimmylovelygeorge@gmail.com*

[§]*mrakeshkrishnan@gmail.com*

Abstract

The global economy has been greatly affected following the origin of the COVID-19 pandemic in December 2019. Not only did it trigger a massive global health and economic crisis, but it also triggered uncommon human habits, such as panic buying, across the globe. When negative emotions such as anxiety, panic, and feelings of confusion impair behaviour, panic buying happens, causing people to buy more items than normal. This chapter attempts to demonstrate how the purchasing activity of individuals is influenced by panic buying behaviour. A Google Forms questionnaire for the collection of data for the research was used to perform an online survey. The study used the panic buying scale introduced by Lins and Aquino (2020b) and the individual difference scale created by Rick *et al.* (2008) to collect data on the panic buying behaviour and individual differences of respondents. The panic buying was measured based on demographic information (gender, age, marital status, income, occupation, and location). An independent sample *t*-test was conducted to identify panic buying behaviour based on demographic factors. Correlation and ANOVA were performed to find the relationship between panic buying and the individual differences of consumers. The findings showed a positive correlation, and the results of the analysis indicate that spendthrifts exhibit a greater panic buying behaviour. The condition of panic buying induces uncertainty in the minds of customers who are likely to purchase more goods. In a panic buying situation, the negative sense of pain of paying reduces. The expectation and apprehension of an increase in price or a lack of stocks produce a condition that helps minimize the pain of paying for essential goods. As the pain of payment reduces, individuals indulge in more acquisitions of essential goods.

Keywords: Panic buying, spending behaviour, spendthrift consumer, tightwad consumer, unconflicted consumer, pain of paying.

Introduction

The COVID-19 pandemic had its origins in Wuhan, a city in China, in late 2019. The virus has currently spread to more than 111 million people, infecting over 220 countries, resulting in a death count above two million as of February 2021 (Worldometer, 2021). The pandemic has influenced everyday life and is hindering the worldwide economy (Outlook India Magazine, 2020). A significant number of people, including those specifically infected by the outbreak and others, have been affected by this pandemic, unable to lead their normal lives. The spread of the virus has been exponential in most countries. Based on the recommendations from scientific researchers and the trends of the virus spread, many countries have brought in very strict rules, such as lockdowns of various places and even the entire country for a certain period (Alvarez *et al.*, 2020; Lancet, 2020; Lau *et al.*, 2020).

Owing to the uncertainty of its effects on everyday life, the COVID-19 pandemic has triggered anxiety and panic. Many researchers predict that the pandemic can also affect people's mental well-being and health (Cullen *et al.*, 2020; Kluge, 2020; Walton *et al.*, 2020). When there is some sort of uncertainty or threat, it is natural for one to feel stressed, frightened, and worried. The same applies to the COVID-19 pandemic. Apart from the concerns about when the pandemic will end, there are restrictions on movement and activities (Moore *et al.*, 2020; Obi *et al.*, 2020). We need to look after both our mental and physical well-being because of the changes that have affected the various aspects of our lives, such as no physical contact with friends and family, online classes for students, and managing kids as well as working from home for parents (Armitage and Nellums, 2020; Cluver *et al.*, 2020; Wang *et al.*, 2020).

The purchasing habit is also affected due to the outbreak of COVID-19. The unpredictable lockdown has affected the daily lives of people and created panic due to the uncertain situation. Large-scale, extreme catastrophies (e.g., floods) or pandemics, such as COVID-19, are often the causes of panic buying. Consumers prefer to shop for necessities and other essential goods that they perceive will help them support themselves during the crisis period in the expectation of product shortages (Yoon *et al.*, 2018). Some may be scared of a large price rise caused by the devastation (Su, 2010). Previous studies have attempted to explain the origins and actions of panic buying behaviour (Xu *et al.*, 2011; Zheng *et al.*, 2020). The spending patterns of consumers are affected as their purchasing habits change. Consumers in the new era of COVID-19 tend to spend less than usual, mainly on daily essential products. Research on spending decisions suggests that the negative emotion of pain of paying influences the spending habits of consumers. Rick *et al.* (2008) proposed that the tendency to experience the pain of paying varies across individual differences. The spending decision of a person is influenced by the emotion a person feels at the time of making purchases. The researcher categorizes people into three categories based on the level of pain of paying, which influences their spending pattern. According to the researchers, *tightwads* are described as individuals who feel extreme pain at the prospect of spending cash and therefore appear to spend less than they would prefer to spend. *Spendthrifts*, at the thought of investing, feel inadequate quantities of discomfort and thus prefer to spend more than they would prefer to pay. When making transactions, unconflicted customers feel a moderate level of discomfort and usually pay what they would ultimately want to pay.

Previous research indicates situations that temporarily decrease the pain of paying tend to increase spending by spendthrifts (Thomas *et al.*, 2011), and circumstances that temporarily raise the pain of paying tend to minimize spending by tightwads (Rick, 2018). This study shows how panic buying behaviour caused by the fear and anxiety of the COVID-19 pandemic tends to influence the spending patterns of individual consumers. It investigates whether there is any relationship between panic buying behaviour and consumers' individual differences, namely tightwad, unconflicted and spendthrift consumers.

Literature Review

Panic buying behaviour

Apart from the health hazards and economic issues all over the world, the COVID-19 pandemic has induced many people to adopt unusual and novel buying behaviours (Kuruppu and De Zoysa, 2020). Many people have started to buy much more items than they usually require due to the change in behaviour caused by the uncertainty and fear of the pandemic; this behaviour is called *panic buying* (Yuen *et al.*, 2020b). In certain circumstances and crises triggered by pandemics, natural disasters such as floods, and other unmanageable and catastrophic eventualities, this mentality of procuring more products arises (Lins and Aquino, 2020a). The purchase quantity of household items, groceries, and essentials increased very much during the lockdown period, indicating a significant increase in panic buying since people were fearing that much more restraints would be introduced and the lockdown would continue (The Economic Times, 2020). This social and herd behaviour of panic buying is socially undesirable because it causes a scenario of stockout in the market due to the purchase of large quantities of daily necessities and medical items (Yuen *et al.*, 2020b). The social security literature suggests that people in low- and high-income groups face fear and panic differently (Wesseler, 2020). The unprivileged and vulnerable people, such as the elderly and poor people, who are in greater need of the products are greatly affected by panic buying (Yuen *et al.*, 2020a). They won't be able to buy the necessities due to the shortage of items. This causes social abnormalities and chaos (OECD, 2020). In the market, particularly in the retail sector, panic buying disrupts supply chain systems (Zheng *et al.*, 2020).

Panic buying is a normal behaviour, as lockdowns force us to work from home and be at home more often, so naturally people look to stock up on products required for daily life. However, some of this panic buying is quite irrational (Lufkin, 2020). Consumer behaviour studies show that people panic buy for three reasons: (i) guilt avoidance, where consumers buy too much because they don't want to be the ones who are left without what they need; (ii) social cues, i.e., when somebody else stocks up, it makes them feel like they should do it too; (iii) anxiety, which is a feeling that the problems caused by the pandemic will not be resolved, so people buy more products to reduce their fear and anxiety (Dholakia, 2020; Dodgson, 2020). The epitome of panic buying gone wrong is when we lose any sort of social consciousness, i.e., when we think of getting all that we need without considering the needs of others (Patent, 2020).

These phenomena of panic buying are comparatively an unexplored and niche area in consumer behaviour research since consumer decisions are controlled by their emotions and social causes (Yuen *et al.*, 2020b). The literature is reviewed with a focus on the causes and reasons for panic buying among the masses all over the world due to the pandemic situation. The literature review suggests that it is possible to categorize the causes for panic buying into the following four key themes: (1) the person's fear of the crisis and the non-availability of necessary items (Frank and Schvaneveldt, 2016; Wang *et al.*, 2020; Zheng *et al.*, 2020), (2) the fear about some unknown factors caused by uncertainty and other emotions (Dulam *et al.*, 2020; Kemp *et al.*, 2014; Larson and Shin, 2018; Sterman and Dogan, 2015), (3) coping behaviour caused by control deprivation (Gao and Liu, 2016; Kemp *et al.*, 2014; Kennett-Hensel *et al.*, 2012; Yoon *et al.*, 2018), and (4) psychological and social factors considering the dynamics of the individual's social network (Kang *et al.*, 2020; Wang *et al.*, 2020; Yap and Chen, 2020; Zheng *et al.*, 2020). In situations, such as the COVID-19 pandemic, people will have a perception of risk. The level of it varies between individuals and mainly depends on their perception of the panic situation, which may be measured by the susceptibility and severity of the situation (Wen *et al.*, 2019; Yuen *et al.*, 2020a). Panic buying is a sort of self-protection behaviour for minimizing the risk before and during a disaster. They believe that the risk can be minimized by storing larger quantities of products to gain a sense of safety and confidence. Individuals can mitigate their public exposure through infrequent shopping activities. It is common for a person to indulge in panic buying to escape the great risk of catching the disease if the fear of spreading the disease is high. Therefore, panic buying can be interpreted as a method of self-protection to improve the well-being of individuals (Gao and Liu, 2016). The apprehension that there may be a scarcity of products in the future may trigger a sense of urgency to procure more things. The individuals may be motivated to panic buy owing to a psychological impulse to avoid an anticipated regret (Sterman and Dogan, 2015).

When a disease outbreak occurs, the common people will undergo emotional distress such as fear, anxiety, and panic (Ballantine *et al.*, 2014; Taylor, 2019). This situation is mainly due to our inability to predict the results of a pandemic outbreak, which threatens human dominance over nature (Sterman and Dogan, 2015). This fear of the unknown is due to the absence of knowledge about the disease crisis affecting health. Thus, uncertainty induces people to imagine the worst, which arouses fear and panic (Freeland, 2020). In order to minimize stress and fear, individuals make panic purchases, which give them a sense of security, at least temporarily. This kind of motivation is not caused by a real necessity for the items purchased, but rather is a way to suppress their negative emotions and stress (Kennett-Hensel *et al.*, 2012; Sneath *et al.*, 2009). Since people are deprived of other chances of enjoyment and entertainment, they turn to panic buying to compensate for them and enjoy indirect satisfaction (Koles *et al.*, 2018). Research has been undertaken to explain a person's behaviour and response to panic buying during this pandemic with the help of behavioural theories. The aims are to understand the psychological process involved in panic buying during the COVID-19 pandemic (Kuruppu and De Zoysa, 2020) and identify controlling measures that can reduce this behaviour (Arafat *et al.*, 2020).

Individual differences of consumers

The action of purchasing goods or services by an individual can cause the pain of parting with cash or savings. The purchasing intention of consumers depends on the subjective component of shopping discomfort or enjoyment. The buying behaviour of consumers depends on the subjective component of buying pain or pleasure. If the pain or discomfort of parting with cash is low, customers will pay out more, and vice versa (Soman, 2001). For the process of a clear trade-off, an individual must possess the skill of impulsive interpretation of the opportunity cost compared to the price of an item. This involves the comparison of enjoying the product currently with the expected upcoming purchase through an effective usage of cash (Becker *et al.*, 1974; Okada and Hoch, 2004). According to various researches working on the behaviours of individuals, plenty of individuals do not think about opportunity costs when dealing with a price (Frederick *et al.*, 2006; Jones *et al.*, 1998; Northcraft and Neale, 1986). In usual scenarios, individuals think about the pain of paying instead of the real opportunity cost, as it is much easier and more satisfying for their feelings. Those individuals who spend less on products are prone to have a high pain of paying, while individuals who have no or little pain of paying tend to pay out more (Rick *et al.*, 2008).

Consequentialist decision-making models presume that at the moment of choosing, feelings encountered are epiphenomenal, merely a by-product of the decision-making process. The only feelings that are known to impact decision-making are those that are likely to arise if different courses of action are taken (Rick *et al.*, 2008). The studies on spending behaviour, however, indicate that individual differences tend to experience an immediate feeling, the pain of paying, which has a strong effect on spending behaviour (Prelec and Loewenstein, 1998). According to Rick (2013), these combinations of low and high levels of payment pain cause individuals to spend in a different way relative to the way they would typically spend. In particular, Rick *et al.* (2008) predict that people who experience extreme pain of paying, the tightwads, close the purchase with a much lower sum than what they would usually have paid. Due to this difficult discomfort of paying, they refrain from buying on several occasions. The spendthrifts, on the contrary, experience less pain than is actually needed to pay and spend much more. Those who experience a natural and moderate pain of paying when spending may not have much difference between their real spending and the ideal spending habits, and such people belong to another category called *unconflicted consumers*. To measure these individual differences, Rick *et al.* (2008) formed a four-item individual difference scale. This scale studies whether customers have difficulty regulating their tendency to overspend or whether they are pressured to spend.

Rick *et al.* (2008) hypothesized that contexts that make spending less unpleasant, mainly by promoting higher spending among tightwads, can minimize individual spending differences. Research on vice and virtue goods was performed in a grocery store by Thomas *et al.* (2011). The outcome showed that for vice goods, when participants paid with credit (the comparatively less painful payment method), individual differences in spending were different. Spendthrifts were oblivious to the system of payment. However, neither tightwads nor spendthrifts were receptive to the payment system for virtue goods. Furthermore, the study explained that decreases in the pain of paying are most likely to minimize disparities among individual differences in consumer spending. Frederick *et al.* (2009), Rick *et al.* (2008), and Thomas *et al.* (2011) indicate that the scale of individual differences is likely to be affected by circumstances that affect the pain of paying. Contexts that minimize the pain of paying, mostly by modifying the actions of spendthrifts, should minimize individual spending disparities and can be minimized in situations that increase the pain of payment but do so mainly by modifying the actions of tightwads.

The COVID-19 pandemic has impacted consumer spending behaviour to a significant degree. As customers hunker down for a sustained period of financial volatility, they expect to continue to transfer their spending into necessities, such as food and household items, and cut down on other discretionary categories (McKinsey, 2020). The pandemic-induced crises have made consumers change their spending habits due to the uncertainty, fear, and anxiety of the coming future.

Hypotheses

1. There is a significant difference in panic buying between male and female respondents.
2. There is a significant difference in panic buying between married and unmarried respondents.
3. There is a significant difference in panic buying across different income groups of respondents.
4. There is a significant difference in panic buying across different occupations of respondents.
5. There is a significant difference in panic buying across different locations of respondents.
6. There is a significant difference in panic buying for individual differences of consumers, namely tightwad, unconflicted, and spendthrift consumers.

Methodology

Procedure

An online survey was conducted to gather the data for the analysis and study. A questionnaire was given to the participants for answering, and through this, the data were collected. Google Forms were used for the preparation of the questionnaire. For this study, only fully answered questionnaires were considered. The selection of the participants was done through snowball sampling (Naderifar et al., 2017) using emails and social network messages.

This questionnaire comprised three sections. The first segment was the demographic section, meant for collecting detailed information regarding the age, gender, marital status, occupation, income, and locality of the participants. The second section was meant for data collection regarding the panic buying behaviour of the participants, for which the panic buying scale was used. Seven Likert scale questions propounded by Lins and Aquino (2020b) were included in this. The third section was for collecting data for studying the individual differences of the participants. The individual differences scale known as the spendthrift–tightwad (ST–TW) scale proposed by Rick et al. (2008) was used.

Panic buying scale

The study uses the panic buying scale, as suggested by Lins and Aquino (2020b). Seven items make up the scale ('Fear drives me to buy more than I normally do; Fear drives me to purchase stuff to store at the household; Panic makes me buy more stuff than I normally do; I panic whenever I think that imported goods can run out of the market, so that's why I tend to buy things in quantity'). There was the following instruction before the scale: 'How will you characterize your purchasing actions during the present outbreak of the COVID-19 pandemic? For each argument, considering [your recent actions during the latest coronavirus pandemic] (consider 1 = strongly disagree and 7 = strongly agree), would like you to point out your degree of disagreement or agreement.'

Individual differences scale

Rick et al. (2008) designed the scale of the individual difference to quantify individual variations in the propensity to pain of paying and to classify three categories of customers: tightwads, spendthrifts, and unconflicted customers. The elements of the scale concentrate on whether customers have trouble monitoring their spending or have difficulty pushing themselves to spend. The scale consists of four elements. The first element uses a scale of 1–11 to measure individual differences among consumers, of which the minimum shows tightwad and the maximum shows spendthrift.

The scale's second item consists of two sub-questions that include two sets of five-point scale explanations and calculations. A scenario and a measurement using a five-point scale are defined in the final item of the scale. Rick et al. (2008) divide the scores of the scale into three equally sized groups of sums, with tightwads as those with scale sums from 4 to 11, unconflicted consumers as those with scale sums from 12 to 18, and spendthrifts as those with scale sums from 19 to 26.

Participants

This study of panic buying was conducted in India. An elite group of 1,020 people, including 514 males and 506 females, participated. The mean age of the participants was 27.75 (an SD of 9.456). Out of the 1,020 participants in the study, 712 were unmarried and 305 were married. The residential status of the participants was as follows: 47.1% were from urban areas, 35.9% from semi-urban areas, and the balance (17.1%) were from rural areas.

Result

The reliability was checked for both the panic buying scale and the scale of the individual differences. Statistical analysis showed high reliability for the panic buying scale (Cronbach's alpha, $\alpha = 0.923$) and the individual differences scale (Cronbach's alpha $\alpha = 0.904$). The data on the responses of the participants show that out of the total 1,020 respondents, 420 have low panic buying behaviour and 600 have high panic buying behaviour.

The panic buying was measured based on demographic information (gender, age, marital status, income, occupation, and location).

An independent sample t-test was conducted to test Hypotheses 1 and 2, i.e., there is a significant difference in panic buying across gender and marital status of respondents. The descriptive statistics and independent sample t-test associated with panic buying across gender and marital status of respondents are reported in Table 1. The distribution was sufficiently normal for the purpose of conducting a t-test (skewness $< |2.0|$ and kurtosis $< |9.0|$) (Schmider et al., 2010). Through Levene's F test, the presumption of homogeneity of variances was checked and satisfied for gender ($F(1018) = 0.824, p = 0.364$) and marital status ($F(1018) = 0.068, p = 0.795$). The independent sample t-test showed a statistically signifi-

Table 1. Descriptive statistics and independent sample *t*-test results of panic buying across gender and marital status of respondents.

								Panic buying				
									Levene's test for equality of variances		*t*-test for equality of means		
		N	M	SD	Skewness	Kurtosis	F	Sig.	t	df	p
Gender	Male	514	3.10	0.841	−0.681	0.304	0.824	0.364	−2.232	1018	0.026
	Female	506	3.22	0.878	−0.501	0.141					
Marital status	Single	712	3.03	0.82	−0.525	0.013	0.068	0.795	−7.642	1018	0.000
	Married	308	3.47	0.879	−0.973	1.387					

cant effect between panic buying and gender of respondents, with $t(1018) = -2.232$, $p = 0.026$ in the score with the mean score for females (M = 3.22, SD = 0.878) higher than for males (M = 3.10, SD = 0.841). Cohen's d, based on Cohen's 1992 guidance, was measured at 0.1395, which has a small effect (Cohen, 1992). The independent sample t-test showed a statistically significant effect for panic buying and marital status of respondents with $t(1018) = -7.642$, $p < 0.001$. The mean panic buying for married respondents (M = 3.47, SD = 0.879) was higher than for unmarried respondents (M = 3.03, SD = 0.820). Cohen's d, based on Cohen's 1992 guidance, was measured at 0.517, which has a medium effect (Cohen, 1992).

In order to test the hypotheses that there is a significant difference in panic buying across occupations, incomes, and locations of respondents, a between-groups ANOVA was performed. The presumption of normality was tested prior to the performance of ANOVA and determined to be satisfied since the distribution of the groups was aligned with a skewness less than |2.0| and a kurtosis less than |9.0|. Table 2 shows the results of ANOVA with panic buying among respondents based on their occupations, income levels, and locations. The independent results of ANOVA with panic buying between the occupations of respondents yield a statistically significant effect: $F(5,1014) = 11.098$, $p < 0.001$. Following the analysis of variance (ANOVA), a test for homogeneity of variance was conducted, revealing statistical significance in the Levene statistics. The *post hoc* comparison test using Dunnett's T3 was selected to test the difference between groups, and the results showed that seven out of the 15 groups were statistically significant. The ANOVA results with panic buying across the incomes of respondents show a statistically significant effect: $F(6,1013) = 17.366$, $p < 0.001$. The test of homogeneity showed significance, i.e., equal variance was not assumed. The *post hoc* comparison test using Dunnett's T3 was performed. The independent results of ANOVA with panic buying between the locations of respondents were not statistically significant ($p > 0.05$).

The individual differences scale score was divided into three equally sized groups of sums. The scale sum from 4 to 11 was classified as tightwads ($N = 273$), consumers with scale sum from 12 to 18 were classified as unconflicted ($N = 431$), and those with a sum scale from 19 to 26 were classified as spendthrifts ($N = 316$) (Rick et al., 2008). The results of Pearson's correlation showed that panic buying was positively correlated with the spendthrift–tightwad scale, with $r = 0.106$ and $p < 0.01$.

Table 2. Descriptive statistics and ANOVA results of panic buying across occupations, incomes, and locations of respondents.

			Panic buying							
		N	M	SD	Skewness	Kurtosis	F	df	p
Occupation	Professionals	130	3.18	0.865	−0.634	0.526			
	Government job	38	2.43	1.112	0.151	−1.596			
	Private job	258	3.35	0.863	−0.744	1.066	11.098	5,1014	0.000
	Business	140	3.31	0.974	−1.116	0.417			
	Others	114	3.19	0.622	−0.887	1.213			
	Students	340	3.02	0.782	−0.097	−0.031			
Income	No income	342	2.91	0.717	−0.322	−0.376			
	Below 1 lakh	132	3.20	0.760	−0.533	−0.340			
	1–3	188	3.10	0.718	−1.023	2.220			
	3–5	110	3.50	0.963	−0.503	−0.242	17.366	6,1013	0.000
	5–7	82	3.17	0.993	−1.220	0.268			
	7–10	88	3.16	1.176	−1.040	−0.347			
	Above 10 lakhs	78	3.84	0.691	−0.335	−0.041			
Location	Urban	480	3.21	0.924	−0.552	0.404			
	Semi-urban	366	3.13	0.778	−0.662	0.069	1.874	2,1017	0.154
	Rural	174	3.08	0.844	−0.627	−0.552			

The descriptive statistics associated with panic buying across the three individual differences of consumers are reported in Table 3. In order to test the hypothesis that there is a significant difference in panic buying across the individual differences of consumers (tightwad, unconflicted, and spendthrift consumers), a between-groups ANOVA was performed. Prior to conducting the ANOVA, the assumption of normality was evaluated and determined to be satisfied since the three groups' distributions were associated with skewness and kurtosis of less than |2.0| and |9.0|, respectively. Furthermore, the assumption of homogeneity of variances was tested and satisfied based on Levene's F test: $F(2, 1017) = 0.686$, $p = 0.504$.

Table 3 shows the result of ANOVA with panic buying as a dependent variable and individual differences as a factor variable. The independent results of ANOVA between the groups yield a statistically significant effect: $F(2,1017) = 5.792$, $p < 0.05$, $\eta^2 = 0.011$. Thus, the null hypothesis of there being no differences between the means was rejected. To evaluate the nature of the differences between the three means further, the statistically significant ANOVA was followed up with three Fisher's LSD *post hoc* tests (Table 4). The difference between tightwad consumers and unconflicted consumers was not statistically significant ($p = 0.110$, $d = 0.126$). The difference between tightwad consumers and spendthrift consumers was statistically significant ($p = 0.001$, $d = 0.155$). The

Table 3. Descriptive statistics and ANOVA results of panic buying across individual differences of consumers (tightwad, unconflicted, and spendthrift consumers).

		Panic buying							
		N	M	SD	Skewness	Kurtosis	F	df	p
Individual differences	Tightwad	273	3.04	0.908	0.081	−0.661			
	Unconflicted	431	3.15	0.833	0.177	−0.442	5.792	21,017	0.003
	Spendthrift	316	3.28	0.844	0.38	−0.626			

Table 4. Fisher's LSD *post hoc* multiple comparisons.

Comparison	p	d
Tightwad–Unconflicted	0.110	0.126
Tightwad–Spendthrift	0.001	0.155
Unconflicted–Spendthrift	0.036	0.273

difference between unconflicted consumers and spendthrift consumers was statistically significant ($p = 0.036$, $d = 0.273$). Based on Cohen's (1992) standards, the sizes associated with the statistically significant effects are considered small.

Discussion and Implications

Panic buying is the inclination of people to stock up on large amounts of necessities, such as food, groceries, medicines, and other items, due to the rapid fear of a potential shortage or price increase. Millions across the globe stockpiled necessities as a precautionary measure in the aftermath of the COVID-19 outbreak before being shut in for an unknown number of days. The study suggests that panic buying due to the COVID-19 pandemic has affected the whole population. The findings show panic buying differs among male and female respondents; female respondents showed greater panic buying behaviour compared to male respondents. Married respondents showed more panic buying than unmarried respondents. The respondents with higher incomes showed greater panic buying behaviour. Regardless of location, all respondent groups showed similar behaviour.

The relationship between panic buying and the individual difference scale shows a positive correlation, which means that as the score on the spendthrift–tightwad scale increases, the panic buying level also increases. This suggests that spendthrifts show higher panic buying behaviour. Panic buying is a pattern of behaviour triggered by crises (in this case, COVID-19), motivated by negative emotions, such as fear and anxiety. The adverse feeling of panic buying affects the negative feeling of pain of paying. As per Rick *et al.* (2008), the pain of paying experienced by spendthrifts is considerably less compared to that experienced by tightwads. The pain of paying decreases as the negative sensation of panic buying rises. The expectation and apprehension over an increase in price or a lack of stocks produce a condition that helps minimize the discomfort of paying for essential goods. As the pain of payment reduces, individuals indulge in the acquisition of more essential goods.

If the problems and challenges due to COVID-19 tend to rise by a considerable amount over a prolonged period of time, people will continue to suffer from elevated levels of anxiety and insecurity, even more so with the possibility of new waves of virus spread. The experience of this pandemic demonstrates to us that it is important that the psychological effects that COVID-19 has on individuals and society are not neglected. Since a pandemic is a danger that creates panic, distress, and confusion, questions are often posed about whether adequate resources will be available or how long economic turmoil will continue. Unnecessarily high purchasing and storing habits may induce supply-overcoming demands, create commodity shortages in the middle of the recession, or even trigger panic purchasing among the public, raising feelings of uncertainty and anxiety.

The possible effect of these stressful emotions on shopping behaviour must be understood by customers, healthcare providers, and government decision-makers, as this helps establish strategies that avoid or reduce mental and economic suffering in the wake of emergencies. Understanding purchase choices affected by dramatic environmental shifts will pave the way in times of disaster to minimize and tackle post-traumatic disorders or the impact of pandemic-related panic.

The findings discussed here show that individual variations in the emotions needed to experience an intense feeling, the pain of paying, have an influential effect on panic buying-induced purchasing and spending behaviour. The situation of panic buying created anxiety and fear of the uncertain future, which reduced the feeling of pain of paying. There may be different waves of panic purchasing if the pandemic is not fully under control, and research carried out after a traumatic event may carry new conclusions regarding it. Investigations should also determine the influence and impact of different types of consumer activity on the retail market, family financial issues, and mental well-being, reflecting more on the history of panic purchasing behaviour. Only a body of qualitative studies, removing shortcuts in the retail market and developing behavioural well-being promotion strategies, will be able to draw any conclusions and indications for public policymakers and health practitioners.

Conclusion

A catastrophic and unprecedented change happened all over the globe due to the outbreak of the COVID-19 pandemic. This resulted in a very uncertain situation where people started panic buying to prevent any eventuality of a shortage or scarcity of essential products due to the lockdown. This drastic change in the behaviour of people caused a disturbance in the retail market and supply chain system. The panic buying tendency affected families' budgets and savings. Due to panic and fear, the spending behaviour of people has changed greatly.

References

Alvarez, F. E., Argente, D., and Lippi, F. (2020). A Simple Planning Problem for COVID-19 Lockdown. *National Bureau of Economic Research.*

Arafat, S. M. Y., Kar, S. K., and Kabir, R. (2020). Possible controlling measures of panic buying during COVID-19. *International Journal of Mental Health and Addiction.* https://doi.org/10.1007/s11469-020-00320-1.

Armitage, R., and Nellums, L. B. (2020). COVID-19 and the consequences of isolating the elderly. *The Lancet Public Health*, 5(5), e256.

Ballantine, P. W., Zafar, S., and Parsons, A. G. (2014). Changes in retail shopping behaviour in the aftermath of an earthquake. *The International Review of Retail, Distribution and Consumer Research*, 24(1), 1–13.

Becker, S. W., Ronen, J., and Sorter, G. H. (1974). Opportunity costs-an experimental approach. *Journal of Accounting Research*, 317–329.

Cluver, L., Lachman, J. M., Sherr, L., Wessels, I., Krug, E., Rakotomalala, S., Blight, S., Hillis, S., Bachmand, G., and Green, O. (2020). Parenting in a time of COVID-19.

Cohen, J. (1992). A power primer. *Psychological Bulletin*, 112(1), 155.

Cullen, W., Gulati, G., and Kelly, B. D. (2020). Mental health in the covid-19 pandemic. *QJM: An International Journal of Medicine*, 113(5), 311–312.

Dholakia, U. (2020). Why are we panic buying during the coronavirus pandemic? *Psychology Today.* https://www.psychologytoday.com/blog/the-science-behind-behavior/202003/why-are-we-panic-buying-during-the-coronavirus-pandemic. March 2020.

Dodgson, L. (2020). A human behavior expert explains 4 psychological reasons why people are panic buying items in bulk during the coronavirus pandemic. *Insider.* https://www.insider.com/why-people-are-panic-bulk-buying-during-the-coronavirus-pandemic-2020-3. March 2020.

Dulam, R., Furuta, K., and Kanno, T. (2020). Development of an agent-based model for the analysis of the effect of consumer panic buying on supply chain disruption due to a disaster. *Journal of Advanced Simulation in Science and Engineering*, 7(1), 102–116.

Frank, B., and Schvaneveldt, S. J. (2016). Understanding consumer reactions to product contamination risks after national disasters: The roles of knowledge, experience, and information sources. *Journal of Retailing and Consumer Services*, 28, 199–208.

Frederick, S., Novemsky, N., Wang, J., Dhar, R., and Nowlis, S. (2006). Neglect of Opportunity Costs in Consumer Choice. Working Paper, Marketing Department, Sloan School of Management.

Frederick, S., Novemsky, N., Wang, J., Dhar, R., and Nowlis, S. (2009). Opportunity cost neglect. *Journal of Consumer Research*, 36(4), 553–561.

Freeland, S. (2020). Why people are panic buying and what can help. *UGA Today*. https://news.uga.edu/panic-buying-and-anxiety-tips/. March 2020.

Gao, C., and Liu, J. (2016). Network-based modeling for characterizing human collective behaviors during extreme events. *IEEE Transactions on Systems, Man, and Cybernetics: Systems*, 47(1), 171–183.

Jones, S. K., Frisch, D., Yurak, T. J., and Kim, E. (1998). Choices and opportunities: Another effect of framing on decisions. *Journal of Behavioral Decision Making*, 11(3), 211–226.

Kang, I., He, X., and Shin, M. M. (2020). Chinese consumers' herd consumption behavior related to Korean luxury cosmetics: The mediating role of fear of missing out. *Frontiers in Psychology*, 11, 121.

Kemp, E., Kennett-Hensel, P. A., and Williams, K. H. (2014). The calm before the storm: Examining emotion regulation consumption in the face of an impending disaster. *Psychology & Marketing*, 31(11), 933–945.

Kennett-Hensel, P. A., Sneath, J. Z., and Lacey, R. (2012). Liminality and consumption in the aftermath of a natural disaster. *Journal of Consumer Marketing*.

Kluge, H. H. P. (2020). Mental Health and Psychological Resilience during the COVID-19 Pandemic. World Health Organisation.

Koles, B., Wells, V., and Tadajewski, M. (2018). Compensatory consumption and consumer compromises: A state-of-the-art review. *Journal of Marketing Management*, 34(1–2), 96–133.

Kuruppu, G. N., and De Zoysa, A. (2020). COVID-19 and panic buying: An examination of the impact of behavioural biases.

Lancet, T. (2020). India under COVID-19 lockdown. *Lancet (London, England)*, 395(10233), 1315.

Larson, L. R., and Shin, H. (2018). Fear during natural disaster: Its impact on perceptions of shopping convenience and shopping behavior. *Services Marketing Quarterly*, 39(4), 293–309.

Lau, H., Khosrawipour, V., Kocbach, P., Mikolajczyk, A., Schubert, J., Bania, J., and Khosrawipour, T. (2020). The positive impact of lockdown in Wuhan on containing the COVID-19 outbreak in China. *Journal of Travel Medicine*, 27(3), taaa037.

Lins, S., and Aquino, S. (2020a). Building a panic buying scale during COVID-19: Preliminary results. https://doi.org/10.13140/RG.2.2.30208.05125.

Lins, S., and Aquino, S. (2020b). Development and initial psychometric properties of a panic buying scale during COVID-19 pandemic. *Heliyon*, 6(9), e04746.

Lufkin, B. (2020). Coronavirus: The psychology of panic buying. https://www.bbc.com/worklife/article/20200304-coronavirus-covid-19-update-why-people-are-stockpiling. March 2020.

McKinsey. (2020). Consumer sentiment and behavior continue to reflect the uncertainty of the COVID-19 crisis. *McKinsey*. https://www.mckinsey.com/business-functions/marketing-and-sales/our-insights/a-global-view-of-how-consumer-behavior-is-changing-amid-covid-19.

Moore, S. A., Faulkner, G., Rhodes, R. E., Brussoni, M., Chulak-Bozzer, T., Ferguson, L. J., Mitra, R., O'Reilly, N., Spence, J. C., and Vanderloo, L. M. (2020). Impact of the COVID-19 virus outbreak on movement and play behaviours of Canadian children and youth: A national survey. *International Journal of Behavioral Nutrition and Physical Activity*, 17(1), 1–11.

Naderifar, M., Goli, H., and Ghaljaie, F. (2017). Snowball sampling: A purposeful method of sampling in qualitative research. *Strides in Development of Medical Education*, 14(3), 1–6.

Northcraft, G. B., and Neale, M. A. (1986). Opportunity costs and the framing of resource allocation decisions. *Organizational Behavior and Human Decision Processes*, 37(3), 348–356.

Obi, S. E., Yunusa, T., Ezeogueri-Oyewole, A. N., Sekpe, S. S., Egwemi, E., and Isiaka, A. S. (2020). The socio-economic impact of covid-19 on the economic activities of selected states in Nigeria. *Indonesian Journal of Social and Environmental Issues*, 1(2), 39–47.

OECD. (2020). COVID-19: Protecting people and societies. https://www.oecd.org/coronavirus/policy-responses/covid-19-protecting-people-and-societies-e5c9de1a/. March 2020.

Okada, E. M., and Hoch, S. J. (2004). Spending time versus spending money. *Journal of Consumer Research*, 31(2), 313–323.

Outlook India Magazine. (2020). How coronavirus pandemic will impact the economy and you. https://www.outlookindia.com/magazine/story/how-coronavirus-pandemic-will-impact-the-economy-and-you/303014. April 2020.

Patent, V. (2020). Panic buying and how to stop it. *OpenLearn*. https://www.open.edu/openlearn/health-sports-psychology/psychology/panic-buying-and-how-stop-it. March 2020.

Prelec, D., and Loewenstein, G. (1998). The red and the black: Mental accounting of savings and debt. *Marketing Science*, 17(1), 4–28. https://doi.org/10.1287/mksc.17.1.4.

Rick, S. (2013). The pain of paying and Tightwaddism: New insights and open questions. *SSRN Electronic Journal*. https://doi.org/10.2139/ssrn.2271900.

Rick, S. (2018). Tightwads and spendthrifts: An interdisciplinary review. *Financial Planning Review*, 1(1–2), e1010. https://doi.org/10.1002/cfp2.1010.

Rick, S. I., Cryder, C. E., and Loewenstein, G. (2008). Tightwads and spendthrifts. *Journal of Consumer Research*, 34(6), 767–782.

Schmider, E., Ziegler, M., Danay, E., Beyer, L., and Bühner, M. (2010). Is it really robust? *Methodology*, 6(4).

Sneath, J. Z., Lacey, R., and Kennett-Hensel, P. A. (2009). Coping with a natural disaster: Losses, emotions, and impulsive and compulsive buying. *Marketing Letters*, 20(1), 45–60.

Soman, D. (2001). Effects of payment mechanism on spending behavior: The role of rehearsal and immediacy of payments. *Journal of Consumer Research*, 27(4), 460–474.

Sterman, J. D., and Dogan, G. (2015). "I'm not hoarding, I'm just stocking up before the hoarders get here": Behavioral causes of phantom ordering in supply chains. *Journal of Operations Management*, 39, 6–22.

Su, X. (2010). Intertemporal pricing and consumer stockpiling. *Operations Research*, 58(4-part-2), 1133–1147.

Taylor, S. (2019). *The Psychology of Pandemics: Preparing for the Next Global Outbreak of Infectious Disease*. Cambridge Scholars Publishing.

The Economic Times. (2020). https://economictimes.indiatimes.com/industry/cons-products/fmcg/people-resorted-to-panic-buying-during-announcement-of-lockdown-or-its-extension/articleshow/75656427.cms?from=mdr. May 2020.

Thomas, M., Desai, K. K., and Seenivasan, S. (2011). How credit card payments increase unhealthy food purchases: Visceral regulation of vices. *Journal of Consumer Research*, 38(1), 126–139.

Walton, M., Murray, E., and Christian, M. D. (2020). Mental health care for medical staff and affiliated healthcare workers during the COVID-19 pandemic. *European Heart Journal: Acute Cardiovascular Care*, 2048872620922795.

Wang, G., Zhang, Y., Zhao, J., Zhang, J., and Jiang, F. (2020). Mitigate the effects of home confinement on children during the COVID-19 outbreak. *The Lancet*, 395(10228), 945–947.

Wen, X., Sun, S., Li, L., He, Q., and Tsai, F.-S. (2019). Avian influenza—Factors affecting consumers' purchase intentions toward poultry products. *International Journal of Environmental Research and Public Health*, 16(21), 4139.

Wesseler, J. (2020). Storage policies: Stockpiling versus immediate release. *Journal of Agricultural & Food Industrial Organization*, 18(1), 1–9.

Worldometer. (2021). Coronavirus update (live). https://www.worldometers.info/coronavirus/.

Xu, C., Bai, T., Iuliano, A. D., Wang, M., Yang, L., Wen, L., Zeng, Y., Li, X., Chen, T., and Wang, W. (2011). The seroprevalence of pandemic influenza H1N1 (2009) virus in China. *PloS One*, 6(4), e17919.

Yap, A. J., and Chen, C. Y. (2020). The psychology behind coronavirus panic buying. *INSEAD Knowledge*. https://knowledge.insead.edu/economics-finance/the-psychology-behind-coronavirus-panic-buying-13451. March 2, 2020.

Yoon, J., Narasimhan, R., and Kim, M. K. (2018). Retailer's sourcing strategy under consumer stockpiling in anticipation of supply disruptions. *International Journal of Production Research*, 56(10), 3615–3635.

Yuen, K. F., Li, K. X., Ma, F., and Wang, X. (2020a). The effect of emotional appeal on seafarers' safety behaviour: An extended health belief model. *Journal of Transport & Health*, 16, 100810.

Yuen, K. F., Wang, X., Ma, F., and Li, K. X. (2020b). The psychological causes of panic buying following a health crisis. *International Journal of Environmental Research and Public Health*, 17(10), 3513.

Zheng, R., Shou, B., and Yang, J. (2020). Supply disruption management under consumer panic buying and social learning effects. *Omega*, 102238.

© 2025 World Scientific Publishing Company
https://doi.org/10.1142/9789811292101_0002

Chapter 2

Purchase Intention and Satisfaction of FMCG Shoppers: Empirical Analysis from a Post-COVID-19 Outlook

Shaply Abdul Kareem[*,§]**, D. Yuvaraj**[*,¶]**, S. Aswini Priya**[*,ǁ]**, Pulidindi Venugopal**[†,**]**, and S. Anjani Devi**[‡,††]

[*]*VIT Business School, VIT, Vellore 632014, India*
[†]*Department of Technology Management, VIT, Vellore 632014, India*
[‡]*GITAM, Visakhapatnam, Andhra Pradesh, India*
[§]*shaplyabdul.kareem2019@vitstudent.ac.in*
[¶]*yuvaraj.d2019@vitstudent.ac.in*
[ǁ]*shanthysekar360@gmail.com*
[**]*pulidindi.venu@vit.ac.in*
[††]*f14anjanids@iima.ac.in*

Abstract

Over the years, prior to the pandemic, the growth of fast-moving consumer goods (FMCG) products increased rapidly, with an increased number of product categories. Though the growth rate was lower in the middle of 2018, the industry managed to sustain itself by lowering the cost of its products and increasing its supplies. The industry again faced a recession during the global pandemic, as there was only demand for disinfectants and hand sanitizers. Hence, this research intends to determine the factors swaying the perception of FMCG buyers after COVID-19. In addition to this objective, the study also determines the satisfaction level of FMCG buyers across unorganized and organized retail outlets in specific provinces of Tamil Nadu. The reliability of the survey instrument was tested by carrying out a pilot study in which 20 FMCG shoppers were chosen to respond to the survey after the COVID-19 pandemic. The results indicated that the instrument is reliable and was thus used further for the final study. A total of 158 FMCG shoppers were included in the final study. The study found that factors such as word of mouth (WoM) and perceived value positively influenced the purchase intention of customers, which in turn impacted their satisfaction levels when purchasing in unorganized or organized stores in the post-COVID-19 scenario. However, factors such as trust and perceived risk did not influence the purchase intentions of consumers after the COVID-19 pandemic.

Keywords: Trust, FMCG shoppers, perceived value, perceived risk, WoM, purchase intention, satisfaction.

Introduction

The Indian retail market is composed of unorganized and organized stores, with about 13.8 million being traditional model neighbourhood stores, and the organized retail stores constituting a share that is about 10% smaller (IBEF, 2020). Recently, the retail industry has undergone a number of transformations, particularly in the regulated sector. Emerging models such as department stores, malls, and hypermarkets have risen in large numbers. Retailing today is more hierarchical in nature, and adopting a chain format that excels in comparison to individually operated stores. The retail landscape is subject to constant change and accelerated progress in the face of greater storage capacity, an improvised retail orientation, and better management of available retail formats (Hollingsworth, 2004).

The retail industry has undergone numerous transformations over time, whether in the mode of service, format, or layout. New formats of retail stores have appeared, such as department stores, FMCG stores, supermarkets, and hypermarkets. This sector has proven to be one of the most successful markets, even with the advent of new entrants from the domestic market. This has contributed to an upsurge in competition, which has fundamentally changed supermarket processes. To compete and retain competition, it is necessary that retailers adapt to the new styles of retail formats. This motivates them to be highly inventive and imaginative in terms of marketing to help them earn respect and value in the trading system. Retailing can be defined as a commercial practice aimed at providing goods or services to those who need them (Berman and Evans, 2001).

Since mid-March 2020, McKinsey has conducted customer surveys across the globe to recognize the effect of COVID-19 on consumer perception and stated behaviour. Many people, who had expected COVID-19 to adversely affect their budgets as well as their everyday lives for at least another four months, became mindful of their spending and purchased less costly goods. As consumers hunker down for a protracted period of financial instability, their spending plans begin to shift primarily toward necessities, such as FMCG and household goods, while scaling back on most discretionary purchases. Although the purchasing intention has risen in a significant number of categories since our first assessment at the end of March, outside of China, it remains low for discretionary items, such as apparel, footwear, and travel. Consumers in China, India, and Korea are reporting good buying plans across a wider variety of categories, including food and distribution, snacks, skin care and cosmetics, non-food baby goods, exercise and well-being, and fuel (McKinsey & Company, 2020).

The outbreak of COVID-19 had pushed people to think more transformatively and, with time, to adjust their shopping habits and focus on saving on the requisite products, including at FMCG stores. The rather sudden and unforeseen occurrence of the pandemic has seriously impacted the retail industry. Almost every retail sector has felt adverse impacts. Shopping patterns among consumers have changed as a result of this pandemic, and it seems to have affected the numerous retail stores that sell the requisite merchandise to households or individuals. Hence, the study aims to determine the purchase intention and satisfaction of FMCG shoppers.

Review of Literature

A shift in the consumers' buying behaviour

Throughout the COVID-19 and post-COVID-19 periods, empty shelves at stores created tremendous problems for customers (Lufkin, 2020). The pandemic impacted the shopping behaviours of consumers. Reddy (2020) suggests that there has been an increase in the traditional method of purchasing. While there was a huge rise in the number of consumers transitioning to online shopping, a greater change in the preference of items was also observed. A significant number of shoppers are now involved in purchasing personal care, sanitary, and medical kits online rather than apparel items. Forsythe (2006) supported the proposed measures of perceived benefits and risks associated with online shopping in terms of construct, convergent, discriminate, nomological, and predictive validity.

Mahadira and Purwanegara (2014) revealed that most of the products and brands have successfully proved that their brands are not merely sensations to attract the attention of consumers but are the real deal that satisfy them. Additionally, the authors stated that the only true motivation for customers to consume or purchase lies in the quality of the brand or the performance of the product itself and that all of the marketing media or communication is just a channel of communication between the brand or product and the consumer. The results reported by Saleem *et al.* (2017) revealed that service quality and trust are directly associated with repurchase intentions by acting as mediators of customer satisfaction.

Banumathi (2018) found that consumer behaviour is largely affected by place, product price, promotion, people's influence, and market-wide factors. However, the effects of these factors also differ from product to product. Konuk (2018) found that store image (SI) has a positive impact on perceived quality (PQ) and trust in organic private label (OPL). The researcher also revealed that PQ and trust in OPL contribute to perceived value (PV).

Goswami and Chouha (2020) specified the important effects of awareness of COVID-19, attitude towards the pandemic, and type of product purchased during shopping on changes in consumer behaviour and priorities in the current crisis. Aamer (2021) revealed that perceived risks, such as financial risk, product risk, security risk, time risk, and social risk, have a significant impact on online purchase intention; however, psychological risk has no impact on online shopping intention. Among these risks, product risk makes a huge contribution to preventing consumers from shopping online. Hossan and Solliman (2021) indicated that tourists' revisit intentions are positively and significantly influenced by destination service quality (DSR), destination reputation, and their perceived trust. Additionally, DSR is positively linked to destination reputation and visitors' trust, which are, in turn, positively affected by destination reputation. The results also revealed that fear arousal negatively moderates the link between destination reputation, holidaymakers' trust, and their intentions to revisit.

Yu *et al.* (2021) found that the perceived risk from COVID-19 and post-traumatic stress disorder have severely negative impacts on revisit intention for hotels, with the ability to regulate emotion found to play a moderating role in this process. Because hotels are used by a diverse group of people in terms of race, nationality, age, and culture, they can rapidly spread diseases, such as COVID-19.

The structure of this chapter is organized as follows. In the following section, we present the methodology, which is followed by data analysis and interpretation and then a discussion. We conclude with limitations and suggestions for future research directions.

Theoretical Model and Research Hypotheses

Figure 1 represents the theoretical model used in the current study.

The following hypotheses are presented:

H1: Perceived value is positively related to the purchase intention of FMCG shoppers in the post-COVID-19 period.

The definition of PV has become more significant in customer behaviour and marketing. One of the first conceptualizations of PV developed by Zeithaml (1998) refers to consumers' overall estimation of the utility of a good (or service) based on their expectations of what is offered and what is given. The primary goal of marketers is to concentrate on growing buyers' desire to purchase a product (Agarwal and Teas, 2001). It has also been known that PV contributes to the propensity to purchase FMCG (Liljander *et al.*, 2009).

H2: Perceived risk is negatively related to the purchase intention towards FMCG shoppers in the post-COVID-19 period.

Bauer (1967) stated that consumer behaviour is associated with risk because, as consumers make purchases, they may receive positive or

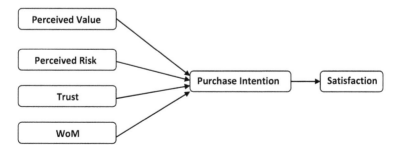

Figure 1. Theoretical model.

negative results that they cannot anticipate. Perceived risk is the subjective aspiration of customers for the loss (Sweeney et al., 1999). This means that any customer behaviour would have effects that they cannot inherently forecast, some of which are at least unfavourable (Liljander et al., 2009).

H3: Trust is positively related to the purchase intention of FMCG shoppers in the post-COVID-19 period.

Trust is described as the consumer's belief that the service provider is trustworthy and that it can be counted on to deliver on its commitments (Sirdeshmukh et al., 2002). Consumer trust may be an important contributor to consumers' purchase intentions (Park and Kim, 2016).

H4: Word of Mouth (WoM) is positively related to the purchase intention of FMCG shoppers in the post-COVID-19 period.

WoM is one of the oldest ways to communicate information (Dellarocas, 2003).

H5: Purchase intention is positively related to customer satisfaction in purchasing FMCG products in the post-COVID-19 period.

Customer satisfaction establishes when an in-store experience is satisfying and allows shoppers to continue shopping with the intention of making a purchase (Brcic, 2016; Porat, 2012; Tynan, 2014).

Methodology

Measurement development

The research model consists of six constructs: perceived value, perceived risk, trust, WoM, purchase intention, and satisfaction. In order to ensure the validity of these constructs, all measurement items have been adapted from existing research and further adjusted to suit the context of FMCG shopping. Nine items of perceived value were modified from Sweeney and Soutar (2001). Five items of perceived risk were modified from Chiu et al. (2014). Three items of purchase intention were modified from Venkatesh and Davis (2000). Three items of satisfaction were adapted from Bhattacherjee (2001) and Cronin et al. (2000). All the items created were measured using a five-point Likert scale (5: Strongly Agree; 1: Strongly Disagree).

The researchers conducted a covariance-based analysis through structural equation modelling using AMOS software, which forms cause–effect relationship models of latent variables using maximum likelihood estimation.

Data collection

Consumers who purchase from both organized and unorganized retail stores in various regions of Tamil Nadu were chosen as sampling units for the study. People from three districts (Ranipet, Tiruvannamalai, and Vellore) were considered as samples. These three districts are economically emerging districts in Tamil Nadu and, according to recent reports, have been severely affected by COVID-19. Convenience sampling was used to empirically examine the purpose, and since the respondents were readily available to obtain the response, this method was found to be efficient and useful. The instrument was pre-tested before proceeding to the final survey. Questionnaires were circulated to 60 people who have a history of making organized and unorganized FMCG purchases. Based on the reliability and factor loading scores, the final data collection was undertaken. This study collected 180 samples from Tamil Nadu. Due to insufficient details, 22 questionnaires were rejected, and a total of 158 eligible questionnaires were considered for analysis. A well-structured questionnaire was used to gather data both online and offline.

Results

Descriptive statistics

Data analysis was carried out with the help of SPSS software version 23 and AMOS version 23. The structure of the data analysis was categorized into two parts: Part I consisted of demographic factors, and Part II consisted of study-related factors.

Interpretation

As noted from Table 1, the majority of the customers are male (80.4%). Most of the respondents belong to the 18–25 age group. Most of the respondents' income level was in the range of Rs. 10,000–16,000, and

Table 1. Demographic profile of respondents.

Demographic	Category	Frequency	Percentage
Gender	Male	127	80.4
	Female	31	19.6
Age (in years)	18–25	53	33.5
	26–30	37	23.4
	31–35	46	29.1
	36–40	17	10.8
	Above 45	5	3.2
Income (in Rupees/month)	Below 10,000	42	26.6
	11,000–15,000	13	8.2
	16,000–20,000	42	26.6
	21,000–25,000	22	13.9
	Above 25,000	39	24.7
Education	SSLC	3	1.9
	HSC	6	3.8
	Diploma	3	1.9
	UG	30	19.0
	PG	104	65.8
	Others	12	7.6
Marital status	Married	78	49.4
	Unmarried	80	50.6
Occupation	Self-employed	17	10.8
	Business	19	12
	Private employee	82	51.9
	Government employee	9	5.7
	Housewife	7	4.5
	others	24	15.2
Location	Rural	39	24.7
	Semi-urban	69	43.7
	Urban	50	31.6
Family structure	Joint family	57	36.1
	Nuclear family	101	63.9

Table 1. (*Continued*)

Demographic	Category	Frequency	Percentage
No. of family member/s	2–3	39	24.7
	4–5	71	44.9
	5–6	25	15.8
	More than 6	23	14.6
What is your preferred Types of retail store?	Supermarket	40	25.3
	Departmental store	44	27.8
	General store	74	46.8
Priority of safety measures	Wearing mask	45	28.5
	Sanities hands	39	24.7
	Social distancing	37	23.4
	Avoid handshake	37	23.4

they had a postgraduate level of education. Of the customers, 50.6% were unmarried, and a majority were working in the private sector. Moreover, 42% of the buyers were located in semi-urban areas, and a majority were from a nuclear family. The family size was predominantly 4–5 in our samples. Of the buyers, 46.8% preferred the general retail stores for groceries. The shoppers prioritized safety precautions during FMCG shopping in the following order: wearing masks, sanitizing hands, social distancing, and avoiding handshakes.

Measurement model results

When performing statistical analyses, it is necessary for the researcher to conduct unidimensionality tests, which should then be followed by validity and reliability tests (Hair *et al.*, 1998). By doing so, the misspecifications can be mitigated (Gerbing and Anderson, 1988), as the validity and reliability tests are dependent on the assumptions made in the unidimensionality test (Nunnally and Bernstein, 1994). Here, the unidimensionality test was performed through confirmatory factor analysis (CFA) for all six factors. The results of the fit indices are presented in Table 2. The chi-square value, which should be between 2 and 4, was found to be 3.255. The other indices and their corresponding thresholds are as

Table 2. Fit indices.

Fit indices	Values	Overall acceptance	Supporting literature
Chi-Square Relative/df	3.255	Acceptable fit	Kline (2005) and Tabachnik and Fidell (2007)
RMSEA	0.062	Good fit	Kaplan (2000), Hu and Bentler (1998) and Steiger (2007)
GFI	0.988	Excellent fit	Marsh and Grayson (1995) and Jarvis et al. (2003)
AGFI	0.982	Excellent fit	Tabachnik and Fidell (2007)
RMR	0.008	Good fit	Hu and Bentler (1995) and Tabachnik and Fidell (2007)
RFI	0.979	Excellent fit	Bollen (1986)
IFI	0.987	Excellent fit	Bentler and Bonnet (1980)
NFI	0.990	Excellent fit	Schermelleh-Engel et al. (2003)
NNFI/TLI	0.991	Excellent fit	Tucker and Lewis (1973) and Jöreskog and Sörbom (1999)
CFI	0.990	Excellent fit	Hu and Bentler (1999)

follows: RMSEA = 0.062 (0.950), GFI = 0.988 (>0.950), AGFI = 0.982 (>0.950), RMR = 0.008 (small value), RFI = 0.979(>0.950), IFI = 0.987 (>0.950), NFI = 0.990 (>0.950), NNFI/TLI = 0.991 (>0.950), and CFI = 0.990 (>0.950). All these fit indices are above the threshold limits, as recommended by the supporting literatures.

Direct effects in AMOS

The model shown in Figure 2 depicts the effects of perceived value, perceived risk, trust, WoM, and purchase intention on the satisfaction of customers.

Purchase intention = (0.320 × perceived value) + (0.454 × WoM)

The above-mentioned equation implies that every unit change in perceived value will result in a 0.320 unit change in purchase intention. Also, every unit change in WoM will result in a 0.454 unit change in purchase intention. The R^2 value for purchase intention is found to be 0.37,

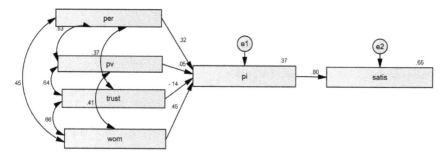

Figure 2. Model with path coefficients.

which means that 37% of the variance in purchase intention is explained by both perceived value and WoM. However, the effects of perceived risk and trust on purchase intention are found to be insignificant.

$$\text{Customer satisfaction} = (0.803 \times \text{purchase intention})$$

The above equation denotes that every unit change in purchase intention will result in a 0.803 unit change in customer satisfaction. Adding to this, the R^2 value for customer satisfaction is found to be 0.65, which implies that 65% of the variance in customer satisfaction is explained by the purchase intention of customers.

Discussion

This study aims to determine the customer purchase intention and satisfaction of FMCG shoppers. Specifically, this research examined the effects of perceived value, perceived risk, trust, and WoM on satisfaction and purchase intention in the FMCG context from a post-COVID-19 perspective. The results of the study point to numerous key findings.

Initially, perceived value contributes to the propensity to purchase FMCG (Liljander et al., 2009). Consumers with higher levels of perceived value are more likely to experience greater satisfaction and develop stronger purchase intentions. In comparison, perceived risk was found to have an insignificant and detrimental impact on purchase intention. The finding is consistent with previous studies (e.g., Lin and Wang, 2015).

Perceived risk means that customers are conscious of possible hazards due to pandemic situations, such as health problems, safety measures, payment ambiguity, and unwarranted product consistency (Chiu et al., 2014).

Table 3. Regression weights.

Relationships			Unstandardized estimates	Standardized estimates	P
Purchase intention	←	Perceived value	0.391	0.320	***
Purchase intention	←	Perceived risk	0.057	0.046	0.613
Purchase intention	←	Trust	−0.175	−0.140	0.167
Purchase intention	←	WoM	0.500	0.454	***
Customer satisfaction	←	Purchase intention	0.664	0.803	***

Note: ***Significance at the 0.001 level.

The perceived risk is then considered to not affect the purchase intention. Consumer trust may be an important contributor to consumers' purchase intentions (Park and Kim, 2016). Hence, the results reveal an insignificant relation between trust and purchase intention (Table 3).

The results showed that the path coefficient of WoM and purchase intention was positive and significant. The positive path coefficient means that WoM would increase the purchase intention. It is critical to establish trust with consumers in order to make repeat sales and convert new customers into regular customers. This highlights, on the one hand, the value of useful practices for businesses to boost customer satisfaction, such as delivering high-quality products, providing a convenient shopping experience, and maintaining a strong relationship with customers. On the other hand, it is equally critical for businesses to provide positive information, create trustworthy relationships with customers, support consumers with more information and services about products, and eventually provide them with shopping satisfaction. It is also important for retailers or businesses to carry out a range of activities to enhance customer satisfaction. Therefore, the results indicate that purchase intention is more significant than customer satisfaction.

Table 4 presents the hypotheses tested among the variables using the different analyses to get the results.

Implications

This research provides beneficial information to both unorganized and organized retailers in better understanding the behaviour of consumers in

Table 4. Results of hypothesis testing.

Hypothesis	Path	Analysis (*p*-value)	Result
H1	Perceived value → Purchase Intention	0.000	Accepted
H2	Perceived risk → Purchase Intention	0.613	Rejected
H3	Trust → Purchase Intention	0.167	Rejected
H4	WoM → Purchase Intention	0.000	Accepted
H5	Purchase Intention → Satisfaction	0.000	Accepted

the post-COVID-19 scenario. The analysis results found an insignificant relationship between trust, perceived risk, and purchase intention. The retailers can mitigate risk and increase trust by following more safety measures, such as cashless payments using UPI and e-wallets, sanitization of stores, wearing gloves while billing the products, door delivery, and kiosk shops. By doing so, retailers can increase trust in the minds of consumers, which consequently leads to increased purchase intention and satisfaction. The study also found a significant relationship between perceived value, WoM, and purchase intention. As stated earlier, retailers can increase safety measures and promotional offers to attract and satisfy customers. This in turn encourages their customers to spread positive WoM about the products and services offered by their outlets.

Conclusion and Future Research

As far as the retail sector is concerned, India is at a junction where both unorganized and organized retailers possess dominating competitive advantages. Both types of retail existed even during COVID-19 due to the demand for disinfectant products and grocery items. Initially, the study intended to explore the factors shaping the perception of FMCG shoppers in the post-COVID-19 scenario. By reviewing the literature, the study found that WoM, perceived risk, perceived value, and trust are the most prominent factors impacting FMCG shoppers' perceptions. Second, the study attempted to examine the relationships between and effects of WoM, perceived risk, perceived value, trust, purchase intention, and satisfaction. The study found that perceived value and WoM have significant effects on purchase intention, which gradually leads to customer satisfaction.

However, the factors of trust and perceived risk do not have any influence on purchase intention.

The study has certain limitations, which will be useful for guiding future research. First, the study covered the most dominant factors influencing the intentions of consumers. Future research can identify other factors that impact the perception of consumers. Second, the study examined the effects in the post-COVID-19 scenario. Future research can test this model during the time of COVID-19 and perform a comparative study between the situations during and after COVID-19. The current study was performed only in three districts of Tamil Nadu. Future research can test this framework across other districts and even entire countries. The study is not restricted to any product category. The factors that influence the buying decision can vary across other product categories. Hence, researchers can apply this model across different product categories.

References

Aamer, W. (2021). Exploring the Moderating Role of Openness to Experience in the Relationship between Perceived Risk and Online Purchase Intention. Doctoral Dissertation.

Agarwal, S., and Teas, K. (2001). Perceived value: Mediating role of perceived risk. *Journal of Marketing Theory and Practice*, 9(4), 1–14.

Banumathi, M. P., & Rani, S. M. (2018). Study on customer's perception and satisfaction towards FMCG products with special reference to Thoothukudi district. *Journal of Emerging Technologies and Innovative Research*, 5(5), 393–404.

Bauer, R. A. (1967). Consumer behaviour as risk taking. In Cox, D. F. (ed.) *Risk Taking & Information Handling in Consumer Behaviour*. Graduate School of Business Administration, Harvard University, Boston.

Bentler, P. M., and Bonett, D. G. (1980). Significance tests and goodness of fit in the analysis of covariance structures. *Psychological Bulletin*, 88(3), 588.

Berman, B., and Evans, J. R. (2001). *Retail Management* (8th edn.). Prentice Hall, Upper Saddle River, N.J.

Bhattacherjee, A. (2001). Understanding information systems continuance: An expectation-confirmation model. *MIS Quarterly*, 25(3), 351–370.

Bollen, K. A. (1986). Sample size and Bentler and Bonett's nonnormed fit index. *Psychometrika*, 51(3), 375–377.

Brcic, J., and Latham, G. (2016). The effect of priming affect on customer service satisfaction. *Academy of Management Discoveries*, 2(4), 392–403.

Chiu, C.-M., Wang, E. T. G., Fang, Y.-H., and Huang, H.-Y. (2014). Understanding customers' repeat purchase intentions in B2C e-commerce: The roles of utilitarian value, hedonic value and perceived risk. *Information Systems Journal*, 24(1), 85–114.

Cronin Jr., J. J., Brady, M. K., and Hult, G. T. M. (2000). Assessing the effects of quality, value, and customer satisfaction on consumer behavioral intentions in service environments. *Journal of Retailing*, 76(2), 193–218.

Dellarocas, C. (2003). The digitization of word of mouth: Promise and challenges of online feedback mechanisms. *Management Science*, 49, 1407–1424. doi: 10.1287/mnsc.49.10.1407.17308.

Forsythe, S., et al. (2006). Development of a scale to measure the perceived benefits and risks of online shopping. *Journal of Interactive Marketing*, 20(2), 55–75.

Gerbing, D. W., and Anderson, J. C. (1988). An updated paradigm for scale development incorporating unidimensionality and its assessment. *Journal of Marketing Research*, 25(2), 186–192.

Goswami, S., and Chouhan, V. (2021). Impact of change in consumer behaviour and need prioritisation on retail industry in Rajasthan during COVID-19 pandemic. *Materials Today: Proceedings*. https://doi.org/10.1016/j.matpr.2020.12.073.

Hair, J. F., Anderson, R. E., Tatham, R. L., and Bleck, W. C. (1998). *Multivariate Date Analysis with Readings*. Prentice Hall, Englewood, Cliff, NJ.

Hassan, S. B., and Soliman, M. (2020). COVID-19 and repeat visitation: Assessing the role of destination social responsibility, destination reputation, holidaymakers' trust and fear arousal. *Journal of Destination Marketing & Management*, 19, 100–495.

Hollingsworth, A. (2004). Increasing retail concentration: Evidence from the UK food retail sector. *British Food Journal*, 106(8), 629–638.

Hu, L. T., and Bentler, P. M. (1999). Cutoff criteria for fit indexes in covariance structure analysis: Conventional criteria versus new alternatives. *Structural Equation Modeling: A Multidisciplinary Journal*, 6(1), 1–55.

IBEF. (2019). Indian Retail Industry Analysis. Retrieved 10 April 2020 from https://www.ibef.org/industry/indianretail-industry-analysis-presentation. January 2019.

Jarvis, C. B., MacKenzie, S. B., and Podsakoff, P. M. (2003). A critical review of construct indicators and measurement model misspecification in marketing and consumer research. *Journal of Consumer Research*, 30(2), 199–218.

Jöreskog, K. G., and Sörbom, D. (1993). *LISREL 8: Structural Equation Modeling with the SIMPLIS Command Language*. Scientific Software International.

Kaplan, D. (2000). *Structural Equation Modeling: Foundations and Extensions*. Sage Publications, Thousand Oaks, CA.

Kline, R. B. (2005). *Principles and Practice of Structural Equation Modeling*. Guilford Press.

Konuk, F. A., et al. (2018). The role of store image, perceived quality, trust and perceived value in predicting consumers' purchase intentions towards organic private label food. *Journal of Retailing and Consumer Services*, 43, 304–310.

Liljander, V., Polsa, P., and van Riel, A. (2009). Modelling consumer responses to an apparel store brand: Store image as a risk reducer. *Journal of Retailing and Consumer Services*, 16(4), 281–290.

Lufkin, B. (2020). Amid the corona virus outbreak, people are flocking to supermarkets worldwide – But are they simply preparing, or irrationally panicking? www.bbc.com/worklife/article/20200304-coronavirus-covid19-update-why-people-are-stockpiling.

Mahadira, F., and Purwanegara, M. F. (2014). A study of brand consumption and consumer satisfaction towards fast-moving consumer goods. *Journal of Business and Management*, 3(1), 61–75.

Marsh, H. W., and Grayson, D. (1995). Latent variable models of multitrait-multimethod data.

McKinsey & Company. (2020). Consumer sentiment and behavior continue to reflect the uncertainty of the COVID-19 crisis. https://www.mckinsey.com/business-functions/marketing-and-sales/our-insights/a-global-view-of-how-consumer-behavior-is-changing-amid-covid-19. July 8, 2020.

Nunnally, J., and Bernstein, I. (1994). *Psychometric Theory*. Mcgraw-Hill, New York.

Park, H., and Kim, Y.-K. (2016). Proactive versus reactive apparel brands in sustainability: Influences on brand loyalty. *Journal of Retailing and Consumer Services*, 29, 114–122.

Reddy, A. (2020). Covid-19 Impact: Consumers Move More towards Digital. www.thehindubusinessline.com/opinion/covid-19-impact-consumers-move-more-towardsdigital/article31337127.ece.

Saleem, M. A., Zahra, S., and Yaseen, A. (2017). Impact of service quality and trust on repurchase intentions–the case of Pakistan airline industry. *Asia Pacific Journal of Marketing and Logistics*, 29(5), 1136–1159.

Schermelleh-Engel, K., Moosbrugger, H., and Müller, H. (2003). Evaluating the fit of structural equation models: Tests of significance and descriptive goodness-of-fit measures. *Methods of Psychological Research Online*, 8(2), 23–74.

Sirdeshmukh, D., Singh, J., and Sabol, B. (2002). Consumer trust, value, and loyalty in relational exchanges. *Journal of Marketing*, 66(1), 15–37.

Steiger, J. H. (2007). Understanding the limitations of global fit assessment in structural equation modeling. *Personality and Individual Differences*, 42(5), 893–898.

Sweeney, J. C., and Soutar, G. N. (2001). Consumer perceived value: The development of a multiple item scale. *Journal of Retailing*, 77(2), 203–220.

Sweeney, J. C., Soutar, G. N., and Johnson, L. W. (1999). The role of perceived risk in the quality-value relationship: A study in a retail environment. *Journal of Retailing*, 75(1), 77–105.

Tabachnik, B. G., and Fidell, L. S. (2007). *Using Multivariate Statistics*. Pearson.

Tucker, L. R., and Lewis, C. (1973). A reliability coefficient for maximum likelihood factor analysis. *Psychometrika*, 38(1), 1–10.

Tynan, C., McKechnie, S., and Hartley, S. (2014). Interpreting value in the customer service experience using customer-dominant logic. *Journal of Marketing Management*, 30(9–10), 1058–1081.

Venkatesh, V., and Davis, F. D. (2000). A theoretical extension of the technology acceptance model: Four longitudinal field studies. *Management Science*, 46(2), 186–204.

Yu, J., Lee, K., and Hyun, S. S. (2021). Understanding the influence of the perceived risk of the coronavirus disease (COVID-19) on the post-traumatic stress disorder and revisit intention of hotel guests. *Journal of Hospitality and Tourism Management*, 46, 327–335. March 2021.

Zeithaml, V. A. (1998). Consumer perceptions of price, quality, and value: A means-end model and synthesis of evidence. *Journal of Marketing*, 52(3), 2–22.

Chapter 3

Predicting Visit Intention after COVID-19 Using Theory of Planned Behaviour

N. Muhammed Sajid[*,§], Meera Peethambaran[†,¶], and K. Jiyas[‡,‖]

School of Management Studies, CUSAT, Kochi, Kerala, India
†IIM Kozhikode, Kerala, India
‡University of Kerala, Thiruvananthapuram, Kerala, India
§sajidnasar@cusat.ac.in
¶meerapeethambaran66@gmail.com
‖nofearsajid@gmail.com

Abstract

The global pandemic COVID-19 has stretched its vicious wings across the world, forcing the entire world to strive hard to come up with solutions to address the situation. There were periods when each day ended with a death toll crossing the count of lakhs (hundreds of thousands). People were left stranded in many places due to travel bans and social distancing in many parts of the world. The travel industry, which is one of the most prosperous industries, was direly affected by the pandemic. In this chapter, we incorporate the theory of planned behaviour in order to predict the travel intentions of tourists in the post-COVID-19 phase. For this, we examine variables such as attitude, subjective norms, and perceived behavioural control. Another independent variable that plays a crucial role in travel intention is perceived risk, which prevents people from travelling from one place to another in fear of the risk (pandemic spread) that they could encounter.

Keywords: COVID-19, visit intention, perceived risk, destination image, intention.

Introduction

The novel coronavirus disease (COVID-19) was first identified in a central city in China named Wuhan, which later spread rapidly to the rest of the world and was declared by the World Health Organization (WHO) as a global pandemic. It is very infectious and, like severe acute respiratory syndrome (SARS), can easily transmit from one human to another (WHO, 2020). It affected the entire population of the world while taking away the right of movement of people due to the strict preventive measures, including grounding of airlines, closure of resorts, and travel restrictions in place in most nations around the world. It is vital to observe that global tourism has been exposed to a wide variety of crises in the past, including the 9/11 terrorist attack in 2001, the SARS outbreak in 2003, the Indian Ocean tsunami in 2005, the global financial crisis of 2008, and the Middle East Respiratory Syndrome (MERS) outbreak in 2015. None of them led to a long-term decline in the global development of tourism, with most of them not even having a notable impact.

However, the pandemic resulted in all of the worldwide locations implementing travel restrictions, approximately 45% absolutely or partially closing their borders, 30% completely or partly suspending global flights, 18% banning the entry of passengers from specific countries or those who have transited via particular destinations, and 7% applying distinctive measures consisting of quarantine or self-isolation for 14 days and visa restrictions (UNWTO, 2020). One of the industries which was jeopardized by this pandemic was the tourism industry. The global tourism industry plays a pivotal role in offering at any time approximately 3% of the world's employment (Ladkin, 2011). By attracting global tourists, tourism contributed extensively to a destination's financial prosperity by accumulating forex earnings, supplying employment possibilities, and improving infrastructure (Li *et al.*, 2018). The significance of the tourism industry for international destinations is properly documented in the existing literature (see, for instance, Dogru *et al.*, 2017; Dogru and Bulut, 2018). Hence, it's highly conspicuous that the tourism industry has a wider effect on the world economy.

The tourism industry has never witnessed such an extreme slowdown. So, boosting it up and bringing it back on track is really a tiresome task. Travel merchandise are associated with greater risk due to not only their tangibility but also that they usually involves higher value and complex choices (Lin *et al.*, 2009). The fear that the pandemic has created in the minds of people will unknowingly control their travel behaviour for an extended period. In this study, we focus on the prediction of the travel behaviour of people after the pandemic against the backdrop of the theory of planned behaviour (TPB). Also, it has been stated that attitude, subjective norms, and perceived behavioural control have a tremendous effect on intention in the course of a pandemic (Zhang *et al.*, 2019). The primary demographic focus of the travel industry has traditionally been families. Nevertheless, amid prevailing uncertainties, individuals tend to manifest more stereotypical inclinations across various aspects, including their preferences related to travel. In this context, a variable called *perceived risk* becomes relevant. Perceived risk reduces the urge to travel to a new place in people who are conscious of their family's health and safety. In such a context, the variable *destination image* plays a different role in attracting tourists to a particular destination with respect to the prevailing pandemic. In this chapter, we concentrate on the question of what can create a similar urge for movement or travel in people by reducing their perceived risk due to COVID-19. We suggest a conceptual framework that could help predict tourists' visit intentions after the COVID-19 pandemic.

Review of Literature and Conceptual Framework

Theory of planned behaviour

The theory of planned behaviour (TPB) is an extension of the theory of reasoned action proposed by Ajzen (1991). It was originally developed to predict consumer behaviour, which in turn helps marketers successfully market their products and services. TPB is based on the notion that human behaviours are formed jointly by three factors: *attitude, subjective norms*, and *perceived behavioural control* (PBC) (Ajzen, 1985). This theory has been efficiently used in various backgrounds to describe or predict human behaviour (Ajzen, 2002), including risk management in natural tourism (Gstaettner *et al.*, 2017), tourists' health risk preventative behaviour (Huang *et al.*, 2020), and tourists' responsible environmental behaviours (Wang *et al.*, 2018). Scholars have also used TPB to study consumer behaviour during or after a pandemic. For example, Zhang *et al.* (2019) used TPB to predict consumers' intentions to consume poultry during an H7N9 outbreak and found a positive correlation between attitude, subjective norms, PBC, and intention. Yang (2015) has used TPB to predict young adults' intentions to get the H1N1 vaccine and found a positive correlation between attitude, subjective norms, and intention.

Attitude indicates individuals' feelings related to exhibiting a behaviour which results from their salient beliefs and outcome evaluations (Ajzen *et al.*, 1980; Kim and Han, 2010). In the context of predicting consumers' intention to visit a location after COVID-19, attitude is defined as the well evaluated or assumed result (which can be either positive or negative) of the visit behaviour of people after COVID-19. With regard to subjective norms, they are a form of perceived social pressure by other social groups that could have a relevant effect on an individual's thought process regarding whether they should or should not exhibit a particular behaviour (Ajzen *et al.*, 1980). In the context of COVID-19, we define subjective norms as the social opinion or pressure a person acquires while choosing a travel destination, which in turn results in their positive or negative behaviour toward travelling to that particular destination. The third predictor of intention is PBC. Ajzen (1991) describes control beliefs as 'the resources and opportunities available to a person must to some extent dictate the likelihood of behavioural achievement.' In the context of predicting consumers' intention to visit after COVID-19, we could define PBC as another antecedent factor that could create a positive drive in the mindset of an individual by focusing on the ease or difficulty of performing the act of travelling without much concern. For example, a person who is travelling to Kerala (a state in India) would be more delightful and less concerned about health issues since the state has created an excellent healthcare system and model which has drastically flattened the curve and was accepted worldwide. Many research studies, in a number of contexts, confirmed that the attitude towards behaviour, subjective norms, and PBC as alien constructs that lead to customer intention and behaviour inside the framework of the TPB or extended TPB (Kim and Han, 2010; Hsu and Huang, 2012; Kim *et al.*, 2013; Ong and Musa, 2011; Quintal *et al.*, 2010; Teng *et al.*, 2015; Paul *et al.*, 2016). In the studies on tourism, many have found that attitude, subjective norms, and PBC have a good-sized impact on intention (e.g., Soliman, 2019; Quintal *et al.*, 2010; Gstaettner *et al.*, 2017). Moreover, Zhang *et al.* (2019) found that attitude, subjective norms, and PBC have a tremendous effect on intention in the course of a pandemic. We, therefore, present the following propositions:

P1a: Attitude is positively related to tourists' visit intentions after COVID-19.

P1b: Subjective norms are positively related to tourists' visit intentions after COVID-19.

P1c: PBC is positively related to tourists' visit intentions after COVID-19.

Derivation of extended TPB

Ajzen (1991) specified that TPB is widely open to extensions of its trails via the inclusion of additional constructs to capture a greater proportion of the variance in intention or behaviour. In addition, new variables added to the original version should be introduced only as per the following principles: (1) they must be conceptually independent from existing variables in the model; (2) they must be imperative elements that affect the decision-making method; and (3) they should be potentially suitable for a selected behaviour. In fact, previous studies have efficaciously extended TPB by including variables which can be believed to be vital in various precise contexts (e.g., Paul *et al.* 2016). At the outset of this background, we're extending the version by including the variable destination image. There were a few other relevant constructs, such as 'anticipated fear,' to be considered while extending TPB in this context. However, from the review of relevant literature, it was noted that safety concerns by tourists can negatively affect destination image with long-standing consequences if they continue to exist unaddressed (Sirakaya *et al.*, 1997). Also, Perpiña *et al.* (2020) have opined that destination image and risk perception have the same faculty to influence travel decisions and behaviours, i.e., studies on destination image focus on the positive aspects of the destination, while studies on risk focus on the negative aspects.

Destination image has been a highly researched subject matter for decades. It refers to the thoughts, beliefs, and impressions that individuals experience about the traits and activities at a destination after studying the facts accrued from different sources over a given period (Assaker *et al.*, 2014; Crompton, 1979; Gartner, 1986). Images that 'drive' perceptions are comparatively more important than tangible assets in motivating consumers to take action (Guthrie and Gale, 1991). It is a valuable knowledge to understand how tourists pick out a destination (Baloglu and McCleary, 1999). Embacher and Buttle (1989) noted that a destination image constitutes the thoughts or concepts held individually or collectively of the destination under investigation. In this context, we define destination image as the thoughts, beliefs, and impressions that individuals and groups received about the safety regarding the spread of any communicable diseases, such as COVID-19, how much a particular destination is free from the diseases, and how equipped the place is in terms of healthcare.

The image construct is often recommended as including two distinct but interrelated components: perceptual/cognitive and affective (Baloglu, 2000). However, in discussing the relationship among destination image and other variables, only a few scholars considered destination image as a single item; for instance, see Baloglu and McCleary (1999), Bigne et al. (2001), and Lee (2009). In analyzing the relationship between the destination image and its constructs, this study also adopts the single-item approach. Previous research in consumer behaviour and tourism have validated a positive correlation between destination image and behavioural intention (Mayo, 1973; Goodrich, 1978; Reibstein et al., 1980; Court and Lupton, 1997). Also, many studies found the image to be an instantaneous antecedent of perceived quality, satisfaction, and behaviour intention (Bigne et al., 2001). Destination image is advanced and created in various ways and has an enormous effect on the selection of a destination (Khan et al., 2016). We, therefore, present the following proposition:

P2: Destination image is positively related to tourists' visit intention after COVID-19.

Perceived risk on COVID-19

Perceived risk is defined as the probability of an undesirable incident that results in viable negative effects on a consumer's behaviour (Laws and Prideaux, 2005). In contrast, perceived risk is also referred to as a customer's perception of the overall negativity of an action that, if it exceeds a specific threshold, might have an effect on tourist behaviour (Mansfeld and Pizam, 2006). Researchers argued that incidences of crime, terrorism, natural disasters, accidents, and epidemics individually or together increase risk perceptions and affect tourist arrival at destinations (Carter, 1998; Chew and Jahari, 2014; Fuchs and Reichel, 2006; Rittichainuwat and Chakraborty, 2009). Irvine and Anderson (2006) found that risk perception, rather than facts or circumstances of real risk, influences tourists' behaviour in keeping away from or cancelling travel to a specific destination. In connection with tourism, studies have recognized five major risks pertaining to this area: terrorism, war and political instability (Sönmez and Graefe, 1998a, 1998b; Richter, 2003), health concerns (Richter, 2003), crime (Dimanche and Lepetic, 1999), and those related to cultural and language differences (Basala and Klenosky, 2001; Vassos, 1997). In this chapter, we address the risk associated with health concerns, i.e., travel after COVID-19. When tourists perceive that there is excessive physical risk involved in travelling to a particular destination, it is evident that they will rethink or cancel their travel plans (Wang, 2009).

Previous research confirms the view that perceptions of risk and safety can directly affect travellers' destination choices in addition to their propensity to visit or stay away from certain destinations (Sönmez and Graefe, 1998a, 1998b; Yavas, 1987). A massive corpus of prior research has highlighted the negative relationship between risk perception and tourists' intention to visit (Çetinsöz and Ege, 2013; Khan *et al.*, 2017; Rittichainuwat, 2008; Promsivapallop and Kannaovakun, 2017). Since risk perception is a critical antecedent determining an individual's visit intention, risk perception should also be taken into consideration as an antecedent as part of the additives of the extended TPB version to better apprehend tourists' intentions to visit after COVID-19.

P3a: Perceived risk from COVID-19 is negatively related to tourists' attitudes.

P3b: Perceived risk from COVID-19 is negatively related to subjective norms.

P3c: Perceived risk from COVID-19 is negatively related to PBC.

P3d: Perceived risk from COVID-19 is negatively related to destination image.

Methodology

Highly recognized databases were used to sort the literature. A thorough examination of areas such as travel and tourism, sociology, psychology, and consumer behaviour was conducted. Databases used for the survey of literature include ScienceDirect, Emerald Insight, Elsevier and Taylor & Francis Online. Keywords such as 'Visit Intention,' 'Destination Image,' 'Pandemic,' and 'Attitude to Intention' were used to retrieve the relevant literature. Along with the above-mentioned databases, we have used Google Scholar, Springer Link, and Sage to identify and define variables used in the conceptual model. In order to obtain facts and estimations about COVID-19 and its impact on tourism, we relied on reports from industries, governments, and the media and other reliable internet sources. However, to retrieve literature related to the conceptual model, only scientific literature of high quality was considered.

Discussion

As referenced in Figure 1, the conceptual framework presented in the chapter is derived on the basis of thoroughly researched secondary data. Indeed, during the extensive literature survey, it was found that previous studies proposed different aspects of intent to visit during a pandemic. However, visit intention during and after COVID-19 is a completely unexplored area. The framework presented here lacks empirical evidence as it has not been tested statistically. Therefore, future researchers can use this model to verify

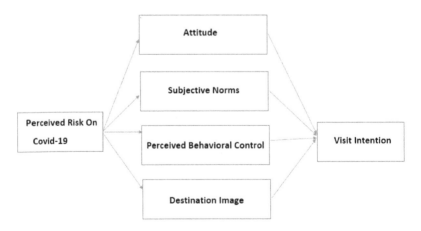

Figure 1. Conceptual model

the correlations in different cultural settings. They could also look into the antecedents of perceived risk from COVID-19, which we did not consider in this study. The model presented above gives a clear relation between different variables which were identified with the help of literature.

Managerial Implications

As evident from the literature, attitude, subjective norms, perceived behavioural control, and destination image have a direct impact on the intention to travel, while the perceived risk of COVID-19 holds an indirect relationship with the intention. It is also evident that the perceived risk of COVID-19 is a predictor of the intention to travel. Therefore, market players in the tourism industry should focus on minimizing the perceived risk of COVID-19 to tourists. Also, marketers should focus on building up a COVID-19-free image for their respective destinations. Digital marketing is a viable method that has an impact on all these factors. Along with these, steps should be taken to positively impact the independent TPB variables, which could be implemented through the use of influencer marketing as a cost-effective strategy.

Conclusion

Based on a systematic literature review, this study, unconventionally, provides a comprehensive set of hypothesized explanatory variables influencing visit intention. This paper clearly explains the relation between variables such as perceived risk, perceived behavioural control, subjective norms, attitude, destination image, and visit intention. The revival of the tourism industry is vital for a developing country, such as India. The contribution of tourism towards the GDP plays a key role in our development. The onset of fear and perceived risk created by the pandemic has seriously affected the industry. Therefore, in order to reinject the craving for travel in people, we have identified certain variables that create or have the potential to create the intention of travelling.

References

Ajzen, I. (1985). From intentions to actions: A theory of planned behavior. In Action control: From cognition to behavior (pp. 11–39). Berlin, Heidelberg: Springer Berlin Heidelberg.

Ajzen, I. (1991). The theory of planned behavior. *Organizational Behavior and Human Decision Processes*, 50(2), 179–211.

Ajzen, I. (2002). Residual effects of past on later behavior: Habituation and reasoned action perspectives. *Personality and Social Psychology Review*.

Ajzen, I., Fishbein, M., and Heilbroner, R. (1980). *Understanding Attitudes and Predicting Social Behavior.* Prentice-Hall, Englewood Cliffs.

Assaker, G., Hallak, R., and Vinzi, V. (2014). An empirical operationalization of countries' destination competitiveness using partial least squares modeling. *Journal of Travel Research*.

Baloglu, S. (2000). A path analytic model of visitation intention involving information sources, socio-psychological motivations, and destination image. *Journal of Travel & Tourism Marketing*.

Baloglu, S., and McCleary, K. (1999). A model of destination image formation. *Annals of Tourism Research*.

Basala, S., and Klenosky, D. (2001). Travel-style preferences for visiting a novel destination: A conjoint investigation across the novelty-familiarity continuum. *Journal of Travel Research*.

Bigne, J., Sanchez, M., and Sanchez, J. (2001). Tourism image, evaluation variables and after purchase behaviour: inter-relationship. *Tourism Management*.

Carter, S. (1998). Tourists' and travellers' social construction of Africa and Asia as risky locations. *Tourism Management*.

Çetinsöz, B., and Ege, Z. (2013). Impacts of perceived risks on tourists' revisit intentions. *Anatolia*.

Chew, E., and Jahari, S. (2014). Destination image as a mediator between perceived risks and revisit intention: A case of post-disaster Japan. *Tourism Management*.

Court, B., and Lupton, R. (1997). Customer portfolio development: Modeling destination adopters, inactives, and rejecters. *Journal of Travel Research*.

Crompton, J. (1979). An assessment of the image of Mexico as a vacation destination and the influence of geographical location upon that image. *Journal of Travel Research*.

Dimanche, F., and Lepetic, A. (1999). New Orleans tourism and crime: A case study. *Journal of Travel Research*.

Dogru, T., and Bulut, U. (2018). Is tourism an engine for economic recovery? Theory and empirical evidence. *Tourism Management*.

Dogru, T., Sirakaya-Turk, E., and Crouch, G. (2017). Remodeling international tourism demand: Old theory and new evidence. *Tourism Management*.

Embacher, J., and Buttle, F. (1989). A repertory grid analysis of Austria's image as a summer vacation destination. *Journal of Travel Research*.

Fuchs, G., and Reichel, A. (2006). Correlates of destination risk perception and risk reduction strategies. *Progress in Tourism Marketing*.

Gartner, W. (1986). Temporal influences on image change. *Annals of Tourism Research*.

Goodrich, J. (1978). The relationship between preferences for and perceptions of vacation destinations: Application of a choice model. *Journal of Travel Research*.

Gstaettner, A., Rodger, K., and Lee, D. (2017). Visitor perspectives of risk management in a natural tourism setting: An application of the theory of planned behaviour. *Journal of Outdoor Recreation and Tourism*.

Guthrie, J., and Gale, P. (1991). Positioning ski areas. *New Horizons Conference Proceedings* (pp. 551–569). University of Calgary, Calgary.

Hsu, C., and Huang, S. (2012). An extension of the theory of planned behavior model for tourists. *Journal of Hospitality & Tourism*.

Huang, X., Dai, S., and Xu, H. (2020). Predicting tourists' health risk preventative behaviour and travelling satisfaction in Tibet: Combining the theory of planned behaviour and health belief model. *Tourism Management Perspectives*.

Irvine, W., and Anderson, A. (2006). The impacts of foot and mouth disease on a peripheral tourism area: The role and effect of crisis management. *Journal of Travel & Tourism Marketing*.

Khan, M., Chelliah, S., and Haron, M. (2016). Medical tourism destination image formation process: A conceptual model. *International Journal of Healthcare Management*.

Khan, M., Chelliah, S., and Ahmed, S. (2017). Factors influencing destination image and visit intention among young women travellers: Role of travel motivation, perceived risks, and travel constraints. *Asia Pacific Journal of Tourism*.

Kim, Y., and Han, H. (2010). Intention to pay conventional-hotel prices at a green hotel – A modification of the theory of planned behavior. *Journal of Sustainable Tourism*.

Kim, Y., Njite, D., and Hancer, M. (2013). Anticipated emotion in consumers' intentions to select eco-friendly restaurants: Augmenting the theory of planned behavior. *International Journal of Hospitality Management*.

Ladkin, A. (2011). Exploring tourism labor. *Annals of Tourism Research*.

Laws, E., and Prideaux, B. (2005). *Tourism Crises: Management Responses and Theoretical Insight*. Psychology Press.

Lee, T. (2009). A structural model to examine how destination image, attitude, and motivation affect the future behavior of tourists. *Leisure Sciences*.

Li, K., Jin, M., and Shi, W. (2018). Tourism as an important impetus to promoting economic growth: A critical review. *Tourism Management Perspectives*.

Lin, P., Jones, E., and Westwood, S. (2009). Perceived risk and risk-relievers in online travel purchase intentions. *Journal of Hospitality Marketing and Management*.

Mansfeld, Y., and Pizam, A. (2006). *Tourism, Security and Safety.* Routledge.

Mayo, E. (1973). Regional images and regional travel behavior. *The Travel Research Association Fourth Annual Conference Proceedings* (pp. 211–218).

Ong, T., and Musa, G. (2011). An examination of recreational divers' underwater behaviour by attitude–behaviour theories. *Current Issues in Tourism.*

Paul, J., Modi, A., and Patel, J. (2016). Predicting green product consumption using theory of planned behavior and reasoned action. *Journal of Retailing and Consumer Service.*

Perpiña, L., Prats, L., and Camprubí, R. (2020). Image and risk perceptions: An integrated approach. *Current Issues in Tourism.*

Promsivapallop, P., and Kannaovakun, P. (2017). A comparative assessment of destination image, travel risk perceptions and travel intention by young travellers across three ASEAN countries: A study of German students. *Asia Pacific Journal of Tourism Research.*

Quintal, V., Lee, J., and Soutar, G. (2010). Risk, uncertainty and the theory of planned behavior: A tourism example. *Tourism Management.*

Reibstein, D. J., Lovelock, C. H., and Dobson, R. D. P. (1980). The direction of causality between perceptions, affect, and behavior: An application to travel behavior. *Journal of Consumer Research*, 6(4), 370–376.

Richter, L. (2003). International tourism and its global public health consequences. *Journal of Travel Research.*

Rittichainuwat, N. (2008). Responding to disaster: Thai and Scandinavian tourists' motivation to visit Phuket, Thailand. *Journal of Travel Research.*

Rittichainuwat, B., and Chakraborty, G. (2009). Perceived travel risks regarding terrorism and disease: The case of Thailand. *Tourism Management.*

Sirakaya, E., Sheppard, A., and McLellan, R. W. (1997). Assessment of the relationship between perceived safety at a vacation site and destination choice decisions: Extending the behavioral decision-making model. *Journal of Hospitality & Tourism Research.*

Soliman, M. (2019). Extending the theory of planned behavior to predict tourism destination revisit intention. *International Journal of Hospitality & Tourism Administration.*

Sönmez, S., and Graefe, A. (1998a). Influence of terrorism risk on foreign tourism decisions. *Annals of Tourism Research.*

Sönmez, S., and Graefe, A. (1998b). Determining future travel behavior from past travel experience and perceptions of risk and safety. *Journal of Travel Research.*

Teng, Y., Wu, K., and Liu, H. (2015). Integrating altruism and the theory of planned behavior to predict patronage intention of a green hotel. *Journal of Hospitality & Tourism.*

UNWTO. (2020). https://www.unwto.org. From https://www.unwto.org/news/covid-19-response-travel-restrictions.

Vassos, M. (1997). Perceived risk and risk reduction in holiday purchases. *Journal of Euro-Marketing.*

Wang, Y. (2009). The impact of crisis events and macroeconomic activity on Taiwan's international inbound tourism demand. *Tourism Management.*

Wang, C., Zhang, J., Yu, P., and Hu, H. (2018). The theory of planned behavior as a model for understanding tourists' responsible environmental behaviors: The moderating role of environmental interpretations. *Journal of Cleaner Production.*

WHO. (2020). www.who.int. From https://www.who.int/emergencies/diseases/novel-coronavirus-2019. January 2020.

Yang, Z. (2015). Predicting young adults' intentions to get the H1N1 vaccine: An integrated model. *Journal of Health Communication.*

Yavas, U. (1987). Foreign travel behaviour in a growing vacation market: Implications for tourism marketers. *European Journal of Marketing.*

Zhang, Y., Yang, H., Cheng, P., and Luqman, A. (2019). Predicting consumers' intention to consume poultry during an H7N9 emergency: An extension of the theory of planned behavior model. *Human and Ecological Risk Assessment: An International Journal.*

© 2025 World Scientific Publishing Company
https://doi.org/10.1142/9789811292101_0004

Chapter 4

A Study on Consumer Behaviour towards Digital Food App Services in India

Kritika Mahensaria* and Supriyo Patra[†,‡,§]

Department of Business Administration/BMS, St. Xavier's College (Autonomous), Kolkata, West Bengal, India

*mahensaria.k@gmail.com
†spatra@sxccal.edu
‡supriyo_patra@rediffmail.com
§drsupriyopatra@gmail.com

Abstract

Digital food apps have gained immense popularity during the ongoing pandemic as the world took a step forward towards going contactless in terms of shopping and delivery. COVID-19 hampered the restaurant business dramatically. However, in times of crisis, digital food delivery applications and their distribution channels served as a bridge between people stuck at home and restaurants operating in order to earn a living and sustain themselves. The **major objective** of this study is to examine **consumers' behaviour towards digital food app services in India**. The study is also aimed at determining awareness-creating sources and understanding the relationship between income and money spent on meals on each occasion. It also focuses on determining the factors influencing consumers' motivation to place orders online.

The **research methodology** focused on **cross-sectional research design**, and primary data were collected from 150 respondents across India from varying demographics with the aid of a structured questionnaire.

The **data analysis** consisted of chi square tests in SPSS, along with graphical methods of analysis and study. The **findings** of our study highlighted that social media is the most preferred source for creating awareness; higher incomes result in inflated spending, with cash on delivery and e-wallets being the preferred modes of payment by the elderly and youth, respectively.

These insights are expected to facilitate brands in understanding the behaviour of their target audience better and in developing effective marketing and promotional strategies. This will help them gain popularity and make the most of the current situation, which is driving people further towards using digital applications.

Keywords: Digital food apps, COVID-19, consumer behaviour, consumer awareness and India.

Introduction

COVID-19 has brought every sector to a standstill, apart from the stores and services that provide essential items. Most companies took drastic measures to remodel their supply chains and restructure their organizations to minimize losses. One of the sectors which initially seemed doomed but prospered later was the digital delivery industry. Food delivery applications extended their services to include supplying essential items, including groceries and medical equipment, along with their usual restaurant deliveries.

With an increase in the adaptation of technology during the pandemic and most of the population effectively under a form of house arrest, the number of people making use of digital technologies increased at an astonishing rate. Comfort and timely delivery are important influencers, as they simplify digital ordering with just a few clicks on a handheld device. Technology, convenience, safety, sanitization, and time efficiency in the delivery of food and essentials are vital reasons for consumers to choose these services.

Mobile applications and food delivery companies provide customers with infinite restaurant and market options, with dishes, groceries, alcohol, and medical supplies available from various parts of the world. Customers enjoy the provision of placing orders from home while payment is made either online or via pay-on-delivery systems. These applications allow and implement a feedback methodology where users can provide their feedback along with recommendations and rate the food received and delivery experience. Another appealing characteristic of these digital food delivery apps is that they are surprisingly cost-effective and offer consumers a wide variety of options to pick from. These service providers have adapted to the challenge thrown at them by the world very well and have henceforth managed to not only survive in these difficult times but also flourish and be more successful.

Scope and relevance

Online food delivery applications offer delivery services; however, the way these services have adapted depends on the awareness and perception of consumers. This research is therefore aimed at understanding this very aspect of consumers' awareness of these digital services and the frequency of their usage based on consumers' income. Further growth of the industry and consumer satisfaction depend on the key factors and unique selling propositions (USPs) of these services.

Need and motivation

Due to the diversity of India, there exist large differences in cultural backgrounds, lifestyles, economic status, religious beliefs, and spending patterns, which consequently give rise to variations in diet and consumption factors. Digital food application services help bridge the gap which exists between food providers and consumers. They also develop a well-established and connected system for the delivery and transfer of commodities. However, the way consumers or customers perceive these applications and their services depends on their backgrounds, needs, culture, and the primary and secondary services provided by these enterprises. Thus, there arises a need to understand purchase behaviour and consumption patterns in order to improve these existing services in terms of consumers' preferences and their sources of awareness. This study aims to address this need.

Objectives

The objectives of the study are as follows:

- to identify the major source of awareness about different food delivery applications;
- to determine the relationship between income and money spent on meals on each occasion;
- to understand the factors important for placing orders for food online.

Literature Review

According to Chavan *et al.* (2015), 'digital restaurants use smartphones to get orders from customers. PDA app has been replaced with smart phones to provide a user interface to display menu or monitor orders.' It emerged from their study that 'with a secured login system, customers have the option of viewing the menu, placing orders, tracking their orders, receiving real-time updates and making online payment, and collecting receipts from gadgets itself thereby increasing their comfort.'

Das (2018) highlighted that 'the doorstep delivery is the highest influencing factor in the use of food ordering applications by end users. Consumers can often benefit from promotions and cash advances.' The study revealed that 'the most successful service provider was Zomato followed by Swiggy.'

Gupta (2020), in his study of online food delivery during the COVID-19 pandemic stated that 'online food delivery services have managed to convince their consumers of food delivery protection. They have also diversified into grocery delivery due to increased demand as a result of panic shopping.'

In the opinion of Hong (2016), in many sectors, 'technological innovation has transformed the business model to expand. Efficient systems of working can help to increase the restaurant's performance and effectiveness.' The online food network is believed to lead restaurant businesses to expand periodically and help them promote new businesses on the internet.

Li *et al.* (2020) highlighted the benefits of online food delivery: 'it provided consumers with ready-to-eat meals while allowing food suppliers to continue working.' They also mentioned that 'online food delivery has changed the way the hospitality industry functions […] It has revolutionised consumption patterns and availability of food nationwide.'

Research Methodology

Research design

A cross-sectional research design was administered in order to collect data from individuals, which varied in demographics such as income, occupation, age, and gender. This thereby ensured diversification in responses.

Data collection

Primary data for the study were obtained using a thoughtfully designed questionnaire, which aided in the analyses of the demographics affecting a consumer's awareness towards digital food delivery apps and the factors influencing the options opted for by them.

Sampling procedure

A convenience sampling procedure was used to gather first-hand data from the available respondents.

Sample size

The respondents' profile included 150 individuals of varying demographics, mostly residing in the cities of Kolkata, Mumbai, and Bengaluru.

Statistical tools

The following statistical tools have been used in the study for analyzing the data. The descriptive statistics technique has been used to determine the frequency of graphical representation of the major source of awareness creation towards these applications and the factors vital for influencing customers' purchase decisions. The Chi-square test has been used to determine the relation between the income of respondents and the average amount of money spent on meals per time.

Data Analysis and Findings

The information collected for this research was from 150 Indian consumers. According to the figures in Table 1, the majority of the respondents are aged 15–30 years (34%), followed by 31–45 years (30%), 46–60 years (26%), and above 60 years (10%). Additionally, the data collected account for 68 male (45.33%) respondents, 77 female (51.33%) respondents, and 5 (3.40%) respondents who prefer not to say. In terms of occupation, the majority of the responses collected are from students, i.e., 38%. This is followed by homemakers (22.67%), service providers (16%), business owners (13.33%), retired individuals (6%), and others (4%).

Table 1. Demographic profile of the respondents.

Demographic categories	Frequency	Valid percentage
Gender		
Male	68	45.33
Female	77	51.33
Prefer not to say	5	3.40
Age (years)		
15–30	51	34
31–45	45	30
46–60	39	26
60+	15	10
Income (Rs.)		
Less than 15,000	34	22.67
15,001–30,000	61	40.67
30,001–45,000	29	19.33
Above 45,000	26	17.33
Occupation		
Student	57	38
Homemaker	34	22.67
Service	24	16
Retired	9	6
Business	20	13.33
Other	6	4

Income classification includes a majority in the Rs. 15,001–30,000 bracket (40.67%), followed by those with less than Rs. 15,000 (22.67%), Rs. 30,001–45,000 (19.33%), and above Rs. 45,000 (17.33%) incomes.

Advertising and marketing play a very important role in determining the success or failure of a concept in general and a business in particular. Hence, informing the potential audience about the availability of the service is of utmost importance. It can be said that when it comes to digital food ordering applications, the most effective method of communication is through social media, which accounted for 67 responses (Figure 1). This can be well justified due to the increasing popularity of social media during the times of the pandemic and its impact on people's minds. Being socially involved and building up a community for oneself have also helped in the marketing of services through word-of-mouth communication (46 responses). It is also seen that these online ordering companies do not advertise as much in newspapers (23 responses), and messages are sent to existing users only to inform them about new deals and sustain their interest (14 responses). These responses can be supported by the fact that, during the pandemic, delivery of newspapers and magazines had come to a halt, and the only source of updates was through one's gadgets.

Relation between the income of respondents and average money spent on meals

H01 (Null Hypothesis): There is no association between the incomes of respondents and the average amount of money spent on meals.

Since the *p*-value from the chi-square statistics in Table 2 is 0.000 < 0.05, we reject the null hypothesis.

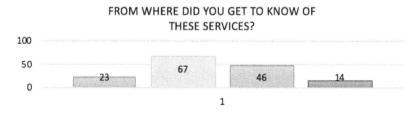

Figure 1. Sources of awareness about these services.

Table 2. Chi-square test results.

	Chi-square test		
	Value	*df*	**Asymp. Sig. (two-sided)**
Pearson Chi-Square	222.313[a]	16	0.000
Likelihood Ratio	215.351	16	0.000
No. of Valid Cases	150		

Note: [a]11 cells (44.0%) have expected counts less than 5. The minimum expected count is 0.09.

We have enough evidence to conclude that there exists an association between income and the average amount of money spent by respondents on meals. From the cross tabulation in Table 2, it can be seen that those who earn above Rs. 45,000 spend more than the expected value of above Rs. 1,200, while they spend less than expected in the Rs. 150–500 category. Those who earn between Rs. 30,000 and 45,000 prefer spending in the range of Rs. 851–1,200 compared to the expected value.

We can rely on the obtained conclusion since a higher level of income does imply higher standards of living and more monetary cushion to spend on meals and essentials with extra delivery charges levied on them. The loss of jobs and reduction in salaries have also reduced purchasing power.

According to Figure 2, for a greater number of respondents (34 individuals), convenience was the most important aspect of online food delivery. The entire concept of online food delivery revolves around the convenience factor, i.e., delivering ready-to-eat food, groceries, and other supplies from restaurants and stores to their doorsteps. Twenty-three respondents chose options availability and low delivery charges as the influencing factors behind their decision to order food through these applications. For 27 individuals, the availability of offers was a concern while ordering food online, which was mostly seen as a trend among young respondents who looked for offers before placing their orders. For 21 respondents, their preferred restaurant having a tie-up with the online food delivery aggregators was most important to them, and they did not want to try out new options. The speed of delivery was a factor of concern for 12 individuals, as they did not want to wait too long for their meal to arrive. Twenty respondents wanted the quality to be on par with what was being served in person at the restaurants. They did not want to make any compromises on the quality whatsoever. Another issue of concern among

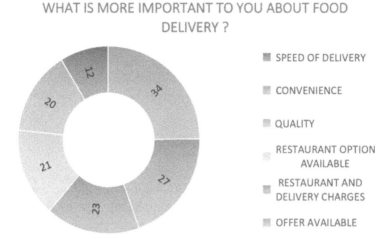

Figure 2. (Color available online) Respondents' answers to 'What is more important to you about food delivery?'

the respondents was the safety and proper sanitization of the goods as well as the delivery executives. These composite factors of food delivery services play an integral role in developing a consumer's mindset towards this entire sector of service offerings. These factors are very personal to every individual and therefore motivate them to opt for such services and adapt to technology.

Recommendations

- Service providers and marketers should make use of social media as their primary mode of advertising, as it proves to be successful in conveying the necessary information about the food delivery applications. With an increase in the use of the internet and smartphones during lockdowns and with the environment prevailing post-COVID-19, marketing policies and strategies should be formed in accordance with consumers' adaptability.
- Since convenience is the most important aspect of food delivery, strategy developers should work on enhancing this factor while simultaneously improving complimentary benefits for consumers, such as promotional offers and reduced delivery charges. Safety and sanitization should be focussed on by service providers in the new normal.

- Marketers should aim to provide a wide range of restaurant options since the amount spent on ordering food per time is co-dependent on the average income of an individual. The higher the income, the higher the monetary cushion. Keeping this in mind, formulators should ensure that alternatives are available for varied income groups to create a larger consumer base and increase sales by capturing a larger portion of the market.

Limitations of the Study

This study has been restricted to 150 respondents due to time constraints and the ongoing pandemic. It is also geographically restricted to certain metropolitan cities only. The study is also conducted among English-speaking respondents since the questionnaire was formulated in English. These might be treated as the limitations of the present study.

Scope for Future Research

This research work can be extended further with greater concentration on service providers' specifications. Comparative analysis between metropolitan cities and rural areas can be conducted to find out differences in the perception of consumers. Psychological analysis based on religion and cultural beliefs can be taken into consideration. Consumer behaviour can be further studied to gain a deeper understanding of the factors influencing their purchase. Purchase analysis on the basis of recurrence in ordering food digitally can be undertaken. Studies on pre-COVID-19 and post-COVID-19 consumer preferences can be carried out to formulate policies. The demographics of the audiences can be analyzed to gain knowledge about their purchase behaviour.

Conclusion

The study highlighted that social media is the most preferred source for creating awareness; higher income results in inflated spending with cash on delivery and e-wallets are the preferred modes of payment by elderly and youth, respectively. The pandemic that emerged in early 2020 acted as a turning point for the online market. The advertisements released on social media and the internet helped marketers gain immense popularity and attention. For people who were stuck at home, the convenience of delivery and offers available were major driving forces towards using these services. It was also understood that there existed an association between income and the average amount of money spent by respondents on meals. Higher income levels result in greater spending due to increased purchasing capacity.

The year 2020 saw the highest fall in income in about a decade, which resulted in low GDP and economic growth. Most households struggled to make ends meet, and with such losses and disrupted jobs, these consumers found it difficult to enjoy the privileges of these services.

These insights are expected to facilitate brands in understanding the behaviour of their target audience better and in developing effective marketing and promotional strategies. This will enable them to gain popularity and make the most of the current situation, which is driving people further towards using digital applications.

References

Chavan, V., Jadhav, P., Korade, S., and Teli, P. (2015). Implementing customizable online food ordering system using web based application. *International Journal of Innovative Science, Engineering & Technology*, 2(4), 722–727.

Das, J. (2018). Consumer perception towards 'online food ordering and delivery services'. *A Study on Consumer Behaviour towards Digital Food App Services in India*, 5(5), 1–12.

Gupta, A. (2020). Online food delivery market in India, online food delivery industry in India. Retrieved February 28, 2021, from https://www.kenresearch.com/blog/2020/05/market-research-report-of-india-online-food-delivery/. May 27, 2020.

Leong Wai Hong. (2016). Food ordering system using mobile phone. A report submitted to BIS (Hons) Information Systems Engineering, Faculty of Information and Communication Technology (Perak Campus), UTAR.

Li, C., Mirosa, M., and Bremer, P. (2020). Review of online food delivery platforms and their impacts on sustainability. *Sustainability*, 12(14), 5528. doi: 10.3390/su12145528.

© 2025 World Scientific Publishing Company
https://doi.org/10.1142/9789811292101_0005

Chapter 5

Consumers' Online Shopping Behaviour: A Post-COVID-19 Analysis in India

Mallika Srivastava[*,§], Mudita Sinha[†,¶], and Biranchi Narayan Swar[‡,∥]

[*]SVKM's Narsee Monjee Institute of Management Studies, Bengaluru, Karnataka, India

[†]Christ (Deemed to be University), Bengaluru, Karnataka, India

[‡]Management Development Institute (MDI), Murshidabad, West Bengal, India

[§]mallikasrivastava123@gmail.com

[¶]mudita.sinha@christuniversity.in

[∥]drbiranchi.marketing@gmail.com

Abstract

The global outbreak of the novel coronavirus disease (COVID-19) has changed the daily lives of citizens across the globe. As the world begins its slow transition from managing the COVID-19 calamity to recovery and the reopening of economies, it's clear that the period of lockdown has had a reflective impact on how people live and how they will continue to lead their lifestyles. The COVID-19 outbreak is not only a health crisis but also one that has invaded our societies and economies. This period will certainly change consumer behaviour in the coming years. However, it is expected that certain behaviours may return to normal after such calamities; nonetheless, since consumers have discovered some new alternatives during this period, they may have changed consumer behaviour. Hence, this study is an attempt to analyze the impact of the COVID-19 pandemic on the Indian economy and the modified behaviour of consumers towards the e-commerce sector in India during this pandemic-induced digitalization.

Keywords: Online shopping, consumers behaviour, COVID-19, Indian consumers, emerging market.

Introduction

The global outbreak of the novel coronavirus disease (COVID-19) has changed the daily lives of citizens across the globe. As the world begins its slow transition from managing the COVID-19 calamity to recovery and the reopening of economies, it's clear that the period of lockdown has had a reflective impact on how people live and how they will continue to lead their lifestyles. The COVID-19 outbreak is not only a health crisis but also one that has invaded our societies and economies. This period will certainly change consumer behaviour in the coming years. Despite the short period since the emergence of COVID-19, a few studies have been conducted, which have primarily focused on the question of how global consumer behaviours have changed during the COVID-19 pandemic. According to Sheth (2020), consumer habits and behaviours are not only habitual but also contextual. This means that natural disasters, such as COVID-19, do interrupt or change consumer habits and behaviours. However, it is expected that certain behaviours may return to normal after such calamities; nonetheless, since consumers have discovered some new alternatives during this period, they may have changed consumer behaviour. This was observed especially with respect to the convenience, affordability, and accessibility of using online shopping during natural disasters (Sheth, 2020). Another recent study conducted by Zwanka *et al.* (2021) reviewed the potential impact of COVID-19 on global traits, buying patterns, and psychographic behaviour. A study by Hall *et al.* (2020) examined the concept of consumption displacement, which refers to a shift in consumption that occurs when consumers experience a change in the availability of goods, services, and amenities to which they are accustomed as a result of an external event. The external event for the study was COVID-19. The study provided evidence affirming the spatial and temporal displacements of consumption based on consumer spending patterns. Jeong *et al.* (2020) surveyed users of contactless services to examine their consumption patterns and confirmed that overall consumer behaviour trends have changed because of COVID-19. E-commerce revenues had increased significantly across the globe (Jeong *et al.*, 2020). Chang (2020) examined the effects of the COVID-19 pandemic on consumer price changes; he expects it to have a prolonged effect.

However, it was observed that the Indian consumers had shown a distinct change in behaviour much before COVID-19, and the pandemic-induced lockdowns have actually quickened the process. These changes were quite prevalent among consumers with some basic expectations of convenience, omni-channel expectations, personalization, etc., and a bias towards healthy living. Now, the advent of the infectious COVID-19 disease has increased online shopping across the globe. If we consider India in particular, it led to a rise in the number of first-time e-commerce users (Deepak, 2020). A web-based cross-sectional study by Chopra *et al.* (2020) and a study by Neger and Uddin (2020) investigated the factors affecting consumers' internet shopping behaviour during the COVID-19 pandemic in Bangladesh. The study measured the influence of product, price, time-saving, payment, security, administrative, and psychological factors on consumers' internet shopping behaviour during the COVID-19 pandemic. The results indicated that all factors, except price and security factors, had a momentous and positive association with consumers' internet shopping behaviour during the COVID-19 pandemic in Bangladesh. Hence, this study is an attempt to analyze the impact of the COVID-19 pandemic on the Indian economy and the modified behaviour of consumers towards the e-commerce sector in India during this pandemic-induced digitalization.

Objectives of the Study

The aims of this study are:

1. to understand the online shopping behaviour of Indian consumers;
2. to explore the determinants of online shopping behaviour of Indian consumers in the post-COVID-19 period.

Research Methodology

In this research, we have adopted both primary and secondary research methods. As a part of secondary research, we have used review of literature and focus group discussions (FGDs). This process helped us identify the items responsible for determining the online shopping behaviour of Indian consumers during the post-COVID-19 period. Through this process, we were able to generate 21 items. With these 21 items, we designed a questionnaire and performed a pilot study among 30 respondents. This study tested the internal consistency of the items, and we subsequently deleted/modified a few items in the present context. Then, to design the final questionnaire, we used 16 items. The data were collected from 250 customers through Google Forms. We used the convenience sampling method to select the samples and a five-point Likert scale, ranging from 1 representing 'strongly disagree' to 5 representing 'strongly agree,' to capture the data. The collected data were analyzed using exploratory factor analysis (EFA) with the principal component method.

Major Findings

EFA extracted five factors, namely security concerns, social concerns, promotional factor, perception factor, and product-specific factor, as shown in Table 1.

In EFA, the KMO value (more than 0.5 with significance) showed that the sample is adequate and acceptable, thus suggesting the appropriateness of the data for factor analysis. With the rotated component matrix, 16 items were rotated using varimax rotation through Kaiser normalization. The results showed that these five factors explained more than 71% of the total variance, and there was no cross-loading on any factor. The reliability test was also done for these factors, and it showed that for all these factors, the alpha values were greater than 0.70.

Implications of the Study

The factors explored in the current study will provide practical guidelines for online retailers to improve their customer experience with respect to online shopping. As each factor is a summation of a few items, the marketers need to focus on those items which contribute the most towards determining the online shopping behaviour of Indian consumers, preferably after COVID-19. The pandemic has impacted consumers and

Table 1. Determinants of online shopping behaviour of Indian consumers in the post-COVID-19 period.

Name of variables/factors	Factor loadings	Total variance explained (%)	Eigen values
Factor 1: Security concerns		32.42	5.19
V13: Secure and convenient payment option	0.724		
V14: Secure transaction process	0.818		
V15: Heavy transactional cash discounts	0.751		
V16: Website is trustworthy	0.777		
Factor 2: Social concerns		13.33	2.13
V10: Contactless delivery	0.822		
V11: Shoppers' maintain social distancing	0.884		
V12: Shop online due to lockdown	0.832		
Factor 3: Promotional factor		11.34	1.81
V4: Affordable delivery charges	0.761		
V5: Online shopping provides me value for money	0.757		
V6: Attractive offers	0.587		
Factor 4: Perception factor		**8.03**	**1.28**
V7: I have interest and like to shop online	0.566		
V8: I have positive attitude and mindset towards online shopping	0.889		
V9: I feel excited while shopping online	0.824		
Factor 5: Product-specific factor		**6.33**	**1.03**
V1: Availability of branded products	0.564		
V2: Excellent product features	0.691		
V3: Availability of product varieties	0.811		

Note: **Extraction method:** Principal component method. **Rotation method:** Varimax rotation method.

transformed their spending patterns, with most consumers restraining themselves and purchasing essential items online during the pandemic. The study will help enhance the level of customer satisfaction with respect to online shopping in India. In addition, the study also provides e-tailers with insights into how they can improve the overall service experience of shoppers during the post-COVID-19 period. The consumption behaviour of online shoppers in India has evolved differently among different consumers from time to time. The current study highlights the determinants of online shopping behaviours of Indian consumers after the COVID-19 pandemic. The overall findings will provide inferences to curate future strategies for adapting to the pandemic situation in consumer purchase behaviour in the Indian e-commerce sector.

References

Chang, M. (2020). The impact of COVID-19 pandemic on consumer price inflation and implications. *Korean Economic and Financial Review*, 25(3), 59–60.

Chopra, S., Ranjan, P., Singh, V., Kumar, S., Arora, M., Hasan, M. S., and Baitha, U. (2020). Impact of COVID-19 on lifestyle-related behaviours — a cross-sectional audit of responses from nine hundred and ninety-five participants from India. *Diabetes & Metabolic Syndrome: Clinical Research & Reviews*, 14(6), 2021–2030.

Deepak, H. (2020, March 25). "Impact of COVID-19 on online shopping in India", *ETRetail*. https://retail.economictimes.indiatimes.com/re-tales/impact-of-covid-19-on-online-shopping-in-india/4115.

Hall, M. C., Prayag, G., Fieger, P., & Dyason, D. (2020). Beyond panic buying: Consumption displacement and COVID-19. *Journal of Service Management*, 32(1), 113–128.

Jeong, H., Kwon, O., Kim, B. S., Bae, J., Shin, S., Kim, H. E., Kim, J., and Lee, H. (2020). Highly durable metal ensemble catalysts with full dispersion for automotive applications beyond single-atom catalysts. *Nature Catalysis*, 3(4), 368–375.

Jo, H., Shin, E., and Kim, H. (2020). Changes in consumer behaviour in the post-COVID-19 era in Seoul, South Korea. *Sustainability*, 2021, 13, 136.

Neger, M., and Uddin, B. (2020). Factors affecting consumers' internet shopping behavior during the COVID-19 pandemic: Evidence from Bangladesh. *Chinese Business Review*, 19(3), 91–104.

Sheth, J. (2020). Impact of Covid-19 on consumer behavior: Will the old habits return or die? *Journal of Business Research*, 117, 280–283.

Whaley, C. M., Pera, M. F., Cantor, J., Chang, J., Velasco, J., Hagg, H. K., and Bravata, D. M. (2020). Changes in health services use among commercially insured US populations during the COVID-19 pandemic. *JAMA Network Open*, 3(11), e2024984.

Zwanka, R. J., and Buff, C. (2021). COVID-19 generation: A conceptual framework of the consumer behavioral shifts to be caused by the COVID-19 pandemic. *Journal of International Consumer Marketing*, 33(1), 58–67.

© 2025 World Scientific Publishing Company
https://doi.org/10.1142/9789811292101_0006

Chapter 6

Substantial Changes in Consumer Buying Behaviour in the Post-COVID-19 World

Tania Chauhan

Research Scholar, HPKVBS, School of Commerce and Management Studies (SCMS), Central University of Himachal Pradesh, Dharamshala, Kangra, H.P., India

taniachauhan08@gmail.com

Abstract

Ever since the emergence of the COVID-19 crisis, the world has seen immense changes, as have consumers' attitudes and behaviours towards their purchasing decisions. Consumers have become more mindful and are making more intuitive choices while purchasing; minimalism and deliberate decision-making are the new normal in consumer buying behaviour. This chapter focuses on understanding how resilience has differed across various segments of customers and how perceptions of purchase decisions have changed. It also attempts to analyze whether or not brand loyalty among customers while making a purchase decision has been impacted. With the help of primary and secondary data analyses, the study suggests that the resilience or capacity to bounce back to pre-pandemic buying behaviour varies among customers depending on their personal experiences with the pandemic and various other demographic factors. In addition, among many consumers, the levels of desire have decreased, and more focus is now on making buying decisions which support a happy and healthy lifestyle, thus reducing materialism and justifying a minimalistic approach to buying. On the other hand, brand loyalty across customers has also been influenced by the pandemic since customers have become more flexible and adaptable to accept other brands, as the scarcity of goods during the pandemic times resulted in substitutions in consumption, thus making consumers less brand-driven and more flexible to accept other brands in order to satisfy their needs. Hence, the research offers insight into consumers' adaptability and acceptance of changing scenarios due to COVID-19 and their behavioural changes towards buying decisions.

Keywords: Consumer behaviour, resilience, minimalism, brand loyalty, deliberate decision-making.

Introduction

Since consumers are the key factors driving and influencing the market, economic instability and uncertainties lead to immense changes in consumer behaviour, thereby impacting the market dynamics and influencing buying decisions. Consumer needs and emotions have been analyzed to observe the shift in their buying decisions from materialism to spiritualism (Mehta *et al.*, 2020). It has been observed that there was a spike in anxiety levels among customers and an unprecedented change in attitudes that not only made them more concerned about the supply of goods at stores but also led them to stockpile essential items at their homes, such as sanitizers, home cleansing products, health-related products, and kitchen-related inventory, due to the fear of product scarcity. This fear led to an increase in the desirability of the products, irrespective of their relevance. Considering the post-COVID-19 scenario, customers are becoming more compassionate, considerate, and empathetic while making purchase decisions which were not prevalent prior to the pandemic and are also prioritizing basic products rather than luxury products, thus exhibiting a shift towards a minimalistic approach. Acee-Eke *et al.* (2020) mention that since consumers are still reluctant to expose themselves to the external environment, the relevance and need for online delivery services have increased immensely.

Impulsive buying decisions across customers were also a very common trait, as there was the fear of inadequate supply of goods, an increase in the price of goods, and getting exposed to the virus, as well as several other insecurities, which altogether resulted in impacting the customer's psychology and hence making them more adaptable and flexible (Naeem, 2021). Mason *et al.* (2020) state that this dramatic shift has not only changed buying behaviours but also affected post-purchase satisfaction levels. Earlier, customers could measure their satisfaction levels on the basis of money spent irrespective of the requirement of the product; however, now, satisfaction levels are measured considering the fulfilment of their needs, thus further making it difficult for marketers to gain customer loyalty. Zwanka *et al.* (2021) highlight the transformational shift to digitalization, where virtual presence has more relevance than physical presence, be it in travel, shopping, learning and developing skills, or various other fields, which together have led to a major psychographic shift. There are prominent changes in the consumption patterns of individuals due to fluctuations in the supply of goods in stores, which led to stockpiling of goods and panic buying, further causing consumption displacement (Hall *et al.*, 2020). The market decline during the COVID-19 period has resulted in an upsurge of new ways and strategies devised by marketers in order to maintain the value of their brands and ensure the existence of their brands in the market. This further points towards the advancement of technologies, which has emerged as the only means by which there can be a transition into the new phase of marketing (Kapur, 2020). Consumers are now more inclined to spend money on health-related products and are focusing more on hygiene. Hence, major changes are observed in product preferences and perceptions among customers (Vijai *et al.*, 2020). Consumers' emotions, such as panic, fear, mindfulness, empathy, and sadness, during the pandemic have led to a drastic shift in their approach towards buying and have resulted in changes in their attitudes (Kirk *et al.*, 2020). The excessive number of purchases of hygiene accessories and toilet paper, resulting in a public upsurge in panic buying, caused a negative social media trend, which also psychologically affected consumers and caused irrational shopping (Leung *et al.*, 2021).

Research Methods

Through various introspective discussions held with the customers and the analysis of the literature comprising the consumer behavioural changes due to the COVID-19 crisis, we have drawn certain conclusions highlighting the trend and various forms of change across customers post-COVID-19.

Conclusion

The COVID-19 crisis has led to massive attitudinal change in consumers, with a minimalistic approach to purchasing emerging as an evident trend. Consumers have become more mindful and less luxury-driven. It has been observed that the resilience of customers varies depending on their personal attributes since many are drastically impacted by COVID-19. A few are marginally impacted, while a few others are not impacted at all, which shows the variation in experiences and hence the variation in buying behaviour as well. Brand loyalty, which was clearly observed in customers prior to the pandemic, has also been affected, as the issues of insecurity, anxiety, panic, and product scarcity resulted in them picking and choosing any required product irrespective of the brand. Furthermore, deliberate decision-making is adopted by customers to add value to the purchase, indicating a change in the earlier norms of purchasing.

Future Research Scope

It has to be critically analyzed to determine whether the considerable changes in consumer buying behaviour will be temporary and for how long, considering the post-COVID-19 scenario. Another question to be answered is whether consumers are shifting to new perceptions and attitudes towards buying. It also has to be analyzed if crises, such as COVID-19, are major drivers of enormous change in the buying behaviour of consumers.

References

Acee-Eke, B. C., Ogonu, G. C., and Chituru, G. (2020). COVID-19 effects on consumer buying behaviour of departmental stores in rivers state, Nigeria. *International Journal of Scientific & Engineering Research*, 11(6), 272–285.

Hall, M. C., Prayag, G., Fieger, P., and Dyason, D. (2020). Beyond panic buying: Consumption displacement and COVID-19. *Journal of Service Management*, 32(1), 113–128.

Kapur, S. (2020). The future of consumer behaviour and brand strategy post Covid 19. *Review of Professional Management*, 18(1), 58–63.

Kirk, C. P., and Rifkin, L. S. (2020). I'll trade you diamonds for toilet paper: Consumer reacting, coping and adapting behaviors in the COVID-19 pandemic. *Journal of Business Research*, 117, 124–131.

Leung, J., Chung, J. Y. C., Tisdale, C., Chiu, V., Lim, C. C., and Chan, G. (2021). Anxiety and panic buying behaviour during COVID-19 pandemic — A qualitative analysis of toilet paper hoarding contents on Twitter. *International Journal of Environmental Research and Public Health*, 18(3), 1127.

Mason, A., Narcum, J., and Mason, K. (2020). Changes in consumer decision-making resulting from the COVID-19 pandemic. *Journal of Customer Behaviour*, 19(4), 299–321.

Mehta, S., Saxena, T., and Purohit, N. (2020). The new consumer behaviour paradigm amid COVID-19: Permanent or transient? *Journal of Health Management*, 22(2), 291–301.

Naeem, M. (2021). Understanding the customer psychology of impulse buying during COVID-19 pandemic: Implications for retailers. *International Journal of Retail & Distribution Management*, 49(3), 377–393.

Vijai, C., and Nivetha, P. (2020, June). A study on coronavirus (COVID-19) impact of consumer buying behavior with special reference to Chennai city. In *International Conference on COVID-19 Studies*.

Zwanka, R. J., and Buff, C. (2021). COVID-19 generation: A conceptual framework of the consumer behavioral shifts to be caused by the COVID-19 pandemic. *Journal of International Consumer Marketing*, 33(1), 58–67.

© 2025 World Scientific Publishing Company
https://doi.org/10.1142/9789811292101_0007

Chapter 7

A Study of Disruptions in Consumer Behaviour and Marketing Strategies in Response to the Pandemic in India

Reetika Jain

Commerce Department, Hansraj College, University of Delhi, New Delhi, India

reetikajain29@yahoo.com

Abstract

The COVID-19 pandemic that engulfed the entire world in the year 2020 was not only an unprecedented rare event but also brought about disruptive changes in consumer behaviour and consequent responses by companies in the form of their preparedness for new norms of consumer behaviour. Companies which were unable to adjust and adapt to the sudden changes posed by the pandemic perished very soon.

The pandemic scenario in India led to a surge in demand for packed and staple food products but, at the same time, a decrease in demand for beverages (cold) and alcoholic and deep-freeze items, such as ice creams. There was a huge demand for previously less-demanded products, such as sanitizers, masks, disinfectants, laundry, and home and personal hygiene products, while visits to restaurants, shopping complexes, malls, and cinema halls declined sharply. Similarly, demand for digital products, such as smartphones and laptops, surged (to facilitate online education or work from home), as did demand for electrical appliances that eased domestic work (such as washing machines and dishwashers), whereas demand for other appliances dropped drastically. E-commerce, e-banking, and e-wallets use skyrocketed, but brick-and-motor stores or offline stores witnessed a steep decline in footfall, some of which were even on the verge of closure or facing merger.

The current study, based on secondary data on consumer behaviour during the pandemic and post-pandemic times obtained by prominent research analyst firms, aims to investigate the changing demand pattern and behaviour of consumers in India. This study also gives an insight into the marketing strategy adopted during different phases of the pandemic in the country, from lockdown to unlocking, in response to consumers' inhibitions to spend on non-essential purchases during the initial phase and a change in the mode of shopping and spending that is becoming the 'new normal.'

Keywords: COVID-19 pandemic, disruption, response, consumer behaviour, marketing strategy.

India's Reaction to the Pandemic

The impact of the pandemic varied from country to country, depending on its geographical spread, the concentration of people, and the promptness of the government in its control measures, such as the number of days of lockdown, strictness in the implementation of COVID-19 safety norms, as well as medical preparedness. India witnessed one of the longest and strictest periods of lockdown compared to countries such as the US and the UK. Yet, its geographical spread coupled with the concentration of people did not produce the expected results of lockdown. A crucial aspect of the success of governments' efforts is how fast people adapt to the new way of behaviour since lockdowns can't be a long-term solution for any economy given the financial burden they put on the government. Another reason for people's inhibitions towards complying with social distancing norms is that they go against our basic social and cultural ethos. Nevertheless, the government's and media's 360-degree awareness campaigns on the dos and don'ts of public behaviour led to a percolation of desired change in the target audience, as was visible during the unlocking phase. This was also possible with stricter enforcement of laws that were passed to punish the offenders.

Consumer Response to Disruptions Caused by the Pandemic

The pandemic situation has led to many shifts in the behaviour patterns of consumers. The gravity of the situation provides a strong impetus for gradual or sudden shifts in behaviour (Kotler and Zaltman, 1971). The four stepping stones that marked the journey of the changes in consumer behaviour through the pandemic to the new normal of life (the desired behaviour) can be studied with respect to the following four stages (Figure 1):

1. Awareness
2. Assimilation
3. Action
4. Adaptation

The movement from the awareness stage to the assimilation stage, then to the action stage, and finally to the adaptation stage was quicker in the current pandemic situation than in any other crisis witnessed in the past. This was so because the crisis unravelled at the global level and not just at the national or regional level.

Behaviour of Indian consumers during lockdown

The massive 360-degree campaign by the government using different forms of media was pivotal in spreading awareness about the novel coronavirus and the ways to protect oneself and one's family both in urban and rural areas. Coupled with the 'Janta Curfew,' the long lockdown periods

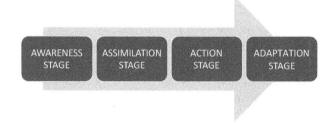

Figure 1. Four stages of behavioural change.

created a significant buzz about the gravity of the pandemic and the consequent social responsibility cast on each person to protect the near and dear ones. As a result, there was quick assimilation of the information disseminated in the campaigns, which became visible in the changed behaviour patterns of the consumers. According to Nielsen, Deloitte, and EY India Reports (2020), the following were some of the prominent changes in consumer behaviour in India:

- increased interest in health, wellness, and ayurvedic products;
- increased demand for masks, sanitizers, hand-wash soaps, and disinfectants;
- priority given to public safety products;
- stockpiling of essential and day-to-day items;
- restricted offline shopping;
- increased online shopping;
- work from home as an alternative to work at office;
- online education and learning as a viable alternative;
- use of do-it-yourself (DIY) appliances for home chores becoming a trend;
- medicines and medical supplies becoming crucial.

Behaviour of Indian consumers post-lockdown ('unlocking' phases)

A true test of whether the desired behaviour has been acquired and practised can be known only when people exhibit that behaviour on their own in a normal situation (Andreasen, 1994). So, when the government began 'unlocking' in May 2020, it was observed that people were largely following the new pattern of conduct in public places (i.e., social distancing, wearing masks, and using sanitizers). Though transgressions were also witnessed, they were seriously taken to task by law and enforcement agencies in the form of fines or reprimands, so that observing the desired behaviour soon became the new normal for the people. This was also needed as the government was slowly moving towards 'unlocking' everything in a phased manner so as to restore livelihoods and businesses to the normal state. Thus, the combination of voluntary and forced measures led the consumers to the action stage during the 'unlocking' phases. They started exhibiting the desired behaviour in marketplaces.

Finally, consumers are said to reach the adaptation stage when they exhibit the desired behaviour automatically when they step out of their homes with masks and sanitizers and maintain social distance in public places on their own. The study by Deloitte, EY India, and Nielsen Reports (2020) revealed the following:

- new behaviour trends adopted by consumers during the lockdown period continued in the post-lockdown phase;
- increased focus by consumers on saving for future and being prepared for the future uncertainties;
- increased preference for contactless delivery as well as home delivery;
- increased use of digital wallets as a payment mode;
- drastic reduction in demand for labour from the unorganized sector during the initial unlocking phase;
- greater demand for washing machines and dishwashers as DIY appliances for home chores continued;
- home cooking became a trending practice;
- increased procurement of local products;
- movements in public places allowed only for those following COVID-19 safety norms;
- slow increase in demand for non-essentials;
- offline shopping showing a minor revival;
- increased investment in digital technologies to facilitate work and education from home;
- increased spending on healthcare and medical essentials.

Planning for unforeseen disruptions: Towards a new normal for businesses

The purpose of seeking insights into the changes in consumer behaviour during the pandemic is to help businesses adapt to the new normal of the market so that they not only survive the current pandemic but also remain agile and are able to withstand any future disruptions with ease. Based on the observed behaviour of Indian consumers during the initial phase of the COVID-19 pandemic, the following businesses proved to be game-changers due to their agility to outperform in the current scenario (Deloitte, EY India, and Nielsen Reports, 2020):

- online healthcare sector to take care of urgent but routine ailments;
- contact-tracing apps to facilitate government mapping of contacts with patients infected by COVID-19;
- robotic technology to disinfect large areas, such as hospitals and other public places, in a short time;
- use of mobile money wallets to avoid the hassles associated with manual cash handling;
- boost to research in drugs as well as vaccine development;
- boost to local as well as ayurvedic products as a result of 'Atmanirbhar Bharat' and 'Vocal for Local' campaigns;
- boost to online education as well as conferencing platforms, such as Zoom, Google Meet, and Microsoft Teams, to facilitate easy transfer of information from schools, colleges, and offices to homes;
- boost to online learning and tutoring apps;
- boost to investments in businesses related to digital platforms, big data analytics, and AI to obtain real-time data regarding consumers;
- boost to e-commerce businesses, such as Amazon and Big Basket, to facilitate contactless shopping and delivery;
- boost to food aggregator apps to facilitate home dining;
- boost to cab aggregator businesses to facilitate contactless essential travel while avoiding public transport.

Conclusion

With continued pressure on costs as well as uncertainty prevailing around businesses, it is essential to make strategic decisions that ensure the current and future sustainability of businesses. The current pandemic situation is just one of many instances highlighting the unpredictability of the future and an eye-opener for businesses to test their preparedness for the future. Agility and investment in disruptive technologies are the twin mantras for the future survival and success of businesses. Only then will businesses be able to shape their destiny on their own rather than being shaped by uncertainties.

References

Andreasen, A. R. (1994), Social marketing: Its definition and domain. *Journal of Public Policy & Marketing*, 13(I) (Spring), 108–114.

Deloitte Insights. (2020). Government's response to Covid-19: From pandemic crisis to better future. www.deloitte.com/insights.

EY India Report 2020. COVID-19 and emergence of a new consumer products landscape in India. www.ey.com/en_in.

Kotler, P., and Zaltman, G. (1971). Social marketing: An approach to planned social change. *Journal of Marketing*, 35(July), 3–12.

Nielsen Report 2020. Covid-19: Evolving consumer dynamics, Edition 4, July 2020. www.nielsen.com.

Chapter 8

A Narrative of Needs Assessment through Psychobiography of COVID-19 Patient by Observing Moment of Truth

Jyoti[*] and Sarvesh Kumar[†]

Himachal Pradesh Kendriya Vishwa Vidyalaya Business School (HPKVBS), School of Commerce and Management Studies, Central University of Himachal Pradesh, Himachal Pradesh, India
[*]*jyoguleria25@gmail.com*
[†]*sarveshkumar@hpcu.ac.in*

Abstract

In response to the growing sensitivity of consumer orientation to the COVID-19 situation, the positioning of products that are relatively relevant to a healthy lifestyle has effectually changed. Before the emergence of the COVID-19 pandemic, both nationwide and individual perceptions of social change and the exchange of offerings shared different indexed reflections in terms of different products at diverse marketplaces. However, during the pandemic, the predominance of global marketing evolved into a new global perception of social change and unique offerings in the marketplace. To understand the objective reality of these new propositions of social change due to the chaotic situation caused by COVID-19, psychobiography investigations play a crucial role. In this era where rapid community spread of viruses can occur, the cognitive development process is relevant to recognize the needs, preferences, and experiences of people. To narrate the needs assessment of COVID-19 patients, we combine psychobiography with ethnomethodology. The unit of investigation will accommodate consumer experiences which indicate pluralism and chronology. The increasing health consciousness in consumer society has created a new stimulus-response capacity between product development, product promotion, and product adoption, subject to needs assessment. The consequences of needs assessment refer to an instrumental conditioning of consumer behaviour, which constitutes the perspectives of the individual, family, and society.

Keywords: Consumer consciousness, need assessment, offerings, product perception, psychography.

Introduction

Globally, the psychosocial consequences of the COVID-19 pandemic are causing radical changes in all individuals (Pakpour *et al.*, 2020). Therefore, recognizing the psychosocial needs of different individuals requires measuring their stimulus-response capacity through their experiences.

The COVID-19 pandemic changed the culture of health and healthy consumption practices in day-to-day life. The psychological cost of infection and poor well-being are both phenomena that create threats to life and community spread among people (World Health Organization, 2020a). Hence, consumer socialization focuses on a healthy lifestyle through traditional and indigenous ethnobotanical resources (AYUSH, 2019). After COVID-19, health has become a matter of survival. Moreover, throughout the world, the pandemic has changed the mindset of every individual before taking any decision.

The COVID-19 pandemic outbreak has resulted in changed perceptions of individuals in terms of risk to life, loss of life, public health, and social measures, complementary to the aspect of well-being of society at large (World Health Organization, 2020b). It should be identical to consumer expectations in terms of product and service adoptions to deal with this problematic phenomenon.

The increasing health consciousness in consumer society has created a new stimulus-response capacity between product development, product promotion, and product adoption, subject to needs assessment.

The consequences of needs assessment refer to the instrumental conditioning of consumer behaviour, which mainly constitutes an individual's perspective.

In consumer behaviour, needs assessment should resonate with the mean of its association. An assessment of consumer needs and their means consists of instrumental drivers or institutions, such as family, society, federal bodies, marketplaces, consumption rituals, and information about the products, ingredients, and their effects on the human body (Kotler *et al.*, 2002; American Marketing Association, 2017; Kotler, 2017). These instrumental drivers have a significant impact on the final decision on where and why to spend?

The principal assumption of being healthy is the subject of having personal care and home care products for primary needs. Hence, the role of healthcare institutions is a subsegment of unsought goods and negative demand. Thus, shifting this social perception into regular demand would increase the role of those firms which deal with the day-to-day offerings of personal and household care products for consumers. After the pandemic situation, the above-mentioned products were considered to be part of the essential category.

In a homogeneous world, age, cultures indicate pluralism and chronology (Solomon *et al.*, 2007). In this chapter, *pluralism* is used to denote the existence of various truths based on the experiences of COVID-19 patients, the fulfilment of basic hierarchical needs through different goods and services available in their geographical locations to support a healthy lifestyle, and the well-being of consumers. By *chronology*, we mean the consumers' search for solutions at a particular location through various means at a particular time as a preventive measure for their well-being and recovery.

It is an appealing practice involving basic lifestyle segmentation. This practice stands for those individuals who share similar ages and experiences. Before the emergence of the pandemic situation due to COVID-19, both nation-wide and individual perceptions of social change, exchange of offerings, and acceptance of products shared different indexed reflections or perceptions.

The conceptualization of regular goods and services is based on consumer consciousness. The turbulence in political, social, economic, historical, and health-related aspects has changed the market scenario. These turbulences have brought about transformations not only in the marketplace but also in the consumer mind. Eventually, these transformations and increasing consumer consciousness towards their health have resulted in changes in terms of new product development, demands, perceptions, and value propositions.

Nielsen (2020) reports that, from personal hygiene products to daily staple goods, the buying behaviour of consumers has started prioritizing the threat of COVID-19 infection. It appears that consumers of different cohorts have become more aware than ever while buying primary care products in the healthcare category.

The domain of sustainable, ethical, and natural consumerism is becoming crucial. It provides information about the following: Why are consumers considering factors such as health, society, risk–benefit consciousness, product-value consciousness, and money-value consciousness within society at large? What part of the disclosure of information is important for firms to mention on their products? How are rational constraints such as product, price, place, promotion, and preferences getting influenced through behavioural aspects, including social norms, loss aversion, reference points, time consistency, endowment effect, and default choices?

The perceived risks of community spread, health risk, and other above-discussed contextual considerations have negative impacts on an individual's mind. To overcome these perceived risks and life risks, many health and social measures have been implemented in all parts of the world. These social measures include: (1) personal protective measures, such as promoting personal hygiene, providing food and dietary supplements, mask wearing, and physical distancing; (2) environmental measures, such as cleaning and disinfection; (3) surveillance and response measures, including contact tracing, isolation, and quarantine; (4) travel, marketplace, and workplace measures. These considerations include the impact on the economy, the purchase behaviour of individuals for their own and their families' benefits, security, mental health, human rights, food security, socioeconomic disparities, the treatment and management of conditions other than COVID-19, and the psychosocial well-being of every individual in the community (World Health Organization, 2020a).

Despite such public health and social measures, the cluster of cases increased with a high fatality rate of transmission. Therefore, it is essential to understand the psychography of individuals, specifically COVID-19 patients, at different levels of a community.

Transmission dynamics

Worldwide, the intensity of the transmission of COVID-19 recorded high fatality rates in infected and suspected cases (Yan *et al.*, 2020). There is now more evidence that COVID-19 is spreading not merely from human to human but also across generations of cases (World Health Organization, 2020a).

The World Health Organization (WHO) (2020b) has divided the transmission dynamics of the novel coronavirus into four categories. First is the clinical criterion under which an individual experiences any three or more symptoms, such as acute onset of fever, cough, fatigue, sore throat, anorexia, coryza, myalgia, and altered mental status. The second criterion is epidemiological, which refers to residing or working in a setting with a high risk of transmission of this virus or travelling in a community transmission/cluster transmission setting anytime within 14 days before symptom onset. The third category considers severe acute respiratory illness in patients, and the last category includes asymptomatic individuals not categorized under the epidemiological criterion following a positive diagnostic test. COVID-19 is a complex phenomenon. The cost of COVID-19 risk is equal to the risk of losing one's own life by getting infected, mental depression, community spread, and the fear of passing the virus to coming generations (Guan *et al*, 2020). The perceived risk of COVID-19 has been embedded in psychological orientation and social construction. This perception increased the level of anger, anxiety, health risk, and susceptibility to social risk, decreased the level of life satisfaction, and contributed to poor credibility towards the healthcare systems of society (Li *et al.*, 2020; Guler and Yilidirim, 2020). Currently, the intensity of transmission in public is expressed in terms of social measures and other contextual considerations; however, these criteria do not meet the expectations of consumers in the sense that the different products offered are unable to provide satisfaction to them given the available resources.

Research Design

Research Methodology: This narrative has been developed by observing a subject who was a COVID-19 patient. The subject's reaction has been examined through the prism of psychography and ethnomethodology. To understand the psychobiography and indexed reflections of the patient, we have used ethnographical methodology with instrumental conditioning of the human brain (Pavlov, 1906; Garfinkel, 1969). By implementing the ethnographic methodology, we can obtain deep insights and sociological reasoning about the life of a COVID-19 patient. Ethnomethodology focuses on how people create and maintain their everyday needs fulfilment via different products and interactions with society in a particular social arrangement. A COVID-19 patient is a part of society. Indeed, the experiences of the individual with the disease have not only affected his perspective but have also had a huge impact on others within the same society who share similar groups or communities.

Research Method: In this psychobiography study of a COVID-19 patient, we have used the observation research method with hypercathexis to present their moments of truth in terms of the perspectives of the individual, family, and society (Freud, 1915). In this type of study, hypercathexis helps us obtain a more inductive understanding of the psychographic situation of an individual and also his group members due to the original situation arising as a result of COVID-19.

Participants: The investigation unit for the following study is the human mind of COVID-19 patients and their psychosocial needs.

Discussion

Fundamentally, to understand the needs assessment of any individual related to any problematic phenomenon, we need to go through the hierarchy of needs given by Maslow. Here, the research insight into the needs assessment of COVID-19 patients emphasized the physiological needs, safety needs, and belongingness needs of an individual, as proposed by Maslow's hierarchy. Every level of this hierarchy demands a specific category of products to meet the expectations of consumers.

The emergence of the COVID-19 pandemic and increasing community spread of COVID-19-positive cases have proportionately shown the negative impact on the psychosocial needs of a vulnerable population, specifically on those individuals and their families who were caught by this virus.

Considering the contextual information about the situation of a COVID-19 patient, we have observed the evolution of the stimulus-response capacity of different institutions. By the word 'institutions,' we mean a family or a society which the individual is a part of, sharing different value propositions. Here, the instrumental stimulus is COVID-19, and we are observing the response of COVID-19 patients in terms of the impact on different institutions, their perception towards product affordability, product adoption, product rejection, product acceptance, availability of resources, healthcare services, and consumption pattern in the choice architecture of consumer behaviour.

Observed moment of truth of COVID-19 patient

By assessing the level of cluster/community transmission of the novel coronavirus, we came to know about the psychological situation of COVID-19 patients as well as their needs at any specific moment. The fear of infection and community spread through various means has made individuals feel insecure, leading to negative word-of-mouth. Amid the fear of getting infected with this virus, the role of social media became an instrumental driving force to condition the minds of individuals. It influenced the mindset of people.

This fear has effectually changed the positioning of consumer products that are relatively relevant to the healthy lifestyle orientation of consumers. People are following social measures for their safety. This has increased the role of the purchase and consumption of products that offer personal health benefits, which has directed attention towards traditional and grassroot knowledge. Now, collective decision-making and product perception are more concerned with herbs and plant-based alternatives available in a particular location. Earlier, these were perceived by consumers to fall under the category of medicines. However, because of the stimulus of COVID-19, consumers have started interpreting them as part of regular use. Therefore, consumer consciousness has begun to support a herbal-health consciousness. In this regard, the WHO's health guidelines for the promotion of herbal products and herbal supplements have prompted the need for new product offerings from the fast-moving consumer goods sector. In this context, health has been defined as part of physiological needs, where food security and sanitation are crucial for survival and a healthy lifestyle.

The present situation in the world has different dynamics for those who have suffered from the COVID-19 virus. The transmission of this virus to the human body through any mode forces the infected patients to isolate themselves from their families and social lives until they test negative. The psychosocial needs, which are culturally embedded, cause the patients to experience a novel emotion. As both patients and consumers, the fear of the virus spreading to their families and society has conditioned a new mindset. This fear of cluster spread has channelized a new learning process for COVID-19 patients. The stimulus of the spreading of the virus within families and society has significantly influenced the perception of new products.

The response capacity to understand psychology is enshrined in different communication modes. The fear of death and the spreading of the virus gave rise to a duality of emotions. The biggest psychological fears for a COVID-19 patient are the fear of losing their lives, concerns about their family members' health, the inability to meet them, access to proper healthcare services and supervision by healthcare practitioners, the response capacity of different institutions, acceptance and sympathy from society, and accessibility to medication and food supplements. Henceforth, the role of time and space for COVID-19 patients should complement the availability, affordability, and accessibility of the desired products and services, facilitating quick recovery.

In order to understand the psychology and duality of emotions of COVID-19 patients, we need a holistic approach. In the above, we have talked about the expectations of COVID-19 patients; however, there remains the question of whether their expectations match their real-time experiences.

The dualities of emotions and feelings associated with this practical problem have indexed reflections and experiences. The indexed reflections and psychography of COVID-19 patients are mainly based on geographical location, resource accessibility, and psychosocial response capacity. This kind of primary process is succeeded by secondary processes (Loewald, 1970).

To understand and narrate these experiences, we need to go through the cognitive development process. For instance, the mode of virus transmission, rapid detection, and surveillance approach adopted by the healthcare service institutions, which could include isolation or quarantine, supervision by local authorities on personal and family hygiene, medication and food supplement prescription, time and space of isolation, psychosocial pressure of discrimination, behavioural aspects of family and society, and a lack of information exchange between different institutions.

While observing and encountering the moment of truth, we found that for all COVID-19 patients, the outlook in society has not been the same. While there is a perceived societal stigma against patients who test positive for COVID-19, the patients' families have proven to be really supportive and understanding.

The indexed reflections of COVID-19 patients share different points of view and dual personalities. These were based on their experiences and interactions with other nodes of their social network. The unsatisfied mindset of patients and their families has disrupted their old consumption habits and behavioural processes in dealing with this outbreak. The outcome of these disruptions can be seen in the autocratic and syncratic decisions of consumers.

Nobody anticipated the life-changing aspects resulting from this outbreak. The product perception due to the impact of this disease is creating and communicating novel cognitive knowledge in society.

Though the stimulus of the practical situation of COVID-19 is similar for all people, the practical actions and circumstances to deal with this in day-to-day life are distinct from person to person, from gender to gender, from society to society, and between different cohorts. With these distinctions, consumer orientation is experiencing a new paradigm of healthy lifestyle segmentation worldwide. This has brought about a shift in the meaning of products. In response to the growing sensitivity of consumer orientation to the COVID-19 pandemic situation, the positioning of products that are relatively relevant to personal growth and life satisfaction has effectually changed.

References

American Marketing Association. (2017). Definition of marketing. Retrieved February 18, 2021, from: https://www.ama.org/the-definition-of-marketing-what-is-marketing/#:~:text=Marketing%20is%20the%20activity%2C%20set,Approved%202017.

Ahorsu, D. K., Lin, C. Y., Imani, V., Saffari, M., Griffiths, M. D., and Pakpour, A. H. (2020). The fear of COVID-19 scale: Development and initial validation. *International Journal of Mental Health and Addiction*, 20, 1537–1545. https://doi.org/10.1007/s11469-020-00270-8.

Arslan, G., and Yıldırım, M. (2020). Meaningful living, resilience, affective balance, and psychological health problems during COVID-19.

Berger, S., and Rejman, K. (2019). Food digestion in Ivan Petrovich Pavlov studies on 115 anniversary of his Nobel Prize and present avenues. *Roczniki Panstwowego Zakladu Higieny*, 70(1), 97–102.

Freud, S. (1915). Observations on transference love. *The Psychoanalytic Technique*, 12(1), 116–130.
Garfinkel, H. (1967). *Studies in Ethnomethodology*. Prentice-Hall, Englewood Cliffs, N.J.
Guan, W. J., Ni, Z. Y., Hu, Y., Liang, W. H., Ou, C. Q., He, J. X., ... and Zhong, N. S. (2020). Clinical characteristics of coronavirus disease 2019 in China. *New England Journal of Medicine*, 382(18), 1708–1720.
Kotler, P., and Gertner, D. (2002). Country as brand, product, and beyond: A place marketing and brand management perspective. *Journal of Brand Management*, 9(4), 249–261.
Kotler, P. (2017). *Principles of Marketing*. Pearson Education, New Delhi.
Loewald, H. W. (1970). Psychoanalytic theory and the psychoanalytic process. *The Psychoanalytic Study of the Child*, 25(1), 45–68.
Li, Q., Guan, X., Wu, P., Wang, X., Zhou, L., Tong, Y., and Feng, Z. (2020). Early transmission dynamics in Wuhan, China, of novel coronavirus–infected pneumonia. *New England Journal of Medicine*, 382(13), 1199–1207.
Ministry of AYUSH (2020). COVID-19 related information. Retrieved September 27, 2020 from: https://www.ayush.gov.in/.
Naja, F., and Hamadeh, R. (2020). Nutrition amid the COVID-19 pandemic: A multi-level framework for action. *European Journal of Clinical Nutrition*, 74(8), 1–5.
Pavlov, I. P. (1906). The scientific investigation of the psychical faculties or process in the higher animals. *Science*, 24(620), 613–619.
Solomon, M., Bamossy, G., Askegaard, S., and Hogg, M. (2006). *Consumer Behaviour: A European Perspective*. Pearson Education, England.
Todes, D. P. (2014). *Ivan Pavlov: A Russian Life in Science*. Oxford University Press, USA.
Usher, K., Durkin, J., and Bhullar, N. (2020). The COVID-19 pandemic and mental health impacts. *International Journal of Mental Health Nursing*, 29(3), 31.
Weil, A. R. (2020). Food, income, work, and more: From the editor-in-chief focuses on food, income, work, and more. *Journal of Health Affairs*, 39(7), 1111.
World Health Organization. (2020a). Public health surveillance for COVID-19. Retrieved December 16, 2020, from https://apps.who.int/iris/bitstream/handle/10665/337897/WHO-2019-nCoV-SurveillanceGuidance-2020.8-eng.pdf?sequence=1&isAllowed=y.
World Health Organization. (2020b). Considerations for implementing and adjusting public and social measures in the context of COVID-19. Retrieved November 4, 2020, from https://www.who.int/publications/i/item/considerations-in-adjusting-public-health-and-social-measures-in-the-context-of-covid-19-interim-guidance.

© 2025 World Scientific Publishing Company
https://doi.org/10.1142/9789811292101_0009

Chapter 9

Digital Migration and Survival of Fashion Industry Post New Normal

Jahanvi* and Meenakshi Sharma†

Birla Institute of Technology Mesra, Noida Campus, Noida, Uttar Pradesh, India

*Jahanvi.0328@gmail.com

†Meenakshi@bitmesra.ac.in

Abstract

The COVID-19 pandemic has disrupted all domains worldwide. Abrupt economic closure, causing universal bankruptcy and a financial crunch as well as social isolation resulting in home confinement, has certainly imposed a major shift in behaviours. Consequently, the behaviour of consumers towards digital platforms during this pandemic is changing rapidly. Retailers and brands have come to grips with many challenges, for instance, related to the supply chain, health and safety, consumer demand, cash flow, marketing, and sales. However, fashion brands have been successfully navigating these challenges, although this will not assure a favourable future, let alone any future at all. Adopting digitalization in their business models is a move that most fashion brands have taken up. The consumers of the fashion industry have lost hope of restoring their wardrobes due to destroyed networks of supply chain and apprehensions about purchase apparel from retail stores. The objective of this research is to study the existing COVID-19 distress which has disturbed the fashion industry, the digital migration of the fashion industry after COVID-19, and the long-term strategies used by companies to compete in the sector post-COVID-19. This research is completely descriptive and based on secondary sources.

Keywords: COVID-19, pandemic, fashion, digitalization, consumer.

Introduction

The COVID-19 pandemic and the following restrictions have hit the global economy hard, leaving scars on many sectors, including the fashion and apparel industry, which is one of the most wasteful consumer businesses globally because of the 'wear-once' attitude of consumers (Raja and Kannappan, 2020). The pandemic years are probably one of the cruellest periods for the worldwide economy since the Great Depression, according to the International Monetary Fund (IMF, 2020). Due to the halt, the industry recorded substantial revenue losses and unemployment for workers in Asia. Many fashion brands have intended to reduce their production; some have had to stop completely, while others have switched to making masks and personal protective equipment (PPE), leading to an unprecedented disruption of commerce. Countries are now commencing to resume their economies; for brands, the trends and the noteworthy decline in sales will contribute to substantial retail overcapacity. This is a major challenge for the fashion industry because the inventory in the outlets has worn out and lost its original appeal. Hence, managing the old stockpile and the new production process is chaotic. However, it is likely to observe a surge in online shopping driven by the perpetual shifts in mindset, shopping preferences, and behaviour of people impacted by COVID-19, including divided spending, quickened adoption of e-commerce, and improved demand for purpose-driven brands and sustainable fashion. Whether these transformations have started to manifest or are in the pipeline, they are no doubt inevitable.

Digitalization is not only a progressively important channel of sales, but returning to the usual form of business is also no longer a possibility for survival. It also supports businesses, helps adapt cost structures, and makes the individual stages of the value chain more improved, quicker, and inexpensive (Gonzalo *et al.*, 2020). The COVID-19 pandemic has left the world in a perplexed state, while the global economy has crumpled, as stated by the World Bank (2020). This pandemic has led brands to redefine their business models and create a more sustainable, radical future to avoid mishaps and damages that could happen post-COVID-19. To curb the spread of the novel coronavirus, many countries drastically limited social life. These restrictions varied from prohibitions on large events and the closure of educational institutions to a temporary shutdown of the economy (Koch *et al.*, 2021). Due to the shutdown of retail outlets, online shopping has filled the void created by the impracticality of visiting a retail store amid the pandemic and also satisfied the needs of consumers. Moreover, it has offered wide variety and convenience to customers. Many companies have succeeded in their digital transition in three months, a process that would typically have taken three years. Owing to social distancing, the footfall of customers in retail stores has reduced, so that a 'no-interaction' economy could begin fostering e-commerce and mechanization to a different level. Nonetheless, successfully addressing the challenges will not guarantee an assured future, let alone any future at all. This is because, once we get through this pandemic, the world will emerge in a very different state compared to the one before the outbreak (Gonzalo *et al.*, 2020).

This chapter studies the effects of COVID-19 on the fashion industry, the benefits of digitalization for the fashion industry, and the long-term strategies of the fashion industry that could help it emerge from the COVID-19 crisis in a state of strength. The structure of the chapter is as follows. In the following section, we review the literature, which involves a theoretical background of COVID-19, an overview of the fashion industry, the impact of COVID-19, the digital migration of the fashion industry, and the long-term and potential influence on the industry's 'next normal.' The review is followed by sections on research methodology, research objectives, and findings. Finally, we end the chapter with discussions, limitations, and future research for academicians and managers.

Literature Review

Theoretical background of COVID-19

The extremely communicable COVID-19 was declared a pandemic by the World Health Organization on 11 March 2020 (Armani *et al.*, 2020). Although its precise beginnings are uncertain, the COVID-19 outbreak is supposed to have arisen in Wuhan, China, in December 2019. The severity of the disease varies from person to person, fluctuating from mild symptoms of fever, coughing, and breathlessness to serious respiratory troubles in critical cases (McMaster et al., 2020). Over 6.9 million people have been affected, claiming more than 400,000 lives in over 200 countries worldwide (Pal and Yadav, 2020). On 3 March, it was estimated that the case fatality rate of COVID-19 was almost 3.4% (World Health Organization, 2020). The death rate is higher among the elderly and those with pre-existing diseases (Zhou et al., 2020).

Fashion industry and the impact of COVID-19

The fashion business has grown remarkably, specifically over the past few years, when the boundaries of the industry started to expand (Djelic and Ainamo, 1999). The changing undercurrents of this industry since then, such as the disappearance of bulk production, surge in the number of seasons of fashion, and modified structural characteristics in the supply chain, have affected retailers' desire for low cost and flexibility in delivery, quality, speed to market, and design (Doyle et al., 2006). Moreover, marketing and capital investment have also been acknowledged as influential forces of competitiveness in the fashion industry. Today's fashion industry is highly aggressive, and the persistent need to 'renew' product collections means that there is an expected move by many vendors to increase the number of 'seasons,' i.e., the occasions when the entire stock within the store is upgraded. With the appearance of smaller collections of clothing, fashion retailers are appealing to consumers to visit their outlets more frequently with the impression of 'Here Today, Gone Tomorrow.' This results in shorter life cycles and high profit margins from the sale of fast-selling clothing, omitting the markdown process altogether (Sydney, 2008; Bhardwaj and Fairhust, 2009).

In order to be cost-effective in the industry, fashion retailers are required to take the 'speed to market' approach to capitalize on fashion that is not yet featured in the stores of their competitors. It is a subject that will continue to describe the fashion industry over the coming decade because its boundary extends over a variety of areas within the industry and will have an uninterrupted effect on the way consumers shop and respond to trends in the future (Sydney, 2008). Fast fashion refers to reasonable apparel collections grounded on existing, high-priced luxury fashion trends, which drives a quick response technique that boosts disposability (Fletcher, 2008). Fashion brands help quench the deep longings of young consumers for luxury fashion in the industrialized world (Joy et al., 2012). Fashion brands demand that store owners have 'five fingers touching the patrons and five fingers touching the factory' (the founder of Zara, cited in Ferdows *et al.*, 2014). They change fashions into goods that could be placed in the market almost instantly, releasing themselves and the patrons from the 'periodic assortment trap,' and, in the process, shifting the conditions surrounding production (Reinach, 2005). The Swedish Hennes & Mauritz (H&M), the Spanish Zara, and the US-based Gap now have around 5,000, 7,412, and 3,345 stores, respectively. The Italian Benetton and several others, such as the Spanish Mango, Forever 21, and the British Topshop, emphasize their vitality in evaluating tens of thousands of fresh designs every year, making clever choices, changing them into merchandise with extraordinary swiftness, and delivering them to their outlets straightaway (D'Avanzo *et al.*, 2004; Tokatli, 2007).

The COVID-19 pandemic is a watershed moment for the apparel industry, characterized by declining sales, cancelled fashion shows, shutdown of retail outlets, furloughed workers, accumulation of unsold stock, and a budding portion of the fashion business tumbling into fiscal agony (Business of Fashion, 2020). People have started to enter a shell, foster new skills, and take good care of where they are living (Donthu and Gustafsson, 2020). The need to buy apparel for weddings, vacations, jobs, and different occasions has come to a standstill. Therefore, fast fashion brands are doomed. They say fashion perishes quicker than a cooked biryani, and the impact of the pandemic on the fashion industry and manufacturing is no different. Industry players have commenced to fix themselves for the new normal (Gandhi, 2020). Factories and brands are left with no option but to demolish or keep hold of superfluous goods already manufactured and layoff their personnel in droves. From Zara to Forever 21, the homepage banners of all fast fashion brands announced major discounts and sales to clear out their inventories. From April to May 2020, sales declined by 60–70% in the fashion business globally, with footfall in retail stores and recreation outlets reducing by 52% in Germany, 59% in Brazil, 44% in the US, and 78% in India.

Simultaneously, manufacturers worldwide faced withdrawals of finished and near-finished orders, which are already causing distressing ripple effects. Bloomberg reports that approximately 1,089 garment factories in Bangladesh, the world's second-largest garment exporter after China, have had orders cancelled worth roughly $1.5 billion due to the pandemic (Fashion Revolution, 2020). As a direct repercussion, 40% of the factories struggled to pay employees, which led to layoffs and closures of factories. The boom of fashion sustainability has also accelerated during the

COVID-19 period as the mindset of people has shifted. They have become more conscious of the ethical aspects of their shopping experience. As noted, activewear and loungewear are trending, and it is expected that the pandemic could completely change the fashion game even after its end. Similar to how the Great Depression and World War II brought about a major transformation in people's wardrobes, COVID-19 will also become a new trendsetter; however, it is up to designers to lead this change (Orlova, 2020). The Vogue editor says, 'I think it's a chance for everyone to look around and to think again about the morals' (Open Access Government, 2020). For post-COVID-19 survival, there is a prerequisite to be extra nimble and trustworthy, giving importance to the three significant basics of rethink, replan, and revamp, which are essential for the fashion industry to plan and measure the industry's achievements (Raja and Kannappan, 2020).

However, despite all this, many brands in the sector came forward to instantly respond and contribute to the fight against COVID-19 and to fulfil the needs of community health. Brands discovered ingenious ways to donate personal protective equipment (PPEs), which are important gear for frontline workers. For instance, Migrolio fabricated and gave away breathing masks in support of the government of Italy, and LVMH (LVMH Moët Hennessy Louis Vuitton SE) manufactured hand sanitizers as part of their scent amenities. Moreover, at the facility level, 10 shoe workshops in Putian manufactured a minimum of two lakh (200,000) face covers each day in place of the sneakers they earlier mass-produced for fashion brands, such as Puma and Nike. Such works are remarkable, given the amount of stress the individual companies and the sector are facing.

Anticipated COVID-19 pandemic impact on global sales of fashion and luxury in 2020

The sales of fashion and luxury oscillated during 2019, decreasing from 59–68% in April to 10–18% in December. Looking towards 2020, a minimum of a 28–38% drop in fashion and luxury purchases was expected, as per the BCG analysis presented in March (Fig. 1).

Digital migration of fashion industry post-COVID-19

The fashion industry, just like any other industry, is being wrung out and is finding ways to fight COVID-19 and mitigate its impact. Forced by the crisis, fashion experts and curators recognized their job of looking for

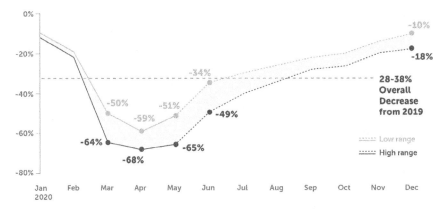

Figure 1. Impact of the Covid-19 pandemic on worldwide fashion and luxury sales in 2020.
Source: Weaving-a-Better-Future-Covid-19-BCG-SAC-Higg-Co-Report.

innovative ways to sustain the fashion culture in accordance with consumer behaviour, which will definitely change once the pandemic is over (Amin, 2020; Singh, 2020). As a result, there is a rise in online events, which have now become supplementary if not mainstream. The world's first completely virtual fashion week, Shanghai Fashion Week, was recently streamed online. According to its organizers, this week-long event created $72 million in online sales and gained a total of 11 million livestream views (Amin, 2020). Similarly, India Couture Week (ICW) went virtual with pre-made shoots showing models in designer wedding attire in a sanitized environment. This not only offered charm and glamour but also reduced the carbon footprint, which the industry has been struggling to reduce for a long time, because people would not be flying thousands of miles from all over the world to attend the shows (Singh, 2020). Speaking of digital events, even the famous Moscow Fashion Week chose to go virtual this time and had over 830,000 people stream it. The Milan Fashion Week combined physical and virtual shows, with Prada successfully pushing the hybrid format (Amin, 2020). In addition, many large-scale events with runway shows have largely migrated online, including Dior and Valentino's Fall/Winter 2020 couture shows and Gucci's latest resort offerings broadcast to viewers over livestream (Kwek, 2021).

'Digital migration' has become a well-known term in the fashion business today, and in the upcoming years, digital transformation innovations will help write the next chapter of progression in the fashion, textile, footwear, and apparel industries. This has aided the fashion brands in staying afloat, as outlets have been shut down, and the situation will continue to be acute during and after the recovery period of COVID-19. Digital transition means using digital technology in order to transform the way a company functions, drive efficiency and evolution in new or existing markets, and add more value to consumers (Mageean, 2020). Customers are avoiding shopping malls even after shops reopened. This shows that some proportion of offline sales could shift to online forever. This not only boosts sales but also entices customers to visit the stores once they reopen (Achille and Zisper, 2020). It is a certainty that coronaviruses can spread through contact during cash transactions, which has become one of the key reasons for patrons to choose digital migration (Auer *et al.*, 2020). Many high-street brands with noteworthy brands like J.Crew, Neiman Marcus, and G-Star RAW have declared insolvency, whereas H&M has announced the permanent closure of roughly 250 stores globally and accelerated its plans to increase digital investment since COVID-19 had moved shoppers with growing online demand (BBC, 2020). Similarly, the popular fashion brand Zara's Spanish owners and one of the world's biggest clothing retailers, Inditex, have suffered a net loss of $465 million, including a €308 million charge for shutting down 1,200 stores worldwide. From 1 February to 30 April, 2020, net sales dropped by 44% due to COVID-19. However, online sales have not felt the sting; in fact, things are contradictory, and sales rose by 50% year-on-year during the quarter and surged to 95% in April, which has provided a small relief (Jolly, 2020).

The equation of fashion and technology today has advanced to a higher stage with some ground-breaking innovations. The fashion-tech industry is trying to come up with innovative products to keep their consumers pleased and secure during this outbreak. For instance, brands such as H&M and Zara, which are fast fashion brands, are bringing out the concept of 3D printing clothes at home as an emerging alternative. Trial rooms, too, feature an alternative in the form of virtual reality (VR) and augmented reality (AR) technologies. These two additions to retail outlets are transforming the way consumers shop. Buyers can not only look at 3D representations of clothing but can also use AR to digitally try on clothes without the hassle of using trial rooms (Roy, 2020).

Leaders of analytics and digitalization (businesses with 30–40% of aggregate sales coming from online platforms, value chain fragments that are pointedly digitized, and integration of offline and online networks to a certain level) are beneficial nowadays but might rapidly drop off if others accelerate their transformations. Whereas, laggards (businesses with online sales contributing a maximum of 20% to overall sales, low intensities of digitalization throughout the value chain, and poor online and offshore functional models) have the opportunity to create a 'total' stake in analytics and digital and potentially capture a profitable market share with lesser investments in capital outflow, which would be a factor of limitation for various fashion companies (Gonzalo et al., 2020). The study makes it clear that the uptick in acceptance of digital services is not a temporary phenomenon. Over 70% of respondents said they would continue using digital services with the same frequency as they did now or even more often. Digital acceptance in Europe jumped from 81% to 95% in the wake of the COVID-19 crisis (Fernandez et al., 2020). COVID-19 has provided a tailwind for development in India's digital economy. The fashion industry asserts a noteworthy share of world economic output; the market has a development of more than three percent per year globally and by 2025 the progression rate is expected to reach five percent per year. The acceleration is mainly driven by emerging markets' demand surge as well as by the e-commerce growth and digitalization era. Nonetheless, digitalization will not be an antidote. Businesses should bifurcate funds to places where the maximum value of the business lies, which can be anywhere in the value chain if not in sales.

Framing the next normal

As times are uncertain, it is imperative for the fashion industry to set long-term strategic actions to compete and potentially influence the fashion industry's 'next normal' (Gonzalo et al., 2020):

1. **Define a pathway:** The digital and analytics transition is an approximately 18–24-month journey which requires motivated aspiration, a definite blueprint, and concrete milestones. A definite plan prioritizes initiatives that combine with actions, which help set up the organizers for the company with the execution of use cases that result in swift gains. A central team is required to help construct a pathway by examining opportunities, allocating budgets, and coordinating execution. Digitalization is much more than an online presence, and rapid pinpointing is essential to choosing and aligning with the main zones.
2. **Provide the experience of omni-channel:** The extensive spread of COVID-19 has uplifted digitalization as a necessity for the fashion industry. Therefore, this opportunity should be seized to make the

online platform the centrepiece of the functional model: shift customer traffic and the engagement generation engine online and influence digital networks to drive retail outlet traffic, and vice versa.
3. **Recognize that personalization is vital:** Customer lifetime value increases with personalization. It has been verified to be even more valuable in subsectors with additional persistent and predictable patterns of purchasing, such as cosmetics. Prioritize according to occasions based on the context of business, advanced analytical skills, and customer segments. Introduce personalization to all delivery stations to guarantee consistency in shopper communications.
4. **Leverage huge database and analytics to handle the supply chain:** The digital and analytics transition has to initiate top-line growth and also meaningfully develop the flexibility, speed, sustainability, and cost of the supply chain. Additionally, systematizing logistics through digital warehouse design and predictive exception management can drastically improve effectiveness. The profits will stream down to patrons in the form of improved availability of products and quicker, inexpensive, and more precise deliveries.
5. **Expand product lines and support functions digitalization:** Digitization throughout the pandemic has proven to be a competitive advantage for brands that were already operating with a progressive approach. For example, those employing technologies such as 3D product design, online selection, digital material libraries, and AI-supported planning have fared better than others throughout the crunch. Their fashion creators can respond quicker to market styles, markedly lessening both costs and time-to-market times, and collaborate remotely across teams. Efficiency can be improved with the digitization of support functions.
6. **Be tech enablers and build data to support the transition:** The data foundation should be solid, which allows for prompt scaling up and advancing compatibility. The usage of cloud infrastructure can help achieve scaling and approach best-in-all facilities. These techniques within companies should keep up with similar nimble timelines and sprints so that they provide a necessary edge and are not the cause for rescheduling.
7. **Retention of best digital personnel:** After the calamity, the monetarily sound brands will perhaps entice the best digital personnel with on-demand profiles, such as data scientists, digital talents, data engineers, and data architects. Holding on to these types of personnel will

require the fashion industry to foster fresh talent acquisition procedures with tailor-made initiatives in recruiting, learning and skill development, and career growth in parallel to what several fashion companies prepare for designers and creative directors.

Therefore, COVID-19 has made 2020 a tough year, with even survival becoming a struggle for some fashion brands. However, this struggle can be addressed if these brands function with understanding and undertake courageous actions in digital and analytics. It is believed that the industry would sustain itself beyond the catastrophe while also creating competitive advantages and bolstering the business for an omni-channel, digitally positioned next normal.

Research Methodology

COVID-19 is a novel occurrence, because of which the economy ground to a halt worldwide. There are various research studies introducing innovative models, concepts, theories, and themes which can be the basis for business firms to rescue themselves if applied and executed in the correct direction.

This is an exploratory study which depends on the careful examination of secondary data from many journals, websites, and databases. This gives us a chance to comprehend the broad concepts and also analytically assess them to bridge the gap. In this study, white papers are mainly considered since they are reliable reports that offer thought-provoking information which can be further reviewed by academicians. Additionally, research papers from reputed journals have been used.

Research Objectives

From the literature review and the published papers, the following research objectives have been framed:

1. to study the effect of COVID-19 on the fashion industry;
2. to study the digital transition of the fashion industry post COVID-19;
3. to study the long-term strategies used by companies to compete in the sector post-COVID-19.

Findings

- It's quite evident that, due to the pandemic, sales of all fast fashion brands have been migrating to digital platforms.
- The outbreak has also caused a mindset shift in the way consumers behave and carry out their actions, directly affecting digital channels and making consumers more digitally prone.
- This pandemic has also changed the buying behaviour of consumers towards apparel. Now, they are more interested in purchasing essential goods, such as groceries and safety- and hygiene-related goods.
- Fast fashion brands worldwide are focusing more on expanding their digital investments than on their retail outlets. Brands which have never had a presence on the digital platform are aiming to be present digitally for customers.
- Many fast fashion brands are coming up with innovative products to engage customers digitally and entice them to make purchases.
- COVID-19 has made consumers conscientious by directing their concerns towards sustainable fashion.

Limitation of the Study and Future Scope

This study has emphasized only fast fashion brands. Future research could investigate how different sectors, such as travel and tourism and educational institutions, react to the present public health disaster in specific regions and also trace this transition over time.

Discussion and Conclusion

COVID-19 has had a critical impact, with the current behaviours and patterns of consumers coming under scrutiny. The whole world has gone through a state of tragedy, with nothing remaining the way it was before. As the pandemic crunch triggered basic economic and societal changes, companies are compelled to comprehend the behaviour of consumers at this specific phase. The trends recognized throughout this pandemic may endure forever, inflicting serious consequences on retail outlets due to an expansion of digitalization. The fashion industry, in particular, suffered falling sales during the outbreak. However, there are still chances for companies to boost their wear and gear sales despite this challenging economic situation. By tactically improving their presence online and making it alluring to consumers' specific shopping motives, fashion companies may mitigate decreasing sales. Although the path ahead is vague and unanswered questions remain as society and governments traverse the outbreak, a major experience of the COVID-19 era will be that safety, health, and wealth are essentially joint pursuits rather than distinct ones. And the fashion industry is not distinctive. To survive a once-in-a-generation economic calamity while taking brave steps despite social and environmental apprehensions will not be hassle-free. But front-runners who efficaciously interlace digitalization into their approaches to business will continue and leave an enduring bequest.

References

Achille, A., and Zipser, D. (2020). McKinsey & Company. Perspective for the Luxury-Goods Industry during—and after—Coronavirus. https://www.mckinsey.com/industries/retail/our-insights/a-perspective-for-the-luxury-goods-industry-during-and-after-coronavirus#.

Ahmed, I., and Berg, A. (2020). The state of fashion 2020: Coronavirus update — It's time to rewire the fashion industry. The State of Fashion 2020: Coronavirus Update — It's Time to Rewire the Fashion Industry.

Amin, R. Digital fashion shows take over the runway. Available at http://everythingexperiential.businessworld.in/article/Digital-fashion-shows-take-over-the-runway/14-10-2020-331401/.

Armani, A. M., Hurt, D. E., Hwang, D., McCarthy, C. M., and Scholtz, A. (2020). Low-tech solutions for the COVID-19 supply chain crisis. *Nature Reviews Materials*, 5, 403–406.

Auer, R., Cornelli, G., and Frost, J. (2020). BIS Bulletin payments. Based on Google community reports and BCG analysis. Available online: https://www.bis.org/publ/bisbull03.pdf.

Bhardwaj, V., and Fairhust, A. (2010). Fast fashion: Response to changes in the fashion industry. *The International Review of Retail Distribution and Consumer Research*. doi: 10.1080/09593960903498300.

Business of Fashion. (2020). The state of fashion 2020: Coronavirus update. Business of Fashion. Accessed 9 April 2020. https://www.businessoffashion.com/articles/intelligence/the-state-of-fashion-2020-coronavirus-update-bof-mckinsey-report-release-download.

D'Avanzo, R., Starr, C. E., and Von Lewinski, H. (2004). Supply chain and the bottom line: A critical link. Outlook, no. 1. www.accenture.com/Outlook.

Devnath, A. (2020). European retailers scrap $1.5 billion of Bangladesh orders. https://www.bloomberg.com/news/articles/2020-03-23/europe-retailers-cancel-1-billion-of-bangladesh-garment-orders.

Djelic, M. L., and Ainamo, A. (1999). The coevolution of new organizational forms in the fashion industry: A historical and comparative study of France, Italy, and the United States. *Organizational Science*, 10.

Donthu, N. and Gustafsson, A. (2020). Effects of COVID-19 on business and research. *Journal of Business Research*, 117, 284–289.

Doyle, S. A., Moore, C. M., and Morgan, L. (2006). Supplier management in fast moving fashion retailing. *Journal of Fashion Marketing and Management: An International Journal*, 10(3), 272–281.

Ferdows, K., Lewis, M. A., and Machuca, J. A. D. (2004). Rapid-fire fulfilment. *Harvard Business Review*.

Fernandez, S., Jenkins, P., and Vieira, B. (2020). Europe's digital migration during COVID-19: Getting past the broad trends and averages. McKinsey Report. https://www.mckinsey.com/business-functions/mckinsey-digital/our-insights/europes-digital-migration-during-covid-19-getting-past-the-broad-trends-and-averages.

Fletcher, K. (2008). *Sustainable Fashion and Textiles: Design Journeys*. Earthscan, London.

Gandhi, F. (2020, May 11). "Apparel industry players prepare for the new normal", *The Hindu Business Line*. https://www.thehindubusinessline.com/economy/fashion-industry-draws-action-plan-for-post-covid-19-situation/article31555037.ece.

Gereffi, G. (2005a). The global economy: Organization, governance, and development. *The Global Economy: Organization, Governance, and Development*. Princeton University Press and Russell Sage Foundation, Princeton.

Gonzalo, A., Harreis, H., Altable, S. C., and Villepelet, C. (2020). Fashion's digital transformation now or never. McKinsey Report. https://www.mckinsey.com/industries/retail/our-insights/fashions-digital-transformation-now-or-never.

Jolly, J. (2020, June 10). "Zara owner to close up to 1,200 fashion stores around the world", *The Guardian*. https://www.theguardian.com/business/2020/jun/10/zara-owner-to-close-up-to-1200-fashion-stores-around-the-world.

Joy, A., Sherry, J. F., Venkatesh, A., Wang, J., and Chan, R. (2012). Fast fashion, sustainability, and the ethical appeal of luxury brands. *Fashion Theory*. doi:10.2752/175174112X13340749707123.

Koch, J., et al., (2021). Looking for talent in times of crisis–The impact of the Covid-19 pandemic on public sector job openings. *International Journal of Information Management Data Insights*, 1(2), 100014.

Kwek, G. (2021). What brands need to be thinking about amid the mass migration to digital. https://www.thefashionlaw.com/what-brands-need-to-think-about-in-light-of-the-mass-migration-to-the-digital-world/.

Mageean, L. (2020). How digital transformation is fundamentally changing the fashion industry. https://www.whichplm.com/how-digital-transformation-is-fundamentally-changing-the-fashion-industry/.

McMaster, M., Nettleton, C., Tom, C., Xu, B., Cao, C., and Qiao, P. (2020). Risk management: Rethinking fashion supply chain management for multinational corporations in light of the COVID-19 outbreak.

Mishra, S. (2020). How fashion and lifestyle industry drew a survival strategy in 2020. https://www.financialexpress.com/brandwagon/how-fashion-and-lifestyle-industry-drew-a-survival-strategy-in-2020/2154832/.

Open Access Government. (2020). Impacts of COVID-19 on the fashion industry. https://www.openaccessgovernment.org/covid-19-fashion-industry/89851/.

Orlova, D. (2020). How will COVID-19 change the fashion industry. https://newseu.cgtn.com/news/2020-05-05/How-will-COVID-19-change-the-fashion-industry--QdWaZBwGCQ/index.html.

Pal, R., and Yadav, U. (2020). COVID-19 pandemic in India: Present scenario and a steep climb ahead. *Journal of Primary Care & Community Health*, 11, 1–4.

Raja, A. S., and Kannappan, S. (2020). Marketing agility and E-commerce agility in the light of COVID-19 pandemic: A study with reference to fast fashion brands. *Asian Journal of Interdisciplinary Research*, 3(4). https://doi.org/10.34256/ajir2041.

Roberts, B. (2020). Designer and supply chain digital revolution: How COVID-19 is changing the fashion industry. https://www.forbes.com/sites/brookerobertsislam/2020/04/13/designer-and-supply-chain-digital-revolution-how-covid-19-is-changing-the-fashion-industry/?sh=4b6ae03f7ccc(20.

Revolution, F. (2020). The impact of COVID-19 on the people who make our clothes. https://www.fashionrevolution.org/the-impact-of-covid-19-on-the-people-who-make-our-clothes/.

Singh, S. (2020). Impact on psychology of fashion after COVID 19. Available at https://www.iknockfashion.com/impact-on-psychology-of-fashion-after-covid-19.

Singh, P. (2020). How green are digital fashion shows? Livemint Report. https://www.livemint.com/mint-lounge/features/how-green-are-digital-fashion-shows-11601625017308.html.

Stanley, M. (2020). Covid-19 to accelerate digital adoption in India. Bloomberg Report. https://www.bloombergquint.com/business/covid-19-to-accelerate-digital-adoption-in-india-jio-helped-spur-internet-usage-morgan-stanley.

The World Bank. (2020). The global economic outlook during the COVID-19 pandemic: A changed world. Retrieved from The World Bank. https://www.worldbank.org/en/news/feature/2020/06/08/the-global-economic-outlook-during-the-covid-19-pandemic-a-changed-world.

Tokatli, N. (2008). Global sourcing: Insights from the global clothing industry—the case of Zara. *Journal of Economic Geography*, 21–38. doi: 10.1093/jeg/lbm035.

WHO (World Health Organization). (2020). WHO Director-General's opening remarks at the media briefing on COVID-19. https://www.who.int/dg/speeches/detail/who-director-general-s-opening-remarks-at-the-media-briefing-on-covid-19. Accessed on 3 March 2020.

Zhou, F., Yu, T., Du, R., Fan, G., Liu, Y., Liu, Z., Xiang, J., Wang, Y., Song, B., Gu, X., and *et al.* (2020). Clinical course and risk factors for mortality of adult inpatients with COVID-19 in Wuhan, China: A retrospective cohort study. https://pubmed.ncbi.nlm.nih.gov/32171076/. Accessed on 18 June 2020.

Chapter 10

Rural Healthcare: Recovery and Resilience through Digital Health Entrepreneurial Foresight in Developing Countries Post-COVID-19

Rahul Khandelwal

Institute of Management Studies Career Development & Research, Ahmednagar, Maharashtra, India

rahulkhandelwal29@rediffmail.com

Abstract

The purpose of the study is to conduct a scoping review aimed at identifying innovative entrepreneurial opportunities in digital healthcare ecosystems in rural areas. The study highlights the barriers to digital health in developing countries. The study serves as a platform for introducing entrepreneurship prospects in the Indian context to other foreign readers in developing countries. This exploratory study explores successful ways of improving market potential in developed countries with respect to digital health. The research offers insights into how a digital health environment could be applied and provides a trajectory that concentrates on key skills and a creative approach. Health service providers need to develop their competencies and skills to accelerate and enhance their entrepreneurial opportunities. The research briefly suggests a creative solution to entrepreneurship in developed countries that can be applied in today's digital arena.

Keyword: Healthcare, digital healthcare, entrepreneurship, developing countries, COVID-19.

Introduction

The COVID-19 pandemic has spread to all countries in the world, and their healthcare systems are increasingly adapting to rising demand. Digital technologies may be used, which can efficiently help organizations after the pandemic through the immediate and wide dissemination of knowledge, monitoring in real time, setting up virtual venues, conferences, or everyday operations, and the provision of patient visits through telemedicine (Clypool, 2020). Due to technological innovation at higher levels, developed countries are able to manage this challenge with digital health in a proper manner; however, the problems in developing countries are enormous in terms of digital health accessibility. India is one of the developing Asian countries, having 70% rural population among 6.5 lakh cities. The Indian general healthcare industry is worth around $100 billion and is forecast to hit $280 billion by 2025 (Chandwani and Dwivedi, 2015). With a compound annual growth rate (CAGR) of 22.9%, India is the first nation to create explicit public targets and pointers pointed towards lessening the quantity of worldwide unexpected losses from non-communicable diseases (NCDs) by 25% by 2025 (Chandwani and Dwivedi, 2015). The digital health market was valued at more than $38.3 billion in 2018 and estimated to grow at a compound annual growth rate (CAGR) in excess of 19% between 2019 and 2025 by Global Market Insights in March 2019 (Kurji *et al.*, 2015). This study investigates the global scenario of digital health and the opportunities it presents. The study also focuses on the current telemedicine situation in India from a rural viewpoint as well as entrepreneurs' prospects post COVID-19.

Overview of study

The COVID-19 pandemic has created significant gaps in the networks for education, health and social security, and the persistence of a major digital divide across developed and developing countries. In order to lower costs and improve the quality of care, developed and established countries have spent considerable capital and will continue to spend on the implementation of digital health systems (Ancker *et al.*, 2019). The pandemic revealed that a lack of adequate health literacy has a significant impact on individuals' availability, reliable access to, and management of healthcare issues, especially in developed countries, and on specific and useful health information. Citizens in these countries have no expertise in reading unfamiliar materials and tools (Kim and Xie, 2017). Almost 70% of the population of India lives in rural areas that lack access to health and infrastructure facilities. Public health access centres in these areas link people to the internet and offer health services via municipal services (Mathur *et al.*, 2017).

Conceptual framework

Digital Health: The use of connectivity and information technology to enhance the health of the public can be characterized by exchanging biomedical and clinical information, the experiences of doctors and patients, and reducing overall costs. The engagement and consent of patients are required by digital health, not only at the doctor's office or hospital.

Digital Health Entrepreneurship: Entrepreneurship contributes by fostering new industries, leading to the economic and social goal of growth (Dana and Manson, 2009). Digital health entrepreneurship is the search for healthcare opportunities characterized by scarce and unrelated resources to build user-defined values by developing, expanding, integrating, or releasing innovative digital health goods, technologies, platforms, and models.

Technology: The set of methods, skills, techniques, and processes used in the manufacture of products or services or in the achievement of goals, such as scientific research, is technology. The awareness of methods, procedures, and the like can be provided by technology, or it can be incorporated into devices that can be run without comprehensive knowledge of their operations.

Barriers for development of digital health

Challenges and barriers in developing countries, such as accessibility, availability, and acceptability, are addressed by Bali (2018). These barriers are becoming particularly troublesome for women, girls, the elderly, and the mentally challenged (Jacob *et al.*, 2012). Although healthcare and regional connectivity have increased, local women remain unable to use the facilities without the quality and cultural demands of the services rendered (Chiang *et al.*, 2013).

Further, some hurdles, such as organizational structure and policy barriers; lack of team champions, including nurses, doctors, and clinical champions; deficiency in telemedicine delivery services, and lack of an IT network; technological barriers, such as high costs of replacing old technologies with new ones, telecommunication expenses, and lack of training; legal barriers, such as malpractice liability; financial barriers; and social barriers, are often seen in the hinterlands of developing countries (Bali *et al.*, 2016). Barriers addressed in some developing countries are as follows: in Jordan, there are legal and financial barriers and a lack of awareness (Buney *et al.*, 2010); in Turkey, the challenges are technical support, security, and cultural (Sharifi *et al.*, 2013); in Iran, the barriers are a lack of professional expertise, cost, and security (Ghani and Jaber, 2015); similar barriers are addressed in Egypt (Hoque *et al.*, 2016); and Kuwait reports challenges of ICT, legal, and confidentiality (Alaslawi *et al.*, 2019). In some Asian countries, the challenges are as follows: in India, the challenges are a lack of awareness, financial, legal, and professional expertise to promote businesses (Chandwani and Dwivedi, 2015); in Sri Lanka, Indonesia, and Malaysia, the barriers are a lack of professional expertise, ICT literacy, and knowledge (Luna *et al.*, 2015); in China, the barriers are policy, privacy, and confidentiality, as explained by Zhai *et al.* (2014) and Wu (2011); in Syria, the challenges are economic constraints and knowledge (Alaslavi *et al.*, 2019); and in Brazil, the hurdles are a lack of strategic plans and professional expertise (Bervell and Sammarraie, 2019). Some earlier studies of telemedicine services in a developing country, India, identified critical factors for their success, highlighting the importance of setting a clear programme goal, government support, adapting a user-friendly interface to ensure connectivity, and measuring cost efficiency and satisfaction with user protocols (Keupp and Gassmann, 2009). Discovered that digital health services in India provide new entrepreneurial opportunities by overcoming the barriers faced in digital health.

Research questions

How can the experiences of developing countries serve as a lesson for developed countries in adapting digital health services?

How can digital health provide entrepreneurship opportunities in developing countries? How can these opportunities be anticipated to deliver digital health services in developing countries?

Need for study

This study tries to bridge the research gap by considering digital health as a tool for consultation and awareness of health issues, providing entrepreneurial opportunities in developing countries such as India, which has a huge rural population. The research highlights developed and developing countries' digital health scenarios while shedding light on the Indian landscape for digital health services. Further, the study reflects on how entrepreneurs should be innovative in delivering digital healthcare services, how technology can improve the quality of healthcare services, and how entrepreneurs in providing healthcare can more efficiently serve the evolving needs of patients despite many obstacles post-COVID-19 pandemic.

Research Methodology

This research study is based on exploratory research involving the examination of digital texts, which include electronic databases, web pages, and emails. Accordingly, journals were classified through a website where the research papers with abstracts related to the research topics that are cited are available and indexed in international databases. A subsequent search was conducted on these international databases, namely Springer Link, Emerald Insight, EBSCO, ScienceDirect, and Google Scholar. In archival research the changeover COVID-19 issue needs to be addressed as the research question in an exploratory or descriptive manner.

After a rigorous review, further analysis of the research papers was performed in the context of conceptual frameworks, including the topics of digital healthcare post COVID-19 in developed and developing countries, digital health scenario in India, entrepreneurship approach to digital health services, discussion and implications, and conclusion with future scope for research.

Digital Health: Developed and Developing Countries' Scenarios

Advance technology in IT, for example, telemedicine, e-welfare, telehealth, and versatile welfare, seemed to minimize costs and clinical failures in public healthcare (Bervell and Samarraie, 2019). In developed countries, particularly in European nations, for example, France, Germany, the United Kingdom, Sweden, and Norway, the viable usage of telemedicine has empowered an expansive selection of the best medical care practices. Non-industrial nations, particularly the Middle Eastern nations, are gaining ground in receiving important data innovation developments, strategies, and rules with the end goal of propelling the utilization of their telemedicine programmes (McCleary et al., 2013). In Australia, the health services devoted to the provision of supplementary mental health services via video conference were refinanced by the Medicare Benefits Schedule (MBS). Related facilities for mental well-being were also provided to the bushfire-impacted residents. In the US, rural areas are managed through video conferencing and are successfully saving the cost of medicine. In Europe, telesurgery is usually regarded as providing assistance to surgery, i.e., the surgeon can see and display the invisible parts of a patient's body (Kurji et al., 2015). China has begun to investigate telehealth and advanced electronic medical services for related uses. Similar initiatives are also seen in some African countries, such as Ghana, Zambia, Tanzania, Rwanda, and Mozambique, where some initiatives have helped these countries transform their health information systems from paper-based records to digital health information systems (Chiang et al., 2013). It is additionally worth referencing that past and current wars in some Middle Eastern nations, for example, Yemen, Iraq, Egypt, and Syria, are a source of constant chaos and insecurity in the area (Ghani and Jaber, 2015). With this in mind, the use of telemedicine in the Middle East has, after some time, drastically improved. Moreover, despite the fact that a great many telemedicine schemes have been delivered in the Middle East since the 1990s (Saudi Arabia and the United Arab Emirates, Iran, Turkey, Kuwait, Bahrain, Iraq, Syria, Oman, Jordan, and Qatar), there has been a lack of improvement and fluctuations in their usage across nations (Bali et al., 2016), and this social challenge is responsible for the powerlessness of telemedicine organizations in most Middle Eastern nations. According to Alaboudi et al. (2016), about 75% of telemedicine programmes in developed countries are abandoned, and this figure is as high as 90% in some countries.

Current Digital Health: Telemedicine Situation in India

The WHO recommends a doctor-to-population ratio of 1:1,000, while in India the actual ratio is just 0.62:1,000. This is because medical education is expensive and exhausting, for a while to come, the expert's image will likely remain poor (Mathur *et al.*, 2017). The objective is to achieve excellent well-being facilities for all Indians through the financially stable and healthy use of ICTs in the field of social welfare. In India, telemedicine consultations are also required in the customary medicinal areas. The national rural telemedicine network AYUSH plans to encourage customary techniques to expand telemedicine to a broader community. The concept of a village resource centre (VRC) (Mathur *et al.*, 2017) was developed by ISRO to provide a variety of administration tools, such as telecommunications, telemedicine, online preference assistance, ranchers' intuitive alert systems, tele-fishing, e-governance, environment protection, and executive's water systems. The VRCs act as learning centres and establish robust emergency clinics, providing access to the services of expert professionals from the cities. Throughout the country, almost 500 of these VRCs have been installed.

Telemedicine: A distinct advantage in the rural regions

Telemedicine can offer a distinct advantage in the provincial regions and among the underserved zones by making it simpler for individuals to consult a specialist (Borup *et al.*, 2006; Venkatesh *et al.*, 2000). Progress in innovation has empowered specialists from metropolitan India to take care of patients in rural zones remotely through video-call discussions (Gopalan *et al.*, 2019; Keupp and Gassmann, 2009). However, video-call conversations are not enough in the case of more recent risks, such as COVID-19. Concerning the pandemic, telemedicine performs a functioning job. Anybody with a cell phone will have 24×7 access to qualified specialists, regardless of which part of the nation they are in (Timpel *et al.*, 2020). Metro urban communities, from where the vast majority of the consultation requests are coming, are also incorporated (Khan *et al.*, 2020). The non-metro urban areas include Ahmedabad, Jaipur, Lucknow, Bhubaneshwar, Indore, Delhi, NCR, Hyderabad, Mumbai, Pune, and

Chennai. Apollo Telehealth currently operates over 700 open private healthcare ecosystems in India, boasting of a wide distribution covering more than 11.4 million lives across Andhra Pradesh, Himachal Pradesh, Uttar Pradesh, and Jharkhand. A modest number of new health technology companies in rustic India are now trying to create an economical basis for telemedicine. The study of the overall image of global developments and problems, which integrates with country-specific systemic variables, translates into opportunities and risks that help build potential adaptation strategies (Saritas and Kuzminov, 2017). The stage has over 2,000 practitioners and more than 45 medical practitioners, super officials, family physicians, and ayurvedic and homoeopathic doctors. New telemedicine companies raised $178.4 million across 16 arrangements, 40% more than in 2018.

Foresight: Digital health entrepreneurship in telemedicine

Telemedicine is expected to create business opportunities worth over $5.4 billion by 2025. The regulations on telemedicine in India, outlined in 2020, have clarified the current market and speculators' guidelines. India is one of the top 10 countries in the world market for telemedicine. The early selection of an administrative system will enable the portion to grow quickly. The extraordinary COVID-19 flare-up exposed the difficulties of customary medical care frameworks in India (Timpel *et al.*, 2020). Because of countrywide lockdowns, residents did not have the option to consult with specialists in person. This circumstance drove the legislature to change the guidelines on remote conveyance of medical care benefits and permit telemedicine by means of video, audio, or text. New companies, for example, Practo and Doc Prime, are driving India's telemedicine market, which is filled with unexplored opportunities. With an expansion in the frequency of way-of-life ailments and rising medical service costs, there is an enormous burden on the customary medical services framework. Inventive advances are permitting welfare associations to upgrade access and decrease the burden on clinics through continuous discussion with specialists via smartphones, tablets, workstations, or PCs (Saebi *et al.*, 2019). India has a shortage of around 600,000 qualified specialists and 2 million medical attendants, according to 2018 reports. India has only one government specialist for every 1,139 individuals, while the

World Wellbeing Association (WWA) suggests a proportion of 1:1,000. The lack of specialists is restricting vis-à-vis counselling among patients. Besides, India likewise has a deficiency of medical clinic beds, which makes hospitalization precarious, and there should be better offices and facilities for situations where patients can be taken care of by means of teleconsultation. Strategic alternatives for research and innovation partners should be devised with a view to implementing new and evolving ways in which research is being organized and carried out (Amanatidou et al., 2016).

Discussion

The reforms prompted by COVID-19 are likely to drive creativity across the globe as a way to discover solutions to the problems encountered by entrepreneurs. The research findings of Hoque et al. (2019) advocate that digital health is the result of ICT and has a significant influence on developed countries' healthcare sector improvements. Governments in many developing countries are highly optimistic that the digital health system can enhance the efficiency, accessibility, and affordability of healthcare. Schroeder (2020) predicts that such a trend can provide everyone with better access to healthcare facilities and promote better coordination among patients, physicians, nurses, and other healthcare staff.

A digital entrepreneur's success becomes more visible with the creation of new business ventures, capitalizing on opportunities, and accelerating new businesses internationally (Jean et al., 2020). The study justifies that a strong digital divide still exists in some countries today and that the digital approaches adopted could leave vulnerable people behind (Lorenz et al., 2019; Oudsheem, 2008). However, there seem to be at least two explanations why, in developing countries, digital health telemedicine might be important. Second, digital health telemedicine is a tool used in developed nations, such as North America and Australia (ILO, 2020), to bring healthcare to rural and isolated areas where there are few physicians and other personnel. In the developed world, there are large rural and remote areas and very few health workers. For example, 24% (15% in Australia) of the total US population is rural, compared to 64% in the developed world and 79% in the least developed countries (Schotter et al.,

2018). There are significant variations in the number of healthcare workers as well as differences in urbanization: there is only one doctor for every 18,000 people in sub-Saharan Africa, compared to one for every 6,000 in the developed part of the world as a whole and one for every 400 in the industrial countries (Lin *et al.*, 2019). Developing countries have large healthcare problems, as both synchronous and asynchronous technologies are used in each country. In Asia and Europe, telemedicine is primarily used to link delivery organizations, while services use patient connectivity via telemedicine in the United States (Jean *et al.*, 2020). For example, different countries in India collaborate with the central administration to set up networks in telemedicine and connect hospitals with digital healthcare providers to improve creative market opportunities after COVID-19.

Implications

Public–private partnership (PPP) operations with small and big entrepreneurs are an effective way to reach foreign markets quicker or at less expense as a result of independent growth (Dana, 2000; Ferreira and Dana, 2017). Stakeholders, including governments (public), can form partnerships with private organizations to provide health services. Through PPPs in the digital health innovation ecosystem, the identified objectives should be formally recorded at an early stage for better delivery of digital health services. The government should establish tie-ups to align with technology, and strategies for combining current systems with the latest applications should be in place to ensure that workflows proceed with existing healthcare applications. Structured preparation can be introduced to ensure that the alignment of current infrastructure with emerging modern health technology is reviewed and provides entrepreneurship opportunities in unexplored rural areas.

Private sector involvement

Private sector entrepreneurship opportunities should tie up with the government and also outsource required services to other entrepreneurs for business growth:

(a) Health apps: Techno-entrepreneurship can also be an assisting tool in providing telemedicine and tracking and self-managing health. Innovation through easy techno-savvy apps in local languages may bridge the gap in awareness about health and serve the digital health technology from local to global scenarios.
(b) Sensor devices: Devices in the form of sensor-equipped kits made by the private sector, as suggested by Pal *et al.* (2005), can log the vital signs of a patient, such as blood pressure, pulse rate, and saturation of blood oxygen. They should be cheap and open to rural people in developing countries. In such cases, the first steps of a normal medical test are replaced by this system. One can test them with this system rather than go to a hospital and give them to a specialist for examination to help assess if an appointment in person is necessary. The smoothness device offers families lower costs to access health treatment and a healthier lifestyle.
(c) Reviewing and monitoring services: Entrepreneurship in innovative methods of monitoring and reviewing the data of patients can provide fresh opportunities in developing countries. Stakeholders need to build mechanisms for analysis and tracking. The stakeholders will perform assessments at designated times. Health practitioners can help with clinical decisions and evaluations of real-world data by providing digitalized solutions. One can obtain information about their hormonal, biological, and anatomical dimensions.

Conclusion

The application of digital health during the COVID-19 pandemic is another example of how entrepreneurs empowered to apply technological innovations can improve the quality of care for patients today while also reducing costs and improving convenience. The study highlights the barriers to digital healthcare and discusses developing and developed countries' health scenarios. In this study, restrictions created by government regulations and the current payment model have prevented wider use of telemedicine despite its demonstrated value to patients. In the healthcare sector today, entrepreneurs neither have the incentive nor the ability to develop alternative practices or delivery models to increase overall efficiency and eliminate waste at the scale needed. It is necessary to foster greater entrepreneurship in healthcare and to dramatically reduce costs, expand access, and enhance the quality of care. These advantages would emerge in developing countries, such as India, which is a growing economy, because of the same dynamics that enable entrepreneurs to increase our living standards, providing employment by creating new health ventures. The healthcare sector also operates in the wider economy, and several market developments, from the creation of emerging technologies to the introduction of digital health services in the midst of the COVID-19 pandemic, have been reported in the previous studies, which illustrate the possible structural benefits provided by entrepreneurial efforts and direct future studies in developing and developed nations, digital well-being, innovation, and digital ecosystems. Market ecosystems encourage startups, use online workshops, and promote regional development, sustainability, economic recovery, and corporate growth post-COVID-19, fostering creativity and entrepreneurial practices.

References

Alaboudi, A., Atkins, A., Sharp, B., Balkhair, A., Alzahrani, M., and Sunbul, T. (2016). Barriers and challenges in adopting Saudi telemedicine network: The perceptions of decision makers of healthcare facilities in Saudi Arabia. *Journal Infection Public Health*, 9(6), 725–733.

Alaslawi, H., Berrou, I., Alhuwail, D., and Aslanpour, Z. (2019). Status and trends of e-health tools in Kuwait: A narrative review. *Journal of Health Information in Developing Countries*, 13(2), 1–21.

Amanatidou, E., Saritas, O., and Loveridge, D. (2016). Strategies for emerging research and innovation futures. *Foresight*, 18(3), 253–275. https://doi.org/10.1108/FS-07-2014-0048.

Ancker, J. S., Grossman, L. V., and Benda, N. C. (2019). Health literacy 2030: Is it time to redefine the term? *Journal of General Internal Medicine*. https://doi.org/10.1007/s11606-019-05472-y.

Bali, S. (2018). Enhancing the reach of health care through telemedicine: Status and new possibilities in developing countries. In *Health Care Delivery and Clinical Science: Concepts, Methodologies, Tools, and Applications*. Information Resources Management Association, (pp. 1382–1397). Accessed 3 December, 2018. doi: 10.4018/978-1-5225-3926-1.ch069.

Bali, S., Gupta, A., Khan, A., and Pakhare, A. (2016). Evaluation of telemedicine centres in Madhya Pradesh, Central India. *Journal of Telemedicine and Telecare*, 22(3), 183–188.

Bervell, B., and Al-Samarraie, H. (2019). A comparative review of mobile health and electronic health utilization in sub-Saharan African countries. *Social Science Medicine*, 232, 1–16. doi: 10.1016/j.socscimed.2019.04.024.

Borup, M., Brown, N., Konrad, K., and Van Lente, H. (2006). The sociology of expectations in science and technology. *Technology Analysis and Strategic Management*, 18(3–4), 285–298.

Burney, S. A., Mahmood, N., and Abbas, Z. (2010). Information and communication technology in healthcare management systems: Prospects for developing countries. *International Journal of Computer Application*, 4(2), 27–32.

Chandwani, R., and Dwivedi, Y. K. (2015). Telemedicine in India: Current state, challenges and opportunities. *Transformation Government People Process Policy*, 9(4), 393–400.

Chiang, C., Adly Labeeb, S., Higushi, M., Mohamed, A. G., and Aoyama, A. (2013). Barriers to the use of basic health services among women in rural southern Egypt (upper Egypt). *Nagoya Journal of Medical Science*, 75(3–4), 225–231.

Claypool, B. (2020). Telemedicine and COVID-19: 6 tips to ace your first visit. *Mental Health Weekly*, 30(17), 5–6.

Dana, L. P. (2000). Creating entrepreneurs in India. *Journal of Small Business Management*, 38(1), 86.

Dana, L. P., and Manson, A. (2009). A study of enterprise in Rankin, where subsistence self employment meets formal entrepreneurship. *International Journal of Entrepreneurship and Small Business*, 7(1), 14–23.

Ferreira, J., and Dana, L. P. (2017). Knowledge spillover-based strategic entrepreneurship. *International Entrepreneurship Management Journal*, 13, 61–67.

Ghani, M. K. A., and Jaber, M. M. (2015). The effect of patient privacy on telemedicine implementation in developing countries: Iraq case study. *Research Journal of Applied Science, Engineering Technology* 11(11), 1233–1237. doi: 10.19026/rjaset.11.2230.

Gopalan, H. S., Haque, I., Ahmad, S., Gaur, A., and Misra, A. (2019). Diabetes care at doorsteps: A customised mobile van for the prevention, screening, detection and management of diabetes in the urban underprivileged populations of Delhi. *Diabetes & Metabolic Syndrome*, 13(6), 3105–3112. https://doi.org/10.1016/j.dsx.2019.11.008.

Hoque, M. R., Bao, Y., and Sorwar, G. (2016). Investigating factors influencing the ad option of e-health in developing countries: A patient's perspective. *Informatics for Health and Social Care*, 42(1), 1–18. doi: 10.3109/17538157.2015.1075541.

International Labor Organization. (2020). As job losses escalate, nearly half of global workforce at risk of losing livelihoods. Downloaded July 13, 2020. https://www.ilo.org/global/about-the-ilo/newsroom/news/WCMS_743036/lang–en/index.htm.

Jacobs, B., Ir, P., Bigdeli, M., Annear, P. L., and Van Damme, W. (2012). Addressing access barriers to health services: An analytical framework for selecting appropriate interventions in low-income Asian countries. *Health Policy and Planning*, 27(4), 288–300.

Khan, N., Qureshi, M., Mustapha, I., Irum, S., and Arshad, R. (2020). *A Systematic Literature Review Paper on Online Medical Mobile Applications in Malaysia*. International Association of Online Engineering. https://www.learntechlib.org/p/218041/.

Keupp, M. M., and Gassmann, O. (2009). The past and the future of international entrepreneurship: A review and suggestions for developing the field. *Journal of Management*, 35(3), 600–633.

Kim, H., and Xie, B. (2017). Health literacy in the eHealth era: A systematic review of the literature. *Patient Education and Counseling*, 100(6), 1073–1082. https://doi.org/10.1016/j.pec.2017.01.015.

Kurji Z., Premani, Z.S., and Mithani, Y. (2015). Review and analysis of quality healthcare system enhancement in developing countries. *The Journal of the Pakistan Medical Association*, 65(7), 6.

Lin, D., Zheng, W., Lu, J., Liu, X., and Wright, M. (2019). Forgotten or not? Home country embeddedness and returnee entrepreneurship. *Journal of World Business*, 54(1), 1–13.

Mair, F. S., May, C., O'Donnell, C., Finch, T., Sullivan, F., and Murray, E. (2012). Factors that promote or inhibit the implementation of e-health systems: An explanatory systematic review. *Bulletin of the World Health Organization*, 90(5), 357–364.

Mathur, P., Srivastava, S., Lalchandani, A., and Mehta, J. L. (2017). Evolving role of telemedicine in health care delivery in India. *Prim Health Care*, 7, 260. doi: 10.4172/2167-1079.1000260.

McCleary-Jones, V., Scheideman-Miller, C., Rev Dorn, J. A., Johnson, B., Overall, M., and Dwyer, K. (2013). Health information technology use and health literacy among community-dwelling African Americans. *The ABNF Journal: Official Journal of the Association of Black Nursing Faculty in Higher Education, Inc*, 24(1), 10–16.

Oudshoorn, N. (2008). Diagnosis at a distance: The invisible work of patients and healthcare professionals in cardiac telemonitoring technology. *Sociology of Health and Illness*, 30(2), 272–288. doi: 10.1111/j.1467-9566.2007.01032.x.

Pal, A., Mbarika, V. W. A. Cobb-Payton, F., Datta, P., and McCoy, S. (2004). Telemedicine diffusion in a developing country: The case of India. *IEEE Transactions on Information Technology in Biomedicine*, 9(1), 59–65.

Rasiah, R. (2006). Information and communication technology and GDP per capita. *International Journal of Internet and Enterprise Management*, 4(3), 1–12. https://doi.org/10.1504/IJIEM.2006.010914.

Saritas, O., and Kuzminov, I. (2017). Global challenges and trends in agriculture: Impacts on Russia and possible strategies for adaptation. *Foresight*, 19(2), 218–250. https://doi.org/10.1108/FS-09-2016-0045.

Saebi, T., Foss, N. J., and Linder, S. (2019). Social entrepreneurship research: Past achievements and future promises. *Journal of Management,* 45(1), 70–95.

Schotter, A. P., Buchel, O., and Vashchilko, T. (2018). Interactive visualization for research contextualization in international business. *Journal of World Business*, 53(3), 356–372.

Schroeder, D. (2020). Turn your Covid-19 solution into a viable business. *Harvard Business Review*. https://hbr.org/2020/07/turn-your-covid-19-solution-into-a-viable-business. Retrieved July 15, 2020.

Sharifi, M., Ayat, M., Jahanbakhsh, M., Tavakoli, N., Mokhtari, H., and Wan Ismail, W.K. (2013). Ehealth implementation challenges in Iranian medical centers: A qualitative study in Iran. *Telemedicine e-Health*, 19(2), 122–128.

Thompson, C. J., Rindfleisch, A., and Arsel, Z. (2006). Emotional branding and the strategic value of the doppelgänger brand image. *Journal of Marketing*, 70(1), 50–64.

Timpel, P., Oswald, S., Schwarz, P. E. H., and Harst, L. (2020). Mapping the evidence on the effectiveness of telemedicine interventions in diabetes, dyslipidemia, and hypertension: An umbrella review of systematic reviews and meta-analyses. *Journal of Medical Internet Research*, 22(3), 16791. doi: 10.2196/16791, PMID:32186516.

Venkatesh, V., and Morris, M. G. (2000). Why don't men ever stop to ask for directions? Gender, social influence, and their role in technology acceptance and usage behaviour. *MIS Quarterly*, 24(1), 115–139.

Wu, I. L., Li, J. Y., and Fu, C. Y. (2011). The adoption of mobile healthcare by hospital's professionals: An integrative perspective. *Decision Support Systems*, 51(3), 587–596.

Zhai, Y. K., Zhu, W. J., Cai, Y. L., Sun, D. X., and Zhao, J. (2014). Clinical- and cost-effectiveness of telemedicine in type 2 diabetes mellitus: A systematic review and meta analysis. *Medicine (Baltim)*, 93(28), 312. https://doi.org/10.1097/MD.0000000000000312.

Chapter 11

Impact of Social Media during COVID-19 Using Binary Logistic Model

Rachna Bansal[*,‡], Prabhat Mittal[†,§], and Priti Verma[*,¶]

Sharda University, Greater Noida, Uttar Pradesh, India
†Satyawati College, University of Delhi, New Delhi, India
‡rachnabansal1984@gmail.com
§profmittal@gmail.com
¶priti.verma@sharda.ac.in

Abstract

The study aims to empirically measure the effectiveness of social media during the COVID-19 outbreak in India. Data are collected from 182 social media users during the COVID-19 outbreak in India. Binary logistic regression is used to determine the influence of the personal utility of social media during the pandemic, the negative role of social media specific to COVID-19, and the general negative role of social media in the overall impact of social media. The binary logistic regression is appropriate for dichotomous outcome variables. The study has considered the impact of social media as an endogenous variable, while personal utility and the negative role of social media are considered exogenous variables. The study also examined any significant differences between different genders and different categories of age on the overall impact of social media during COVID-19.

Keywords: Social media, COVID-19, binary logistic.

Introduction and Literature Review

In December 2019, there was an outbreak of the fatal novel coronavirus disease (COVID-19), which started in Wuhan, China, and rapidly spread to almost every part of the world. Millions of people fell ill, and a large number died across the world. The World Health Organization (WHO) declared the outbreak a global health emergency. Then, on 11 March 2020, the organization declared the COVID-19 outbreak a global pandemic (WHO, 2019). To confine the spread of the virus, several countries across the world announced partial or full lockdowns. It was an unprecedented emergency for the current generation.

In this unexpected, barely once-in-a-generation emergency situation of a global lockdown caused by the COVID-19 pandemic, which curtailed physical mobility and confined people within their homes, social media emerged as a ray of hope. During earlier emergency situations, the WHO recognized the significance of social media and pronounced that it 'may be used to engage the public, facilitate peer-to-peer communication, create situational awareness, monitor and respond to rumours, public reactions and concerns during an emergency, and facilitate local-level responses' (WHO, 2017). Social media has influenced human life in an unprecedented manner during the past decade. Almost no part of life is untouched by it. The use of social media is multidimensional: it provides information, connects people, and is a source of entertainment, connectivity, and information. Research done during earlier epidemics had already revealed social media's effectiveness in providing people with timely information, facts and figures, and pertinent suggestions (Omrani and Shalhoub, 2015).

People were already anxious to update themselves with knowledge or information related to COVID-19, especially medical information. Here, the literature and infographics exponentially disseminated through social media platforms helped the target audience (Chan *et al.*, 2020). Social media was found to be one of the main channels that helped people keep up to date with COVID-19 information (Bao *et al.*, 2020).

Research revealed that social media emerged not only as a strong means of information dissemination but also as a means of social and emotional support for people in crisis during the COVID-19 pandemic. Further, it was increasingly used by both parents and children as an informational and emotional support tool (Drouin, 2020).

Distancing was central to checking the spread of COVID-19 (Tian et al., 2017), but it raised concerns about human well-being, as social isolation and the resulting sense of loneliness carry a negative impact on human well-being (Brooks et al., 2020). The sudden lockdown led to isolation, loneliness, and depression, which badly affected social human relationships and the death rate (Holt-Lunstad et al., 2015). Thus, psychologists were concerned about the acceleration of an already existing and increasing feeling of loneliness (Brody, 2020), as it is risky for mental health.

Confinement within the home, social distancing, and quarantine became the normal norms of society for public health and to contain the spread of the virus. This physical isolation, combined with economic instability, the fear of infection, and stress regarding future uncertainty, had a deep impact on the mental health of people, making research in this area a significant requirement (Brooks et al., 2020; Holmes et al., 2020). Some researchers chose to focus on the effects of COVID-19-related stress in adolescents (Findlay and Arim, 2020) because of their increased longing for freedom and their friend circles (Brown and Larson, 2009), which were affected by physical distancing. However, people of all age groups were bound to be affected, as human beings are social creatures, and human or social interaction decreases the issues created by stress on physical and mental health (Nausheen et al., 2007).

People are inherently social; however, the sudden lockdown prompted by the COVID-19 pandemic necessitated physical distancing and home confinement. This posed a challenge to human well-being because face-to-face interaction has a great positive impact on well-being and is closely linked to human health (Fiorillo, 2011), happiness (Diener, 2002), and satisfaction (Mehl, 2020). However, technology-driven social media is still a way people can connect (Sun et al., 2020). Previous research says that technology-mediated communication in any form, be it oral, visual, or written text, lessens feelings of loneliness, reduces negativity (Teo, 2019), and is linked to overall well-being.

Therefore, in this time of physical disconnect and resulting mental stress, numerous organizations, agencies, associations, and governments, along with certain other recommendations, strongly suggested social networking through online interactions and using social media, while cautioning against excessive news consumption (Canadian Mental Health Association, 2020; Canadian Psychological Association, 2020). Researchers also recommended virtual connections through social media for the mental well-being of people during the COVID-19 lockdown (Pancani et al., 2020).

To assuage stress and anxiety caused by COVID-19 and the ensuing lockdowns, the American Psychological Association (2020) also advocated sustaining virtual social connections through various tools provided by social media platforms and apps. They also suggested that during the pandemic, sharing beneficial information with near and dear ones through social media may be helpful in controlling stress and anxiety.

Along with numerous positive aspects of the use of social media to cope with the problems caused by the COVID-19 crisis, there has been simultaneous cautionary advice against that excessive use of media, as this may raise stress and anxiety (Garfin *et al.*, 2020) because during emergencies, people also articulate their negative emotions and experiences, including fear, anxiety, and grief over the deaths of near and dear ones, which are contagious (Kramer, 2014). Researchers found that misinformation and fake data about COVID-19 also inundated social media and fuelled groundless fears among people (Xinhua, 2020), which affected their mental health.

On the whole, the review of literature shows various perceived benefits and disadvantages of social media during the global pandemic. This study aims to study the effectiveness of social media during COVID-19. A conceptual model (Figure 1) is proposed, and various hypotheses are established to test the relationship between the dependent and independent variables.

Hypothesis 1: The perceived utility of social media positively influenced the impact of social media during COVID-19.

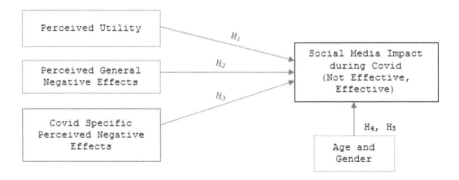

Figure 1. Conceptual model.

Hypothesis 2: The perceived general negative effect of social media negatively influenced the impact of social media during COVID-19.

Hypothesis 3: The perceived COVID-19-specific negative effects of social media negatively influenced the impact of social media during COVID-19.

Hypothesis 4: The age of respondents influenced the impact of social media during COVID-19.

Hypothesis 5: The gender of respondents influenced the impact of social media during COVID-19.

Variables

Dependent Variable: The dependent variable is considered dichotomous, with '1' denoting 'effective' (social media impact) and '0' otherwise, i.e., 'not effective.'

Independent Variables: These variables are the perceived utility of social media, the perceived general negative effect of social media, the perceived COVID-19-specific negative effects of social media, age, and gender.

Data Collection

Social media users were considered the target population in this study. The data were collected online using the snowball sampling method. A 14-item structured questionnaire was developed and used to collect data from respondents. Questions related to age, gender, and the average number of hours spent on social media were asked in the first part of the questionnaire. A total of 262 responses were received, and 180 usable responses were selected for further analysis. Out of the questions, 13 were related to the personal utility of social media during COVID-19, such as how social media was helpful in establishing connections with people, discovering new hobbies, connecting with family and friends, creating awareness about the pandemic, and providing learning opportunities, and how it proved to be a blessing.

Three questions asked whether social media affected respondents' focus on work, whether the respondents felt health issues due to excessive use of social media, and about the role of social media in spreading negativity and hatred.

Specific to the negative experiences of people during COVID-19, four questions were asked about the increased addiction to social media during the pandemic, the increase in hatred and racism during the pandemic, the creation of panic regarding the COVID-19 outbreak, and the increase in fake news related to COVID-19. Respondents were asked to rate these statements on a scale of 1–5, with 1 indicating 'strongly disagree' and 5 indicating 'strongly agree.'

Results and Discussions

The respondents' demographic characteristics are shown in Table 1. Age-wise classification shows that the participation of the age group 30–45 is highest in using social media (61%), followed by the age group of below 30 (30.2%), and least participation by people aged above 45 (8.8%). Gender-wise classification clearly shows that 54.4% of the total respondents were female, and the remaining 45.6% were male. Most of the

Table 1. Characteristics of respondents.

Demographic factor	Count	%
Age		
Below 30	55	30.2
30–45	111	61.0
Above 45	16	8.8
Gender		
Female	99	54.4
Male	83	45.6
Average hours spent on social media		
Less than one hour	24	13.2
1–3 hours	86	47.3
3–5 hours	35	19.2
More than 5 hours	37	20.3

respondents (47.3%) spend on average 1–3 hours on social media, and 20.3% of the respondents use it for more than 5 hours. Only 13.2% of respondents spend less than one hour on social media, and 19.2% use social media for 3–5 hours. The Cronbach value of all the dimensions indicated acceptable levels of reliability of constructs, i.e., a Cronbach alpha of 0.7 (Hair *et al.*, 2014).

To test the hypotheses, binary logistic regression was performed, and the results of the analysis are summarized in Table 2. In the current study, social media ('1': effective and '0': not effective) has been considered the dependent variable, whereas the age and gender of respondents, perceived utility of social media, perceived general negative effects of social media, and perceived COVID-19-specific negative effects of social media were the independent variables. Regression coefficients and their statistical significance obtained using 'enter logistic regression method' are included in Table 2. The impact of the five independent variables on determining the effectiveness of social media is also shown in Table 2.

We see from the above table that the estimated model is

$$SME = -6.801 - 0.306 GNE - 0.203 CSN + 3.548 PU - 0.327 GEN\,(1) + 2.987 Age\,(1) + 2.927 Age\,(2) \quad (1)$$

where **GNE** denotes general negative effects, **CSN** denotes COVID-19-specific negative effects, **PU** denotes perceived utility of

Table 2. Results of logistic regression analysis.

	B	S.E.	Wald	df	Sig.	Exp(B)
General negative effects	−0.306	0.371	0.678	1	0.410	0.737
Covid specific negative effects	−0.203	0.395	0.263	1	0.608	0.817
Perceived utility	3.548	0.631	31.587	1	0.000	34.753
GEN (1)	−0.327	0.592	0.305	1	0.581	0.721
AGE			5.639	2	0.060	
AGE (1)	2.987	1.333	5.024	1	0.025	19.823
AGE (2)	2.927	1.246	5.518	1	0.019	18.663
Constant	−6.801	1.910	12.680	1	0.000	0.001

social media, **GEN (1)** denotes gender ('1': male and '0': female), **AGE (1)** equals '1' if age in group 30–45 and '0' otherwise, and **AGE (2)** equals '1' if age in group above 45 and '0' otherwise.

The regression slope coefficient of the perceived utility of social media ($b = 3.548$, $p < 0.01$) is positive and statistically significant; thus, H1 is supported. The regression slopes of general negative effects ($b = -0.306$, $i > 0.05$) and COVID-19-specific negative effects (-0.203, $p > 0.05$) are not statistically significant; hence, H2 and H3 are not supported.

The age of respondents has been classified into three categories ('1': less than 30, '2': 30–45, and '3': above 45 years), which were transformed into two dichotomous variables: (i) Age1 ('1': 30–45 and '0': otherwise) and (ii) Age2 ('1': above 45 and '0': otherwise). The results indicate that Age1 media ($b = 3.548$, $p < 0.01$) and Age2 media ($b = 3.548$, $p < 0.01$) are statistically significant. This confirms that people above 30 years of age were significantly impacted by social media during the pandemic.

The coefficient of gender is non-significant ($b = -0.327$, $p = 0.581 > 0.05$). Thus, we can conclude that gender has no statistically significant impact on explaining social media effectiveness. Hence, H5 is not supported.

Out of the five hypotheses tested in this study, two are supported. Hypothesis 1, which suggests that the perceived utility of social media has a strong influence on the effectiveness of social media during the global pandemic. People find social media extremely useful for connecting with family and friends, discovering new hobbies, and making new connections. Social media also proved to be very effective in spreading awareness among people about COVID-19 issues, and people explored new learning opportunities with the help of social media. These results are well in line with the previous research findings discussed in the literature review (Bao *et al.*, 2020; Chan *et al.*, 2020; Omrani and Shalhoub, 2015).

Hypotheses 2 and 3, which proposed that the perceived negative effect of social media would have a negative influence on its effectiveness are not supported by the results of the study. These findings are not consistent with the previous studies, which concluded that social media can give rise to stress, anxiety, negative emotions, and fear among people and may spread misinformation (Garfin *et al.*, 2020; Kramer, 2014; Xinhua, 2020). This study did not find any significant influence of gender in explaining social media effectiveness, whereas the results indicated that people in older age groups found it extremely useful during COVID-19.

References

American Psychological Association. (2020). Five ways to view coverage of the coronavirus. https://www.apa.org/helpcenter/pandemics. Accessed March 19, 2020.

Bao, Y., Sun, Y., Meng, S., Shi, J., and Lu, L. (2020). 2019-nCoV epidemic: Address mental health care to empower society. *The Lancet*. 7 February, 2020. https://doi.org/10.1016/S0140-6736(20)30309-3.

Brody, J. E. (2020, March 23). Taking steps to counter the loneliness of social distancing. *The New York Times*. https://www.nytimes.com/2020/03/23/well/family/coronavirus-loneliness-isolation-social-distancing-elderly.html.

Brooks, S., Webster, R., Smith, L. E., Woodland, L., Wessely, S., Greenberg, N., and Rubin, G. J. (2020). The psychological impact of quarantine and how to reduce it: Rapid review of the evidence. *Lancet* (Lancet Publishing Group), 395, 912–920. Retrieved from http://dx.doi.org/10.1016/S0140-6736(20)30460-8.

Brown, B. B., and Larson, J. (2009). Peer relationships in adolescents. In Steinberg, R. M. L. (ed.) *Handbook of Adolescent Psychology: Vol. 2. Contextual Influences on Adolescent Development*, 3rd edn. Wiley, Hoboken, NJ, pp. 74–103.

Canadian Mental Health Association. (2020). CMHA offers tips to support mental health amid concerns of COVID-19 pandemic. Retrieved from https://ontario.cmha.ca/news/cmha-offers-tips-to-support-mental-health-amid-concerns-of-covid-19-pandemic/.

Canadian Psychological Association. (2020). Psychology works fact sheet: 19. Retrieved from https://cpa.ca/docs/File/Publications/FactSheets/PW_HelpingTeensCopeWithImpacts_COVID-19.pdf.

Chan, A. K. M., Nickson, C. P., Rudolph, J. W., *et al.* (2020). Social media for rapid knowledge dissemination: Early experience from the COVID-19 pandemic. *Anaesthesia*.

Diener, E., and Seligman, M. E. P. (2002). Very happy people. *Psychological Science*, 13, 81–84. doi: 10.1111/1467-9280.00415.

Drouin, M., McDaniel, B. T., Pater, J., and Toscos, T. (2020). *Cyberpsychology, Behavior, and Social Networking*, 23(11). Published Online: 6 November 2020. https://doi.org/10.1089/cyber.2020.0284.

Fiorillo, D., and Sabatini, F. (2011). Quality and quantity: The role of social interactions in self-reported individual health. *Social Science & Medicine*, 73, 1644–1652. doi: 10.1016/j.socscimed.2011.09.007.

Garfin, D. R., Silver, C. R., and Holman, A. E. (2020). The novel coronavirus (COVID-19) outbreak: Amplification of public health consequences by media exposure. *Health Psychology*, 39, 355–357. http://dx.doi.org/10.1037/hea0000875.

Holt-Lunstad, J., Smith, T. B., Baker, M., Harris, T., and Stephenson, D. (2015). Loneliness and social isolation as risk factors for mortality: Ameta-analytic review. *Perspectives on Psychological Science*, 10, 227–237. http://dx.doi.org/10.1177/1745691614568352.

Kramer, A. D., Guillory, J. E., and Hancock, J. T. (2014). Experimental evidence of massive-scale emotional contagion through social networks. *Proceedings of the National Academy of Sciences USA*, 111(24), 8788–90. doi: 10.1073/pnas.1320040111. pmid:24889601.

Mehl, M. R., Vazire, S., Holleran, S. E., and Clark, C. S. (2010). Eavesdropping on happiness: Well-being is related to having less small talk and more substantive conversations. *Psychological Science*, 21: 539–541. doi: 10.1177/0956797610362675.

Nausheen, B., Gidron, Y., Gregg, A., Tissarchondou, H. S., and Peveler, R. (2007). Loneliness, social support, and cardiovascular reactivity to laboratory stress. *Stress*, 10, 37–44. https://doi.org/101010.1080/10253890601135434.1080/10253890601135434.

Omrani, A. S., and Shalhoub, S. Middle East respiratory syndrome coronavirus (MERS-CoV): what lessons can we learn? *Journal of Hospital Infection*, 91(3), 188–196. 22 August 2015. https://www.journalofhospitalinfection.com/article/S0195-6701(15)00306-0/fulltext.

Pancani, L., Marinucci, M., Aureli, N., and Riva, P. (2020). Forced social isolation and mental health: A study on 1006 Italians under COVID-19 quarantine. Retrieved from http://dx.doi.org/10.31234/osf.io/uacfj.

Sun, R., Rieble, C., Liu, Y., and Sauter, D. (2020, December 30). Connected despite lockdown: The role of social interactions and social media use in wellbeing. https://doi.org/10.31234/osf.io/x5k8u.

Teo, A. R., Markwardt, S., and Hinton, L. (2019). Using Skype to beat the blues: Longitudinal data from a national representative sample. *The American Journal of Geriatric Psychiatry*, 27, 254–262. doi: 10.1016/j.jagp.2018.10.014.

Tian, H., Liu, Y., Li, Y., Wu, C.-H. H., Chen, B., Kraemer, M. U. G. G., *et al.* (2020). An investigation of transmission control measures during the first 50 days of the COVID-19 epidemic in China. *Science*, 368(80), 638–642. doi: 10.1126/science.abb6105.

WHO (2019). https://www.who.int/europe/emergencies/situations/covid-19.

World Health Organisation, Geneva. (2017). https://apps.who.int/iris/bitstream/handle/10665/259807/9789241550208, www.who.int.

Xinhua. Bat soup, biolab, crazy numbers … Misinformation "infodemic" on novel coronavirus exposed. http://www.xinhuanet.com/english/2020-02/04/c_138755586.htm. Accessed March 21, 2020. https://www.liebertpub.com/doi/full/10.1089/cyber.2020.0284.

© 2025 World Scientific Publishing Company
https://doi.org/10.1142/9789811292101_0012

Chapter 12

Digital Transformation for Recovery, Resilience, and Adaptation Post-COVID-19 in India

G. V. Sobha* and P. Sridevi†

Department of Management Studies, National Institute of Technology, Tiruchirappalli, Tamil Nadu, India
*sobhagv@gmail.com
†psridevi@nitt.edu

Abstract

The global outbreak of the novel coronavirus disease, COVID-19, started in December 2019 in Wuhan City of China and spread worldwide very soon. The public was cautioned to take responsive actions, such as frequent handwashing, wearing a face mask, social distancing, and avoiding mass gatherings. Countries have adopted lockdowns and stay-at-home recovery strategies to control the transmission of the disease. In March 2020, India declared a nationwide lockdown to contain the COVID-19 pandemic. The economic and social factors of the country were affected. Businesses, schools, shopping malls, entertainment, transport, beauty clinics, gyms, and sports stadiums came to a standstill for a few months. This chapter focuses on how India responds to the pandemic and the associated economic and social issues through a literature study. It provides insights into the country's recovery and resiliency to uplift the economy by adopting different strategic levels in business operations during the post-COVID-19 period. The chapter describes specific technological initiatives taken by various states of the country to tackle the pandemic and provides a few insights into post-COVID-19 management strategies for future resilience and adaptation to the new normal.

Keywords: COVID-19, new normal, adaptation strategy, e-business, post-COVID-19 management strategy, digital transformation.

Introduction

In December 2019, the first coronavirus disease (COVID-19) case was observed in China's Wuhan City, which is considered the origin of the life-threatening viral outbreak. Initially, the country suspected pneumonia with unknown causes of respiratory symptoms. Later, samples of suspected patients were sent for further investigation to labs. They traced common symptoms of virus exposure to the wholesale seafood market in Wuhan. Soon, the virus had spread to different cities, and the number of cases increased exponentially. On 31 December 2019, China notified the outbreak to the World Health Organization (WHO) and declared the closure of the seafood market from 1 January 2020 until further notice, and on 11 January 2020, China reported its first fatal case (Anbesh *et al.*, 2020).

Meanwhile, the disease spread to other countries through people who visited Wuhan during the outbreak. On 23 January 2020, the Chinese government decided to lockdown, putting in place restrictions on entry and exit to the cities where the virus had spread. Moreover, the airports of different countries arranged screening mechanisms to detect infected people and place them in isolation for recovery. India evacuated her citizens from China by arranging special flights; they were tested for COVID-19 and isolated for 14 days. The number of positive cases reported in China and the rest of the world increased at an exponentially fast pace. India recorded its first case on 30 January 2020 in the state of Kerala: a student who returned from Wuhan University, China. Subsequently, a greater number of cases were reported in different regions of India. Later on, on 11 March 2020, the WHO declared COVID-19 a pandemic (Sohrabi *et al.*, 2020). Most of the world's countries declared lockdown for months, and a few countries implemented extended lockdowns to contain the virus. Before the lockdown, people rushed to make bulk purchases of essential items from supermarkets, which they believed would be necessary to meet their needs during the lockdown. This affected many other people who were about to purchase essential items that went out of stock or became scarce.

Moreover, due to lockdowns, all the industries were shut down, and their previous production lots stagnated because of interruptions in the supply chain, all logistics went down, and all transportation modes were cancelled. When a business' primary operation is interrupted, the outcome of the business value chain declines. There was a massive demand for essential items, and when companies responded with limited or no supply of essentials, it resulted in economic and social loss.

Along with the pandemic, the country faced economic distress too. The chapter aims to address the following questions: How did India respond to tackling COVID-19 and handling the economic pain? What strategies or business plans were adopted for recovery from the pandemic and the resilience of India post-COVID-19? What adaptation strategy should India follow for its transformation to the new normal and for becoming resilient for future India?

The chapter is organized as follows. The following section gives an overall picture of the COVID-19 pandemic, its origin, transmission, and impact. In the subsequent sections, we discuss how different states of India tackled COVID-19 using technology to overcome the pandemic and describe how businesses took strategic decisions to recover, become resilient for the future, and adapt to business sustainability during and after the pandemic. In the final section, we conclude that careful strategic planning by mapping the environment and capabilities will help the nation transform and adopt technological innovations and be resilient for the long-term sustainability of businesses and the post-COVID-19 world's economy.

COVID-19

COVID-19 is one of the infectious diseases caused by a new virus that originated in wild bats and belongs to the SARS-CoV subgroup (De Wit *et al.*, 2016; Reusken *et al.*, 2013; Lu *et al.*, 2015). COVID-19 causes mild upper respiratory infections, which include the common cold. It was found that the infectious disease transmits viruses from one person to another through the respiratory droplets produced during sneezing and coughing (Yuan *et al.*, 2009). These infected droplets have an incubation period of 2–14 days. During this period, if a person touches an infected person and then touches his nose, eyes, or mouth, the virus can be transmitted to another person (Goh *et al.*, 2019). Moreover, the droplets don't travel more than six feet and don't linger in the air (Cai *et al.*, 2020). Hence, the rate of transmission of the virus depends on the location. The infected person exhibits common symptoms such as cough, high fever, and fatigue, whereas dyspnoea and diarrhoea are uncommon features observed in a few cases (Lupia *et al.*, 2020). The virus can be detected by identifying common symptoms and diagnosing blood samples and specimens of stool. COVID-19 can also be detected by collecting a specimen of saliva and mucus (Ali *et al.*, 2020). There were no drugs developed for treating COVID-19; however, many practitioners have suggested a few antiviral treatments and treatments for Middle East Respiratory Syndrome (MERS) and severe acute respiratory syndrome (SARS) can be used for COVID-19 treatment (Zhang and Liu, 2020). Later, other compounds of drugs were used as an alternative drug for treating COVID-19 (Harapan *et al.*, 2020). People suffering from chronic diseases are highly vulnerable to COVID-19, which may cause death. In addition to that, people who have infectious diseases, respiratory diseases, and cardiovascular and cancer diseases are recommended to take precautionary steps to prevent COVID-19. Since there were no vaccines available, it is crucial to prevent the infection at an early stage by adopting a few prudent mechanisms (Ali *et al.*, 2020). If found infected, certain precautions such as self-isolation, using alcohol-based sanitizers, wearing masks and gloves, and frequent handwashing with alcohol-based sanitizers or soap will minimize the spread of the virus to the surroundings (Harapan *et al.*, 2020). Different countries have developed and tested vaccines, which have been deployed based on a person's health condition.

How India Responded to COVID-19

The pandemic has affected India and the whole world, with more than 117 million confirmed cases and 2.6 million deaths by March 2021 (Katz *et al.*, 2021). India responded to COVID-19 in a way reserved for war, depression, or natural disasters. Unlike other countries, India has much broader challenges, including managing its population density of more than 1 million, inadequate healthcare infrastructure as prescribed by the WHO, business discontinuity, sudden job loss, vulnerability to an economic shock, etc.

Despite the challenges, India has taken several measures to contain the spread of the virus by:

(i) imposing a nationwide lockdown from 25 March to 31 May 2020;
(ii) setting up 100% medical screening for domestic and international travellers as well as tracking and tracing of COVID-19 patients;

(iii) increasing the number of testing laboratories;
(iv) facilitating local manufacturing of personal protective equipment (PPE) kits;
(v) providing a fiscal package worth $270 million to help the economically vulnerable sections, including the general public, focus on micro-, small-, and medium-sized enterprises (MSMEs), employees, and entrepreneurs to sustain the economy (World Economic Forum, 2020).

The Smart Cities mission launched by the Indian government played a crucial role in response to COVID-19, including the development of an integrated command and control centre (ICCC) platform as "COVID-19 War Rooms" to coordinate and monitor various cities and states. The ICCCs integrate civil society, local businesses, and other operations on a single platform to collaborate across the cities. The ICCCs usually consist of coordinated functions, including city surveillance, disaster management, solid waste management, traffic management, and street lighting (Rathor, 2020).

Some of the technology solutions adopted by smart cities with the help of ICCCs are as follows:

- **information dissemination** through social media, web portals, mobile applications, public address systems (PASs), and variable message displays (VMDs);
- **setting up health facilities**, such as e-doctor for online consultation and prescriptions, telemedicine support, remote capacity building, and training for healthcare workers;
- **managing lockdown** in terms of facilitating the delivery of essentials through online vendors, geographic information systems (GIS)-based tracking of supply vehicles, ensuring food and shelter for economically weaker sections through GIS-based tracking systems to map the demand and supply of food and the use of Google Forms by non-government organizations (NGOs), restaurants, and private organizations, as well as online food donation;
- **contact tracing and tracking** suspected and positive cases identified using GIS mapping and heat maps, dashboards for real-time visualization, mobile application tracking, statistical tools, and simulation models.

Technologies such as traffic integrated management systems (ITMSs), drone surveillance, self-registration platforms, and interactive voice response systems (IVRSs) were used for monitoring and communication.

Artificial intelligence (AI)-based real-time analysis of surveillance footage was employed for social distancing violations. ICCC enables real-time and evidence-based decision-making for the authorities by using machine learning, image processing, and AI (NITI Aayog, 2020; World Economic Forum, 2020).

Role of Technology during COVID-19 in Different States of India

Along with COVID-19, another challenge India faced was an increase in lockdown violations across the country, which poses a problem for front-line workers to ensure safety and security. Such activities further cause the spread of COVID-19. The government has taken few technological initiatives to make citizens stick to lockdowns and battle against the pandemic (Bajpai *et al.*, 2020).

Cluster containment strategy in Agra

To battle against the pandemic, Agra has come up with a containment strategy using a technology tool suite that reduced the number of positive cases to single digits per day. As part of the Agra Smart City (ASC) mission, cities with vast CCTV infrastructure were deployed under an ICCC). All districts and medical control rooms, grocery delivery help desks, etc., were monitored and controlled. In addition to these strategies, Agra introduced a few more initiatives to contain the pandemic, including a lockdown monitoring app, the 'Sarvam Setu' app, a grocery information portal, a GIS-based dashboard, the 'eDoctor-Seva' app, and smart health centres. Table 1 provides various technological applications initiated during COVID-19 in Agra (Raval, 2020b).

An integrated tech platform in Chhattisgarh

The IT department of the Chhattisgarh government established an integrated platform in partnership with CISCO. All the home quarantine, contact tracing, sample collection, and quarantine centre details are entered directly by the field staff. The integrated platform has an auto alert system that ensures smooth data flow between various verticals of the

Table 1. Various technological initiatives taken in Agra.

Technological initiatives	Description
Lockdown monitoring app	AI-enabled video analytics capture images of mass gatherings when people violate social distancing norms and send alerts to the nearest police station. The alert provides information related to the time, photograph, and location where the lockdown was violated. After 15 days of functioning, the app generated 7,247 alerts that helped the police department control the situation.
Sarvam Setu app	This app can be used under any distress, alerting a rescue operation team when the distressed person presses the SOS button on their mobile phone.
Grocery information portal	To ensure doorstep delivery of groceries, vegetables, and fruits, ASC launched a grocery information portal on their website. The GIS and RFID tags available in the portal fetch information about the top vendors. The residents can order their essential needs from local vendors through the portal and get things delivered to their doorsteps. Zomato and Big Bazaar joined hands with ASC to facilitate door delivery.
GIS-based dashboards	To identify hotspots, a GIS-based COVID-19 tracker dashboard was created. It monitors and updates positive, negative, and recovered cases, daily count, age and gender of the affected, and the pandemic trend. It also provides the quarantine centres and their updated information.
eDoctor-Seva app	This application enables doctors and patients to have video consultations. More doctors are added under the AYUSH scheme, and patients can upload their old reports for consultation, and they can download the prescriptions signed by doctors after consultation.
Smart health centres	Smart health centres are established, where doctors under e-Doctor seva can offer their services, face masks and sanitizers are provided at reasonable prices, and medicines can be home delivered free of cost to citizens.
Area of focus post lockdown	The state can continue to monitor, and the trend could be identified using analytics. They also planned to focus on an integrated platform that brings major departments, such as medical, defence, district magistrate, police, security surveillance, waste management, and online grocery, to a single platform.

health department. Through this technology, the state has been able to achieve an 81% green-zone area.

Some of the technologies used during the pandemic period included drone cameras and the portal cghaat.in for online ordering of grocery and vegetables. Raipur Smart City works hand in hand with a start-up that used their cameras to identify people who aren't wearing masks. The state government made efforts to introduce video-based consultation to reduce load on the outpatient department. Later they launched a telemedicine service to Surajpur district (OPD; Raval, 2020a).

Disinfection in Varanasi using special drones

Invest India is a national investment promotion agency that has collaborated with the AGNI Mission and the agency's Business Immunity Platform (BIP) (Invest India, Business Immunity Platform, n.d.). The collaboration facilitated the use of specially designed drones, which support the authorities in spraying disinfectants in crowded and vulnerable areas and protecting city dwellers while reducing human contact to keep frontline workers safe in the state of Varanasi (Express Computer, 2020a).

Pune Smart City adopted GIS and predictive analytics, heat maps, and apps

To fight COVID-19, Pune Smart City Development Corporation's (PSCDCL) command and control centre has opened new containment zones, blocked specific roads, and deployed teams for field surveys. To keep track of home quarantine, an app called 'Sanyam' was installed on the mobile phones of the quarantined people, with GPS always enabled. This app keeps track and collects the data of their geolocations, and if they breach the threshold area, the command centre executive will alert them with a green or red alert depending on the distance they breached. The state was also taking care of foreign travellers through counselling and enquiring about their health-related problems, which provided psychological support to lead their routine lives. A GIS analytical tool was used to collect various data, such as positive cases, deaths, and recovered cases, which was then superimposed on maps that the command centre could access through dashboards (Raval, 2020c). The most crucial part is coordinating the actions to make the efforts of various teams successful. For that, the district collector, health department, and government act as a central system for all operations. They found contact tracing is the most energy-consuming operation done through call detail record (CDR) files.

Geofencing and geotagging technologies, development of direct transfer of money apps, use of social media and drones by Jharkhand

During the lockdown, the migrant labourers faced hardships while travelling to their homes and in getting food and materials. Many social organizations and individuals arranged food and other essentials for the migrants. A few state governments developed apps for the direct transfer of money into the accounts of the migrants to help them through the crisis. The government has also used geofencing and geotagging technologies to help identify the migrants (Raval, 2020d). Also, the use of drones helped monitor lockdown and the movement of people in the containment zones.

Moreover, to ensure the safety of the frontline health workers who take care of COVID-19-infected patients, they developed a collaborative robot called Co-Bot, which would transfer both medicine and food to patients. This cut down human contact in the hospital isolation facility (Barik, 2020). The Jharkhand police used social media to communicate and resolve the public's grievances during the pandemic and handle the outbreak of the deadly disease. The police department shared WhatsApp helpline numbers with the public for them to share their feedback and grievances. They also used unmanned aerial vehicles (UAVs) or drones to monitor the lockdown and ensure that no one violated the law. In addition to that, drones were used to warn people who moved around unnecessarily and used the automatic number plate recognition (ANPR) system to identify lockdown violators (Dass, 2020a).

Integrated platform Sehat Sathi app developed by Rajasthan government partnered with healthcare app 'Aayu'

To control the spread of COVID-19, the Rajasthan government partnered with a healthcare start-up called MedCord. MedCord worked with the 'Aayu and Sehat Sathi app' integrated platform to facilitate people consulting doctors and getting their medicines online, irrespective of their geographic limitations. This integrated solution provides tremendous help for people with disabilities and older people who were helpless during the lockdown (Express Computer, 2020c).

Supply chain information management system, use of geofencing, drones, Telemed app, development of COVID-19 testing kit, and an anti-fake news division in Kerala

Kerala was the first state in the country to report a COVID-19 infection. Yet, they were able to reduce the number of cases far better than other states in the earlier stage, although the numbers saw an immense increase after the lockdown. Kerala received much praise from the rest of the country for their use of cutting-edge technology to facilitate the services provided to the citizens, be it during the calamities it has seen in the past or the current pandemic. Due to the lockdown in the country, supply chain operations in India were interrupted. Kerala, being a consumer and dependent state, faced disturbances in the deliveries of rice, grain, etc. However, the state decided to devise an integrated supply chain information management system (SIMS) to ensure and keep track of daily essential commodities and their stock levels with wholesale and retail traders in every district of Kerala. They also leveraged an E-Way bill system through the Goods and Service Tax Network (GSTN), in which the database of the trader will be replicated in the supply chain information management system (SIMS). The system helps replenish their stock levels if they find any shortages of commodities across Kerala. The state is also planning to upgrade its system with advanced analytics and a blockchain platform to make SIMS more transparent and secure (Raval, 2020e).

The police department of Kerala used ICT to a great extent to track people violating the lockdown and keep citizens at their homes. They have adopted drones fitted with sirens and flashlights, geofence-based home quarantine solution app, and a telemedicine platform to watch out lockdown and social-distance violations. Keeping people under quarantine to tackle the spread of COVID-19 is a huge challenge for the state. Hence, the cyber cell of Kerala Police, 'Cyberdome,' has developed a platform for the surveillance of quarantined people using geofencing, which tracks people who have had close contact with those infected by COVID-19, and those who break the protocol are monitored. A geofence is a virtual boundary set up around a geographical location that uses the global positioning system (GPS), RFID tags, Wi-Fi, or a person's mobile phone to track their location. Suppose the person who has been quarantined is moved to some other place or is found violating the protocol. In that case, the geofence will fetch the location of the person and provide an alert to the police authorities immediately. The state's police department joined hands with the Indian Medical Association and launched a telemedicine mobile app called 'blueTeleMed' that facilitates free video consultations with doctors. After consultation, an e-prescription will be provided, and if required, patients will be referred to other hospitals along with an e-pass. The app helps patients consult with doctors on time and travel to other hospitals using the e-pass during the lockdown (Dass, 2020b).

Another technological innovation in medical science was the development of a diagnostic kit that confirms COVID-19 within two hours at a low cost. This testing kit was designed and developed by the Sree Chitra Tirunal Institute for Medical Sciences and Technology, Trivandrum. It diagnoses the N Gene of SARS-CoV-2, which provides confirmation and showed an accuracy of 100%. The development of the kit, named 'Chitra GeneLAMP-N,' was funded by the Department of Science and Technology (DST). The test results match those of the RT-PCR test (Express Computer, 2020b).

In addition to the efforts taken to keep people inside their homes, the government of Kerala has opened an anti-fake news division to combat fake news and their creators, which spread during the COVID-19 pandemic. The objective of the anti-fake news division is to expose fake news and provide authentic government information and educational content to help people become more alert and sensitive to misinformation. The anti-fake news division always keeps an eye on such misinformation that spreads among the public. It offers a provision for any individual to send any complaint through WhatsApp or to check whether the information they received on social media sites, such as Facebook, Twitter, and WhatsApp groups, is true or false. Also, based on the gravity of a fake news complaint and its circulation, the division will forward the complaints to the Kerala Police to caution people and take strict action against repeat offenders (Dass, 2020d).

Bhubaneswar promoted the TickMe app for ordering essential goods online

To keep citizens at their homes and maintain social distancing during the extended lockdown until May 2020, the Bhubaneswar Municipal Corporation (BMC) decided to promote the 'TickMe' app to enable people to place online orders for groceries, medicines, or food from restaurants. The app will notify the buyer when the order is ready for pickup or delivery. It also helps local traders manage their delivery times and make the process more effective. This innovative app was designed by a team based in North Carolina, US, led by a graduate from IIT Kanpur. It can be operated on Android- or iOS-based mobile phones without OTPs (Dass, 2020c; Indian Express, 2020).

Use of Aarogya Setu IVRS facility and drones to fight COVID-19 in Tamil Nadu

The Tamil Nadu state government collaborated with the central government to launch the Aarogya Setu interactive voice response system (IVRS) for non-smartphone users, whereas smartphone users can download the app. This system works by responding to a toll-free number which citizens can call. Several questions with options are posed to the citizens, and based on their response, the system could categorize the call as 'no risk,' 'low risk,' or 'high-risk.' Upon categorization, the concerned district team will support the citizen in terms of medication, quarantine, or hospitalization, whichever is required. In addition to the Aarogya Setu IVRS facility, the state used drones in partnership with a start-up, Garuda, to disinfect hospitals and other public places. Other conventional technologies, such as trend analysis, GIS, and hotspot monitoring systems, are also leveraged. The Tamil Nadu e-Governance Agency (TNeGA) provides technological support to the health department by providing software to manage hospital beds, inventory, quarantines, call centre operations, etc. The workflow of such software is designed in such a way that unresolved problems will remain on the radar of the respective officials. Also, the geospatial data will be operational on the dashboard for effective decision-making (Raval, 2020f).

Delhi government offers free online medical consultation through a cloud-based platform

The COVID-19 outbreak affected healthcare infrastructure across the globe, making it difficult for people to consult the doctor and visit the hospital for non-emergency medical issues. The public was in fear of visiting the hospital, as most of the hospitals were designated to treat

COVID-19. The Delhi government collaborated with the 'CallDoc' app, a cloud-based platform created by Oncall Medicare Pvt. Ltd., to help people in such a situation and provide them with 24×7 online medical consultations free of cost. Such an initiative saved people from the trouble of physically travelling to hospital and reduced the transmission of the virus in hospitals. More than 100 doctors from different parts of Delhi offered their services free of cost through this app. Patients could quickly consult the doctors from home at their convenience and connect through video or voice calls using the app. Also, they can upload and download test reports and prescriptions through the app (IANS, 2020).

Impact of COVID-19 on Business: Shifting Business Models

India has taken numerous technological initiatives to recover from the impacts of COVID-19 and become resilient enough to continue battling against economic and social losses by adapting strategies to the current realities. After the lockdown, the country geared up to resume work by adopting preventive measures, such as wearing masks, washing hands, avoiding crowds, and maintaining social distance from one another, which have become the new normal. To tide over the loss that occurred due to the pandemic, India has to devise better strategies based on the nation's capabilities and constraints. Formulating plans requires careful analysis of the global economy and identifying how India can respond to it. The whole world has realized how deadly the COVID-19 crisis was and the speed at which the disease spread across the entire world in a short time. While the scientific community initiated research for prevention and cure to enable recovery from the crisis, the business and management community developed strategic plans for the economic impact of the crisis. Due to lockdown, the first impact was the sudden drop in demand and supply, leaving many organizations to shut down, and many struggled to survive and were forced to look for alternative strategic plans (Breier *et al.*, 2021). While the pandemic imposed challenges on business organizations, on the one hand, it led them to explore innovative ideas to reframe their business models aimed at surviving the crisis.

When the business environment changes, it finds ways to devise strategic plans for the sustainability of the business. Porter and Miller (1985) argued that information technology would play a strategic role in an industry characterized by the information intensity of products, services, or the value chain, or, in other words, to what extent information processing is required to effectively and efficiently manage business process activities. Product information intensity refers to the extent to which customers use information to select and purchase the product. Product information intensity varies from one industry to the other. Some industries, such as cement, construction, and mining, have lower information intensity than others, such as textiles, banking, finance, education, news, and media. For example, information intensity associated with textiles involves size, colour, pattern, material, etc. IS researchers have emphasized that an assessment of existing and potential information intensity of product and process of a firm, indicates the extent of IT investments that a firm may benefit from, extent to which the firm can go online and make delivers of its product and services (Liang *et al.*, 2004; Seetharaman, 2020). During the pandemic, many countries imposed restrictions on industries, as there is closer proximity of people while working. The industries that manufacture physical goods involving highly intensive labour were forced to minimize their operations or shut down temporarily. However, in most countries, firms that produce essential physical products were permitted to manufacture them, as they are necessary for everyday life. Again, the 'essential products' are subjective, as they become essential for one country but may not be so for another country.

However, irrespective of country, a common demand was found for essential products, such as food, pharma, fuel, banking, and bazaar. Industries such as retail and hospitality explored ways to reduce the movement of people or physical proximity during delivery or distribution. So, through strategic planning, industries tried to leverage technology to serve their customers by maintaining COVID-19 regulations in the industry.

Banking and media

During the lockdown, the two other inevitable industries that took advantage of the complete digitization of their services were banking and media. They were the early technology adopters; therefore, they reaped the benefits without feeling the negative business impacts of COVID-19. There has been a significant increase in online banking services and digital payments during and after COVID-19. The public depends on the media to know about the updates of COVID-19 and the lockdown restrictions. Hence, the viewership of television increased significantly (Breier *et al.*, 2021).

Moreover, there has been a surge in consumption of streaming video-on-demand services, such as Amazon Prime and Netflix, and online gaming was at its peak. Social media, including Facebook, Instagram, and YouTube was also flooded with content. Users engage in social media platforms to showcase their creativity and generate content, making the media industry a prime differentiator. Certain entertainment forms in media that demand physical space were not considered 'essential' services to everyday living, such as movies, series, collaborative art performances, museums, etc., which were affected by COVID-19 and the lockdown restrictions for collective gathering. A few came up with innovative ideas to leverage their digital presence and reach their audience, whereas others who believe in live performances could not make it possible through media adoption (Seetharaman, 2020).

Digital India is one of India's policy focuses, providing public services and a digital economy. Due to the pandemic, the country took to rapid adoption of technology to meet the needs of the people, which has accelerated digital transformation (Rathor, 2020). Prior to the pandemic, the public was suspicious about the usage and acceptance of the digital economy. However, COVID-19 has forced people to change the way they spend money, and we could see a behavioural change in digital platforms for public and personal transactions. This enabled the country to adopt future online services without much effort. During the pandemic response phase, Indians widely used the Unified Payments Interface (UPI), an existing digital infrastructure that enables domestic payments across digital payment businesses. For contact tracing, the Aarogya Setu app was used in crisis response (NITI Aayog, 2020; Raval, 2020f). Thus, adopting technology for every service ensures procedural transparency and effective grievance mechanisms for customer support.

Hospitality and mobility

The hospitality industry is one of the sectors that faced the negative impact of COVID-19. As countries restricted collective gathering to overcome COVID-19, consumers were forced to stay away from hotels, restaurants, and homestays, which are primarily meant for leisure and not considered essential services. Though restaurants provide food, which is an essential resource, during the lockdown, regular restaurant-goers have shifted their preferences to off-premise dining, food pickups, ready-to-eat meals, home deliveries, etc. This shift in their deliveries allowed restaurants to stay profitable and retain their ability to scale up and innovate their services, meeting customers' demands quickly. Also, the mobility industry was abruptly stopped by the lockdown measures. Ride-hailing, ride-sharing, and vehicle-sharing platforms in various countries went idle. On the other hand, India and other countries were experimenting with a new business model of lease-to-own vehicles fitted with IoT devices to perform diagnosis remotely.

Education sector

COVID-19 disrupted the education system for the first time in history. India has seen a paradigm shift in the education system from traditional face-to-face teaching and learning to online learning due to COVID-19. Several lockdowns, social distancing, and an increasing number of cases led the country to close schools, universities, training institutions, and higher education facilities. Online distance learning creates several challenges for both educators and learners. The education system was not prepared for such uncertain situations, and as a result, it was compelled to adopt online learning. Educators facilitate online teaching using various platforms such as Microsoft Teams, Google Classroom, Canvas, Zoom, and Blackboard. These platforms enable educators to create course content, video, audio, assignments, quizzes, discussion forums, and share files in different formats (Pokhrel and Chhetri, 2021). When technology adoption benefits many other businesses and services, the education sector strived hard to adapt. This is because, in education, there are various subjects which address different needs. So, one-size-fits-all pedagogy will not be suitable for all subject areas in online learning. Students with a fixed mindset find it difficult to adapt to and engage with online learning productively, which creates psychological and emotional distress. Though the education sector under this emergency was coping with the new normal, researchers found that accessibility, affordability, flexibility, learning pedagogy, educational policy, and life-long learning were the few challenges in e-learning. Many students faced issues with internet connections, and those from economically backward sections could not afford online learning devices. The productivity and performance of students will be affected by the reduced contact hours with their teachers (Sintema, 2020). Moreover, exposure to longer screen time poses health issues for children. There will be other psychological, social, and economic repercussions in the life of a student.

There is a common assumption that the shift in business models will not persist once normalcy resumes and that every industry will revert to their earlier business models. That may happen yet. Nonetheless, the radical change in their businesses during the pandemic has allowed the industry to realize the potential to expand their boundaries using technology. Such a response to the situation sets an example for the firm to be more agile and swift in developing new capabilities and strategies for redesigning product development, processes, supply chains, technology adaptation, etc. Agility and radical change will create value for businesses, thereby helping them survive when uncertainty looms.

Challenges in Technology Adoption during COVID-19

Technical know-how

Not all cities had a COVID-19 war room to coordinate and monitor the operation of the city. In that case, it was forced to establish a new centre in the city. Hence, establishing a new ICCC would be difficult if there was no one with sound technical knowledge.

Capacity building and training of COVID-19 war room staff

Cities that are newly creating war rooms may employ less-trained people to operate them. They have to prepare the workers and volunteers with local partner organizations through video conferencing facilities.

Designing solutions

Officials find it challenging to design a technical solution that responds to the pandemic, such as predicting the spread of the virus, identifying vulnerable areas, tracking new cases, contact tracing, etc.

Technical challenges

Several technological solutions are available to address this particular problem. However, choosing the best solution among the alternatives in a short span of time is difficult. Also, it takes time to understand the issues of deployment and the compatibility of the solution with the existing system.

Administrative challenges

In order to perform the activities, there was a limited workforce to train the healthcare workers, nurses, and volunteers for data entry. Since a large volume of data flows from various sources, it isn't easy to manage or sort data in a particular format. There is no standard template or standard operating procedure for operators to provide quality data. Moreover, implementing several initiatives at a time requires special permissions (World Economic Forum, 2020). Facing such challenges, India's response to COVID-19, its search for ways to address the challenges strategically and quickly adapting to the strategy will make it more resilient post-COVID-19. The above challenges in technology regulation and COVID-19 management recovery operations can be resolved by ensuring data protection and security, standardization and interoperability, institutional coordination among agencies, adequately staffed technology and data management, adopting objectives for providing citizen services, and multiple messaging channels for citizens. Adopting these measures will strengthen IT and data governance capabilities, make agencies agile, and improve resilience in the face of crises.

Regulatory framework for technology and data governance

Though India has a technological infrastructure, there are a few challenges related to standardization and interoperability between technology solutions. Adopting standards ensures formulating an evidence-based response to the pandemic. Extensive use of citizen data demands measures for citizen data privacy while handling and managing data. Most countries do not have data protection regulations. However, the generally accepted and widely adopted data protection regulation is the European General Data Protection Regulation (GDPR), which remains applicable for the pandemic. India has no specific standard or regulation on citizen data protection and security. Currently, the Bureau of Indian Standards (BIS) and Smart City Mission (SCM) work closely to develop Indian smart cities. However, Indian cities comply with the provisions of the "Information Technology (Reasonable security practices and procedures and sensitive personal data or information) Rules, 2011" that govern and manage the sharing of sensitive and non-sensitive personal or government data.

Conclusion

COVID-19 is a life-threatening virus that had infected the whole world, leading to the common practice of wearing a mask. Countries strived hard to contain the virus by declaring lockdowns phase by phase, following preventive measures such as wearing masks, hand washing with an alcohol-based liquid, social distancing, etc. In addition, the pandemic pulled down the economy, leaving people and countries in distress. This chapter provides insights about COVID-19, how India tackled it, and its impact on business. The chapter also discussed how a powerful adaptation strategy would help India battle the economic downturn. The pandemic has forced most industries to adopt technology for their survival, and the government initiatives in digital transformation have revealed the benefits and challenges of technology adaptation. Ensuring data protection and security, solving interoperability, and framing data governance and regulations will enhance the digital transformation of India to cope with potential future pandemics. The extensive analysis of the capabilities and constraints to map with the outcomes needs strategic thinking and strategy formulation. Improving capabilities will make an institute more agile and improve its resilience for the future.

References

Arshad Ali, S., Baloch, M., Ahmed, N., Arshad Ali, A., and Iqbal, A. (2020). The outbreak of Coronavirus Disease 2019 (COVID-19) — An emerging global health threat. *Journal of Infection and Public Health*, 13(4), 644–646. https://doi.org/10.1016/j.jiph.2020.02.033.

Bajpai, N., Biberman, J., and Wadhwa, M. (2020). ICT Initiatives in India to Combat COVID-19 ICT India Working Paper #32. Retrieved from https://

economictimes.indiatimes.com/news/politics-and-nation/indias-covid-19-recovery-rate-improving-.

Barik, S. (2020, April 14). Jharkhand to use collaborative robot in COVID-19 isolation facility to cut down human interference. *The Hindu*. Retrieved from https://www.thehindu.com/news/national/other-states/jharkhand-to-use-collaborative-robot-in- covid-19-isolation-facility-to-cut-down-human-interference/article31335881.ece.

Breier, M., Kallmuenzer, A., Clauss, T., Gast, J., Kraus, S., and Tiberius, V. (2021). The role of business model innovation in the hospitality industry during the COVID-19 crisis. *International Journal of Hospitality Management*, 92, 102723. https://doi.org/10.1016/j.ijhm.2020.102723.

Cai, J., Sun, W., Huang, J., Gamber, M., Wu, J., and He, G. (2020). Indirect virus transmission in cluster of Covid-19 cases, Wenzhou, China, 2020. *Emerging Infectious Diseases*, 26(6), 1343–1345.

Dass, V. (2020a). Social media, drones come in handy for Jharkhand police in enforcing lockdown. Retrieved 24 April 2020 from Express Computer website: https://www.expresscomputer.in/egov-watch/social-media-drones-come-in-handy-for-jharkhand-police-in-enforcing-lockdown/53579/.

Dass, V. (2020b). The Kerala way: Use of geofencing, drones, telemed app to tackle Covid-19. Retrieved 24 April 2020 from Express Computer website: https://www.expresscomputer.in/news/the-kerala-way-use-of-geofencing-drones-telemedicine-app-to-tackle-covid-19/52853/.

Dass, V. (2020c). US designed TickMe app to help people order essential goods online in Bhubaneswar. Retrieved 24 April 2020 from Express Computer website: https://www.expresscomputer.in/egov-watch/us-designed-tickme-app-to-help-people-order-essential-goods-online-in-bhubaneswar/53286/.

Dass, V. (2020d, April). Coronavirus-hit Kerala unveils anti fake news division to keep rumour-mongers at bay. Retrieved 25 April 2020 from Express Computer website: https://www.expresscomputer.in/egov-watch/coronavirus-hit-kerala-unveils-anti-fake-news-division-to-keep-rumour-mongers-at-bay/53083/.

De Wit, E., Van Doremalen, N., Falzarano, D., and Munster, V. J. (2016). SARS and MERS: Recent insights into emerging coronaviruses. *Nature Reviews Microbiology*, 14(8), 523–534. https://doi.org/10.1038/nrmicro.2016.81.

Express Computer. (2020a). COVID-19: Disinfection in Varanasi using special drones. Retrieved 24 April 2020 from Express Computer website: https://www.expresscomputer.in/indiaincfightscovid19/covid-19-disinfection-in-varanasi-using-special-drones/53896/.

Express Computer. (2020b). COVID-19 testing: Chitra GeneLAMP-N confirms COVID-19 test results in 2 hours. Retrieved 24 April 2020 from Express Computer website: https://www.expresscomputer.in/egov-watch/covid-19-testing-chitra-genelamp-n-confirms-covid-19-test-results-in-2-hours/53297/.

Express Computer. (2020c). Rajasthan Govt partners with healthcare App 'Aayu' to tackle COVID-19. Retrieved 24 April 2020 from Express Computer website: https://www.expresscomputer.in/industries/healthcare/rajasthan-govt-partners-with-healthcare-app-aayu-to-tackle-covid-19/53474/.

Goh, G. K., Dunker, A. K., Foster, J. A., and Uversky, V. N. (2019). Rigidity of the outer shell predicted by a protein intrinsic disorder model sheds light on the COVID-19 (Wuhan-2019-nCoV) infectivity. *Biomolecules*, 19(M), 2019–2021.

Harapan, H., Itoh, N., Yufika, A., Winardi, W., Keam, S., Te, H., Megawati, D., Hayati, Z., Wagner, A. L., and Mudatsir, M. (2020). Coronavirus disease 2019 (COVID-19): A literature review. *Journal of Infection and Public Health (2020)*, 2020 (March), 136486. https://doi.org/10.1016/j.jiph.2020.03.019.

IANS. (2020). Delhi govt ties-up with CallDoc app to offer free online medical consultation. Retrieved 24 April 2020 from Express Computer website: https://www.expresscomputer.in/news/covid-19/delhi-govt-ties-up-with-calldoc-app-to-offer-free-online-medical-consultation/53172/.

Indian Express. (2020, April 17). TickMe app to help people order essentials in Bhubaneswar. *The New Indian Express*. Retrieved from https://www.newindianexpress.com/cities/bhubaneswar/2020/apr/17/tickme-app-to-help-people-order-essentials-in-bhubaneswar-2131311.html.

Invest India, Business Immunity Platform. (n.d.). Retrieved 30 June 2020 from https://www.investindia.gov.in/bip#sections-11.

Jamwal, A., Bhatnagar, S., and Sharma, P. (2020). Coronavirus disease 2019 (COVID-19): Current literature and status in India. *Preprints*, 4. https://doi.org/10.20944/preprints202004.0189.v1.

Katz, R., Graeden, E., Phelan, A., and Carlson, C. (2021). Covid-19. Retrieved 24 March 2021 from Strategic Intelligence, World Economic Forum website: https://intelligence.weforum.org/topics/a1G0X000006O6EHUA0?tab=data.

Liang, T. P., Lin, C. Y., and Chen, D. N. (2004). Effects of electronic commerce models and industrial characteristics on firm performance. *Industrial Management & Data Systems*, 104(7), 538–545. https://doi.org/10.1108/02635570410550205.

Lu, G., Wang, Q., and Gao, G. F. (2015). Bat-to-human: Spike features determining 'host jump' of coronaviruses SARS-CoV, MERS-CoV, and beyond. *Trends in Microbiology*, 23(8), 468–478. https://doi.org/10.1016/j.tim.2015.06.003.

Lupia, T., Scabini, S., Mornese Pinna, S., Di Perri, G., De Rosa, F. G., and Corcione, S. (2020). 2019 novel coronavirus (2019-nCoV) outbreak: A new challenge. *Journal of Global Antimicrobial Resistance*, 21, 22–27. https://doi.org/10.1016/j.jgar.2020.02.021.

Pokhrel, S., and Chhetri, R. (2021). A literature review on impact of COVID-19 pandemic on teaching and learning. *Higher Education for the Future*, 8(1), 133–141. https://doi.org/10.1177/2347631120983481.

Prasad, U., Sarwal, R., Gopal, M., and Vinod, P. (2020). *Mitigation and Management of COVID-19 Practices from india's states and Union Territories.* National Institution for Transforming India (NITI) Aayog, New Delhi. https://doi.org/10.7910/DVN/7MHJEM.

Rathor, M. (2020). Digital India 2.0: Govt transforms with emerging technologies. Retrieved 24 April 2020 from Express Computer website: https://www.expresscomputer.in/egov-watch/digital-india-2-0-govt-transforms-with-emerging-technologies/53199/.

Raval, A. (2020a). Chhattisgarh fights COVID-19 with an integrated tech platform. Retrieved 24 April 2020 from Express Computer website: https://www.expresscomputer.in/indiaincfightscovid19/chhattisgarh-fights-covid-19-with-an- integrated-tech-platform/53899/.

Raval, A. (2020b). COVID-19: How technology played a role in Agra's acclaimed cluster containment strategy. Retrieved 24 April 2020 from Express Computer website: https://www.expresscomputer.in/indiaincfightscovid19/covid-19-how-technology-played-a-role-in-agras-acclaimed-cluster-containment-strategy/54016/.

Raval, A. (2020c). GIS and predictive analytics, heat maps, apps empowers Pune smart city to fight COVID-19. Retrieved 24 April 2020 from Express Computer website: https://www.expresscomputer.in/indiaincfightscovid19/gis-and-predictive-analytics-heat-maps-apps-empowers-pune-smart-city-to-fight-covid-19/53786/.

Raval, A. (2020d). Jharkhand develops app to transfer cash to migrant labourers. Retrieved 24 April 2020 from Express Computer website: https://www.expresscomputer.in/indiaincfightscovid19/53660/53660/.

Raval, A. (2020e). SIMS: Kerala's hack for supply chain distress in the times of COVID-19. Retrieved 24 April 2020 from Express Computer website: https://www.expresscomputer.in/egov-watch/sims-keralas-hack-for-supply-chain-distress-in-the-times-of-covid-19/53410/.

Raval, A. (2020f). Tamil Nadu uses Aarogya setu IVRS facility, drones to fight COVID-19. Retrieved 24 April 2020 from Express Computer website: https://www.expresscomputer.in/egov-watch/tamil-nadu-uses-aarogya-setu-ivrs-facility-drones-to-fight-covid-19/53280/.

Reusken, C. B. E. M., Haagmans, B. L., Müller, M. A., Gutierrez, C., Godeke, G. J., Meyer, B., … Koopmans, M. P. G. (2013). Middle East respiratory syndrome coronavirus neutralising serum antibodies in dromedary camels: A comparative serological study. *The Lancet Infectious Diseases*, 13(10), 859–866. https://doi.org/10.1016/S1473-3099(13)70164-6.

Seetharaman, P. (2020). Business models shifts: Impact of Covid-19. *International Journal of Information Management*, 54(June), 1–4. https://doi.org/10.1016/j.ijinfomgt.2020.102173.

Sintema, E. J. (2020). Effect of COVID-19 on the performance of grade 12 students: Implications for STEM education. *Eurasia Journal of Mathematics, Science and Technology Education*, 16(7), 1–6. https://doi.org/10.29333/EJMSTE/7893.

Sohrabi, C., Alsafi, Z., O'Neill, N., Khan, M., Kerwan, A., Al-Jabir, A., ... Agha, R. (2020). World Health Organization declares global emergency: A review of the 2019 novel coronavirus (COVID-19). *International Journal of Surgery*, 76, 71–76. https://doi.org/10.1016/j.ijsu.2020.02.034.

World Economic Forum. (2020). Technology and Data Governance in Cities Indian Cities at the Forefront of the Fight against COVID-19.

Yuan, H., Cas, X., Ji, X., Du, F., Zhou, X, He, J., Xie, Y., and Zhu, Y. (2009). A current emerging respiratory infection: Epidemiological and clinical characteristics, diagnosis and treatments of COVID-19. *Diagnosis and Treatments of COVID-19. SSRN Electronic Journal*, (C), 2005–2009.

Zhang, L., and Liu, Y. (2020). Potential interventions for novel coronavirus in China: A systematic review. *Journal of Medical Virology*, 92. https://doi.org/10.1002/jmv.25707.

Chapter 13

COVID-19: A Blessing in Disguise for Social Commerce in India

Dawn Jose[*,‡] and E. Sulaiman Ebrahimkunju[†,§]

*St. Joseph's College of Engineering & Technology,
Pala, Kerala, India*

†*School of Management and Business Studies,
M. G. University, Athirampuzha, Kerala, India*

‡*dawnjos@outlook.com*
§*sulaim25@yahoo.co.in*

Abstract

Social commerce (SC), the successor to e-commerce, has already started making waves across the globe. The COVID-19 pandemic and the accompanying lockdowns seem to have acted as a catalyst for embracing SC in India, as customers are relying more on contactless purchases. The article investigates the status of SC activities in order to understand the trend and its growth potential. The study is conducted in the state of Kerala, India — a market with high internet and mobile penetration coupled with a large proportion of young customers.

Keywords: Social commerce, social media, e-commerce, buying behaviour.

Introduction

The world witnessed disruptive changes in the technological environment during the past two decades. It won't be an exaggeration to state that an internet-based, data driven era has arrived. Riding on this new technology wave, social media (SM) emerged as a powerful medium, connecting millions of people. The power of SM prompted marketers to make 'social' a key communication strategy, if not the core communication strategy. Social commerce (SC), the new 'avatar' of e-commerce, has already made its presence felt in markets such as China and the US and is fast spreading to developing countries. According to the GSMA report, SC sale of goods and services amounted to $720 billion in 2020. SC sales in China are rising consistently each year and are expected to reach $474.81 billion in 2023 (eMarketer). The US accounted for 80.1 million SC buyers in 2020 and will grow another 12.9% to 90.4 million in 2021 (Insider Intelligence). India, one of the major economic powers in the world, was seen as being left behind by her counterparts in terms of SC adoption. According to a Bain & Company report, India's SC sector, which is currently valued between $1.5 and $2 billion in gross merchandise value (GMV). However, the COVID-19 pandemic has made considerable changes to the buying behaviour of consumers. Contactless shopping seems to have caught the imagination of consumers in India. The authors have made an attempt to see if the pandemic and the accompanying lockdown have acted as a blessing in disguise for SC growth in India. The study was done in the state of Kerala, India, which possesses an ideal environment for such growth with high internet penetration, excellent mobile network coverage, widespread smartphone usage, and a young, educated population.

Literature Review

SC is widely regarded as an outgrowth of e-commerce. According to Friedrich (2015), the origin of SC can be traced back to e-commerce pioneers, such as Amazon and eBay, in the 1990s, and more specifically to Yahoo launching Shoposphere in 2005. Shoposphere enabled customers to curate a shopping list, give recommendations, and buy products. SC is defined as a form of internet-based SM that allows people to actively participate in the marketing and selling of products and services in online marketplaces and communities (Stephen and Toubia, 2009). Thus, SC empowers consumers to be the king in its true spirit. According to Liang and Turban (2012), at the heart of SC lie SM technologies, community interactions, and commercial activities. It could be understood as an all-powerful amalgamation of technology, society, and commerce, inviting the dedicated attention of industry as well as academia. Customers have embraced new communication channels, such as microblogs and SM, for sharing shopping experiences, asking for opinions, and, more importantly, making decisions (Vázquez *et al.*, 2014). Thus, it becomes important for marketers to explore more about how consumers are making use of SC. Hajli (2013) proposed three constructs defining SC: recommendations, ratings and reviews, and forums and communities. These constructs are widely used to measure SC. Social platforms, such as Facebook, Instagram, and Pinterest, have actively integrated SC features, enabling consumers to seamlessly transact through the SM. A study conducted by Makmor and Alam (2017) in the UK established positive effects of recommendations and referrals, forums and communities, and ratings and reviews on purchase intention. Consumers take into account the positive and negative reviews posted and compare the information to arrive at a final purchase decision (Catedrilla, 2017).

Study Objectives

The study was undertaken with the broad objective of understanding the usage and popularity of SC, especially during the COVID-19 pandemic period. The specific objectives of the study are:

- to understand the status of SC in the country and to evaluate its potential for growth;
- to study SM habits and the usage of SC during the lockdown period;
- to learn about the SC activities of the respondents;
- to know if SC usage is different among Generation Y and Generation X;
- to identify factors in favour of and against SC;
- to understand the preferred SM platforms for SC transactions.

Research Methodology

The study was done in the state of Kerala, India, using an online survey. A Likert-scale questionnaire was used. In order to measure the variable SC, a standardized scale proposed by Hajli and Julian (2015) was used. Five hundred and ten responses were collected and processed. The following two criteria were set as prequalifiers for respondents: (a) they must have an active SM account on at least one of the SM platforms considered in the study, namely Facebook, Instagram, and Pinterest; and (b) they must be born between 1965 and 1996 (inclusive of both years). The study was conducted during the period of lockdown in Kerala, April–June, 2020. Primary and secondary data were relied upon in arriving at the conclusions.

Results and Discussion

Social commerce usage

The COVID-19 pandemic and the accompanying lockdown have triggered the use of SM in general and SC in particular. Referring to Figure 1, based on our data, 510 respondents were surveyed. Out of these respondents, the majority (28.2%) indicated a 20–30% rise in SC usage. This was followed by a group (24.3%) that reported a 10–20% increase in SC use over the specified time. A good number of respondents suggested that their SC transactions went up by 30–50%, indicating a faster growth prospect in the days to come.

The results indicate that the right time has come for SC to emerge as a major force. Marketers must understand this and strategize to capitalize on this emerging trend by integrating SC into their business models.

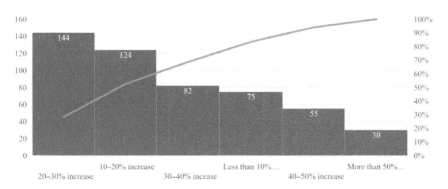

Figure 1. Increase in SC usage.

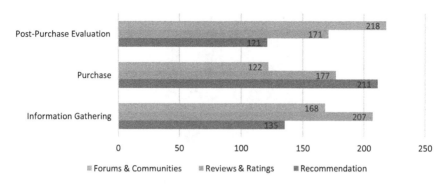

Figure 2. (Color available online) SC usage during the decision-making stages.

Use of SC in consumer decision-making

SM users actively use recommendations, reviews and ratings, and forums and communities during various phases of consumption decision-making, including information gathering, purchase, and post-purchase evaluation.

The scale used for measuring the SC construct showed high reliability with a strong Cronbach's alpha value (0.832). During the information gathering phase, the usage of reviews and ratings is more popular (40.5%), followed by the participation in forums and communities (32.9%) and listening to recommendations (26.6%). In the purchase phase, recommendations are used more (41.4%), followed by reviews and ratings (34.7%) and participation in forums and communities (23.9%). During the post-purchase evaluation phase, forums and communities are more popular (42.8%), followed by reviews and ratings (33.5%), recommendations (23.7%) (see Figure 2). Understanding the consumer decision-making process and utilizing suitable SC strategies for each stage is the key to success. Integrating SM into brand pages can act as an easy source of reliable information for consumers.

Social commerce activities

Referring to Figure 3, a majority of respondents, specifically 334 individuals (65.5%) out of a total of 510, confirmed that they had made purchases through SM throughout the lockdown time and actively participated in SC activities. The most often engaged social commerce activities are ratings and reviews, accounting for 45.5% of user participation. This is

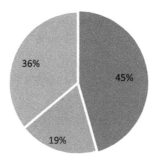

- Rating & reviewing products
- Participating in Forums and Communities
- Giving recommendations to friends

Figure 3. SC activities.

followed by recommending products to friends, which accounts for 35.8% of activity. Participating in forums and communities is the least frequent activity, with a participation rate of 18.7%.

The data suggest that SC is here to stay. Consumers may be encouraged to participate more in SC by providing them with suitable rewards for SC engagement.

SM platform and product category

Having a brand presence on SM platforms is critical to brand success in the changing media environment. It becomes important for marketers to evaluate the capabilities of each platform and design-appropriate strategies. Instagram is the most preferred SM platform for SC, followed by Facebook and Pinterest.

It is also worth noting that there are differences in preference for an SM platform depending on the product category under consideration.

Referring to Figure 5, Instagram is the most favoured social media network for the fashion sector, with a preference rate of 42%. Facebook follows with a preference rate of 35.1%, while Pinterest comes in third with a preference rate of 22.9%. For financial products and services, Facebook is the most favoured platform, with a preference rate of 55.1%. Instagram comes next with a preference rate of 29.6%, followed by Pinterest with a preference rate of 15.3%. Regarding electronics and appliances, Facebook is the most favoured platform (55.7%), with

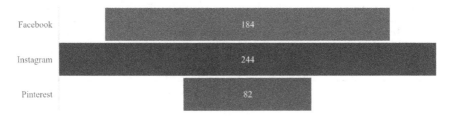

Figure 4. Prefered SM Platform for SC.

Figure 5. Preferred platform — Product Category.

Instagram coming in second (33.5%) and Pinterest in third place (10.8%). 42.4% of respondents expressed a preference for using Instagram mostly for purchasing groceries and food items. Pinterest has a market share of 35.9%, whereas Facebook has a market share of 21.7%. Facebook dominates the travel/hotel/stay sector with a market share of 37.3%, surpassing Pinterest's 33.7% (see Figure 4). Instagram follows closely after with a share of 29%. Marketers must possess a comprehensive understanding of the appropriate strategy for each individual product category. Marketers may get superior outcomes by adopting a tailored approach.

SC usage among Generation Y and Generation X

The SC usage by Generation Y and Generation X was particularly studied. According to Pew Research Centre (2018), Generation X is defined as those born between 1965 and 1980, while Generation Y (also referred to as Millennials) are those born between 1981 and 1996 (Pew Research Centre).

Referring to Table 1, the *t*-test revealed that there is a statistically significant difference in the factor SC among the different generations of respondents (a t value of 4.493 and a p value of 0.000). Since the calculated p value is less than 0.05, the null hypothesis is rejected, and the

Table 1. Independent sample *t*-test, generation of respondents, and the usage of SC.

Description		Descriptive statistics			*t*-test results	
Factor	Age/Generation	N	Mean	Std. deviation	t	Sig. (two-tailed)
SC	GEN Y	413	3.6449	0.93869	4.493	0.000
	GEN X	97	3.1581	1.04759		

alternate hypothesis 'the usage of SC varies significantly among Generation X and Generation Y' is accepted. The mean value results show that the usage of SC constructs, namely forums and communities, ratings and reviews, and recommendations, is higher among Generation Y (a mean of 3.6449) compared to Generation X (a mean of 3.1581). The understanding has relevance in a market such as India, which has a sizeable presence of Generation Y customers. It is advisable to form uniquely designed communication strategies for both Generation X and Generation Y, keeping in mind their communication preferences and specific needs. Promotional strategies encouraging Generation X to participate more in SC must be initiated to lure them in.

Factors favouring SC usage

The study also sheds some light on the factors which favour SC usage. For most respondents, convenience and ease of use top the list (36.3%), followed by the possibility of finding better deals (32.5%) and peer influence (31.1%).

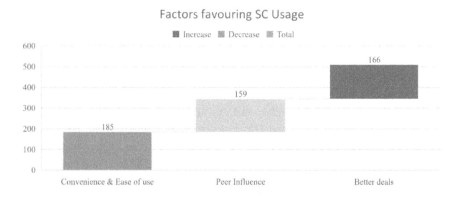

Marketers must deeply ponder factors that are critical to SC success, such as the ones identified in this study. 'Trust' is identified as a challenge in SC usage by most respondents. It is important to identify trustworthy influencers to promote products and services. This can help win the trust of consumers and encourage them to actively participate in SC. Offering a differential advantage while shopping through SM platforms can attract more customers.

Conclusion

The study reveals that the COVID-19 pandemic and the accompanying lockdowns have acted as a blessing in disguise for the SC to take off in India. Consumers appear to be comfortable shopping through SM platforms. Recommendations, reviews and ratings, and forums and communities have significant influence during the various phases of consumption-related decision-making. SC will be a win-win strategy for both consumers and marketers. SC replacing e-commerce seems no longer a distant dream.

References

Bain & Company, Inc. (2020). The future of Commerce in India. Retrieved from https://www.bain.com/globalassets/noindex/2020/bain_report_unlocking_the_future_of_commerce_in_india.pdf.

Catedrilla, J. (2017). Filipino consumers' decision-making model in social commerce. In *21 Pacific Asia Conference on Information Systems*, Langkawi. Retrieved 9 February 2020 from http://h7p://aisel.aisnet.org/pacis2017/112.

Friedrich, T. (2015). Analyzing the factors that influence consumers' adoption of social commerce – A literature review. In *21 Americas Conference on Information Systems*, Puerto Rico, pp. 1–14. Retrieved 5 February 2019 from https://www.researchgate.net/publication/279975923_Analyzing_The_Factors_That_Influence_Consumers%27_Adoption_Of_Social_Commerce_-_A_Literature_Review.

GSM Association. (2019). Social commerce in emerging markets: Understanding the landscape and opportunities for mobile money. Retrieved from https://www.gsma.com/mobilefordevelopment/wp-content/uploads/2019/12/Social-commerce-in-emerging-markets.pdf.

Hajli, N. (2013). A research framework for social commerce adoption. *Information Management & Computer Security*, 21(3), 144–154. doi: 10.1108/IMCS-04-2012-0024.

Insider Intelligence. (2021). In China, social commerce makes up 11.6% of retail ecommerce sales. Retrieved 4 February 2021 from https://www.emarketer.com/content/china-social-commerce-makes-up-11-6-of-retail-ecommerce-sales.

Liang, T.-P., and Turban, E. (2011). Introduction to the special issue social commerce: A research framework for social commerce. *International Journal of Electronic Commerce*, 16(2), 5–13. doi: 10.2753/JEC1086-4415160201.

Makmor, N., and Alam, S. S. (2017). Attitude towards social commerce: A conceptual model regarding consumer purchase intention and its determinants. *International Journal of Economic Research*, 14(22).

Pew Research Centre. (2018). Definitions. Pewresearch.org. Retrieved 1 August 2020 from https://www.pewresearch.org/methods/demographic-research/definitions/.

Social Commerce 2021. Insider Intelligence. (2021). Retrieved 12 February 2021 from https://www.emarketer.com/content/social-commerce-2021.

Stephen, A. T., and Toubia, O. (2009). Deriving value from social commerce networks. *Journal of Marketing Research*, 47(2). doi: 10.2139/ssrn.1150995.

Vázquez, S., García, Ó. M., Campanella, I., Poch, M., and Fisas, B. (2014). A classification of user-generated content into consumer decision journey stages. *Neural Networks*, 58, 68–81. http://dx.doi.org/10.1016/j.neunet.2014.05.026.

© 2025 World Scientific Publishing Company
https://doi.org/10.1142/9789811292101_0014

Chapter 14

Purchasing Criteria of Wealthy Single Urbanites with Respect to Mobile Phone Accessories: A Post-COVID-19 Study

Harshvardhan N. Bhavsar

Institute of Management Studies Career Development and Research, Ahmednagar, Maharashtra, India
harshvardhanbhavsar@yahoo.co.in

Abstract

The mobile phone accessories market is booming in response to a surge in smartphones, the 'work from home' culture induced by the COVID-19 era, and an increasing focus on aesthetics by young consumers. Moreover, increasing internet penetration and online retailing trend in India are helping the mobile phone accessories market flourish. Wealthy single urbanities (WSUs) are the new superconsumers. In the post-COVID-19 era, this group of consumers is adapting to the new culture of working from home and limited direct social interactions with friends and family. With the requirements of working from home, these individuals are spending heavily on mobile phones and their accessories. The current study thus tries to identify the most significant factors that influence mobile phone accessory purchase decisions among WSUs. The research also tries to find out if there exists any association between gender and the monthly purchases made by WSUs with respect to mobile phone accessories. The sample size for this study was 210, and the research was conducted in Pune City in Maharashtra State. The data were analyzed using Garrett's ranking technique and the chi-square test performed using the SPSS software. The research found that social influence, compatibility, and brand name were the three important factors that influenced WSUs while purchasing mobile phone accessories. The research also found that there is no association between gender and the monthly purchases made by WSUs. These critical outcomes of the study could help mobile phone accessory companies formulate more suitable policies to make accessories more socially influential as well as work on the key outcome that their mobile accessories should be compatible with the majority of the available mobile brands. The study also reveals that companies should focus on the branding aspect, as the brand name is also an important factor that influences customers' purchase decisions.

Keywords: Garrett's ranking, mobile phone accessories, post-COVID-19, purchasing criteria, wealthy single urbanities.

Introduction and Statement of the Problem

The mobile phone accessories market is booming in response to a surge in smart phones, the 'work from home' culture induced by the COVID-19 era, and an increasing focus on aesthetics by young consumers. Moreover, increasing internet penetration and online retailing trends in India are helping the mobile phone accessories market flourish (Allied Market Research, 2019). Mobile phone accessories, such as batteries, headphones/earphones, portable speakers, chargers, memory cards, power banks, battery and protective cases, screen guards, selfie sticks, pop sockets, and USB cables, are some of the products that are in huge demand among young adults.

Recently, a new class of 'superconsumers' was identified in India (Nielson, 2018). This new class is named 'wealthy single urbanities' (WSUs). WSUs are people who are wealthy, i.e., earning above Rs. 50,000 per month, who are single and live in urban cities. These superconsumers spend a lot of money on apparel, devices, holidays, health services, etc. They are called superconsumers as they have handy disposable income, which they spend on purchasing products of their choice.

This study tries to determine the purchasing criteria of these WSUs, particularly in the post-COVID-19 era. In this era, this group of consumers is adapting to the new culture of working from home and limited direct social interactions with friends and family. With the requirements of working from home, these individuals are spending heavily on mobile phones and their accessories. This research aims to understand how the purchase decisions for mobile accessories are made by these superconsumers and what factors influence their decisions.

Review of Literature

WSUs have emerged as the new superconsumers. This category of consumers spends a lot of money on fashion accessories, mobile accessories, apparel, devices, and health-related services. Many researchers in the past have tried to study the factors that influence customers in buying mobile phones and accessories.

Katz and Sugiyama (2006), in their research work, tried to find out the relationship between mobile phones and fashion among college users in the US and Japan. They found that young people use mobile phones as a way of expressing their sense of self and perceive others through a 'fashion' lens. Katz and Aakhus (2002) had earlier noted a similar observation in their research, where they found that the technological function of a new tool is not necessarily the most important consideration when people decide to buy a new tool.

Fortunati (2002), in her research, considered the mobile phone's social implications in Italy, focusing on its aesthetic dimension. She attributes its success to its 'fashionableness.' She suggests an interesting point that mobile phone ownership and its use communicate 'about' the person. In the past, numerous scholars have paid special attention to the way in which young people use mobile phones (e.g., Kasesniemi and Rautiainen, 2002; Ling and Yttri, 2002; Skog, 2002). Green (2003) argued that young people negotiate the social and cultural values of the mobile phone 'in relation to identity, difference, independence, and interdependence' (p. 213).

In the recent past, studies on factors influencing customers while purchasing mobile phones have been conducted. These factors are very similar to those that customers consider while purchasing mobile accessories. Sata (2013), in her research, found that price, social group, product features, brand name, durability, and after-sales services are the six important factors that influence customers when buying a new mobile phone.

A similar attempt was made by Samanta and Banerjee (2016), where they compared the choice of purchasing a mobile phone made by Indian and US-based customers. Their study found that price is the pivotal factor that an Indian consumer primarily considers, whereas an American buyer stresses brand name.

Kaushal and Kumar (2016), in their study, found that compatibility, dependency, and social influence were the factors which significantly affected the purchase intention of smartphone consumers. In a similar context, Bugyei (2020), in her research, found that branding, price, technical features, and the quality of phones were the key factors that affected purchase decisions in Ghana.

The above literature review shows that considerable research has been conducted on the factors influencing customers while purchasing mobile phones. Also, research considering mobile devices as fashion statements has been conducted. However, very limited research has been conducted on factors influencing customers while purchasing mobile phone accessories. Also, studies on WSUs are limited with respect to mobile phone accessories. This study deals with this research gap and proposes to study factors influencing the purchasing criteria of WSUs with respect to mobile phone accessories in the post-COVID-19 era.

Objectives of the Study

This study aims:

1. to identify the most significant factors that influence purchase decisions among WSUs with respect to mobile phone accessories and
2. to find an association between gender and monthly purchases made by WSUs with respect to mobile phone accessories.

Hypotheses of the Study

H_0: There is no association between gender and monthly purchases made by WSUs with respect to mobile phone accessories.

H_a: There is an association between gender and monthly purchases made by WSUs with respect to mobile phone accessories.

Methodology

The detailed research methodology used in the current research is as follows:

(i) Research design: descriptive research design;
(ii) Research location: Pune City;
(iii) Type of data: both primary and secondary data;
(iv) Instrument for primary data collection: questionnaire;
(v) Secondary data sources: review of literature, including international and national scholarly papers, conference proceedings, peer-reviewed articles, magazines, newspapers, reports, books, and internet sources;
(vi) Sample size: 210;
(vii) Sampling method: convenience sampling;
(viii) Statistical techniques used:
   a. Garrett's ranking technique,
   b. Chi-square test.

Data Analysis and Interpretation

Ranking of factors that affect purchase decisions amongst WSUs

Table 1 shows the ranking of factors that affect purchase decisions among WSUs. In the table, respondents ranked the given factors from 1 to 9 according to their preferences, where rank 1 was the most preferred and rank 10 was the least preferred. The factors that respondents were asked to rank were brand name, price, quality, style, design, discount, product features, compatibility, and social influence. The results showed that the rankings were widely distributed. So, to further understand which were the most important factors, according to the respondents, in purchasing mobile phone accessories, Garrett's ranking technique was used.

Garrett's ranking technique

In order to determine the most significant factor, according to the respondents, Garrett's ranking technique was used. With the help of Garrett's table, the estimated percentage position was converted into scores. Then, for each factor, the scores of each individual were added, and then the

Table 1. Ranking of factors that affect purchase decisions among WSUs with respect to mobile phone accessories.

Factors	Ranking									Total
	1	2	3	4	5	6	7	8	9	
Brand name	36	38	31	28	21	13	14	11	18	210
Price	12	14	15	27	36	38	21	24	23	210
Quality	13	13	37	35	25	13	24	34	16	210
Style	25	17	26	31	27	29	39	1	15	210
Design	21	22	21	33	35	26	12	28	12	210
Discount	19	16	23	32	29	13	27	29	22	210
Product features	27	21	17	36	31	28	19	18	13	210
Compatibility	41	25	39	32	24	16	9	17	7	210
Social influence	53	41	32	21	15	8	12	14	14	210

Table 2. Percentage position of ranks assigned and their respective Garrett's table values.

Rank	Percentage position	Garrett's table value
1	5.51	81
2	16.66	69
3	27.62	62
4	38	56
5	50	50
6	61.14	44
7	72.2	38
8	83.33	31
9	94.44	19

total and mean values of the scores were calculated. In Table 2, the percentage position of ranks assigned 1–9 and their respective Garrett's table values are given.

By applying Garrett's ranking technique, Garrett's table values were obtained for each of the nine ranks. Garrett's table values were then multiplied by the rankings given to each factor by the respondents. The total score, mean score, and thus the final rank obtained are shown in Table 3.

Table 3. Calculation of Garrett's value and ranking.

Factors	Rankings									Total	Mean score	Rank
	1	2	3	4	5	6	7	8	9			
Brand name	2,916	2,622	1,922	1,568	1,050	572	532	341	342	11,865	56.50	3
Price	972	966	930	1,512	1,800	1,672	798	744	437	9,831	46.81	9
Quality	1,053	897	2,294	1,960	1,250	572	912	1,054	304	10,296	49.03	7
Style	2,025	1,173	1,612	1,736	1,350	1,276	1,482	31	285	10,970	52.24	5
Design	1,701	1,518	1,302	1,848	1,750	1,144	456	868	228	10,815	51.50	6
Discount	1,539	1,104	1,426	1,792	1,450	572	1,026	899	418	10,226	48.70	8
Product features	2,187	1,449	1,054	2,016	1,550	1,232	722	558	247	11,015	52.45	4
Compatibility	3,321	1,725	2,418	1,792	1,200	704	342	527	133	12,162	57.91	2
Social influence	4,293	2,829	1,984	1,176	750	352	456	434	266	12,540	59.71	1

In Table 3, it is seen that, according to respondents, 'social influence' was the most important factor, with a total score of 12,540 and a mean score of 59.71. This was followed by 'compatibility' and 'brand name,' with mean scores of 57.91 and 56.50, respectively. 'Discounts' and 'price' were the least important factors, with mean scores of 48.70 and 46.81, respectively.

Chi-square test

A chi-square test was done to check the hypothesis that there was an association between gender and monthly purchases made by WSUs. The chi-square test was conducted using SPSS software. The results are shown in Table 4.

A Pearson chi-square test was conducted to examine whether there was an association between gender and monthly purchases made by WSUs with respect to mobile phone accessories. The results revealed that there was no association between the two variables. Hence, the null hypothesis (H_0) was accepted and the alternate hypothesis (H_1) was rejected (chi-square value = 1.138, $df = 3$, $p < 0.05$).

Discussion, Conclusion, and Managerial Implications

After COVID-19, the demand for mobile phone accessories, such as noise-free headphones, batteries, ear buds, chargers, mobile stands, etc.,

Table 4. Chi-square test results.

	Value	df	Asymp. Sig. (two-sided)
Pearson chi-square	1.138	3	0.768
Likelihood ratio	1.125	3	0.771
Linear-by-linear association	0.025	1	0.874
N. of Valid cases	210		

is increasing. The rise in work from home culture and the increasing time spent on mobile phones are important factors that have contributed to the increasing demand for mobile accessories. Therefore, it was imperative to identify the factors that affect the purchase decisions of customers with regard to mobile phone accessories.

This study focused on identifying these key purchasing criteria, with an emphasis on new superconsumers, i.e., WSUs. In the study, Garret's ranking technique was used to identify the most influencing factors, and the chi-square test was used to find the association between gender and monthly purchases made by WSUs with respect to mobile phone accessories. From the findings obtained, the study concludes that 'social influence,' 'compatibility,' and 'brand name' were the three most important factors that influence purchase decisions among WSUs. The study also concludes that there is no association between gender and the monthly purchases made by WSUs.

These critical outcomes of the study could help mobile phone accessory companies formulate more suitable policies to make accessories more socially influential as well as work on the key outcome that their mobile accessories should be compatible with the majority of the available mobile brands. The study also reveals that companies should focus on the branding aspect, as brand name was also an important factor that influences customers' purchase decisions.

References

Allied Market Research Report, 2019. Available at: https://www.alliedmarketresearch.com/mobile-accessories-market. Accessed on 12 November 2020.

Bugyei, G. (2020). Factors influencing consumers' purchase decision of mobile phones in the Mfantsiman municipality of Ghana. *Journal of Information Engineering and Applications*, 10(4), 21–33.

Dhanavandan, S. (2016). Application of garret ranking technique: Practical approach. *International Journal of Library and Information Studies*, 6(3), 135–140.

Fortunati, L. (2002). Italy: Stereotypes, true and dalse. In Katz, J. E., and Aakhus, M. (eds.) *Perpetual Contact*. Cambridge University Press, Cambridge, pp. 42–62.

Kasesniemi, E., and Rautiainen, P. (2002). Mobile culture of children and teenagers in Finland. In Katz, J. E., and Aakhus, M. (eds.) *Perpetual Contact*. Cambridge University Press, Cambridge, pp. 170–192.

Katz, J. E. and Aakhus, M. (eds.) (2002). *Perpetual Contact*. Cambridge University Press, Cambridge.

Katz, J. E., and Sugiyama, S. (2006). Mobile phones as fashion statements: Evidence from student surveys in the US and Japan. *New Media and Society*, 8(2), 321–337.

Kaushal, S. K., and Kumar, R. (2016). Factors affecting the purchase intension of smartphone: A study of young consumers in the city of Lucknow. *Pacific Review Business International*, 8(12), 1–16.

Ling, R., and Yttri, B. (2002). Hyper-coordination via mobile phones in Norway. In Katz, J. E., and Aakhus, M. (eds.) *Perpetual Contact*. Cambridge University Press, Cambridge, pp. 139–169.

Samanta, J., and Banerjee, N. (2016). A comparative study on factors affecting consumer's choice on purchasing a cellular phone across India & US. *International Journal of Business and Social Research*, 6(6), 59–67.

Sata, M. (2013). Consumer buying behavior of mobile phone devices. *Journal of Marketing and Consumer Research*, 4(2), 8–15.

Skog, B. (2002). Mobiles and the Norwegian teen: Identity, gender and class. In Katz, J. E., and Aakhus, M. (eds.) *Perpetual Contact*. Cambridge University Press, Cambridge, pp. 255–273.

New Super Consumers. Available at: https://timesofindia.indiatimes.com/business/india-business/new-class-of-single-urbanites-emerges-as-super-consumers/articleshow/65466005.cms. Accessed on 2 November 2020.

Nielsen Report 2018. Available at: https://www.nielsen.com/in/en/insights/report/2018/wealthy-single-urbanites-go-premium/. Accessed on 2 November 2020.

Chapter 15

Indian Teens' Buying Behaviour towards E-Commerce

Ruchika Dawar[*], Sonika Siwach[†], and Sapna Sehrawat[‡]

*Fashion Management Studies,
National Institute of Fashion Technology Jodhpur,
Rajasthan, India*
[*]*ruchika.dawar@nift.ac.in*
[†]*sonika.siwach@nift.ac.in*
[‡]*sapna.sapna1@nift.ac.in*

Abstract

E-commerce in India has been experiencing remarkable growth, successfully changing the way people transact. The pandemic has accelerated the shift towards a more digital world and triggered changes in online shopping behaviours that are likely to have lasting effects. Social media has become integral to the teen market's online shopping experience. Food and clothing are the primary sources of expenditure among teenagers, followed by health and personal care for girls and video games for boys. Of the adolescent spending, 42% is directed to social uses, such as food, video games, music, movies, events, or books; 38% to clothing, accessories, or shoes; and 15% to beauty and personal care. The research was conducted to study the factors that affected teenagers' online shopping. This objective led to the formation of a questionnaire which focuses on collecting information on the current e-commerce trends of

Indian teenagers. The study was conducted online, involving those in the age group ranging from 13 to 19 years over a period spanning two weeks. The study focuses on determining gaps in the Indian market for teenagers in order to cater to them in a better way.

Keywords: Teen market, online shopping, market gap, shopping experience.

Introduction

E-commerce is the process of buying and selling tangible products and services online. It involves two or more parties exchanging data or currency to process a transaction. Young demography, increasing internet and smartphone penetration, and relatively better economic performance are some key drivers of this sector.

The growth story of India continues — a story of tremendous growth. To the extent that one can be as conservative as one can, the gross domestic product (GDP) is seen increasing from 6% to 7% a year, with consumption expenditures expected to rise by a factor of three to reach $4 trillion by 2025. With a nominal year-over-year expenditure growth of 12%, which is more than double the anticipated global rate of 5%, India is poised to become the third-largest consumer market by 2025.

E-commerce has transformed the way business is done in India. The Indian e-commerce market is expected to grow to $188 billion by 2025 from $46.2 billion as of 2020. By 2030, it is expected to reach $350 billion. Propelled by rising smartphone penetration, the launch of 4G networks, and increasing consumer wealth, the Indian e-commerce market is expected to grow to $200 billion by 2026 from $38.5 billion in 2017 (IBEF, 2022).

A **teenager**, or **teen**, is someone who is between 13 and 19 years old.

The life of a teenager seems to change daily. Constantly exposed to new ideas, social situations, and people, teenagers strive to develop their personalities and interests during this time of great change. Before their teenage years, these adolescents focused on school, play, and gaining approval from their parents.

The perception of teenagers as cool, trendsetting, and influential was — and still is — just as much a creation of commerce and media as a reflection of reality. Teenage music, fashion, and language ripple across the rest of society, supercharged by industries established to profit from them.

Objectives, Scope, and Limitations

Objectives of the study

The objectives of the study were:

- to evaluate the teen market and buying behaviour towards e-commerce in India;
- to evaluate the brand choices, trends, price points, competition mapping, white gaps, and shopping challenges for teens.

Scope of the study

The study can be used to understand the current e-commerce trends among Indian teenagers. The findings of the study can also help gauge the popular sites teenagers prefer to engage in for online shopping. Based on the preferences of teenage buyers, these websites can fine-tune their services to improve their online business prospects.

Limitations of the study

The study was limited only to those teenagers who directly engage in shopping online, whereas those who buy on behalf of teenagers were not included.

Literature Review

Teenagers are brand-conscious but not necessarily brand-loyal. Friends, whose opinions they value, heavily influence buying behaviour. Peer approval of purchases is very important, especially for girls. A Piper Jaffray report states that friends had the most influence over teen purchase decisions, and about 50% of both males and females said social media influenced them. Shopping is a core social activity for teenage girls, who are more likely to be swayed by celebrities than boys. Almost 40% of teenage girls sign up for emails from their favourite brands to receive information about sales and promotions. Sharing is common: 65% say that when their favourite brands have a sale, they want to share the information with their best friend or sister, and 57% say that when they find a new brand or trend, they tell a best friend or sister. About 80% prefer to share the information by texting or calling rather than posting to social media platforms. As for celebrities' influence, 43% are influenced by the style of celebrities. Teens have short attention spans, especially regarding advertisements. They filter out a good deal of the messages and are often doing several other things while shopping online, especially if they are on a mobile device. Messaging that is concise, transparent, and has a point is necessary to garner their attention. It can be time-consuming to keep up with the changing inclinations of teenagers, but they do have substantial purchasing power (Kaplan, 2013).

The term "digital natives" has been used to describe Generation Z. They are the first generation to always have the internet at their disposal. They grew up in a world that is seamlessly connected. As much as 41% of teens identify an athletic apparel brand as their preferred clothing brand, with Nike topping the list (Kaplan, 2017), and 70% of teens prefer to shop at their favourite stores online. Teens are shopping more via the internet and at brick-and-mortar outlet stores and less at speciality stores. Teens have to come up with more of their own resources, which may account for them shopping less at pricier speciality stores. When it comes to online shopping, teens are outspending their parents. Shoppers aged between 13 and 18 spent at twice the rate of adults. Teen confidence in online shopping for consumer goods extends across the retail landscape. Amazon.com is the most frequented site. Teens also frequent speciality retailers looking for discounts and unique items — sites their parents may not be familiar with (Amato-McCoy, 2017).

Loosely defined as people born between the mid-1990s and the early 2010s, Gen Z has never known a world without the internet or smartphones. For them, social media is second nature. According to marketing experts, that very much shapes how they buy things, even in real life. The way that teenagers shop now is totally different from before — brands and trends mostly gain steam over social media — and yet remain very much the same. They're into clothes, makeup, and getting pizza with their friends.

Gen Z considers the brands they support to be a reflection of their values, and the products they buy are a way of telling the world how they wish to be perceived. Teens: they're just like us (Brooke, 2018).

Methodology

Research design

The study is both quantitative and qualitative in nature. The nature of the research is both descriptive as it clearly defines the demographic segment, and our analysis is based on the data derived from various sources to perform competitor analysis, understand market trends, and also launch a teen-specific platform in the market. It is exploratory, as a few assumptions have been made to analyze market sizing for potential growth and sales.

Method of data collection

Primary and secondary data are used:

- **Primary data:** Conducted primary research (group discussions, personal interviews, and questionnaires) to identify customer preferences and the top-performing e-commerce platforms for the age group of 13–19.
- **Secondary data:** Conducted detailed analysis of the teen market by reviewing brand websites, journals, case studies, papers, research databases, etc.

Sample size: 200 teenagers in the age group of 13–19 years.

Analysis

The concerned demographic for this research amounted to a total of 105 respondents. Out of the 105 teens who took the survey, 67.3% were girls and 28.8% were boys. The age group considered for the survey was 13–19, with 13–15-year-olds accounting for 32.7% and 16–19-year-olds accounting for 67.3%.

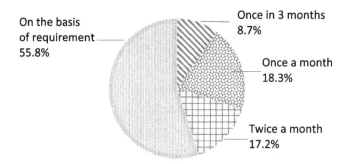

Figure 1. Frequency of shopping.

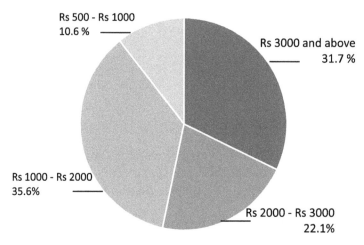

Figure 2. Amount spent per shopping session.

The teen segment shopped the most on the basis of requirement, i.e., during occasions/festivals, followed by once or twice a month (Figure 1). Assuming the average basket size is 2–3 articles, teens' spending power lies in the range Rs. 1,000–2,000 the most while shopping, followed by the range of more than Rs. 3,000 and Rs. 2,000–3,000 (Figure 2). It can be inferred that the teenage segment is willing to spend somewhere in the range of Rs. 500–800 per product.

Most teenagers prefer to shop offline at local stores or flea markets in their area (Figure 3), followed by e-commerce platforms and multi-brand outlets, such as Shopper Stop and Lifestyle. It can be inferred that teens

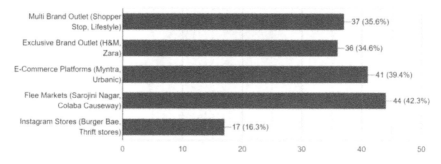

Figure 3. Most preferred shopping destination.

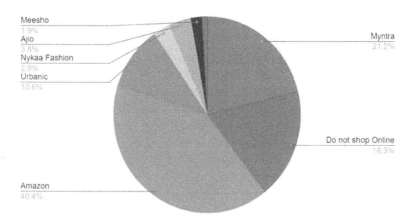

Figure 4. Most preferred e-commerce platform.

look for options under one roof. One major factor influencing the selection decision is the ease of trial and selection.

As of now, teens mostly prefer Amazon, followed by Myntra and Urbanic to shop online (Figure 4).

Teens have a strong inclination towards e-commerce and would want to have a dedicated platform to shop from (Figure 5), considering the ease of navigation.

Teens online presence

The teen segment is an underserved segment in the market, with limited brands/labels catering to it. The teenage years are a phase of transitioning

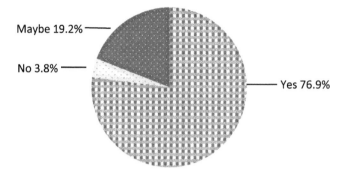

Figure 5. Requirement of teen-specific category on e-commerce application.

from childhood to adulthood during which they go through the process of taking control of their lives. This is a period of transition, with physical and sociological changes converging. This is the time when the child acquires a smartphone and begins using social media. The pandemic accelerated the virtual lifestyle and transitioned the shopping culture to the virtual sphere. The transition to virtual source of education during the pandemic forced parents to grant access to smartphones to their kids as early as 12/13 years of age.

The following are some of the different facets of teens:

1. **Augmented Reality:** An average teen spends 3–6 hours on social media daily, with Instagram and YouTube being the most used apps for entertainment, socialization, expression, and information. These two apps are the most influential for teens and are used for general browsing, songs, entertainment videos, and informative videos. Both platforms provide awareness of fashion trends. Instagram provides more insights since it gives easy access to communication and also enables users to explore new stores and shopping experiences. It is followed by Snapchat, Pinterest, and Facebook as we move towards older teens.
2. **Amalgamated Identity:** Social media acts as a way of expression for teens; therefore, they present a layered personality. A layered personality does not mean faking, but rather a kind of identity that shows off the best version of oneself to the world.

3. **'Glocal' Existence:** Teens are exposed to Indian and international influences through OTT, music, food, and fashion. International influence has more impact on Indian teens through consumption of its content, including Korean, Japanese, and American, and a huge impact is made by Westernized and fusion wear styles and body image. This, however, generates intergenerational tension in small towns and conservative families. Parents are unable to fathom the depth of the impact of global exposure. With time, both parents and teens are striving to compromise, adapt, and bridge the gap.
4. **Privileged and Pragmatic:** Teens expect quick gratification from the immediacy of their online lives; they are impatient and quick to consume and move on. They believe in making informed choices, such as checking reviews before buying anything, and are in a data-rich environment where they are aware of their needs and wants.
5. **Vulnerability:** Teens tend to not trust easily and are privacy conscious. Teens of age 12/13 on social media are prone to being hurt by comments that impact their self-image. They feel pressure to project a positive, confident, and powerful image to the world through their social media activity.

Teens fashion evolution analysis

Male and female teens have different sets of needs arising from their attitudes and environments. Therefore, it was important to study the choices of both girls (Table 1) and boys (Table 2), with further segregation into early teens (12–14) and late teens (15–19).

Pain points

Size and Fit:
Issue: The body is still growing and body curves are not fully developed; therefore, finding the right fit becomes a challenge. The transition from size charts based on age groups to adult sizing charts creates confusion. One's body size may fall between clothing sizes, and a lack of size consistency across brands limits options.

Current workaround: Shopping offline to be able to try out clothing across the kids and adult sections makes decision-making easy.

Table 1. Evolution of a teenage girl's fashion identity.

	12–14 years	15–19 years
Traits	The age group represents an underconfident and confused state of mind, with lifestyle choices regulated largely by school, connecting with friends in the vicinity, and occasional partying or sleepovers.	The age group represents a more liberated and independent lifestyle, with increased time spent with friends and more occasions.
Goal	The goal is to become confident, express emotions, and be accepted by peers and parents.	The goal is now to experiment, try new things, and be different from the peer group in order to make an impact on society.
Media	It plays a crucial role in shaping decisions, from cartoons, such as *Doraemon* and *Crayon Shin-chan*, to soap operas and movies, such as *Family Man*, *Squid Game*, and *Emily in Paris*.	The consumption choices change from cartoons to content in the form of reality shows, such as *MTV Roadies* and *Splitsvilla*, and other OTT shows.
Fashion inspiration	The constant need for validation and attention comes as a challenge during this phase of life. Fashion inspiration comes from self-assured older siblings, cousins, and friends and are at a stage when they discover influencers on social media.	Fashion inspiration comes from fashion icons and influencers, brand websites, shopping fashion apps, peers, and Instagram.

Fashion trends	The age group is considered a beginner in the fashion world and is a learning stage where they experiment with different styles appropriate for different occasions. Mixing and matching and experimentation are done to find the appropriate fit.	The age group is considered an adopter of fashion. The stage revolves around adopting trends and creating a unique style for oneself.
Demands	The girls in this age group look for the right fit and comfort and do not focus on budget.	The girls in this age group are more concerned with the trends and fit of the garment. The budget thus becomes more important.
Shopping behaviour	The age group browses online for information and mainly prefers buying offline after ensuring the right fit. Online purchases are supervised by mothers.	Purchases are still skewed to favour offline. The age group usually browses and buys online, and the payment is usually done by mothers.
Shopping apps	Instagram and Facebook stores are usually visited. Very limited access to and use of e-commerce stores, such as Amazon and Myntra. Shopping apps are usually used on parents' mobile phones.	Multiple shopping apps on mobile to trace the best deal on different brands. Family influences account for shopping on Amazon. Spending power still rests with parents.
Brands	The relationship with brands is nascent but evolving. They are more focused on styles than brands, but leading brands, such as Zara and H&M, set their fashion taste. They begin to explore portals such as Amazon, Myntra, Meesho, and Urbanic.	Brands such as Zara and H&M, Westside, Lifestyle, and Forever21 drive their style concepts. These are largely offline. Online brands such as Myntra, Ajio, Urbanic, and Nykaa have become default online options.

Table 2. Evolution of teenage boys' fashion identity.

	12–14 years	15–19 years
Traits	The age group represents itself as boys with a limited lifestyle revolving around school and playing cricket/football as a hobby. The media accessible and enjoyed by this age group revolves around gaming and sports.	The age group represents itself as men when the body starts growing. The attitude grows more responsible and self-aware. Life choices are more fitness-oriented. Social media starts playing a major role in order to socialize with interests in more adventurous and funny content.
Fashion	The fashion interest is more sports driven. The age group is physically underdeveloped and aspires to be taller/muscular. They aspire to look older and therefore emulate their favourite sports stars. They are not bothered by fashion as they are unsure of what would suit them in terms of colours and body type.	Fashion and experimenting with looks begin to interest them. The body transitions make them feel more self-assured. Occasions to go out and explore arise, and thus, fashion helps create an identity and feel inclusive.
Demands	For younger teens, comfort is non-negotiable. They are more inclined towards sports and therefore unconcerned about looks.	The older teens would trade comfort for a proper fit. Trade-offs between semi-formal/smart casual are made in order to attract the opposite sex or to settle in with the group of friends.
Fashion inspiration	Influenced by sports stars, young movie actors, and singers, such as Virat Kohli and Tom Holland.	Influencer group expands to include more style-based icons, such as Zayn Malik and Harry Styles.
Shopping apps	Very low use of shopping apps. May browse occasionally in search of particular shoes. Seeks approval of parents to make a purchase if the right product is found.	More into browsing on apps such as Amazon and Myntra. Takes purchasing power into their hands if the product is within their budget, otherwise convinces siblings/parents to buy for them.
Brands	Brand understanding is tenuous. They seek comfort over brands. Parents and older cousins/siblings are key sources of information; therefore, the choices are influenced by them instead of peers.	Connects with brands in order to gain a sense of class, status, and identity. Influenced by celebrities and peers in making purchasing decisions about brand choices.

Style Gaps:
Issue: Taste matures fast but retains some childhood elements. Therefore, toggling between child and adult styles creates confusion. The brands with the right sizes usually end up not being able to cater to the trend.

Current workaround: Try both adults' and kids' sections to find the appropriate style.

Culture Clashes:
Issue: Convincing mothers to accept more modern styles in smaller towns or conservative families. The generation gap makes the choices made by the teens difficult to accept for the parents.

Current workaround: Educating mothers about the changing trends and styles. Gives decision-making to mothers on traditional outfits.

Pain points

Finding the balance between comfort and fit:
Issue: They are constantly playing sports and involved in other activities; therefore, the body keeps changing. A good fit is therefore that which is closest to current fashion. They are unsure of colours, styles, and what works on their changing body types.

Current workaround: They tend to buy clothes that are a size larger to make do with the outfit or completely rely on the choice of their parents.

No say in buying decision-making:
Buying decisions rely on parents, while teens have no say in them. With little pocket money, they would rather spend it on food than clothes. Buying decisions shift from mothers for boys aged 12–14 to fathers for boys aged 15 and above with changes in dynamics and ease of communication.

Competitive brand analysis and gap mapping

Customer profile

The analysis helped study the customer profile in order to cater to the segment better. The age group includes 13–19-year-old girls and boys with 'student' as a profession. The style revolves around streetwear, casual wear, Y2K, and sporty. The fashion role models for this age group are celebrities, including Khushi Kapoor, Ananya Pandey, and Justin Bieber, and influencers, such as Komal Pandey. The post-pandemic hobbies revolve around consuming internet content, such as television series (*Euphoria, Emily in Paris*, and K-Dramas) and K-pop music. The consuming habits include shopping once or twice a month accompanied by and taking parents' approval for ages up to 15 years, or e-commerce platforms and Instagram stores offering COD options with peer group approvals for the age group beyond 15.

Brands catering to the Indian teen market

The Indian teen market is very niche and has a limited number of brands that cater to the segment (Figure 6). The brands are divided into established and emerging brands. The established brands are further divided into pocket-friendly and expensive brands. Established brands are those that hold credibility in the Indian market and are widely accepted by teens, whereas pocket-friendly brands include those that are budget-friendly for teens' spending power. Emerging brands include brands that are tapping into the Indian teen-specific market. The brands fit the criteria for affordability and trend savvy.

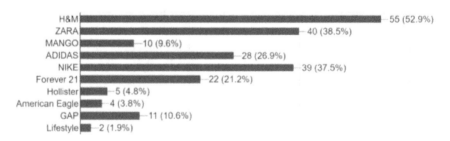

Figure 6. Brands preferred by teens.

Established Brands: Pocket-friendly brands such as Urbanic, H&M (Divided), Forever 21, Aeropostale, UCB, and American Eagle. Expensive brands such as Nike, Zara, Mango Teens, Tommy Hilfiger, Hollister, Superdry, Abercrombie & Fitch, and Gap.

Emerging Brands: Freakins, Burger Bae, Bonkers, BlueBrew, HerSheInbox, Off Duty, Nomad, and Madish.

Learnings and Suggestions

There is a need for a special platform that addresses the needs of teenagers, as they have a different set of needs compared to the mainstream audience.

Beginner mindset: They are beginners in fashion and online shopping and hence have special needs. The target segment would therefore be a 12–16-year-old mindset since they are in a transitional phase and do not readily find styles and sizes for themselves.

Different aesthetic/fashion needs: Their tastes are informed by the fact that they are on the cusp of childhood and adulthood: designs, ensembles, and accessories they want are slightly different.

Different purchase dynamics: They make associative purchases with parents or siblings.

The range of merchandise for boys revolves around athleisure and is sports-driven, while for girls, the range revolves around specific aesthetic-based styles. While boys radiate towards athletic brands, such as Nike, Adidas, and HRX, girls radiate towards brands such as H&M, Zara, and Shein.

The teen segment gravitates towards ease of navigation of products; therefore, the use of simple and efficient filters and search bars with appropriate tagging for age groups is important, as is the use of visual and icon-driven navigation.

Those in the age group of 12–16 are inquisitive and therefore seek knowledge. They love to experiment and mix and match in order to find their own sense of style. They are therefore building and learning about ensembles. Providing them with knowledge alongside the options to purchase makes their purchasing decisions easier.

A strong communication method, prominently through social media platforms such as Instagram and influencer marketing, is needed to push forward teen stores and highlight their presence to the target audience.

Through the study and gap analysis, it is observed that there is an opportunity for e-commerce platforms to have a separate store or category to cater to teenagers.

A teen store with styling tips and fashionable lookbooks would be a shopping heaven for Gen-Z shoppers to cater to their specific fashion and style needs and to offer unique and absorbing experiences to this customer cohort. This platform needs to have a different vibe. It should be a young and playful store.

Conclusion

The study reveals the way teenagers think and behave when shopping online. In the online shopping platforms, a digital market is presented before them in place of a real market. They do not make impulsive purchases; rather, their decisions are affected by a number of reasons. Their buying decision-making is therefore influenced by one major factor: the ease of navigation. Teenagers in today's time want quick responses to their problems and therefore switch between different e-commerce platforms that cater to their requirements. The study has proved that if these factors are not considered seriously by a company, they may decide to look for alternatives. The study analyzed the gaps in the market for the teenage segment after careful analysis of their requirements and brand choices that cater to the segment.

Although some will argue that tailoring e-commerce sites to attract the teen market isn't as valuable because teens don't have direct buying power when it comes to online shopping, they are nonetheless extremely influential when it comes to the consumption patterns of their parents.

References

Amato-McCoy, D. M. (2017, October 15). Study: Teens twice as likely to shop online than adults. Retrieved from https://chainstoreage.com/technology/study-teens-twice-likely-shop-online-adults.

Bloomenthal, A. (2021, September 16). Electronic Commerce (Ecommerce). Retrieved from https://www.investopedia.com/terms/e/ecommerce.asp.

Brooke, E. (2018, September 24). Teen shopping habits, explained by teens. Retrieved from https://www.vox.com/the-goods/2018/9/24/17861398/gen-z-shopping-habits-juul-glossier.

IBEF. (2022, April). E-Commerce Industry in India. Retrieved from https://www.ibef.org/industry/ecommerce#:~:text=In%202022%2C%20the%20Indian%20e,in%20internet%20and%20smartphone%20penetration.

Kaplan, M. (2013, June 13). Teenage Online Shopping Trends. Retrieved from https://www.practicalecommerce.com/Teenage-Online-Shopping-Trends.

Kaplan, M. (2017, May 11). Teen Shopping Habits and Trends. Retrieved from https://www.practicalecommerce.com/teen-shopping-habits-and-trends.

© 2025 World Scientific Publishing Company
https://doi.org/10.1142/9789811292101_0016

Chapter 16

Revamping Hospitality and Tourism: A Review of Service Quality Perceptions Post-COVID-19

Chahat Jain[*,‡], Pallavi (Joshi) Kapooria[†,§], and Saurabh Singh[†,¶]

[*]*Indian Institute of Management, Indore, Madhya Pradesh, India*

[†]*Prestige Institute of Management and Research, Indore, Madhya Pradesh, India*

[‡]*chahatmjain@gmail.com*

[§]*pallavi_kapooria@pimrindore.ac.in*

[¶]*saurabh_singh@pimrindore.ac.in*

Abstract

While COVID-19 has brought the hospitality industry to a halt, the industry's unwavering efforts to introduce technical advances and new safety standards will ensure that it bounces back with greater vigour as it emerges from the crisis. The anticipated growth from the optimistic travel and hospitality sectors has turned downwards due to the outbreak of COVID-19. The pandemic has enforced border restrictions, and travel bans across the globe have thwarted the sector. Hospitality is a people-based sector and has hence been affected the worst (Hoisington, 2020). The tourism and hotel industries are globally affected by the COVID-19 crisis, especially in countries with low incomes (Oh, 1999). At times like this, the sustainability and growth of the tourism and hospitality industries are challenging. Thus, it becomes crucial for brands to know which service quality dimension is most important to customers. The current chapter is based on a conceptual framework drawn from the SERVQUAL model and Kotler's layers of products and services. This study is an in-depth review of the research done on service quality dimensions in the hotel industry, and it suggests the probable shift of customer focus across these dimensions post-COVID-19. The study aims to assess customer needs from the perspective of different layers of services and describes how brands can change their outlook on the way these services are perceived and delivered in post-COVID-19 times so as to effectively revamp the business. In light of customers' shift in their service quality needs, the chapter highlights the opportunities for the emerging concept of homestays and also suggests that research on the concept of homestay, considering its huge relevance in post-COVID-19 times, is very limited and can be explored through empirical studies of different stakeholders.

Keywords: Homestay, hospitality, service quality, SERVQUAL, tourism.

Introduction

COVID-19 has brought the hospitality industry to a halt; however, the persistent efforts of the entire industry to leap back with technological innovation, government support, safety, and sanitization will lead it out of the crisis. Hospitality and tourism are crucial components of the economy for employment generation and revenue generation from foreign exchange. The ARR of the hotel industry in India stood at Rs. 5,844.81 in FY 2019 as against Rs. 5,527 in FY 2016 and is expected to reach Rs. 6,707.46 by FY 2024, expanding at a compound annual growth rate (CAGR) of 3.16% during the FY 2020–FY 2024 period (Bateson, 1977). The travel, tourism, and hospitality sector created 330 million jobs in 2019 across the world, i.e., one in every 10 jobs that were generated. The expected growth from the promising travel and hospitality sector has turned downwards due to the outbreak of COVID-19. The imposed border restrictions and travel bans continue to negatively affect the sector. The hospitality industry, being a people-based industry, is critically affected (Hoisington, 2020). The tourism and hotel industries are globally affected by the COVID-19 crisis, with countries with low incomes being severely affected (Oh, 1999). On the upside, authorities began to focus on the largely untapped domestic tourism market once again, which provided some short-term relief to 2020's tourism receipts. With unemployment rates skyrocketing across the board, over the short-to-medium term, domestic tourism-related activities will likely be minimal. The industry is perilously looking forward to government support to sustain and recover in the upcoming few years. The government is making continuous efforts to boost the travel industry. For the survival and growth of the business, it is essential to attract and retain customers. To achieve that, it's vital to have high customer satisfaction (Coyles and Gokey, 2002; Hung *et al.*, 2003; Rao and Kelkar, 1997). Multiple studies have proved that hotel service quality is certainly an important predictor of customer satisfaction. Thus, for higher customer satisfaction, it's important to have an unswerving level of service quality in terms of service production and delivery (Venkateswarlu and Babu, 2016; Marković and Raspor, 2013; Oh, 1999; Pisnik and Milfelner, 2009). Thus, it becomes crucial for service providers to know which service quality dimensions are significant for customers.

Impact of pandemic on hotel industry

Following the COVID-19 pandemic, the hospitality industry is facing unique challenges. Lockdowns, stay-at-home orders, travel bans, and social distancing are crucial to reducing COVID-19 infections; however, these have resulted in an economic slowdown, a significant drop in demand for the travel and hospitality businesses, and the temporary closing of several hospitality establishments (Bartik *et al.*, 2020). All restaurants had to close their dining services, and their operations were limited to deliveries and takeaways. The travel bans and lockdowns drove a sudden drop in hotel stays and occupancy that led to millions of job losses. According to the Federation of Associations in Indian Tourism and Hospitality, the Indian tourism industry could experience 38 million job losses, which is approximately 70% of its total workforce, due to COVID-19. Due to the pandemic, up to three-quarters of India's hospitality and tourism sector suffered financial distress, which is estimated to be as much as Rs. 15 lakh crore. According to the Travel and Tourism Association of Goa, the state will lose over Rs. 1,000 crore (Rs. 10 billion) and approximately 60,000–75,000 lost their jobs due to COVID-19. As of March 23, 2020, Kerala reported that its 7,022 hotels and homestays had remained closed.

Government initiatives

With the introduction of a few initiatives, such as the Pilgrimage, Rejuvenation and Spiritual Augmentation Drive (PRASAD), Swadesh Darshan schemes, Bharat Parv, and Dekho Apna Desh, the Ministry of Tourism has been promoting Indian tourism. Dekho Apna Desh is hailed as one of the best campaigns to attract and engage all Indians across the world. India's hotel sector is attracting significant investment from international hotel brands looking to expand across the country, especially in tier II and tier III cities. A report from the Federation of Indian Chambers of Commerce & Industry (FICCI) suggested that the government should encourage domestic and foreign investments to reinvigorate the travel industry. The report also suggested that the government should allow 100% foreign direct investment (FDI) in the industry for its revival. Also, several initiatives to develop key tourist areas and transport links will continue to fuel growth in this sector.

The New Normal: Hospitality Industry Revamping for Their Survival

Due to COVID-19, cleanliness and hygiene in hotels have gained significance due to the fact that infections can spread by merely touching surfaces carrying the virus (WHO, 2020). Another way of virus transmission is through aerosols that could be produced by central ACs (Zhang *et al.*, 2020). So, it is important to place AC ducts in hotels in such a way that the guests are not exposed to direct air flow (Diwan, 2020). In the post-COVID-19 period, it is essential to screen guests and staff using thermal imagers on a regular basis (Kachru, 2020). Studies have indicated that visible safety and sanitization protocols including sanitization at entry points, social distancing, frequent cleaning of high-touch points, and well-trained staff in COVID-19 protocols are a few significant safety measures customers expect from a hotel (Gursoy *et al.*, 2020). To revamp the industry, FICCI and OYO collaborated to develop and design online certification courses and training for hotel staff and owners. The purpose of this course is to guide owners and professionals in maintaining and implementing high standards of safety, hygiene, sanitation, and operational effectiveness (Zhang *et al.*, 2020).

Concept of Services

Services are often described with unique characteristics, such as heterogeneity, intangibility, perishability, and inseparability (Bateson, 1977; Gronroos, 1990; Zeithaml and Bitner, 1996). Quality is often defined as satisfying customers' requirements (Ghobadian et al., 1994). Until the early 1980s, the main focus of research was on the physical attributes of products and their quality. However, since mid-1980, researchers have been conducting studies on service features and service quality attributes (Chase, 1998). Parasuraman et al. (1985) defined service quality as the gap between customers' expectations and perceptions of quality. A few of the factors affecting customer expectations are brand image, previous experience, and the price of the service (Gronroos, 1984; Johnston and Heineke, 1998). Service quality is mainly centred on service delivery with respect to customers' needs and expectations (Lewis et al., 1994). Various studies have confirmed that hotel service quality is certainly an important predictor of customer satisfaction (Coyles and Gokey, 2002; Hung et al., 2003; Rao and Kelkar, 1997; Lee et al., 2000). Moreover, there is a correlation between service quality, customer satisfaction, and stay intention (Lee et al., 2001). Hence, it is significant for hoteliers to know important service quality dimensions. True service quality cannot be produced except when it is measured; therefore, it's crucial to measure service quality (Souca, 2011). The nature of service is complex, and hence the evaluation and measurement of service quality become much more complex (Souca, 2011).

Concept of service quality dimensions

The most prevalent model to measure customer satisfaction is the SERVQUAL model. This model was developed by Parasuraman et al. (1985). SERVQAL is considered a multidimensional study (Brogowicz et al., 1990; Ekinci, 2002). Since its development, it has been widely applied in diverse kinds of businesses to measure service quality (Buttle, 1996). The SERVQUAL model is generally applied to evaluate the gap between customers' and service providers' expectations and perceptions. This approach facilitates evaluating the gap in exceptions and perceptions while highlighting service quality and the service delivery gap

(Mangold and Emin, 1991). SERVQUAL is produced to reveal various aspects of business service quality and its strengths and weaknesses (Tan and Pawitra, 2001). Initially, when Parasuraman et al. developed SERVQUAL, it had ten dimensions:

1. Reliability
2. Responsiveness
3. Competence
4. Access
5. Courtesy
6. Communication
7. Credibility
8. Security
9. Understanding/knowing the customer
10. Tangibles.

Then, Parasuraman et al. (1988), assorted them into five unique dimensions:

1. Reliability
2. Assurance
3. Tangibles
4. Empathy
5. Responsiveness.

SERVQUAL is also known as RATER. Service quality is considered low when customer expectations exceed their perceptions of experienced service delivery. The SERVQUAL scale is created in the structure of a survey comprising 22 service traits, assorted into the five service quality dimensions, related to customers' perceptions and expectations of services (Parasuraman et al., 1988). Marković and Raspor (2013) pointed out that important perceived service quality dimensions are reliability, empathy and competence of staff, accessibility, and tangibles. Fah and Kandasamy (2011) suggested that reliability, assurance, tangibility, and empathy influence customer satisfaction. The most important dimension is assurance. Assurance means guests should feel safe and secure in a hotel and the hotel staff should be knowledgeable and courteous (Wong et al., 1999). Kitapci et al. (2013) suggested that the four most important service quality dimensions are empathy, assurance, responsiveness, and tangibility. These dimensions influence satisfaction, and the results of customer satisfaction are revisitation and positive word-of-mouth marketing (WOM) (Sandeep and Ruchika, 2019). The key to promoting the hotel industry in these tough times of COVID-19 is assurance about the safety of guests and proper sanitization (Diwan, 2020). The service quality in the hospitality industry should be reviewed and revised as per customers' expectations, as their needs tend to change as per the environment (Prakash and Jhawar 2018). The COVID-19 pandemic has led travellers to feel fear, worry, and anxiety. Hence, it has become more crucial to show empathy (Jiang, 2019). Due to the pandemic, travellers will most likely prefer hotels that reassure hygienic and clean accommodations and services (Jiang and Wen, 2020).

The five product levels developed by Philip Kotler in his book, *Marketing Management*, provide insight into the different levels of products associated with consumer needs. At each product level, there is a value addition for the consumer.

The five product levels are:

1. **Core benefit**: The basic need or want of consumers that will be satisfied after the consumption of the product or service.
2. **Generic product**: A version of the product comprising solely those features or attributes necessary for it to function.
3. **Expected product**: The set of features or attributes that consumers usually expect and agree to when they buy a product.
4. **Augmented product**: Any additional feature, attribute or product variations, and services that aid the product/service in differentiating itself from its competitors.
5. **Potential product**: All developments, transformations, and augmentations a product might undergo in the future. This will aid growth and customer loyalty and will delight customers in the long run.

Hotel industry's perspective before COVID-19

The core objective of a hotel is to provide a bed to relax or sleep in. In a generic product, a hotel has to provide a bed, a bathroom, a towel, and a wardrobe. In the expected product, this would include a clean room, clean bedsheets and towels, and a clean bathroom. The augmented product would include the facilities of toiletry kits, complimentary breakfast, and tea or coffee. The potential product level includes providing virtual check-in and complimentary gifts. The focus of travellers is now on hygiene, cleanliness, and sanitization. Hygiene is going to be a must-have for travellers. Corporates, when selecting a hotel, want to make sure that is meets the highest standards of safety. Hotels will have to assure guests of their safety (Lau, 2020).

Hotel industry's perspective after COVID-19

This pandemic has forced every sector to make drastic changes and adapt to the situation. In the hotel industry, the core objective has been changed to providing a clean bed, sanitization, and safety. In the expected product, this would include high-speed internet services, as COVID-19 has made virtual meetings and offices the new normal. The potential product level would include contactless services and more innovative services. The importance of the model is that it will aid service providers in understanding their customers' needs and wants and in providing a competitive edge.

Technology as a survival tool

Prakash and Jhawar (2018) suggested that, for the survival and growth of the hotel industry, it's essential to adopt the latest technology. To revamp this worst-hit industry, it has become important to adapt and develop new technologies and equipment to protect the staff and guests from infection (Lau, 2020; Davahli et al., 2020). Before COVID-19, person-to-person contact was appreciated, but post-COVID-19, scenarios have changed. Contactless service and high standards of hygiene are a few must-haves for hotel guests (Lau, 2020). Innovative solutions such as antibacterial doorknobs and automated check-ins will be embraced by customers; artificial intelligence can be adopted by hotels for complete cleaning and sanitization tasks. This will lead to more contactless services and fewer chances of virus transmission (Huang and Rust, 2018). Automated check-ins can decrease human contact chances and avoid crowds in the lobby. Virtual menus and paperless or online payment systems can decrease human touch points and enhance the service quality experience. For guests to access the premises and hotel rooms, hotels can think of facial recognition or QR code scans as a potential contactless technology. Voice-activated virtual assistants, such as Google Home and Amazon Echo, can be used by guests to turn lights on or off, set the preferred room temperature, etc., within their rooms.

Homestays as an emerging trend and preference post-COVID-19

Homestays provide a good opportunity for budget travellers and allow them to explore local tastes with a homely feel and care. After analyzing the humongous opportunity in India, branded hospitality chains, such as OYO Rooms, Airbnb, and Mahindra Holidays, started homestays (Sandeep and Ruchika, 2019). According to the tourism department, until 31 December 2019, the total number of homestays in Himachal Pradesh was 2,189. The little tribal district of Lahaul-Spiti received a huge response in preference of homestays. Currently, it has 258 homestays. This also indicates that today's visitors prefer to explore destinations away from the hustle and bustle of the city and stay at places which are more local, cultural, and homely. Homestays are taking precautionary measures for the safety of guests. To ensure safety, a few homestays had made RT-PCR COVID-19 testing mandatory for their staff as well as guests.

Academic and Managerial Implications

The impact of this crisis had unfavourable effects on staff, operations, and customers. Hence, using prior theoretical and conceptual frameworks may help future research. Due to the impact of COVID-19, it is important to provide a new perspective and insights that can aid the industry in the transformation of services and operations due to the shift in customers' needs and wants. This study widens the scope of new research on concepts, strategies, models, and approaches that contribute to the sustainability and growth of the hospitality industry in the era of COVID-19. This study offers a sound conceptual contribution yet with practical implications for the hospitality industry in light of COVID-19.

Conclusion

The study concludes that empathy and assurance are the most important service dimensions perceived by customers. The study also sheds light on the layers of product sanitization and safety as expected products and AI and robotics as augmented products. Additionally, in a health crisis such as COVID-19, the fear of infection can be a major issue; a virus can be transmitted not only between guests and hotel staff but also between guests themselves. With this concern, homestays become relatively safe due to smaller number of guests and staff (Jiang and Wen, 2020). With customers' shift in their service quality needs, the chapter highlights the emerging scope of homestays. Furthermore, it suggests that the research on homestays, considering their enormous importance in post-COVID-19 times, is limited and can be explored through empirical studies of various stakeholders. This research can be useful for hoteliers in understanding customer needs and expectations. This study will help the owners of hotels improve service quality. Knowing the important service quality dimensions can help hotel owners and managers more effectively allocate resources. Furthermore, this research has great importance in this period of global crisis for one of the worst-hit industries, i.e., the hotel industry. This study opens up an opportunity for further research on the enormous potential for homestays after COVID-19, as they offer the dimensions of assurance and empathy. Other research areas can be on the application of machine learning and AI in the hospitality industry for its recovery and resilience. Hence, in the upcoming research, we propose to take up an empirical analysis of the post-COVID-19 impact on customers' perceptions of homestay preferences.

References

Bateson, J. E. G. (1977). Do we need service marketing? In *Marketing Consumer Services: New Insights*. Marketing Science Institute, Cambridge, MA.

Coyles, S., and Gokey, T. C. (2002). Customer retention is not enough. *The McKinsey Quarterly*, 2, 80–89.

Diwan, G. A. (2020). Sanitization and safety will be key to promote industry post Covid19. Business World. Retrieved from https://search.proquest.com/magazines/sanitization-safety-will-be-key-promote-industry/docview/2393632321/se-2?accountid=49670.

Fah, L. K., and Kandasamy, S. (2011). An investigation of service quality and customer satisfaction among hotels in Langkawi. In *Proceedings of International Conference on Management (ICM 2011)*, Penang, Malaysia, pp. 731–749.

Gronroos, C. (1990). *Service Management and Marketing: Managing the Moments of Truth in Service Competition*. Lexington Books, Lexington, MA.

Hoisington, A. (2020). 5 insights about how the COVID-19 pandemic will affect hotels. Available at: https://www.hotelmanagement.net/own/roundup-5-insights-about-how-covid-19-pandemic-will-affect-hotels.

Huang, M., and Rust, R. T. (2018). Artificial intelligence in service. *Journal of Service Research*, 21(2), 155–172.

Hung, Y. H., Huang, M. L., and Chen, K. S. (2003). Service quality evaluation by service quality performance matrix. *Total Quality Management and Business Excellence*, 14(1), 78–88.

Jiang, Y. (2019). A cognitive appraisal process of customer delight: The moderating effect of place identity. *Journal of Travel Research*, 59(6), 1029–1043. doi: 10.1177/0047287519872827.

Jiang, Y., and Wen, J. (2020). Effects of COVID-19 on hotel marketing and management: A perspective article. *International Journal of Contemporary Hospitality Management*, 32(8), 2563–2573. http://dx.doi.org/10.1108/IJCHM-03-2020-0237.

Marković, S., and Janković, S. R. (2013). Exploring the relationship between service quality and customer satisfaction in Croatian hotel industry. *Tourism and Hospitality Management*, 19(2), 149–164.

Oh, H. (1999). Service quality, customer satisfaction and customer value: A holistic perspective. *International Journal of Hospitality Management*, 18, 67–82.

Pandey, D., and Joshi, P. R. (2010). Service quality and customer behavioral intentions: A study in the hotel industry. *California Journal of Operations Management*, 8(2), 72–81.

Parasuraman, A., Zeithaml, V. A., and Berry, L. L. (1985). A conceptual model of service quality and its implication. *Journal of Marketing*, 49(Fall), 41–50.

Parasuraman, A., Zeithaml, V. A., and Berry, L. L. (1986). SERVQUAL: A multiple-item scale for measuring customer perceptions of service quality. Report No. 86-108, Marketing Science Institute, Cambridge, MA.

Parasuraman, A., Zeithaml, V. A., and Berry, L. L. (1988). SERVQUAL: A multi-item scale for measuring consumer perceptions of the service quality. *Journal of Retailing*, 64(1), 12–40.

Parasuraman, A., Zeithaml, V. A., and Berry, L. L. (1991). Refinement and reassessment of the SERVQUAL scale. *Journal of Retailing*, 67, 420–450.

Parasuraman, A., Zeithaml, V. A., and Berry, L. L. (1993). Research note: More on improving service quality measurement. *Journal of Retailing*, 69(1), 140–147.

Parasuraman, A., Zeithaml, V. A., and Berry, L. L. (1994). Reassessment of expectations as a comparison standard in measuring service quality: Implications for future research. *Journal of Marketing*, 58, 111–124.

Pisnik Korda, A., and Milfelner, B. (2009). The importance of perceived value in evaluating hotel guest satisfaction: The case of Slovenia. *Acta turistica*, 21(1), 73–94.

Rao, C. P., and Kelkar, M. M. (1997). Relative impact of performance and importance ratings on measurement of service quality. *Journal of Professional Services Marketing*, 15(2), 69–86.

Venkateswarlu, G., and Babu, K. J. (2016). The role of service quality variables in tourism industry. *KIMI Hospitality Research Journal*, 1(1), 1–4. Retrieved from https://search.proquest.com/scholarly-journals/role-service-quality-variables-tourism-industry/docview/2356794716/se-2?accountid=49670.

Zeithaml, V. A., and Bitner, M. J. (1996). *Services Marketing*. McGraw-Hill, New York, NY.

Zhang, S., Diao, M., Yu, W., Pei, L., Lin, Z., and Chen, D. (2020). Estimation of the reproductive number of novel coronavirus (COVID-19) and the probable outbreak size on the Diamond Princess cruise ship: A data-driven analysis. *International Journal of Infectious Diseases*, 93, 201–204.

Chapter 17

Sustainable Development through Green Marketing: Application and Its Environmental Importance

Pavnesh Kumar* and Ravindra Kumar†

*Department of Management Sciences,
Pandit Madan Mohan Malaviya School of
Commerce & Management Sciences,
Mahatma Gandhi Central University,
Motihari, Bihar, India*
*dr.pavnesh@gmail.com
†ravindra2019bbau@gmail.com

Abstract

The approach to sustainable development through green marketing focuses on the systematic and scientific study of making products and services for the betterment of the whole of humankind and the environment. The boom in environmental marketing has meant more scrutiny of multinational companies looking to differentiate themselves. No longer limited to ecolabels and recycled packaging, green marketers have been forced to raise their game in transparent and creative ways. The modern corporate world has focused on eco-innovation and actual corporate responsibility commitments to enhance their environmentally friendly policies. According to **Mahatma Gandhi, 'Earth provides enough to**

satisfy every man's need but not any man's greed.' We observe that environmental concerns manifest in many actions on the planet. A proper survey in 2008 indicated that 58% of US consumers try to save electricity at home, 46% recycle newspapers, 45% return bottles or cans, and 23% buy products made from or packed in recycled materials, while people's responses vary in their own nature of environmental sensitivity in the modern era. We observed that human overpopulation, hydrology, intensive farming, land use, natural disasters, water pollution, and nuclear issues are some of the urgent issues of sustainable development that we must focus on through the green marketing approach in the modern corporate world.

Keywords: Sustainable development, green marketing, corporate world, eco-friendly.

Introduction

Sustainable development through green marketing is the need of the time to beautify the environment on Earth. The planet's raw materials consist of the infinite, the finite renewables, and the finite nonrenewables. Finite nonrenewable resources — oil, coal, platinum, zinc, and silver — pose particularly serious problems as the point of deflation approaches, while firms making products that require these increasingly scarce minerals face substantial cost increases. Conversely, firms engaged in research and development have an excellent opportunity to develop substitute materials.

According to Polonsky, 'green marketing as all activities designed to generate and facilitate any exchanges intended to satisfy human needs or wants , such that the satisfaction of these needs and wants occurs with minimal detrimental impact on the natural environment.'

According to Philip Kotler, 'marketing is a term that originate with the evaluation of the needs & terminates with the satisfaction of the needs with supply of products at right time, right place & acceptable price.'

Thus, we can say that green marketing is a systematic and scientific process of making products and services for the betterment of the whole of humankind and the environment. Green marketing includes a broad range of activities, including product modifications, changes to the production process, packaging changes, and modifying advertising. Green marketing consists of a holistic marketing concept where the production, marketing, consumption, and disposal of products and services happen in a systematic manner which is less detrimental to the environment while spreading awareness about global warming, the harmful impact of pollutants and nonbiodegradable solid wastes, etc.

According to Pride and Ferrell, 'Green marketing, also alternatively known as Environmental marketing and sustainable marketing refers to an organization's efforts for designing, promoting, pricing and distributing products that will not harmful for environment and whole of mankind.'

Review of Literature

Karna *et al.* (2003): To achieve eco-friendliness with competitive advantages, phenomena must be implemented in the global environmental market. Environmental marketing is totally focused and hypothesized on green values by implementing appropriate marketing strategies and must be logically connected.

Kaur *et al.* (2004): Environmental marketing includes logical and mandatory measures taken in the modern global world. All business firms must focus on eco-friendly activities by practising green marketing throughout the world via sustainable development policies. Green consumerism is critical for healthy environmental progress and corporate environmental benefits.

Ilangovan and Azhagaih (2006): This paper focuses on green marketing and the protection of environmental practices. Current green marketing practices are not sufficient for sustainable development, so the government must act as initiators in this area. The focus of corporate strategy must be based on consumer protection as well as green marketing, keeping in mind the welfare of the whole of humankind. The strategy of proactive marketing is very helpful for corporate marketing.

Dande and Brahma (2008): Green Ventures India is a subsidiary of the asset management firm Green Ventures International, based in New York. They announced a $300 million fund specifically for India, intended to facilitate carbon credit trading and renewable energy products.

Bearse (2009): This study focuses on sustainable development through green practices by following the leadership perspective for the welfare of consumers as well as producers. The corporate world is completely focused on modern marketing styles and strategies to go green. For competitive advantage, it is mandatory to follow the government's norms of go-green concepts.

Christian (2011): It is based on socioeconomic green material analysis in the global market. It identifies the implications for improving and developing green retail approaches in the corporate world. It describes the importance of promoting and offering the brand value of products for the benefit of consumers and provides a fundamental basis for green practices.

Teng *et al.* (2011): This study focuses on consumer benefits from purchasing green materials and food items for the welfare of socioeconomic development in Malaysia. This study mainly focused on the theory of planned consumer behaviour. It also provides insight into the green practices that offer benefits to consumers while meeting their needs and demands in Malaysia.

Nitin (2011): This paper focuses on consumer awareness of using cars which are environmentally friendly in nature in the state of Maharashtra in India. The study indicates the awareness of the use of environment-friendly cars and other green automobiles, which are promoted with the help of the central and state governments' rules and regulations in India. It is based on sustainable development through green marketing practices.

CSR strategy preview — For top trends (2016): In light of the ambitious climate change targets set in the Paris Agreement, discussions about supply chain management, ethical corporations, and investment disinvestment become very relevant for the protection of the environment in the modern era. Ten years ago, Hollywood launched several green campaigns, including the 'Go Green' campaign and Earth Day. According to the Worldwide Science report, solid waste amounted to 1,744,700 pounds, wastewater reached 13,413,923 gallons, greenhouse gases totaled 4,331,760 pounds, and the production of recycled paper for printing consumed 2,250 tons of trees. The green theme of the 2009 Vanity Fair issue aimed to raise awareness about eco-friendly business practices.

Objective

The current study focuses on the following aspects:

- to focus on sustainable development through green marketing;
- to reduce the global warming of the Earth;
- to establish a healthy environment through green marketing.

Methodology

Green marketing aims to establish an environment where humankind can live their lives with happiness, enjoy full and healthy lives, and live in an eco-friendly manner forever. This chapter is based on a number of relevant literature reviews and their applicable outcomes. This literature review constitutes a qualitative approach. The analysis carried out in this study is based on secondary data. To spread these messages and raise awareness about the effects of green marketing, we have taken the help of newspapers, magazines, journals, the internet, books, seminars, and conferences to facilitate a healthy discussion and analysis through this study. We know that global warming is the biggest issue threatening human existence on planet Earth in the modern era. Hence, people should be aware and make Earth a better place for humankind and other species of nature through harmonious coexistence.

Conceptual framework

Green marketing is a systematic and scientific process of making products and services for the betterment of the environment and the whole of humankind.

Green marketing can be defined as 'a holistic & responsible strategic management process that identifies, anticipates, satisfies and fulfil stakeholders needs, for a responsible reward, that does not adversely affect human or natural environmental well-being' (Charter, 1992, p. 394).

According to Charter and Polonsky, 'Green Marketing is the marketing or promotion of the product based on its environmental performance or an improvement there off in very effective manner.'

Green marketing is not a simple task; it is challenging to meet the satisfaction of the needs, wants, and demands of customers through

Figure 1. Model of green marketing.

eco-friendly promotion, production, and advertising of products and services towards sustainable development through green marketing in the world (see Figure 1).

We focus on the effects of green marketing that are not harmful to our surroundings, i.e., the environment. We also believe that by reducing global warming, it will have a positive effect on the planet, contribute to the welfare of the whole of humankind, and provide betterment for a happy and joyous life journey.

Green marketing is crucial to maintain the environment of our surroundings for living in a way which gives us satisfactory and healthier and more pleasurable life globally and finally.

The green consumer

Consumers are the lifeblood of green marketing. Consumers who are aware of their surroundings and very conscious of using products which are good for the environment can be called 'green consumers.'

Typically, a green consumer is:

- inconsistent,
- generally a woman,
- a person who is likely to be more concerned about the environment, and
- aware of their surroundings.

Green marketing process

It is a systematic and scientific process of action. It focuses on an eco-friendly environment while also meeting the needs and wants of consumers. The green marketing process is such a platform to make the cycle of production and promotion of products in the modern era to make the Earth a green heaven to live in (see Figure 2).

Importance of green marketing

- Green marketing should be eco-friendly.
- Green marketing should follow the government's rules and regulations.

Figure 2.   Green marketing process.

- Green marketing should include corporate social responsibility.
- Green marketing should satisfy the needs, wants, and demands of customers.
- Green marketing should consider the cost factor associated with waste disposal or reductions in material usage, which force firms to modify their behaviour.
- Green marketing should be implemented to outperform competitors by becoming more eco-friendly (also see Figure 3 for more information).

The five S's of green marketing success are:
- satisfaction of stakeholders' needs,
- safety of products and processes,
- social and environmental-friendliness,
- sustainability of its activities,
- superior in meeting customers' needs and wants.

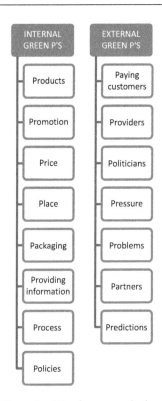

Figure 3. P's of green marketing.

The 5P's of green marketing are:
1. Promotion
2. Product
3. Price
4. Place
5. Packaging.

The first four components were introduced by McCarthy and are collectively called the 'marketing mix.'

In addition to the first four P's, one more 'P' known as 'packaging,' was added to the marketing mix by Khan (see Figure 4). Hence, the marketing mix with the 5 P's in the modern era is applicable to the field of green marketing mix.

1. **Products:** In the marketing mix, the first element is the product (see Figure 5). A product is anything that can be offered to the market for attention, acquisition, use, or consumption that can satisfy the needs, wants, and demands of the customers at acceptable prices.

   Products are of four types :
   - convenience products,
   - shopping products,

Figure 4. Diagrammatical presentation of marketing mix.

- speciality products,
- unsought products.
  ✓ Products made from recycled goods, such as Quick N Tuff housing materials made from recycled broccoli boxes.
  ✓ Products that can be recycled or reused.
  ✓ Products with green labels as long as offer substantiation.

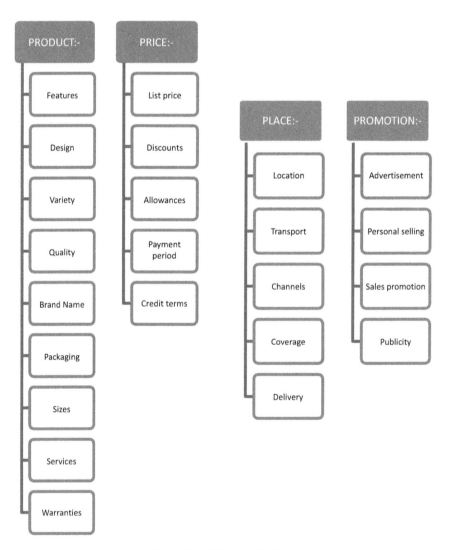

Figure 5. 4 P's of marketing.

2. **Price:** The second element is the price, which significantly affects the volume of sales. It is one of the biggest challenges to fix the prices of products which are acceptable to customers while being profitable to businessmen or entrepreneurs. Environmentally responsible products, however, are often less expensive when product life-cycle costs are taken into consideration.
3. **Place:** The place mix is the physical distribution of products at the right time and right place. It refers to finding out the selling sources (wholesalers, agents, and retailers), inventory control, storage facilities, warehousing, and transportation to provide products in a very easy way. It can be achieved through in-store promotions and using eco-friendly recycled materials.
4. **Promotion**: Promotion consists of the many activities undertaken by an enterprise to communicate and promote its products to the target market in an easy way. The different methods of promoting a product are through advertisement, personal selling representatives, sales promotion, and publicity to make customers aware and to satisfy marketing requirements.
5. **Packaging:** Packaging does the job of silent selling. It should be very attractive, safe, and eco-friendly. Good packaging is an indicator of quality, and maintaining the standards of products inspires customers by promoting sales in a scientific manner. Good packaging makes products more durable and effective.

Challenges in Green Marketing

Need for Standardization: We know that only 5–6% of marketing messages communicated through green campaigns are entirely true, and there is a lack of standardization to verify such claims. Currently, there are no standardizations in place to certify products as organic. A standard quality control board should be framed for such labelling and licencing in favour of the environment.

New Concepts: We should always try our best to introduce new concepts of green marketing for the betterment of customers and the environment. It should be very carefully done to promote the sale of products.

Avoiding Green Marketing Myopia: The first rule of green marketing is to focus on customer satisfaction at all levels of needs and wants.

Products should be eco-friendly but also highly beneficial to customers, offered at acceptable prices, and available at the right place and right time; otherwise, they will lose their market acceptability.

Golden Rules for Green Marketing for Sustainable Development

1. **Know Your Customers:** The customers should always be made aware of the products' benefits, and be provided with facilities. This should be taken seriously.
2. **Educating Your Customers:** Marketing people should always be aware of customers' needs and wants, informing them about the environmental impact of using green products.
3. **Being Genuine and Transparent:** The aims of marketing people should be genuine and transparent in preserving the environment while satisfying customers' demands. Marketing people should keep in mind their profits too.
4. **Giving Your Customers an Opportunity to Participate:** Customers are the backbone of a business. Hence, marketing people should take effective actions to provide customer satisfaction through eco-friendly measures.

Some Problems with Going Green

Although a large number of firms are using green marketing, there are a number of potential problems which need to be addressed:

- Clearly state the environmental benefits and customer benefits.
- Explain the environmental characteristics.
- Explain how benefits are achieved in an effective way.
- Devise strategies to outperform competitors while ensuring they are more eco-friendly.
- Use meaningful terms and pictures when labelling products.
- Follow government regulations, which should be designed to provide customer satisfaction.
- Develop guidelines to control environmental marketing messages and their truthfulness.

Conclusion

Sustainable development through green marketing is not simply one more approach to marketing but has to be pursued with much greater awareness for the betterment of the environment and for the whole of humankind globally. Therefore, it is crucial to establish a healthy environment on the planet through green marketing.

Green marketing promotes eco-friendly businesses and contributes to consumers' healthier and happier lives. We assumed that companies such as McDonald's, Nike, GE, and Dupont were successfully implementing and embracing sustainable development practices and achieving better greening of their surroundings through green marketing to reduce global warming of the planet. The government should promote practices such as greater recycling of newspapers, saving electricity, recycling waste, planting more trees on both sides of the roads in cities, constructing sewage treatment plants, and maintaining the cleanliness of rivers to focus on sustainable development through green marketing. It is a challenge to promote a better environment in the world effectively and globally. Finally, we conclude by saying that sustainable development through green marketing is the lifeblood for the betterment of the environment and the whole of humankind for their healthy, wealthy, and happy lives forever globally.

References

American Marketing Association (AMA). (2010). About AMA. History of the American Marketing Association. Retrieved 10 October 2010, from http://www.marketingpower.com/AboutAMA/Pages/History.aspx.

Azhagaiah, R., and Ilangovan, A. (2006). Green marketing and environmental protection. *Indian Journal of Marketing (IJM)*, 19–21. January 2006.

Bearse, S., Capozucca, P., Favret, L., and Lynch, B. (2009). Finding the green in today's shoppers sustainability trends and new shopper insights. Deloitte Development LLC.

Bowman, J. (2009, March). Green branding: Cashing in on the eco-market. *WIPO Magazine*. Retrieved from http://www.wipo.int/wipo_magazine/en/2009/02/article_0011.html.

Brunnermeier, S. B., and Cohen, M. A. (2003). Determinants of environmental innovation in US manufacturing industries. *Journal of Environmental Economics and Management*, 45(2), 278–293.

Fuentes, C. (2012). Green Marketing at the Store: The Socio-Material Life of a t-Shirt. Research in Service Studies Working Paper No 14, pp. 1–29.

Jain, S. K., and Kaur, G. (2004). Green marketing. An attitudinal & behavioural analysis of Indian consumers. *Global Business Review*, 5(2), 187–205.

Joshi, N., and Mishra, D. P. (2011). Environment friendly car: A study of consumer awareness with special reference to Maharashtra State. *Information Management and Business Review*, 2(2), 92–98. February 2011.

Karna, J., Hanson, E., and Juslin, H. (2003). Social responsibility in environmental marketing planning. *European Journal of Marketing*, 37(5/6), 848–873.

Kotler, P. *Marketing Management*. The Millennium Edition Prentice Hall of India Pvt. Ltd., New Delhi.

Teng, P. K., Rezai, G., Mohamed, Z., and Shamsudin, M. N. Consumers' intention to purchase green foods in Malaysia. *International Conference on Innovation, Management and Service*, Vol. 14.

Chapter 18

Effect of Subjective and Objective Knowledge on Consumers' Willingness to Purchase Health Insurance during COVID-19 Pandemic

Tanuj Mathur

Amity Business School, Amity University, Lucknow Campus, Uttar Pradesh, India

tanujmathur10@gmail.com

Abstract

Consumers' knowledge is suspected to play a key role in influencing their behaviour. The aim of this study is to investigate the impact of consumers' different types of knowledge on their willingness to purchase health insurance plans during the COVID-19 pandemic. For this, an empirical test is done using data from 203 consumer respondents collected online from various cities in India. A multiple regression technique was used to assess the impact of different knowledge types on consumers' willingness to purchase. The findings revealed that consumers' objective knowledge rather than subjective knowledge plays an important role in influencing their willingness to purchase health insurance plans during COVID-19 in India.

Keywords: Consumer knowledge, objective knowledge, subjective knowledge.

Introduction

The perceived risk and fear of the COVID-19 pandemic are extremely high. People are afraid of the fatal consequences of the pandemic, including losing their jobs, becoming severely ill, transmitting the disease to family or acquaintances, being a cause for others' deaths and suffering, bearing heavy medical bills, and general financial loss (Conway et al., 2020; Spitzmuller et al., 2020). Therefore, people search for products through which they could financially protect themselves from the economic burden arising out of the uncertainties of the COVID-19 pandemic. In this regard, 'health insurance' is identified as a viable mechanism to provide coverage for medical expenses in the case of health emergencies during the COVID-19 pandemic.

There has been considerable research examining consumer willingness to purchase health insurance in a variety of situations (Liu and Chen, 2002; Annear et al., 2011; Lim et al., 2007). However, to date, little research has examined the effect of objective and subjective knowledge on consumers' willingness to purchase health insurance during the COVID-19 pandemic.

The global health insurance industry has enjoyed decades of stable growth, even in times of previous global health crises, such as polio in 1952, Ebola in 2013, severe acute respiratory syndrome (SARS) in 2002, and swine flu in 2009. Worldwide, the health insurance industry has witnessed a steady growth in coverage, which increased at an approximate compound annual growth rate (CAGR) of 4.7% (Fior Markets, 2020). However, according to healthcare experts, the current global pandemic, which has spread to 221 countries, infected over 11.7 million people, and caused close to 2.6 million deaths since December 2019, is estimated to raise the subscription rate of health insurance plans.

In the past nine months, the Indian health insurance segment has registered a nearly 14.5% growth in premium collection (IRDA, 2021). According to insurance experts and executives, growth in insurers' premium income is an outcome of consumers' knowledge and favourable judgement about health insurance products in controlling their health-related expenses during the occurrence of any illness in times of pandemic. Given the novelty of the increase in health insurance premiums, the purpose of the current study is to delve deeper to understand consumers' knowledge levels and examine the effects of different knowledge types — objective and subjective — on consumers' willingness to purchase health insurance.

Background and Literature Review

Consumer knowledge: Objective and subjective knowledge

Researchers have considered consumer knowledge to be an important construct in understanding consumer behaviour. The way consumers gather and organize information and, ultimately, what products they purchase and use are significantly influenced by their level of knowledge. Besides knowledge effects on consumers' information search and analysis, studies have found the impact of knowledge level on quality judgements and price acceptance, as well as on the relative use of tangible and intangible product cues (Rao and Sieben, 1992; Rao and Monroe, 1988; Cordell, 1997).

Traditionally, consumer knowledge has been measured as a unidimensional construct, though recent studies have distinguished two components of consumer knowledge: objective and subjective knowledge. Objective knowledge is the accurate information about the product class stored in the consumers' long-term memory, whereas subjective knowledge is the consumers' perceptions of what or how much they know about the product class.

Objective knowledge is usually measured through an unbiased testing procedure, whereas subjective knowledge is self-assessed. In the past, researchers have supported the validity of both measures (Park and Lessig, 1981). While objective measures can best detect true knowledge, subjective measures may well define consumer strategies and heuristics because subjective measures are based on what consumers think they know. Although both measures closely correlate, their distinctiveness descends from their antecedents: objective knowledge relies largely on stored information on a product class, whereas subjective knowledge relies more on product-related experience (Park et al., 1994).

Several studies have compared the objective and subjective measures of consumer knowledge in various product settings and found contrasting differences between the two (Rudell, 1979). In one study, Brucks (1985) found that subjective knowledge influences information search strategies and showed that, with an increase in the level of subjective knowledge, there is an observable decrease in consumers' utilization of salespersons' recommendations. Also, studies have found that higher levels of objective knowledge are related to higher perceived importance and receptivity to newly acquired information.

Although it is clear from past studies that both objective and subjective knowledge have different effects on behaviours, such as information search and processing, several research issues remain. Little research has focused on the effects of objective and subjective knowledge constructs on consumers' willingness to purchase.

Hypothesis and Model Development

Knowledge about health insurance in particular plays a certain role in effectuating consumers' willingness to purchase health insurance. It makes sense to differentiate between 'subjective knowledge' and 'objective knowledge.' In a health insurance context, 'objective knowledge' can be defined as the real knowledge consumers have about the features, benefits, advantages, and processes of health insurance, while 'subjective knowledge' is what individuals think they know about these. By making this distinction, researchers can understand which form of knowledge plays a more important role in influencing consumers' willingness to purchase health insurance. In their study, Radecki and Jaccard (1995) noted that what consumers believe they know about a product should be some function of what they really do know. This means that when a consumer thinks that health insurance would cover post-operative medicine expenditures even after the patient's discharge, such belief formation should have taken place due to their factual understanding of the post-hospitalization coverage clause in their policy. Thus, there exists a certain possibility of a positive and significant relationship between objective and subjective knowledge. Contrastingly, studies by Bruck (1985), Alba and Hutchinson (2000), Park *et al*. (1995), and Carlson *et al*. (2009) have concluded that the correspondence between the constructs of subjective and objective knowledge is not high. In general, it occurs because consumers are overconfident about themselves; thus, their level of overall subjective knowledge exceeds their objective knowledge, expressed, for instance, as the percentage of correct responses to a list of factual knowledge questions. Further, findings about the comparison between the impact of knowledge types on behaviour are often contradictory, i.e., which is a better predictor of behaviour — subjective or objective knowledge. Nevertheless, studies by Feick *et al*. (1992), Pieniak *et al*. (2006), and Zang and Liu (2015) have found subjective knowledge to be the stronger motivator of behaviour than objective knowledge. In a similar vein, studies by House *et al*.

(2004), Park *et al.* (1994), Ellen (1994), and Guo and Meng (2008) also found subjective knowledge to positively predict consumers' willingness towards products. Nonetheless, the prior studies that compared the differential impact of knowledge type on behaviour have largely concentrated their attention on simple, low-risk products, which are less involving, unlike health insurance. Thus, the above factors prompted us to revisit this in the context of health insurance products, which are technically complex, more sophisticated, and demand greater consumer involvement. Therefore, we propose the following hypotheses:

H1: There is a modest relationship between objective and subjective knowledge with regard to health insurance products.

H2: There is a positive impact of objective and subjective knowledge on consumers' willingness to purchase health insurance.

H3: Objective knowledge, in comparison to subjective knowledge, is a stronger predictor of consumers' willingness to purchase health insurance.

Research Method

Data collection

The data were collected through an online survey, wherein a pretested, structured questionnaire was mailed to 3,000 respondents in India. The database used in the study consists of respondents who had previously invested in insurance schemes during the financial year 2019–2020. A total of 212 of 3,000 survey forms were returned, of which 203 were useful for the purpose of analysis. The response rate stood at 6.8%. The respondents were clearly informed in the mail that those who are not currently subscribed to any health insurance plan or do not possess any form of employer-based health insurance scheme will be allowed to participate in the survey. This is done to avoid bias and ensure parity among respondents. Age, gender, marital status, educational background, and respondents' residing location zone were selected as the demographic variables in the study. Further, it is worth noting that the respondent selection procedure and non-probability sampling measures did not result in statistically

Table 1. Descriptive details of sample.

Category	Mean/Percentage
Age	52.32
Education	
Undergraduate level	50.74%
Graduate level	49.26%
Gender	
Male	51.23%
Female	48.76%
Marital status	
Unmarried	48.28%
Married	51.72%
Income	
Less than Rs. 250,000	18.71%
Rs. 250,001 to Rs. 500,000	22.66%
Rs. 500,001 to Rs. 750,000	16.75%
Rs. 750,001 to Rs. 1,000,000	22.66%
Rs. 1,000,001 & above	19.21%
Number of observations	203

representative samples and thus restricted us from making any kind of generalization to the overall population. However, the sample covered a wide range of consumers from varied parts of the country. The sample characteristics are given in Table 1.

Measures development

The measurement scales and the items were borrowed from earlier studies and adopted herein for the purpose of the study. However, a minor modification in the items' wordings was made to better assess India's health insurance situation in times of COVID-19. *Subjective knowledge* about health insurance was assessed using three items developed by Pieniak *et al.* (2010). All the items in the scale were measured on a seven-point Likert scale ranging from 'totally disagree' (1) to 'totally agree' (7). Referring to Table 2, *Objective knowledge* about health insurance, in

Table 2. Correlation matrix.

	Objective knowledge	Subjective knowledge	Willingness to purchase health insurance
Objective knowledge	1.000		
Subjective knowledge	0.1623	1.000	
Willingness to purchase health insurance	0.312	0.170	1.000

general, was measured with seven true/false questions, in which the following five statements were true: (1) health insurance plan covers the expenses related to 24 hours of hospitalization from COVID-19 infection; (2) health insurance plan covers medicine expenses after hospital discharge; (3) health insurance covers ambulance expenses; (4) health insurance covers household expenses during COVID-19 illness; and (5) health insurance provides coverage against COVID-19 to all family members. Two of the statements were false, namely: (1) health insurance pays the full sum insured on insureds' death from COVID-19; and (2) health insurance takes care of the hospitalization expenses of any third person infected from COVID-19 by the insured. These questions were adapted from the studies of Pieniak *et al.* (2010), Zang *et al.* (2015), House *et al.* (2004), and Mishra and Kumar (2011), which were done in different contexts. We preferred not to include a 'don't know' answer, as it forces respondents to think and make up their minds about proposed statements. The 'correct answer' was given one point, and the sum of these points was used as a measure of objective knowledge. Thus, the computed score for the final objective knowledge measure ranged from 0 to 7. *Willingness to purchase* health insurance was measured by asking respondents how likely they are to purchase it based on their judgements about the evaluated object. A three-item scale was developed to assess the willingness of respondents to purchase health insurance. For this purpose, a seven-point Likert scale ranging from 'very less likely' (1) to 'very likely' (7) was used. The detailed scale items for the construct variables are provided in Table 3.

Results and Discussion

In this study, the mean of subjective knowledge is reported between 3.96 and 4.14 on the seven-point scale. The objective knowledge items obtained 54.68%, 52.22%, 48.77%, 50.74%, 57.14%, 49.26%, and 50.25% correct responses (Table 3). These results were found to be consistent with those of House et al. (2004). This indicates that, on average, respondents answered three-fourths of the questions correctly. The measure of objective knowledge moderately correlates ($r = 0.162$) with the measure of subjective knowledge (H1). This result indicates that a correspondence between the two types of knowledge exists but is not high, which corroborates the results of a previous study

Table 3. Descriptive mean of subjective knowledge items and percentage correct versus wrong answers on the objective knowledge items.

	Mean	Correct answer	% of correct response	% of wrong response
Subjective knowledge				
Compared with a common man I know a lot about health insurance	3.96	—	—	—
I know a lot about what coverages are provided by health insurance	4.14	—	—	—
People known to me consider me as a health insurance expert	4.07	—	—	—
Objective knowledge	—			
(1) health insurance plan covers the expenses related to 24 hours hospitalization from COVID-19 infection	—	True	54.68	45.32
(2) health insurance plan covers medicine expenses after the hospital discharge	—	True	52.22	47.78
(3) health insurance covers ambulance expense	—	True	48.77	51.23
(4) health insurance covers household expenses during COVID-19 illness	—	True	50.74	49.26
(5) health insurance provide coverage against COVID-19 to all family members	—	True	57.14	42.86
(6) health insurance pays full sum insured on insureds death from COVID-19	—	False	49.26	50.74
(7) health insurance takes care of the hospitalization expense of any third person infected from COVID-19 by the insured	—	False	50.25	49.75

Table 4. Result of multiple regression.

Variables	Model 1	Model II	Model III
Control variables			
Age	0.012 (0.007)	0.012 (0.008)*	0.012 (0.007)
Education	−0.046 (0.231)	−0.002 (0.239)	−0.012 (0.230)
Gender	−0.116 (0.232)	−0.089 (0.240)	−0.097 (0.230)
Marital status	0.144 (0.235)	0.153 (0.244)	0.191 (0.235)
Income	0.002 (0.083)	0.030 (0.087)	−0.014 (0.083)
Objective knowledge	0.596 (0.130)***		0.557 (0.130)***
Subjective knowledge		0.287 (0.116)**	0.210 (0.113)*
F statistics	4.11	1.58	4.06
P-value	0.000	0.154	0.000
Degrees of freedom	196	196	195
R-square	0.111	0.046	0.127

Note: * means significance level; ***$p < 0.001$, **$p < 0.05$, *$p < 0.10$; values in () represents standard errors.

(Alba and Hutchinson, 2000). Therefore, it is construed that what people think they know may not very strongly match what they actually know. The H2 examined found support in the study. It reflects that both objective (0.596, $p = 0.00$) and subjective knowledge (0.287, $p = 0.05$) do have a significant influence on consumers' willingness to purchase health insurance. Further, H3 also found support in the study. This indicates that, in comparison to subjective knowledge (0.210, $p = 0.10$), objective knowledge (0.557, $p = 0.00$) is a stronger predictor of consumers' willingness to purchase health insurance (Table 4). This result was contrary to the studies that compared the differential effects of each knowledge type on behaviour.

Conclusion

This study found many interesting findings by conducting an empirical study based on the data collected from India. In a similar vein to certain earlier findings (House et al., 2004; Pieniak et al., 2010), the current study shows that a moderate correspondence exists between consumers' subjective and objective knowledge. On the contrary, consumers' objective knowledge is found to have a stronger influence on their willingness to purchase health insurance than subjective knowledge. That is to say, it is objective knowledge rather than subjective knowledge that is a determinant of the willingness to purchase health insurance among consumers in India.

References

Alba, J. W., and Hutchinson, J. W. (2000). Knowledge calibration: What consumers know and what they think they know. *Journal of Consumer Research*, 27(2), 123–156.

Annear, P. L., Bigdeli, M., and Jacobs, B. (2011). A functional model for monitoring equity and effectiveness in purchasing health insurance premiums for the poor: Evidence from Cambodia and the Lao PDR. *Health Policy*, 102(2–3), 295–303.

Brucks, M. (1985). The effects of product class knowledge on information search behavior. *Journal of Consumer Research*, 12(1), 1–16.

Carlson, J. P., Vincent, L. H., Hardesty, D. M., and Bearden, W. O. (2009). Objective and subjective knowledge relationships: A quantitative analysis of consumer research findings. *Journal of Consumer Research*, 35(5), 864–876.

Cordell, V. V. (1997). Consumer knowledge measures as predictors in product evaluation. *Psychology & Marketing*, 14(3), 241–260.

Conway III, L. G., Woodard, S. R., Zubrod, A., and Chan, L. (2020). Why are conservatives less concerned about the coronavirus (COVID-19) than liberals? Testing experiential versus political explanations.

Ellen, P. S. (1994). Do we know what we need to know? Objective and subjective knowledge effects on pro-ecological behaviors. *Journal of Business Research*, 30(1), 43–52.

Fior Markets. (2020, September 30). https://www.globenewswire.com/. Retrieved from https://www.globenewswire.com/news-release/2020/09/30/2101076/0/en/Global-Health-Insurance-Market-Is-Expected-to-Reach-USD-2021-62-billion-by-2027-Fior-Markets.html.

Fredrica, R. (1979). Consumer food selection and nutrition information.

Guo, L., and Meng, X. (2008). Consumer knowledge and its consequences: An international comparison. *International Journal of Consumer Studies*, 32(3), 260–268.

House, L. O., Lusk, J., Jaeger, S. R., Traill, B., Moore, M., Valli, C., Morrow, B., and Yee, W. (2004). Objective and subjective knowledge: Impacts on consumer demand for genetically modified foods in the United States and the European Union.

Insurance Regulatory and Development Authority of India (IRDA) (Hyderabad). (2020). *Annual Report.*

Lim, J. H., Kim, S. G., Lee, E. M., Bae, S. Y., Park, J. H., Choi, K. S., Hahm, M. I., and Park, E. C. (2007). The determinants of purchasing private health insurance in Korean cancer patients. *Journal of Preventive Medicine and Public Health*, 40(2), 150–154.

Liu, T. C., and Chen, C. S. (2002). An analysis of private health insurance purchasing decisions with national health insurance in Taiwan. *Social Science & Medicine*, 55(5), 755–774.

Park, C. W., and Lessig, V. P. (1981). Familiarity and its impact on consumer decision biases and heuristics. *Journal of Consumer Research*, 8(2), 223–230.

Park, C. W., Feick, L., and Mothersbaugh, D. L. (1992). Consumer knowledge assessment: How product experience and knowledge of brands, attributes, and features affects what we think we know. *ACR North American Advances*.

Park, C. W., Mothersbaugh, D. L., and Feick, L. (1994). Consumer knowledge assessment. *Journal of Consumer Research*, 21(1), 71–82.

Pieniak, Z., Verbeke, W., Brunsø, K., and Olsen, S. O. (2006). Consumer knowledge and interest in information about fish. In *Seafood Research from Fish to Dish: Quality, Safety and Processing of Wild and Farmed Fish*, pp. 229–241.

Rao, A. R., and Monroe, K. B. (1988). The moderating effect of prior knowledge on cue utilization in product evaluations. *Journal of Consumer Research*, 15(2), 253–264.

Rao, A. R., and Sieben, W. A. (1992). The effect of prior knowledge on price acceptability and the type of information examined. *Journal of Consumer Research*, 19(2), 256–270.

Radecki, C. M., and Jaccard, J. (1995). Perceptions of knowledge, actual knowledge, and information search behavior. *Journal of Experimental Social Psychology*, 31(2), 107–138.

Spitzmuller, M., Park, G., Van Dyne, L., Wagner, D. T., and Maerz, A. (2020). When do you benefit? Differential boundary conditions facilitate positive affect and buffer negative affect after helping others. *European Journal of Work and Organizational Psychology*, 1–13.

Zhang, M., and Liu, G. L. (2015). The effects of consumer's subjective and objective knowledge on perceptions and attitude towards genetically modified foods: Objective knowledge as a determinant. *International Journal of Food Science & Technology*, 50(5), 1198–1205.

© 2025 World Scientific Publishing Company
https://doi.org/10.1142/9789811292101_0019

Chapter 19

Modelling Challenges Faced by the Retail Sector in the COVID-19 Outbreak

Subhodeep Mukherjee[*,§], Chittipaka Venkataiah[†,¶],
Manish Mohan Baral[*,∥], and Sharad Chandra Srivastava[‡,**]

[*]*Department of Operations, GITAM Institute of Management,
GITAM (Deemed to be University),
Visakhapatnam, Andhra Pradesh, India*

[†]*School of Management Studies,
Indira Gandhi National Open University,
New Delhi, India*

[‡]*Department of Industrial and Production Engineering,
Guru Ghashidas Vishwavidyalaya (A Central University),
Bilaspur, Chhattisgarh, India*

[§]*subhodeepmukherjee92@gmail.com*
[¶]*venkatchitti@gmail.com*
[∥]*manishmohanbaral.31@gmail.com*
[**]*sharadscs2@gmail.com*

Abstract

The COVID-19 pandemic has hit the Indian economy very severely, and most organizations face many challenges in coping with this situation. The retail industry has also been hit very severely due to the COVID-19 pandemic. The rise of the pandemic is having a negative effect on short- and medium-term retailers, and earnest procedures and strategies for retailers are required. Many countries announced a lockdown to break the chain of the virus, which resulted in the closure of retail stores; moreover, even after lockdowns were removed, customer footfall decreased. This research is conducted to study the challenges faced by retail sectors due to the COVID-19 pandemic. A literature review was performed from the available literature, and the following five challenges were identified for the research: lack of supply chain flexibility, lack of government support, shortage of workforce, lack of balance in supply and demand, and change in consumer behaviour. A questionnaire is developed for the research in the retail industry. Data were collected from the retail, floor, departmental, and store managers. The questionnaires were sent to 459 respondents, but only 303 returned usable questionnaires that were valid for analysis. For the data analysis, exploratory factor analysis and structural equation modelling (SEM) were performed. The model developed showed a good fit, and all the hypotheses considered in the research were accepted. The current research will also serve as a base for conducting future research using the SEM approach in several other segments and from other nations' perspectives. This research can be further extended to other sectors where the pandemic has hit the hardest.

Keywords: COVID-19, retail store, challenges, structural equation modelling, lockdown.

Introduction

The social, political, and financial changes from COVID-19 (COV-19) are noticeable. Worldwide, infection control reactions incorporated shutting down superfluous organizations, social distancing, more modest public get-togethers, indefinitely deferring games and sporting activities, and cancelling meetings. Supply chains (SCs) were helpless in delivering products, as their weaknesses and absence of operational deftness became obvious (Baral *et al.*, 2023; Ivanov and Dolgui, 2020). Globalization, offshoring, and lean-based proficiency went under expanding examination. Truly, investigations have been initiated with the endeavour of helping associations gain an upper hand under ideal models of relative preferred position — discovering areas with preferences in expenses and assets (Koch *et al.*, 2020). In any event, for the time being, leanness and productivity were met with ill will, questions, and apprehensions (Mukherjee *et al.*, 2023; Valdez-Juárez *et al.*, 2021).

Retailing has changed drastically in the most recent years because of continuous digitization, which empowered expanded development in the retail area. Retailing is immediately moving from customarily available and multichannel practices to 'omni-channel' (Ailawadi and Farris, 2017). The rise of the COV-19 pandemic has had a negative effect on short- and medium-term retailers; therefore, earnest procedures and strategies for retailers are required (Kang *et al.*, 2020). While retailers ordinarily need a current limit and adjust to developments, for the most part, inventive and intuitive innovations and frameworks for selling merchandise and ventures are accessible and developing quickly to help clients and retailers (Pantano *et al.*, 2020).

As an outcome of the uncommon control measures, purchasers are shopping unexpectedly. The 'shortage impact' has significantly affected value versatility and accumulating propensities, while customary obstacles, for example, holding up occasions and saw swarming, are presently endured, as seen by long lines to enter stores (Baral *et al.*, 2022; Ratten, 2020). A few retailers are diffusing messages about the accessibility of food and restricting the number of things to purchase per shopper, actualizing new sorts of online administrations and home conveyance, however frequently with unsuitable outcomes for buyers' feelings of prosperity (Tran, 2021). Additionally, numerous online supermarkets acquainted virtual lines with a limited quantity of clients to be taken care of while (as on account of Ocado in the UK) and gave needy conveyance openings to helpless or older clients (for example, Waitrose in the UK).

The rest of the chapter is divided as follows. The subsequent section discusses the literature review, followed by sections on the research framework and hypothesis, research methodology, data analysis, and discussion. The final section is the conclusion.

Literature Review

Retailers are considered an integral piece of the SC wardrobe by purchasers, whose job could prove pivotal as they may come under intense pressure to supply essential products (Nordas, 2007). It becomes essential to circulate items rapidly and effectively from uninfected conveyance communities to retail locations (Mukherjee *et al.*, 2022; Verma and Gustafsson, 2020). As COV-19 spread constantly, the stock of actual merchandise required to secure buyers' strength was tested when contrasted with typical conditions (Kumar *et al.*, 2020). It has been accounted for that retail locations are confronting limited imperatives and an abundance of request issues because of evolving requirements. Retailers are communicating the troubles faced by their retail locations due to COVID-19 (Sarkis, 2020).

This brought up a worldwide vulnerability to SARS in 2003 because of the absence of adaptability that affected the conventional SC framework and global travel industry in the Asian region (Chowdhury *et al.*, 2020b). It was observed that 'trust issues between SC players,' 'helpless framework,' 'absence of effective data trade framework,' 'nonappearance of remuneration,' and 'illicit practices' were hindrances that determined the direction of the influenza pandemic in 2006. A pandemic is considered an essential vulnerability that turns out to be quite unsafe because of less responsiveness, untrustworthy offices, and inconsistent transportation arrangements (Chowdhury *et al.*, 2021). A demonstrating system gave a mediation technique to anticipate the flare-up effect on SCs (Ivanov and Dolgui, 2020; Mukherjee *et al.*, 2022; Roy *et al.*, 2023). The examination uncovers that self-isolation, separation of infected individuals, contact tracing, and safe burial practices are the extraordinary measures that lessen the transmission pace of such infections (Sharma and Joshi, 2020).

SCs have traditionally been thought to consist mostly of retail associations. By giving them the knowledge they need to make further predictions, it fulfils their interests and provides genuine interest (Essuman *et al.*, 2020). Even though retailers are viewed as a fundamental partner of SCs, the literature relating the pandemic scourge to the retail industry is scant (Mukherjee *et al.*, 2022; Queiroz *et al.*, 2020). The pandemic flare-up has been referenced as a natural danger to the SCs that causes a deficiency in interest and interruption of retail associations because of the inaccessibility of items (Ivanov and Das, 2020). COVID-19 emerged as an unexpected shock that affected the efficiency of worldwide SCs (Morgan *et al.*, 2021). An investigation revealed that SC execution has a straightforward correspondence with the span of interruption and showed that it relies on schedule, disturbance spread scale, and accessibility of offices (Hosseini *et al.*, 2019). The value of SC practicality and adaptability is especially important in extreme situations like the COVID-19 pandemic study done on 5,800 private ventures discovered that 43% of retail sources were briefly shut down, as they are more vulnerable to COVID-19 flare-ups. Because of movement limitations, isolation protocols, and processing plant closures, retailers confronted issues keeping up operational coherencies both offline and online.

Research Framework and Hypothesis Development

The challenges faced by the retail sector due to COV-19 are as follows:

(1) **Lack of supply chain flexibility (SCF):** Numerous organizations have improved the adaptability of their SCs to react quickly and adequately in an uncertain climate (Chowdhury *et al.*, 2021). In any case, improving adaptability is exorbitant; the association has been battling to discover the equilibrium point between adaptability and vulnerability (Roggeveen and Sethuraman, 2020). The absence of required adaptability and responsiveness brought about an expanded lead time that further lulled the stock of basics (Cariappa *et al.*, 2020). It had been proposed that a decent connection with the provider may improve responsiveness during harsh conditions.

H1: SCF influence CRS.

(2) **Lack of government support (GS):** During a pandemic, alongside the public authority, numerous private offices are attempting to fulfil basic needs of customers or the network (Richards and Rickard, 2020). Although both players were working autonomously, the maker has been operating under the danger of misfortune because of questionable interest (Rowan and Galanakis, 2020). For instance, during flu immunization, numerous clinical associations faced adversity because of an unexpected lessening altogether (Manivannan and Kannappan, 2020). This might be the motivation behind why numerous parts of the world are confronting an absence of crucial clinical gear for COV-19 (Mahendra Dev and Sengupta, 2020). It had been recommended that an arrangement of motivators from the public authority and even cost-sharing agreements may address this sort of operational issue (Adel, 2020).

H2: GS influence CRS.

(3) **Shortage of manpower (SMP):** Because of COV-19, the world is confronting a critical decrease in labour that may break worldwide SCs. After the lockdown declaration, India faced specific deficiencies that swayed the inventory of merchandise (Chowdhury *et al.*, 2020b). Similarly, study by Subashini *et al.* (2020) addresses the issue of a shortage

of skilled and knowledgeable workers who can handle these healthcare emergencies.

H3: SMP influence CRS.

(4) **Lack of balance in supply and demand (BSD):** This is a significant issue looked at by retailers because of the COV-19 pandemic (Kumar *et al.*, 2020). This is because SCs were unable to respond to requests owing to an abrupt increase in demand coupled with supply deficiencies worldwide (Sharma *et al.*, 2020). For instance, the announced absence of responsiveness and adaptability essentially explains market interest disturbances, as it is noted that the pandemic outbreak consistently led to SC interruptions (Sarkis, 2020).

H4: BSD influence CRS.

(5) **Change in consumer behaviour (CB):** Amid vulnerability, shoppers' conduct changes fundamentally (Pagano *et al.*, 2021). They purchase more basic necessities. The unexpected change in buying conduct expands interest in specific products. As manufacturers were not prepared for this unexpected change, it became difficult to satisfy the demand in such a brief period (Brydges *et al.*, 2020). Customers' eagerness to stock up on basic needs increased due to COV-19, which led to further disturbances in SCs (Chowdhury *et al.*, 2020a). As these essentials are vital for survival, shoppers may become aggressive, prompting retail stores and distribution centres to employ additional security (McMaster *et al.*, 2020).

H5: CB influence CRS.

Research Methodology

Sampling

Responses were collected through a structured questionnaire from the retail managers, operation managers, departmental managers, and store managers of various retail stores. The sample was selected from each strata through the stratified random sampling method, as it allows population harmony between the subpopulations (Hair *et al.*, 2010). The questionnaires were sent to 459 respondents, but only 303 returned usable questionnaires that were valid for analysis. To avoid common method bias, the research team took several fundamental precautions during the pre-data collection stage. A note was mentioned at the beginning of the questionnaire indicating that the survey is intended for academic research and that data confidentiality will be maintained.

In the gathered dataset, the first cleansing was accomplished through case screening, which was followed by factor screening, so that clarification regarding the variability of the information could be achieved. It is required to follow this cycle so that there were no missing qualities in the dataset. However, after the data were collected, the research team applied Harman's single-factor test. Exploratory factor analysis (EFA) was performed, and the results show that the first factor explains the maximum variance (32.763%) below the recommended value of 50% (Roy *et al.*, 2022).

Demographics of the respondents

Leedy and Ormrod (2014) stated that a cross-sectional plan includes testing and looking at individuals from a few diverse segment gatherings. This methodology empowers the researcher to gather basic information simultaneously (Mukherjee and Chittipaka, 2022).

Table 1 shows the demographics of the respondents. A questionnaire method was used. The respondents' characteristics with respect to gender showed that 57% were male respondents, followed by 43% female respondents. In terms of their current positions, 29% were store managers,

Table 1. Demographics of the respondents.

Sl. No.	Characteristics	Percentage
I	**Gender**	
A	Male	57
B	Female	43
II	**Respondents current position**	
A	Retail manager	23
B	Operation manager	27
C	Departmental manager	21
D	Store manager	29

followed by 27% who were operation managers, 23% as retail managers, and 21% as departmental managers.

Results

Reliability and validity

Cronbach's alpha

The reliability test was performed for each factor based on Cronbach's alpha (α) value, which assesses the reliability of the constructs. The values of all indicators or dimensional scales should be above the recommended value of 0.70 (Nunnally and Bernstein, 1994). A seven-point Likert scale was utilized in preparing the structured questionnaire. To analyze the information collected, SPSS 20.0 and Amos 22.0 were used. The construct SCF has four indicators: SCF1, SCF2, SCF3, and SCF4, and its α value is 0.830; GS has three indicators: GS1, GS2, and GS3, and its α value is 0.850; SMP has three indicators: SMP1, SMP2, and SMP3, and its α value is 0.840; BSD has three indicators: BSD1, BSD2, and BSD3, and its α value is 0.724; CB has four indicators: CB1, CB2, CB3, and CB4, and its α value is 0.862. Hence, all the values are within the threshold.

Composite reliability

Composite reliability (CR) was also measured for all the components. It is measured for internal consistency and reliability because of its ability to provide better results (Henseler *et al.*, 2009). The construct CB has a CR value of 0.896; SCF has a CR value of 0.886; GS has a CR value of 0.902; SMP has a CR value of 0.909; and BSD has a CR value of 0.844. The five constructs' CR values are greater than 0.7, indicating that the composite reliability measures are reliable (Hair *et al.*, 2010).

Exploratory factor analysis

The KMO value for this research is 0.859. The minimum level set for this statistic is 0.60 (Tabachnick and Fidell 2007). The significance value is 0.000, which is less than 0.05, i.e., the probability value level is acceptable. Meyers *et al.* (2013) indicate that a variance accounted for by its factors needs to meet the lower limit by 50%. The extraction method used was principal axis factoring. Only the eigenvalues with values greater than one were extracted, as they explain the maximum variance. For the components, the percentages of total variance explained by the components are as follows: component 1: 36.474%, component 2: 10.816%) component 3: 9.209%, component 4: 8.290%, and component 5: 6.619%. The cumulative percentage of total variance explained by all four components is 71.409%. The rotated component matrix is important for interpreting the results of the analysis. Rotation helps in grouping the items, and each group contains more than one item at least, which simplifies the structure. Hence, this is the aim of rotation. In this research, we have achieved this aim. This helps us identify the cross-loadings on more than one group, which can then be corrected by removing those items which are cross-loaded. In this research, loadings having values less than |0.40| are suppressed because loadings greater than |0.40| are typically considered high. So, eventually, we achieve a simple structure. There are 17 total variables, which were grouped under five different components. The rotation method used was varimax rotation. All 17 variables listed were grouped under five different components. CB1, CB2, CB3, and CB4 are grouped under the first component with values of 0.837, 0.843, 0.851, and 0.771, respectively. SCF1, SCF2, SCF3, and SCF4 are grouped under the second component with values of 0.838, 0.769, 0.779, and 0.862, respectively. GS1, GS2, and GS3 are grouped under the third component with values of 0.832, 0.769, and 0.779, respectively. SMP1, SMP2, and SMP3 are grouped under the fourth component with values of 0.839, 0.958, and 0.803, respectively. BSD1, BSD2, and BSD3 are grouped under the fifth component with values of 0.845, 0.878, and 0.672, respectively.

Confirmatory factor analysis (CFA) was performed in the next stage, through which constructs identified from the literature survey can be tested to determine how well the variables represent the constructs. Structural equation modelling (SEM) was used for testing the model fit of the proposed research model (Byrne, 2010). An additional thorough trial of building legitimacy is the purported factorial legitimacy, which depends on the factor investigation's outcomes. Its primary role is to characterize the basic structures among the factors identified for the examination (Hair et al., 2010). If the analysis shows normal structures within these factors, this could be demonstrative of construct validity (CV) (Moerdyk, 2009) and, explicitly, factorial validity.

Construct validity (CV)

A significant logical idea to assess the validity of a measure is to develop a CV. CV is the degree to which a test quantifies a concept or development expected to be quantified. CV is generally tested by estimating the relationship in appraisals derived from a few scales. No cut-off characterizes a CV (DeVellis *et al.*, 2003).

This research's primary goal was to analyze structural components, which is a CV that includes the investigation of interior connections among things or subscales corresponding to a specific measure, utilizing such factual examinations as correlation, exploratory and confirmatory factor analysis, and reliability analysis.

Convergent validity

It is measured by using the average variance extracted (AVE). According to Fornell and Larcker (1981), AVE should be greater than 0.5 for convergent validity. Table 2 represents the AVE values for the constructs. All the values are more significant than 0.5, which satisfies convergent validity for all the constructs.

Divergent or discriminant validity

To evaluate this validity, Fornell and Larcker (1981) suggested that the construct's AVE should be greater than the square of the correlation between that construct and other constructs. Table 2 represents the values for construct correlation and AVE. The variance extracted and the squared correlation for CB and SCF are 0.670 and 0.235; CB and GS are 0.717

Table 2. Construct correlation and AVE.

		Variance extracted between factors				
	AVE	CB	SCF	GS	SMP	BSD
CB	0.826	1				
SCF	0.812	0.670	1			
GS	0.867	0.717	0.706	1		
SMP	0.866	0.716	0.705	0.752	1	
BSD	0.798	0.660	0.648	0.695	0.694	1

and 0.184; CB and SMP are 0.716 and 0.161; CB and BSD are 0.660 and 0.153; SCF and GS are 0.706 and 0.202; SCF and SMP are 0.705 and 0.096; SCF and BSD are 0.648 and 0.040; GS and SMP are 0.752 and 0.126; GS and BSD are 0.695 and 0.102; SMP and BSD are 0.694 and 0.073, respectively; hence, the value of variance extracted is more than the squared correlation value. As a result, divergent or discriminant validity is satisfied.

Structural equation modelling

To test the hypotheses, SEM was used (Byrne, 2010). AMOS 22.0 was utilized for this research because of its powerful graphic representations and user-friendly interfaces. The results of the significant paths of the model are described here. Figure 1 represents the final and latent variables and their indicators, mediating variables, and dependent variables. There are five latent variables. The latent variables along with their indicators are as follows: SCF: lack of supply chain flexibility has four indicators, SCF1, SCF2, SCF3, and SCF4; GS: lack of government support has three indicators, GS1, GS2, and GS3; SMP: shortage of manpower has three indicators, SMP1, SMP2, and SMP3; BSD: lack of balance in supply and demand has three indicators, BSD1, BSD2, and BSD3; CB: change in consumer behaviour has four indicators, CB1, CB2, CB3, and CB4. The lone dependent variable is CRS: challenges in the retail sector due to the COV-19 pandemic, which has four indicators, CRS1, CRS2, CRS3, and CRS4.

The value of chi-square is 374.703, and the degree of freedom is 174. The estimations of absolute fit indices are: CMIN/Df is 2.153, where CMIN represents the chi-square value, and Df represents the degree of freedom, and the value is less than 3, which is the accepted threshold value. The root mean square approximation (RMSEA) is 0.062; the comparative fit index (CFI) is 0.937; the Tucker–Lewis coefficient (TLI) is 0.924; the goodness of fit index (GFI) is 0.897; the adjusted goodness of fit indices (AGFI) is 0.864; the normed fit index (NFI) is 0.890; and the incremental fit index (IFI) is 0.938, all of which have values within the threshold level and are acceptable (Byrne, 2010).

Discussion

COV-19 has impacted many industries and firms all over the world, and they are still struggling (Gössling *et al.*, 2021). This research aims to study

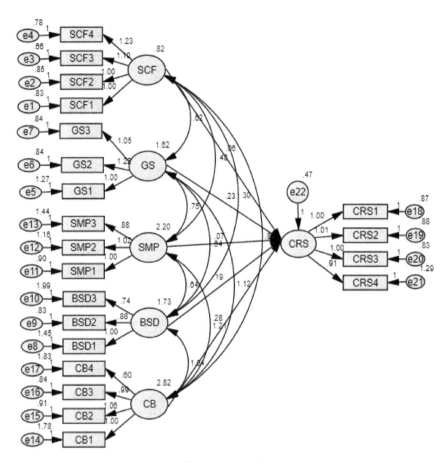

Figure 1. Model.

the retail sector's challenges due to the COV-19 pandemic in India. For this research, a literature review was done to first identify the challenges arising from the COV-19 pandemic. A questionnaire was developed for the study. The target population was mainly employees working in retail stores across India. For analysis, EFA and SEM were used. A model was developed, which showed a good fit.

The five components' Cronbach's alpha and composite reliability values were above 0.7, which is the recommended level (Nunnally, 1978; Hair et al., 2010) for the factors. The construct's KMO value was 0.859, which is also above the recommended level of 0.6 (Hair et al., 2010). This validates the data for factor analysis. The total variance explained was

71.409%, and in the rotated component matrix, the variables were grouped under five groups. Only the loadings which are above |0.40| were considered in this research because those were considered to be typically high and hence more significant (Hair et al., 2010). For further analysis in this research, five components were utilized. The component SCF stands for a lack of supply chain flexibility. SCs are intended to work in a steady and controlled climate to improve their effectiveness (Dannenberg et al., 2020). An unexpected change makes SCs eccentric and causes interruptions (Hall et al., 2020). SCF comprises four sub-components: SCF1, SCF2, SCF3, and SCF4, with values of 0.838, 0.769, 0.779, and 0.862, respectively, which shows that it has very high loadings (>|0.40|). The component GS stands for a lack of government support. SC accomplices consistently bear the danger of abundance creation and questionable interest (Rude, 2020). There is no cost-sharing and misfortune agreement to give relief to SC players (Pagano et al., 2021). GS comprises three sub-components: GS1, GS2, and GS3, with values of 0.832, 0.769, and 0.779, respectively, which show very high loadings (>|0.40|). The component SMP stands for a shortage of manpower. The issue emerges because of the relocation of labourers to their old neighbourhood, government rules to diminish COV-19 disease, and the dread of contamination (Richards and Rickard, 2020). SMP comprises three sub-components: SMP1, SMP2, and SMP3, with values of 0.839, 0.958, and 0.803, respectively, which show very high loadings (>|0.40|). The component BSD stands for a lack of supply and balance. There was an extraordinary expansion sought after by some SCs (e.g., staple products, covers, and sanitizer) that was not satisfied by restricted stockpile, as this pestilence hit most nations at the same time (Lehberger et al., 2021). BSD comprises three sub-components: BSD1, BSD2, and BSD3, with values of 0.845, 0.878, and 0.672, respectively, which show very high loadings (>|0.40|). The component CB stands for change in consumer behaviour. Buyers' purchasing conduct has changed radically (O'connor, 2020). It is currently centred on medical accessories and basic everyday merchandise. The accumulation of these products is creating superfluous tension for retailers (Hand, 2020). CB comprises four sub-components: CB1, CB2, CB3, and CB4, with values of 0.837, 0.843, 0.851, and 0.771, respectively, showing that it has very high loadings (>|0.40|).

Based on EFA, SEM was performed in AMOS 22.0. The value of chi-square is 374.703, and the degree of freedom is 174. The estimations of absolute fit indices are as follows: CMIN/Df is 2.153, where CMIN represents the chi-square value and Df represents the degree of freedom, and the value is less than 3, which is the accepted threshold value. The root mean square approximation (RMSEA) is 0.062; the comparative fit index (CFI) is 0.937; the Tucker–Lewis coefficient (TLI) is 0.924; the goodness of fit index (GFI) is 0.897; the adjusted goodness of fit indices (AGFI) is 0.864; the normed fit index (NFI) is 0.890, and the incremental fit index (IFI) is 0.938, all of which have values within the threshold level and are acceptable (Byrne, 2010).

Conclusion

This research aimed to identify the challenges faced by the retail industry due to the COV-19 pandemic. As we all know, due to and after the lockdown, customer footfall in retails stores decreased. In the lockdown period, retail stores remained closed, as ordered by the government. In this scenario, the purchasing behaviour of customers changed a lot; they started purchasing online. After the lockdown, when stores opened, they faced many challenges, including a lack of SC flexibility, a lack of workforce, a lack of supply and demand, and a change in purchase behaviour. For this research, a literature review was performed to identify the challenges in the retail sector. A questionnaire was developed for the study. The target population that mainly worked in the retail store consisted of retail managers, store managers, floor managers, and departmental managers. The collected data were analyzed using EFA and SEM. The model developed showed a good fit, and all five hypotheses were accepted in the research.

This research can be further extended to other sectors where the pandemic has hit the hardest. This research can also be carried out in other developing or developed countries, and the results can be used to perform a comparative study.

References

Adel, R. (2020). Smart retailing in COVID-19 world: Insights from Egypt, 71–94 (October).

Ailawadi, K. L., and Farris, P. W. (2017). Managing multi- and omni-channel distribution: Metrics and research directions. *Journal of Retailing*, 93(1), 120–135. https://doi.org/10.1016/j.jretai.2016.12.003.

Baral, M. M., Mukherjee, S., Nagariya, R., Singh Patel, B., Pathak, A., and Chittipaka, V. (2022). Analysis of factors impacting firm performance of MSMEs: Lessons learnt from COVID-19. *Benchmarking: An International Journal* (ahead-of-print). https://doi.org/10.1108/BIJ-11-2021-0660.

Baral, M. M., Mukherjee, S., Singh, R. K., Chittipaka, V., and Kazancoglu, Y. (2023). Exploring antecedents for the circular economy capability of micro, small and medium enterprises: An empirical study. *Business Strategy and the Environment*. https://doi.org/10.1002/BSE.3448.

Brydges, T., Heinze, L., Retamal, M., and Henninger, C. E. (2020). Platforms and the pandemic: A case study of fashion rental platforms during COVID-19. *Geographical Journal*. https://doi.org/10.1111/geoj.12366.

Cariappa, A. G. A., Acharya, K. K., Adhav, C., Ramadas, S., and Ramasundaram, P. (2020). Pandemic led food price anomalies and supply chain disruption: Evidence from COVID-19 incidence in India. *SSRN Electronic Journal*. https://doi.org/10.2139/ssrn.3680634.

Chowdhury, M. T., Sarkar, A., Paul, S. K., and Moktadir, M. A. (2020a). A case study on strategies to deal with the impacts of COVID-19 pandemic in the food and beverage industry. *Operations Management Research*. https://doi.org/10.1007/s12063-020-00166-9.

Chowdhury, M. T., Sarkar, A., Saha, P. K., and Anik, R. H. (2020b). Enhancing supply resilience in the COVID-19 pandemic: A case study on beauty and personal care retailers. *Modern Supply Chain Research and Applications*, 2(3), 143–159. https://doi.org/10.1108/mscra-07-2020-0018.

Chowdhury, P., Kumar Paul, S., Kaisar, S., and Abdul Moktadir, M. (2021). COVID-19 pandemic related supply chain studies: A systematic review. *Transportation Research Part E: Logistics and Transportation Review*, 148, 102271. https://doi.org/10.1016/j.tre.2021.102271.

Dannenberg, P., Fuchs, M., Riedler, T., and Wiedemann, C. (2020). Digital transition by COVID-19 pandemic? The German food online retail. *Tijdschrift Voor Economische En Sociale Geografie*, 111(3), 543–560. https://doi.org/10.1111/tesg.12453.

Essuman, D., Boso, N., and Annan, J. (2020). Operational resilience, disruption, and efficiency: Conceptual and empirical analyses. *International Journal of Production Economics*, 229, 107762. https://doi.org/10.1016/j.ijpe.2020.107762.

Gössling, S., Scott, D., and Hall, C. M. (2021). Pandemics, tourism and global change: A rapid assessment of COVID-19. *Journal of Sustainable Tourism*, 29(1), 1–20. https://doi.org/10.1080/09669582.2020.1758708.

Hall, M. C., Prayag, G., Fieger, P., and Dyason, D. (2020). Beyond panic buying: Consumption displacement and COVID-19. *Journal of Service Management*. https://doi.org/10.1108/JOSM-05-2020-0151.

Hosseini, S., Ivanov, D., and Dolgui, A. (2019). Review of quantitative methods for supply chain resilience analysis. *Transportation Research Part E: Logistics and Transportation Review*, 125, 285–307. https://doi.org/10.1016/j.tre.2019.03.001.

Ivanov, D., and Das, A. (2020). Coronavirus (COVID-19/SARS-CoV-2) and supply chain resilience: A research note. *International Journal of Integrated Supply Management*, 13(1), 90–102. https://doi.org/10.1504/IJISM.2020.107780.

Ivanov, D., and Dolgui, A. (2020). Viability of intertwined supply networks: Extending the supply chain resilience angles towards survivability. A position paper motivated by COVID-19 outbreak. *International Journal of Production Research*, 58(10), 2904–2915. https://doi.org/10.1080/00207543.2020.1750727.

Kang, J., Diao, Z., and Zanini, M. T. (2020). Business-to-business marketing responses to COVID-19 crisis: A business process perspective. In *Marketing Intelligence and Planning*. Emerald Group Holdings Ltd. https://doi.org/10.1108/MIP-05-2020-0217.

Koch, J., Frommeyer, B., and Schewe, G. (2020). Online shopping motives during the COVID-19 pandemic — Lessons from the crisis. *Sustainability*, 12(24), 10247. https://doi.org/10.3390/su122410247.

Kumar, M. S., Raut, D. R. D., Narwane, D. V. S., and Narkhede, D. B. E. (2020). Applications of industry 4.0 to overcome the COVID-19 operational challenges. *Diabetes and Metabolic Syndrome: Clinical Research and Reviews*, 14(5), 1283–1289. https://doi.org/10.1016/j.dsx.2020.07.010.

Lehberger, M., Kleih, A. K., and Sparke, K. (2021). Panic buying in times of coronavirus (COVID-19): Extending the theory of planned behavior to understand the stockpiling of nonperishable food in Germany. *Appetite*, 161, 105118. https://doi.org/10.1016/j.appet.2021.105118.

Manivannan, A. S. R., and Kannappan, S. (2020). Marketing agility and e-commerce agility in the light of COVID-19 pandemic: A study with reference to fast fashion brands. *Asian Journal of Interdisciplinary Research*, 3(4), 1–13. https://doi.org/10.34256/ajir2041.

Mahendra Dev, S., and Sengupta, R. (2020). Impact of Covid-19 on the Indian Economy: An Interim Assessment.

McMaster, M., Nettleton, C., Tom, C., Xu, B., Cao, C., and Qiao, P. (2020). Risk management: Rethinking fashion supply chain management for multinational corporations in light of the COVID-19 outbreak. *Journal of Risk and Financial Management*, 13(8), 173. https://doi.org/10.3390/jrfm13080173.

Morgan, A. K., Awafo, B. A., and Quartey, T. (2021). The effects of COVID-19 on global economic output and sustainability: Evidence from around the world and lessons for redress. *Sustainability: Science, Practice, and Policy*, 17(1), 77–81. https://doi.org/10.1080/15487733.2020.1860345.

Mukherjee, S., Baral, M. M., Chittipaka, V., and Pal, S. K. (2022). A structural equation modelling approach to develop a resilient supply chain strategy for the COVID-19 disruptions. In *Handbook of Research on Supply Chain Resiliency, Efficiency, and Visibility in the Post-Pandemic Era*. IGI Global, pp. 242–266. https://doi.org/10.4018/978-1-7998-9506-0.ch013.

Mukherjee, S., Baral, M. M., Chittipaka, V., Pal, S. K., and Nagariya, R. (2022). Investigating sustainable development for the COVID-19 vaccine supply chain: A structural equation modelling approach. *Journal of Humanitarian Logistics and Supply Chain Management* (ahead-of-print). https://doi.org/10.1108/JHLSCM-08-2021-0079.

Mukherjee, S., Baral, M. M., Venkataiah, C., Pal, S. K., and Nagariya, R. (2021). Service robots are an option for contactless services due to the COVID-19 pandemic in the hotels. *Decision*, 48(4), 445–460. https://doi.org/10.1007/s40622-021-00300-x.

Mukherjee, S., and Chittipaka, V. (2022). Analysing the adoption of intelligent agent technology in food supply chain management: An empirical evidence. *FIIB Business Review*, 11(4), 438–454. https://doi.org/10.1177/23197145211059243.

Mukherjee, S., Chittipaka, V., and Baral, M. M. (2023). Risks that impacted the agriculture supply chain during the COVID-19 pandemic. *Managing and Strategising Global Business in Crisis*, 121–136. https://doi.org/10.4324/9781003295068-11.

Mukherjee, S., Venkataiah, C., Baral, M. M., and Pal, S. K. (2022). Analyzing the factors that will impact the supply chain of the COVID-19 vaccine: A structural equation modeling approach. *Journal of Statistics and Management Systems*, 1–16. https://doi.org/10.1080/09720510.2021.1966955.

O'connor, K. (2020). The challenges and opportunities created by a global pandemic's effects on consumer shopping behavior within the fashion retail industry. Undergraduate Honors Theses, University of San Diego. https://doi.org/10.22371/03.2020.003.

Pagano, M. S., Sedunov, J., and Velthuis, R. (2021). How did retail investors respond to the COVID-19 pandemic? The effect of Robinhood brokerage customers on market quality. *Finance Research Letters*, 101946. https://doi.org/10.1016/j.frl.2021.101946.

Pantano, E., Pizzi, G., Scarpi, D., and Dennis, C. (2020). Competing during a pandemic? Retailers' ups and downs during the COVID-19 outbreak. *Journal of Business Research*, 116, 209–213. https://doi.org/10.1016/j.jbusres.2020.05.036.

Queiroz, M. M., Ivanov, D., Dolgui, A., and Fosso Wamba, S. (2020). Impacts of epidemic outbreaks on supply chains: Mapping a research agenda amid the COVID-19 pandemic through a structured literature review. *Annals of Operations Research*, 1–38. https://doi.org/10.1007/s10479-020-03685-7.

Ratten, V. (2020). Coronavirus (Covid-19) and entrepreneurship: Cultural, lifestyle and societal changes. *Journal of Entrepreneurship in Emerging Economies.* https://doi.org/10.1108/JEEE-06-2020-0163.

Richards, T. J., and Rickard, B. (2020). COVID-19 impact on fruit and vegetable markets. *Canadian Journal of Agricultural Economics/Revue Canadienne d'agroeconomie*, 68(2), 189–194. https://doi.org/10.1111/cjag.12231.

Roggeveen, A. L., and Sethuraman, R. (2020). How the COVID-19 pandemic may change the world of retailing. *Journal of Retailing* (Elsevier Ltd.), 96(2), 169–171. https://doi.org/10.1016/j.jretai.2020.04.002.

Rowan, N. J., and Galanakis, C. M. (2020). Unlocking challenges and opportunities presented by COVID-19 pandemic for cross-cutting disruption in agri-food and green deal innovations: Quo Vadis? *Science of the Total Environment* (Elsevier B.V.), 748, 141362. https://doi.org/10.1016/j.scitotenv.2020.141362.

Roy, R., Babakerkhell, M. D., Mukherjee, S., Pal, D., and Funilkul, S. (2022). Evaluating the intention for the adoption of artificial intelligence-based robots in the University to Educate the Students. *IEEE Access*, 10, 125666–125678. https://doi.org/10.1109/ACCESS.2022.3225555.

Roy, R., Chekuri, K., Prasad, J. L., and Mukherjee, S. (2023). Discussing the future perspective of machine learning and artificial intelligence in COVID-19 vaccination: A review. In *Applications of Computational Intelligence in Management & Mathematics*, pp. 151–160. https://doi.org/10.1007/978-3-031-25194-8_12.

Rude, J. (2020). COVID-19 and the Canadian cattle/beef sector: Some preliminary analysis. *Canadian Journal of Agricultural Economics/Revue Canadienne d'agroeconomie*, 68(2), 207–213. https://doi.org/10.1111/cjag.12228.

Sarkis, J. (2020). Supply chain sustainability: Learning from the COVID-19 pandemic. *International Journal of Operations and Production Management*, 41(1), 63–73. https://doi.org/10.1108/IJOPM-08-2020-0568.

Sharma, M., and Joshi, S. (2020). Digital supplier selection reinforcing supply chain quality management systems to enhance firm's performance. *TQM Journal.* https://doi.org/10.1108/TQM-07-2020-0160.

Sharma, R., Shishodia, A., Kamble, S., Gunasekaran, A., and Belhadi, A. (2020). Agriculture supply chain risks and COVID-19: Mitigation strategies and implications for the practitioners. *International Journal of Logistics Research and Applications*, 1–27. https://doi.org/10.1080/13675567.2020.1830049.

Subashini, J. M., Devi, S. K., and Kavitha, D. S. (2020). Apparel industry — The new normal. *Research Journal of Textile and Leather*, 59–63. https://doi.org/10.46590/rjtl.2020.010301.

Tran, L. T. T. (2021). Managing the effectiveness of e-commerce platforms in a pandemic. *Journal of Retailing and Consumer Services*, 58, 102287. https://doi.org/10.1016/j.jretconser.2020.102287.

Valdez-Juárez, L. E., Gallardo-Vázquez, D., and Ramos-Escobar, E. A. (2021). Online buyers and open innovation: Security, experience, and satisfaction. *Journal of Open Innovation: Technology, Market, and Complexity*, 7(1), 37. https://doi.org/10.3390/joitmc7010037.

Verma, S., and Gustafsson, A. (2020). Investigating the emerging COVID-19 research trends in the field of business and management: A bibliometric analysis approach. *Journal of Business Research*, 118, 253–261. https://doi.org/10.1016/j.jbusres.2020.06.05.

© 2025 World Scientific Publishing Company
https://doi.org/10.1142/9789811292101_0020

Chapter 20

Pioneering Digital Marketing: How Service Sector Companies in Bangladesh are Re-redesigning Their Marketing Strengths

Preeti Mehra[*,‡] and Tanvirul Islam Mahim[†,§]

[*]*Marketing Mittal School of Business Lovely Professional University Punjab, India*
[†]*HT Global Ltd., Dhaka, Bangladesh*
[‡]*Preeti.23746@lpu.co.in*
[§]*mahim@htadvisory.org*

Abstract

Pioneering marketing is one of the contemporary approaches to marketing. It is a collective approach that emphasizes incessant enhancement and the attainment of success. It is a very reactive approach that emphasizes proactivity. It is a newer concept, and businesses are gradually getting themselves acclimatized to this approach. In Bangladesh, the education sector is evolving. People are now not sticking to basic academic education and have rather shifted to pursuing higher studies as well. It is a great opportunity for education consultancy firms to entice customers and offer them diverse services that will fulfil these demands. It has been observed that these consultancy firms are using different marketing approaches to create awareness of their services and also serve their customers in a better way. This is an agile way of marketing. The study explores digital marketing strategies that are followed by education companies in Bangladesh to achieve better outcomes. An attempt has also been made to understand how they are reengineering their marketing efforts. Institution owners or managers are assessed based on their attitudes towards marketing efforts. The sample consisted of 10 education consultancy firms promoting higher education for diverse students. The study was conducted in Dhaka City, Bangladesh. Firms were of the view that customers preferred their services due to their utmost service quality. Brand name and additional value-added services were cited as the most noteworthy factors.

Keywords: Education, agility, reengineering, digital, strategies, value-added services.

Introduction

Pioneering marketing approaches are followed by businesses to promote their products and services. Marketing itself is not unanimous; therefore, there are diverse approaches to marketing. Agile marketing is one of the contemporary approaches to marketing. It is a collective approach that emphasizes incessant enhancement and the attainment of success. It is a very reactive approach that emphasizes proactivity. It is a newer concept, and businesses are gradually getting themselves acclimatized to this approach. In Bangladesh, the education sector is evolving. People are now not sticking to basic academic education and have rather shifted to pursuing higher studies as well. It is a great opportunity for education consultancy firms to entice customers and offer them diverse services that will fulfil these demands. It has been observed that these consultancy firms are using different marketing approaches to create awareness of their services and also serve their customers in a better way. This is an agile way of marketing.

Literature Review

The review has been divided into two parts: marketing strategy approach and digital marketing approach. Studies highlighting the significance of marketing strategies and the use of marketing campaigns, digital marketing, and other modes of creating brand awareness have been discussed.

Marketing strategy approach

Ghahnavieh (2018) opined that the business world is incessantly fluctuating. To reduce the impact of environmental forces, prosperous businesses must pay consideration to three significant matters, including the extension of globalization, the expansion of modern technology, and the economic crisis. The target market is the specific collection of customers to whom the product or service is directed. A marketing combination is an arrangement of features that a company can control to affect consumers who buy their products. Marketing managers have a tendency to highlight marketing campaigns, and marketing is seen as the company's most vital assurance. Within this organizational context, social affairs activities are not seen as equal partners with marketing; however, in a practical sense, they are a set of responsibilities intended to help direct marketing functions. Negative developments in the media industry have a direct influence on the marketing communication approaches adopted by advertising agencies. In fact, marketing organizations have begun to redesign marketing communications by focusing on marketing public relations, such as from traditional advertising media to modern methods of public relations marketing, digital public relations, and shared public relations (Papasolomou *et al.*, 2014). The presence of the internet today, the discovery of intelligent communication devices, the appearance of social networking systems, and the development of digital television have taken the field of communication to another level, creating a more sophisticated, knowledgeable, and mature market. Marketing public relations allow professionals to assimilate marketing and public relations tools with advanced and creative methods to promote interaction between institutions, brands, the media, and the public.

Marketing can help companies improve products and services that fulfil the requirements of the target market in their business. Good promotion assists consumers appreciate why a product or service is enhanced or distinct from a competitor's. Marketing managers create marketing strategies to help companies achieve their sales goals. They conduct enquiries, assess product requirements, develop pricing approaches, recognize target audiences, and identify the best ways to reach them. The objective is to contribute to the planning theory of the existing marketing strategy by providing more information on the identification and selection of target markets, the combination of marketing, and the marketing plan. Ghahnavieh (2018) stated that, regardless of whether the company is minor or huge, marketing strategy development plays a significant role in determining what products or services are offered and how they are sold. The lack of adequate marketing actions in an organization will prevent senior managers from determining the agile market environment. Similarly, without marketing, potential consumers will never identify the business. Therefore, companies must focus on their businesses and acquire a brand there. It should help people know more about it and remember it.

Marketing strategies include positioning and positioning decisions based on consumer market division, product, price, delivery, and promotional decisions. Marketing approaches designed to develop long-term relationships with customers can reduce time to market and accelerate cash flow. In addition, they can benefit from the low-price understanding of trustworthy customers to increase cash flow through a steady relationship-based income stream or to reduce cash flow variability (Juttner et al., 2010). The marketing approach is intended to offer innovative and high-quality products at affordable prices. Furthermore, despite limited customer participation, the company will be able to communicate widely and use a wide range of distribution channels to preserve relationships. Marketing strategies also support the advancement of high-quality products.

Digital marketing approaches

The emergence of digital marketing methods is happening due to a tempestuous market, the augmentation of worldwide competition, thought-provoking customers, the swift development of state-of-the-art technologies, and the intricate changes caused by unruly innovations. More or less rapid automations, focused on flexibility and profound business indulgence, can be discovered as a result of this. This vulnerable active arrangement provides real-time monitoring of international communications and customer actions worldwide. Hendrix (2014) stated that the alteration of the marketing system requirements is a result of the pioneering attitude of marketing organizations. Customers place themselves at the heart of this new digital marketing plan. The fundamentals and relationships of the system must be unambiguously envisioned to foster contact between the customer and the product, postulate personal emotional involvement, and add worth to the customer.

Digitization has transformed the buying decision process. Customers pursue information, evaluate products and services, communicate with organizations, and then procure. The transformation process that replaces the traditional purchasing decisions of customers is called the decision-making process of the digital consumer. Due to the development of information technology, after the changes in the preceding periods, marketing is moving towards a new generation, 'Marketing 4.0.' New-generation products are required because customers are observing products that meet not only their basic needs but also their wants and apprehensions (Hendrix, 2014).

They must also meet the inspiration and ethics that were well defined in Marketing 3.0. In addition, they must be part of the manufacturing process, a unique feature of Marketing 4.0. This new generation is available for digitally advanced organizations.

One of the benefits of online marketing is that it can measure interactions with customers more precisely than outdated marketing. Many of the online marketing networks have their own private methodical tools that meet a number of vital marketing criteria. Alford and Page (2015) mentioned in their paper that the arrangement of a shortage of time and how to practice these tools and assimilate the information they offer in their marketing are major obstacles for owner-managers to adopt more marketing techniques. Owner-managers are interested in testing and learning, experimenting with online marketing networks, and equipping themselves with information to achieve tangible benefits. Owner-managers say they are more interested in attracting better attention than measuring existing online marketing impacts and establishing a long-standing approach. Owner-managers openly accept the benefits of adopting marketing models. However, this does not include the level of recognition of business models. In addition, people are aware of how marketing technology can support market positioning. Due to the lack of technical skills and, in particular, the lack of goal setting and measurement, the ability of business possessor executives to convert their positive views on the use of marketing technology to clarify plans is hindered (Alford and Page, 2015). This is an obstacle to achieving all the assistances of the use of technology in marketing.

The appearance of social networks based on the internet allows hundreds or even thousands of companies to communicate about products and services. They are defined as a set of internet-based uses built upon social networks, Web 2.0 ideas, and technologies that allow the formation and interchange of user-generated content. Several social networking applications have been established to enable user interaction on the internet. Vassileva (2017) stated that digitization changes the purchasing decision procedure, including the search for customer information, the consideration and evaluation of products and services, the interaction with organizations, and the purchase.

Social networks have become an important part of the human lifecycle and have concerned the consideration of marketing specialists. Social networks have been recognized as an important tool for today's inbound–outbound hybrid marketing communications portfolio. Today's social media revolution has turned the internet into a policy to promote the exchange of information between users (Vassileva, 2017). Social networks offer marketing specialists a unique opportunity to investigate and analyze customer communication and collaboration of behaviour patterns in social systems, allowing them to develop appropriate marketing campaigns, particularly brand-oriented marketing communications.

Agile marketing

Customer transfer has become very important as it is a material chance to emphasize a customer-oriented approach and is no longer just a commercial priority. Furthermore, it is no longer a network and a mobile device but a new- and last-generation digital cross-channel. Yusoff *et al*. (2019) stated that the total strength of all consumers constitutes market influence, and market forces can affect the market. In addition, marketing is about straightforwardness and understanding why someone desires a product or service. Marketing really makes things easier. The ease of marketing knowledge directs consumerism. Therefore, it works very well when the marketing information is simple, easy to appreciate, and clear. Practice is the basic concept of agile marketing. It is designed to offer customer value in the digital ecosystem with agile marketing, technology, immediate marketing, digital knowledge delivery, customized solutions, information acceleration, incorporated systems, and strategic speed development. Taking these factors into account, agility and the need to respond were determined.

Agile marketing promotes inter-functional collaboration, sharing objectives, and training teams. Achieving goals is a fast-learning process.

This is the strategic marketing method where marketing teams work together to recognize high-value projects to focus on joint efforts. Agile marketing permits marketing teams to quickly issue content and then redesign them according to their performance. Gera *et al.* (2019) stated that, through agile marketing, businesses can react to market changes and regulate their attitudes accordingly. Simply put, agile marketing is a multifunctional event where members of different departments work together to take advantage of marketing prospects and make variations to marketing plans based on dynamic environments. This is a procedure that emphasizes discovery, testing, and execution of a variety of core projects related to corporate marketing.

One of the advantages of using agile marketing is that it assists in generating high-quality jobs with a common vision, which is divided into small projects. The team meets every day to verify project work and detect deviations. They are determined to eliminate avoidable procedures. This leads to generalization. The agile marketing team fulfils daily tasks and communicates with each other at each stage, so that they can easily identify themselves in the first stage in case of any problems (Gera *et al.*, 2019).

Diverse combinations of management may be appropriate for diverse points of market confusion or demand ambiguity. In particular, market-oriented organizations and businesses can work productively in turbulent and shifting surroundings (Cadogan, 2012). It is for this reason that they have the ability to help companies create innovative products and procedures and react to shifting surroundings. Likewise, learning organizations can recognize market opportunities and remain sensitive to market variations.

Methodology

We adopted a practical approach to conduct the research and reach a meaningful conclusion. Two specific research objectives are defined.

The first objective is to explore digital marketing strategies followed by education companies in Bangladesh to achieve better outcomes. The second objective is to determine the ways they are adopting to reengineer their marketing efforts. Institution owners or managers are assessed based on their attitudes towards marketing efforts.

For this research study, data were collected in a systematic manner through a well-structured questionnaire. The questionnaire consists of two sections involving both qualitative and quantitative questions. The first section is designed to collect personal information, and the second section is designed to collect data about their approaches to marketing their services.

The sample consisted of 10 education consultancy firms promoting higher education for diverse students. The study was conducted in Dhaka City, Bangladesh. The data were processed using various statistical techniques.

Analysis

Specific marketing plan

A marketing plan is a premeditated guide map for companies to form, perform, and monitor their marketing strategies over a period of time. It may comprise distinct marketing approaches for several marketing teams throughout the business, but not all marketing plans address the same corporate objectives. It includes additional marketing approaches to support it. It is an outline used to create all marketing strategies that help attach each approach to larger marketing operations and business objectives. The development of a marketing plan can be implemented by the business as a first resource.

As seen in Figure 1 or Table 1, all the businesses have their own marketing plans. It denotes that they are quite sure about their businesses and marketing objectives, as well as the way to attain those objectives.

Figure 1. Specific marketing plan.

Table 1. Responses in regard to specific marketing plan.

Particulars	No. of responses	Percentages
Yes	10	100%
No	0	0%

The inclusion of a marketing plan into the overall business plan helps a business get better outcomes on time and maintain its market status over the years. Above all, a specific marketing plan leads to a way towards the achievement of corporate goals over time.

Basis for targeting customers

Target marketing is an approach that divides large markets into minor segments that focus on a precise customer base within that audience. It identifies a subset of clients grounded on their distinctive features and emphasizes serving those customers. In place of trying to enter the market, companies are using target marketing to focus their energies on connections with specific and defined groups in the market. Companies can also benefit from business segments taking into account factors such as sector, business size, or annual proceeds. Through market segmentation, businesses can understand their target markets more specifically. They can emphasize on a smaller percentage of clients who will benefit most from their products.

A perusal of Figure 2 or Table 2 shows that 40% of firms expressed that the basis of their targeting was the education level of the prospects. Age and income level were the next most considered basis. Location has been considered less by education consultancy firms in Bangladesh. These education consultancy firms are focused on the higher education for students; it is quite common that they consider the education level of their customers to determine whether they are eligible to receive the services offered by them. Furthermore, age can influence the interest of the customer, and income level is required to assess whether the customer has the financial ability to receive the service as a whole.

Budget allocation to promote the services

A sophisticated budget with facilitation services provides a rich sense of trend for the organization of marketing efforts. It allocates finances

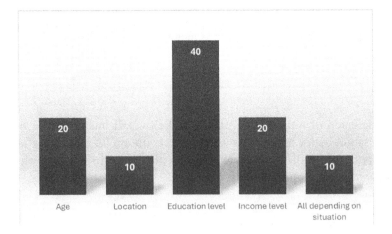

Figure 2. Basis for targeting customers.

Table 2. Responses in regard to the basis for targeting customers.

Particulars	No. of responses	Percentages
Age	2	20%
Location	1	10%
Education level	4	40%
Income level	2	20%
All depending on situation	1	10%

Figure 3. Responses in regard to the basis for targeting customers.

more efficiently. It provides the basis for evaluating the actual outcomes. If the company recognizes the amount in the financial plan, it will better understand which marketing channels can maximize the return on the marketing investment.

As seen in Figure 3 or Table 3, most of the education consultancy firms allocate almost 10% of their targeted sales for promotional

Table 3. Responses in regard to the basis for targeting customers.

Particulars	No. of responses	Percentages (%)
5% of target sales	1	10
10% of target sales	6	60
15% of target sales	0	0
20% of target sales	1	10
30% of target sales	2	20

activities. A business has other expenses as well. Therefore, it is very standard to allocate 10% of targeted sales for this purpose. In contrast, a few businesses employ 30% of their targeted sales for promotion of their services, which is an aggressive approach since the allocation of so much amount to only one nature of expenditure may lead to shortages of supply for other expenditures.

Promotional strategies followed to attract customers

There is no doubt that all companies must adopt some sort of marketing approach to reach a compact client base. It will bring about more sales when the business adopts a good marketing strategy. A good status in this interconnected world has proven to be a key way to differentiate. Good marketing assists in capturing information and metrics to get more information about the target market so that strategies can be better targeted.

Of the respondents, 50% informed that they prefer social media marketing as their promotional strategy (Figure 4 or Table 4). The remaining respondents gave identical responses for the other suggested strategies. This means that social media marketing has become one of the most popular choices for marketing to promote services. It offers various interactive options for the marketers to customize their options as well as target their markets. Thus, it has become so widespread nowadays.

Length of performing promotional activities

A compact schedule of marketing strategies is fundamental to designing a good marketing approach. The marketing approach timeline lists the steps necessary to successfully implement the approach. It permits companies

Figure 4. Promotional strategies followed to attract customers.

Table 4. Responses in regard to promotional strategies followed to attract customers.

Particulars	No. of responses	Percentages (%)
Advertising	1	10
Social media marketing	5	50
Personal selling	1	10
Sales promotion	1	10
Public relations	0	0
Direct marketing	1	10

to implement policies gradually and carefully, so that each stage follows the previous stage. The products require a smart seller to sell quickly to their target audience. Despite this, many markers have failed, one of the main reasons for which is the absence of a solid marketing approach. If they had had a solid marketing program, despite the intense competition, selling their products would have been easy.

As seen in Figure 5 or Table 5, almost 50% of respondents run their promotional strategies for only one week. Since the education sector is also becoming more challenging day by day, it is now difficult to attract and retain customers. Therefore, marketers devise short-term strategies and then customize them, considering the latest demand trends for their services.

Figure 5. Length of performing promotional activities.

Table 5. Responses in regard to length of performing promotional activities.

Particulars	No. of responses	Percentages (%)
One day	0	0
One week	5	50
One month	3	30
Two months	1	10
Depends on service specification	1	10

Biggest selling point

A selling point, also known as a single sale offer, is the core of making a good or service superior to that of a competitor. Communicating this evidently and quickly in online marketing is one of the means of attracting probable customers to the business. A single point of sale identifies the company's distinctive place in the market and becomes the core of the business: the significance it provides and the issue it cracks. A solid perspective clearly shows the specific benefits that other opponents do not provide and highlights the benefits.

Almost 40% of respondents think that their customers prefer their services due to their service quality (Figure 6 or Table 6). Brand name and additional value-added services were cited as the next most probable causes. These features attract customers to the business and compel them

Figure 6. Biggest selling points.

Table 6. Responses in regard to the biggest selling points.

Particulars	No. of responses	Percentages (%)
Brand name	2	20
Service warranty	1	10
Service quality	4	40
Discounted offers	1	10
Additional value-added services	2	20

to receive its services. Therefore, deciding the biggest selling point is itself a challenge for the business.

Conclusions and Recommendations

In the present-day era, it is quite inconceivable for a business to sustain itself without the accomplishment of any marketing efforts for its products or services. It was observed that educational consultancy firms are working systematically towards the creation of specific marketing plans and are targeting the right customers with the required levels of education, age, and income.

The identification of a single selling point by these firms and communicating this evidently and quickly in online marketing is one of the means of attracting probable customers to the business. A single point of sale identifies the company's distinctive place in the market and becomes the core of the business. Firms were of the view that customers preferred their services due to their utmost service quality. Brand name and additional value-added services were cited as the next most probable causes. This was an appealing factor that led them to adopt strategies, leading to brand image creation. Promotional offers were adopted and instantly offered to the prospects.

Most importantly, most of them articulated that the prospects expressed their agility through social media marketing because they consider that it offers various facilities to reach customers easily, get connected with them, and serve them timely. In contrast, it is also observed that few businesses are overspending on marketing approaches. It is recommended to them that they also shift to social media marketing because it provides more services at lower costs. Above all, it helps a business create a strong brand image and provide distinct offers to customers.

References

Alford, P., and Page, S. (2015). Marketing technology for adoption by small business. *The Service Industries Journal*, 35(11–12), 655–669.

Cadogan, J. (2012). International marketing, strategic orientations and business success. *International Marketing Review*, 29(4), 340–348.

Gera, G., Gera, B., and Mishra, A. (2019). Role of agile marketing in the present era. *International Journal of Technical Research & Science*, 4(5), 40–44.

Ghahnavieh, A. (2018). The influence of marketing factors on the marketing strategic planning in SNOWA corporation. *Business and Management Studies*, 4(4), 51.

Hendrix, P. (2014). How digital technologies are enabling consumers and transforming the practice of marketing. *Journal of Marketing Theory and Practice*, 22(2), 149–150.

Juttner, U., Christopher, M., and Godsell, J. (2010). A strategic framework for integrating marketing and supply chain strategies. *The International Journal of Logistics Management*, 21(1), 104–126.

Papasolomou, I., Thrassou, A., Vrontis, D., and Sabova, M. (2014). Marketing public relations: A consumer-focused strategic perspective. *Journal of Customer Behaviour*, 13(1), 5–24.

Vassileva, B. (2017). Consumer activities and reactions to social network marketing. *Management*, 12(2), 133–144.

Yusoff, Y., Alias, Z., Abdullah, M., and Mansor, Z. (2019). Agile marketing conceptual framework for private higher education institutions. *International Journal of Academic Research in Business and Social Sciences*, 9(1), 1052–1058.

Chapter 21

Enhancing Resilience in Times of COVID-19 Crisis: Evidence from Indian Hotel Industry

Sukhpreet Kaur[*], Deepa Guleria[†], and Gurvinder Kaur[‡]

Thapar Institute of Engineering and Technology, Patiala, Punjab, India
[*]sukhpreetkaur358@gmail.com
[†]deepa03guleria@gmail.com
[‡]gurvinder@thapar.edu

Abstract

Employees are considered the most critical resource for any organization. The COVID-19 crisis was never expected by anyone across the globe. The hotel industry is one of the worst hit sectors of the Indian economy. This study aims to explore how the hotel industry developed organizational resilience to survive the first wave of the COVID-19 crisis. For this purpose, survey forms were distributed to a total of 130 human resources (HR) managers/general managers. The survey was distributed and administered via Google Forms. The findings identified 10 broad themes around which the responses were received. The themes were further grouped into three categories: before lockdown phase, during lockdown phase, and after lockdown phase. The results shed light on how HR practices can help revive the hotel industry's workforce.

The results can prove helpful in dealing with the any prodigious situations that may occur in near future due to changing environments.

Keywords: COVID-19, employees, hotel industry, human resource practices, resilience.

Introduction

COVID-19 has affected business operations globally, thereby causing a huge dent in the world's economy. To put the facts straight, the economic effects of the crisis have already been estimated to be five times severe than those of the Global Financial Crisis of 2008 (OECD, 2020). Because of their high vulnerability, the tourism and hotel industries are among the worst hit sectors due to COVID-19. Travel restrictions and norms of social distancing have forced tourism and hospitality businesses to shut down, putting the jobs of over 100 million at risk (World Travel & Tourism Council, 2020). Such a crisis forces businesses to develop resilience capacity to stand against adverse economic situations and survive for the long term. One argument highlights that resilient organizations contribute to resilient communities (Prayag *et al.*, 2020). Extending this argument, Lee *et al.* (2013) explain that if organizations are not prepared to respond to crisis and emergency situations, neither will the suprasystems or communities they belong. Thus, hotel managers (human resource, or HR, managers/general managers) must adopt a resilience-oriented management approach. Preparation should not only be restricted to provide response to anticipated crises but also for after-crisis situations to maximize the opportunities and enhance business competitiveness (Tibay *et al.*, 2018; Lee *et al.*, 2013).

Over the past two decades, HR management (HRM) has evolved from the traditional function of managing labour to a more strategic role of enhancing employee sustainability and strengthening organizations, especially during emergency situations (Bustinza *et al.*, 2019; Naznin and Hussain, 2016). Despite the role of HR in building an organization's resilience capacity, it has not been well studied in the tourism literature, especially for the hotel industry (Brown *et al.*, 2017; Hall *et al.*, 2017). The study aims to understand the specific HR practices (HRPs) which were adopted by the hotel industry to build its resilience capacity during the times of the COVID-19 crisis. The contribution of this study is twofold. First, the study aims to highlight the importance of HR in building the linkage between resilience activities and the hotel industry. Second, a process-based framework of HR-induced resilience practices will be devised to mitigate the effects of future crises.

Literature Review

Organizational resilience

It is defined as an organization's ability to learn and develop situation-specific responses and ultimately engage in activities which capitalize on disturbing circumstances that may also threaten the existence of any organization (Lengnick-Hall et al., 2011, p. 244). Over the past few years, organization resilience has emerged as one of the most sought-after contemporary issues in business (Prayag et al., 2020). Resilience may be considered reactive or proactive in nature. Some authors (Kamalahmadi and Parast, 2016) explain resilience as an answer to disruptions in a business environment, whereas others associate it with preparedness before the event of disruptions. Gilly et al. (2014) justify resilience as an organization's reactive and proactive ability to prepare and act in new ways to seek stability in a turbulent business environment. There is a fine line of difference between resilience and crisis management. Resilience would be more about an organization's ability to cope with any unforeseen event, whereas crisis management would be linked with changes arising from extraordinary situations (Prayag et al., 2020). Resilience is a dynamic process to cope with changes, starting from prior arrangements to during and finally after management activities. Crisis management, however, operates on a crises-to-processes basis (Williams et al., 2017).

Business revolves around survival, adaptation, and innovation by primarily focusing on cost reduction and activities pertaining to operational adjustments (Dahles and Susilowati, 2015). A resource-based organizational resilience approach, coupled with a capital-based approach (Brown et al., 2018), will be valuable in explaining the hotel management perspective for unforeseen situations, such as the COVID-19 pandemic. Capital is of six types: economic, social, physical, social, human, natural, and cultural. Capital can be drawn from and nurtured by organizational resilience by working around people, processes, and partnership elements (Hall et al., 2017). For this study, organization resilience is linked with a resource-based theory proposed by Barney (1991). The interlinkage of the concept includes all the fundamental resources, including finance, human capital, networking, and core values (Biggs et al., 2015). Human capital strategies for establishing resilience have always been a matter of interest for scholars in the fields of organization behaviour and general management (Lengnick-Hall *et al.*, 2011).

HRM in troubled times

HRM can help organizations by alerting them to operational capabilities in troubled times and developing interventions to improve collective and individual performances to bounce back from crisis-like situations (Hillyard, 2000). Some studies have observed organizations adopting cost-reduction activities, such as layoffs, payroll cuts, recruitment freezes, and downsizing, to maintain the entire system (Teague and Roche, 2014; Santana *et al.*, 2017). Other studies have focused on rebuilding capabilities to face the turbulent business environment rather than solely adopting cost reduction measures (Teague and Roche, 2014). A classic example of the latter would be the workings of the hotel sector in Madrid during the 2008 financial crisis. The hotel industry focused on increasing marketing and promotional activities to attract more guests rather than focusing on cost-cutting measures (Del Mar Alonso-Almeida and Bremser, 2013). Technical and behavioural employee-focused practices are two categories of HRPs which can be applied and altered during times of crisis (Teague and Roche, 2014). Technical practices refer to cost and mechanical reduction activities, whereas behavioural practices focus on employee motivation and commitment. Building on this perspective, this study focusses on creating a set of HRPs for developing resilience capabilities among the employees to boost the revenue of the hotel industry while overcoming the crisis.

Methods

Data collection and sample

Data were collected from three top tourism spots in North India. The tourism spots were selected from Himachal Pradesh. Himachal Pradesh is known as the 'Land of Gods.' It is also known as 'A Destination for all Reasons and Seasons' (Himachal Tourism, 2021). According to the website of Himachal Tourism (2021), the following two tourist spots attracts the maximum number of tourists in the state: Shimla and Kullu Valley. Both the spots have good connectivity, with many national and international tourists visiting daily. Due to heavy tourist traffic, the hotel industry in these districts has also grown exponentially. For the purpose of this study, all the hotels registered with the Himachal Pradesh government were considered. In order to gain reliable information about the preparation before lockdown, the fall of events during lockdown, and revival strategies post upliftment of lockdown, HR/general managers were the key informants of the study. HR/general managers were selected because they are responsible for the implementation of various HR activities, including recruitment and selection, training and development, performance appraisal, and managing compensation policies. Additionally, HR managers plan, decide the work flow, and execute the HR activities for the employees.

A cover letter and survey instrument were prepared for the study and communicated online to the managers. To explain the objectives and methodology of the study, the Google Meet platform was used. To obtain the most reliable and accurate information, all the hotels ($N = 1671$) were considered for the study. To encourage participation, biweekly reminders and supplementary sheets were provided, explaining the statements in a better manner. However, only 670 hotels agreed to participate in the study. One HR/general manager was considered from each hotel. Thus, 470 questionnaires were delivered via Google Forms. Out of 470 questionnaires, only 293 were received. 163 questionnaires showed missing information and were filled carelessly. Thus, a total of 130 responses from HR/general managers were finally selected. Simple random sampling technique was followed. Data collection was done during the first two months of 2021, ranging a span of approximately eight weeks.

Measurement

A semi-structured questionnaire was designed. The questionnaire was broadly divided into two sections. Section one deals with the individual experiences of the respondents. Section two deals with the effects and revival strategies pertaining to the organization. The questionnaire had three types of questions: open-ended questions, multiple-choice questions, and Likert scale-based questions (Table 1). The open-ended questions were analyzed using a qualitative data analysis software (Nivivo v.12, QSR International). The responses were read repeatedly to decode the true information. The responses were coded using an inductive approach (Johnson and Onwuegbuzie, 2004). Many responses revealed overlapping between different codes. The next level of analysis involved identifying

Table 1. Question phrasing and modality for COVID-19 research survey.

Questions	Response type
Section one: About you	
1. What is your gender?	Multiple-choice
2. Specify your job title.	Open-ended
3. In which region do you work?	Multiple-choice
4. Which option best describes your general well-being during lockdown?	Likert-scale
5. Which option best describes your general productivity during lockdown?	Likert-scale
Section two: About organization	
6. Explain the preparation of your organization for lockdown.	Open-ended
7. How did your organization respond to lockdown?	Open-ended
8. Were there any challenges faced by the organization during lockdown? If yes, please specify.	Open-ended
9. Explain your views on new normal.	Open-ended
10. Do you think crisis like COVID-19 will change the investment priorities in resilience activities? If yes, please specify.	Open-ended
11. Please share your views/thoughts on relating COVID-19 experience.	Open-ended

and constructing themes from the responses received. The entire process was carried out by two researchers individually. Finally, the codes developed by each researcher were evaluated simultaneously, and the ones which were of similar nature were ultimately considered, providing validation to the themes. For multiple-choice questions and Likert scale-based questions, IBM SPSS (v. 25) was used.

Analysis

There were 10 coded themes. They were: Health & Safety, Positive Psychology, Organization Culture, Leadership, Business Vision & Mission, Talent Management, Job Relocation, Performance Appraisal, Employee Participation, and Affective Commitment. Each code was reread to categorize it under the correct theme. As a result, three themes encompassing 11 codes were created: before lockdown phase, during lockdown phase, and after lockdown phase strategies. The proportion of male to female respondents was 58.4% male to 40% female (with 1.6% preferring not to say).

Results

To meet the objectives, the responses were divided into three specific timelines centred on the crisis: before lockdown phase, during lockdown phase, and after lockdown phase. The following discussions highlight the responses of hotel managers (more specifically, general managers).

Before lockdown phase

Health and safety

The focus before the lockdown was on precautionary items to lower infection risk and ensure the safety of staff and guests. The provision of hand-sanitizer stalls, face masks, and protective gloves was implemented to prevent the spread of COVID-19. These preventive measures instilled a sense of confidence and relief in the guests. Flexible work schedules and work from home options were other preventive measures. Health-related issues among employees were given significant importance. Minimizing human-to-human contact was also ensured.

Positive psychology

Along with physical health, mental health was also given prime priority. This encompasses employee well-being, a central pillar of employee resilience (Hall *et al.*, 2017; Khan *et al.*, 2019). Frequent and open communication channels between management and employees helped with stress management. The management was open to employee feedback regarding operational improvements. Cooperation was also found to push employees into expressing solidarity among themselves and managers. Sharing trust and values facilitated the development of human resource capabilities (Luthans *et al.*, 2007). Employee well-being can be further enhanced by providing indirect benefits to the workers. For example, health insurance in such times is considered the most desirable benefit to promote employee resilience. Lessening working hours and highlighting and encouraging employees to take accrued leave will not only lower business costs but also reduce the fear of losing their job among employees.

During lockdown phase

Affective commitment

Social engagement-centric practices during training generally help bring the workforce together (Leana III and Van Buren, 1999). This helps build emotional bonds among employees. Some responses indicated that their hotels maintained the normal course of training even during the economic slowdown because it helped improve employee interaction and welfare. Training and development activities also helped build mutual hope, positivity, and beliefs. This phase witnessed a shift from external to internal training, thereby harnessing an organization's capabilities to their fullest. In-house training can prove highly beneficial while looking for internal promotions.

Employee participation

Soft practices, such as diffused accountability and employee participation, can also prove useful for enhancing employee resilience. The responses highlighted the need for an empowerment-induced environment for improved decision-making. Such a scenario will improve the output of employee participation activities. Others marked the need for disseminating correct and clear information so that they could act, learn, and respond accordingly. The results broadly shed light on the importance of effective communication to maintain and improve employee involvement and commitment.

After lockdown phase

The first sign of relief for the Indian hotel industry was observed in July 2020 ('Unlock Phase 2.0'), when social distancing rules were partially lifted. Tourist places were opened. Although international borders continued to restrict the entry of tourists, domestic tourism was encouraged during the recovery phase. The key aspects of this phase included the following.

Leadership

Employee-oriented sharing and ethical values helped informants regarding resilience-based HRPs. Most of the responses highlighted employees' fears concerning welfare activities. However, businesses displayed ethical behaviour and concern for subordinates, highlighting two significant leadership qualities that are particularly important in service organizations (Ehrhart, 2004; Mullins, 2016).

Organization culture

The responses indicated that the policies required to survive the COVID-19 crisis were people-centred. In people-centric organizations, the central focus is on the betterment of individuals (Mullins, 2016). Many individuals acknowledged the essential role of employees in delivering good services and increasing profitability (Fulford and Enz, 1995). They felt that caring during tough times would increase loyalty and commitment. People-oriented values have been found to be one of the best antecedents of employee commitment.

Business mission and vision

Another important factor influencing resilience practices was the focus on business vision and mission. During the crisis, the long-term strategies stemmed from the company's charted business mission and values manual. These act as a beacon for the company during tough times. HR managers work in alignment with the charted values to nurture a highly skilled and committed workforce. They felt that maintaining the current workforce was essential for developing business activities, despite the burden of labour costs.

Talent management

It is one of the finest business strategies to develop a competitive advantage (Phillips and Edwards, 2009). During this period, businesses were having a tough time finding a qualified and suitable workforce because their best employees were looking for jobs in sectors which were not badly hit by COVID-19. Measures to retain employees after the COVID-19 crisis proved to be one of the major challenges.

Job relocation

The revival phase witnessed a restructuring of business units, with many more hotels focusing on attracting domestic tourists. This caused managers to hire individuals or rehire temporarily removed employees to ensure more productivity with limited number of staff. Some job roles were even allowed to work from home or in hybrid form.

Performance appraisal

Performance appraisal of employees was an important measure taken by managers. Reopening after a long gap created pressure on businesses to meet the high expectations of customers and thereby win back their business. Frequent performance appraisals kept employees on their toes and were much needed to enable quick business recovery.

Discussions and Conclusion

This study attempted to provide useful insights into the strategies employed to develop organizational resilience through the lens of HRPs. The results included subthemes which were found useful in deriving theoretical and managerial contributions.

This study has four main theoretical contributions. First, it highlights the contribution of resilience capabilities in the wake of the global health crisis, focusing on lockdown, which was applied in many countries. Second, this study offers a process-based approach to considering the stages in the development of organizational resilience. Defensive and offensive responses were measured and interpreted accordingly. Notably, the practices followed during lockdown were both defensive and offensive in nature and possessed the capabilities to initiate change in the organization. Finally, the study highlighted practices which can be deployed at all stages of a crisis to survive and recover. For example, *health and safety* have to be given prime importance during all stages of work.

With the second wave of the COVID-19 crisis, businesses had to gear themselves up to face multiple obstacles and challenges. The results revealed how managers and employees reacted to the crisis and managed potential risks during different stages of lockdown. The proposed framework provides guidelines for businesses to develop action plans to respond to current or future crises. Notably, entrepreneurs should be aware of the interaction of resilience stages, implying that the measures businesses adopt to achieve coping capabilities significantly affect their adaptive capabilities in the recovery phase. Finally, the study emphasized the importance of internal business management factors, such as leadership, organizational culture, vision, and financial support, highlighting that managers must find a balance between what is possible and what is practical during a crisis. It is also hoped that these resilience HRPs will sustain these businesses during the prodigious situations that may occur in near future due to changing environments or resultant of COVID-19.

References

Barney, J. (1991). Firm resources and sustained competitive advantage. *Journal of Management*, 17(1), 99–120. https://doi.org/10.1177/014920639101700108.

Biggs, D., Hall, C. M., and Stoeckl, N. (2012). The resilience of formal and informal tourism enterprises to disasters: Reef tourism in Phuket, Thailand. *Journal of Sustainable Tourism*, 20(5), 645–665. https://doi.org/10.1080/09669582.2011.630080.

Brown, N. A., Rovins, J. E., Feldmann-Jensen, S., Orchiston, C., and Johnston, D. (2017). Exploring disaster resilience within the hotel sector: A systematic review of literature. *International Journal of Disaster Risk Reduction*, 22, 362–370. https:// doi.org/10.1016/j.ijdrr.2017.02.005.

Bustinza, O. F., Vendrell-Herrero, F., Perez-Arostegui, M. N., and Parry, G. (2019). Technological capabilities, resilience capabilities and organizational effectiveness. *The International Journal of Human Resource Management*, 30(8), 1370–1392. https://doi.org/10.1080/09585192.2016.1216878.

Dahles, H., and Susilowati, T. P. (2015). Business resilience in times of growth and crisis. *Annals of Tourism Research*, 51, 34–50. https://doi.org/10.1016/j.annals.2015.01.002.

Del Mar Alonso-Almeida, M., and Bremser, K. (2013). Strategic responses of the Spanish hospitality sector to the financial crisis. *International Journal of Hospitality Management*, 32, 141–148. https://doi.org/10.1016/j.ijhm.2012.05.004.

Ehrhart, M. G. (2004). Leadership and procedural justice climate as antecedents of unit-level organizational citizenship behavior. *Personnel Psychology*, 57(1), 61–94. https://doi.org/10.1111/j.1744-6570.2004.tb02484.x.

Fulford, M. D., and Enz, C. A. (1995). The impact of empowerment on service employees. *Journal of Managerial Issues*, 7, 161–175.

Gilly, J. P., Kechidi, M., and Talbot, D. (2014). Resilience of organisations and territories: The role of pivot firms. *European Management Journal,* 32(4), 596–602.

Hall, C. M., Prayag, G., and Amore, A. (2017). *Tourism and Resilience: Individual, Organisational and Destination Perspectives.* Bristol, Blue Ridge Summit: Channel View Publications. https://doi.org/10.21832/9781845416317.

Leana III, C. R. and Van Buren, H. J. (1999). Organizational social capital and employment practices. *Academy of Management Review,* 24(3), 538–555. https://doi.org/10.5465/amr.1999.2202136.

Chapter 22

Clustering and Topic Modelling of Business Research Trends during COVID-19

Rohit Bhuvaneshwar Mishra* and Hongbing Jiang[†]

*School of Management Engineering,
Zhengzhou University, Zhengzhou, China*

*rohit.bnmishra123@gmail.com

[†]*jhbymx@zzu.edu.cn*

Abstract

During COVID-19, a substantial amount of research literature was published in the field of business research. The new challenges posed by the pandemic tested the resilience of businesses as they tried to find ways to adapt to new business practices during COVID-19. To aid business stakeholders and researchers in understanding the pandemic's impact on businesses, this study used a variety of methods to analyze a corpus of business-related articles published during COVID-19. To begin, an unsupervised clustering algorithm was used to group research papers similar to each other. We combined the t-distributed stochastic neighbour embedding (t-SNE) and k-means clustering for our research. We clustered the articles into 20 clusters using the elbow method to define the optimum number of clusters. Following the clustering of the literature, we used latent Dirichlet allocation to perform topic modelling on each cluster. We identified 457 topics from the 20 clusters obtained from *t*-SNE *k*-means clustering. To these 20 clusters, we manually assigned research themes such as technology, healthcare, economy, finance, supply chain management, education, travel and tourism, trade, mental health, emerging technology, energy sector, policy, workplace and employee, and strategic decision-making. Additionally, co-occurrence analysis was used to determine the relationships between keywords. The abstract text from all included studies was used to create a network map of co-occurrences. We concentrated on the word "business" to highlight the relationships and the direction of keyword connections. Finally, we provide a word cloud of the abstract text and a world cloud derived from the topic modelling keywords. At the end of the chapter, we check the clustering efficiency using the stochastic gradient descent classifier, and we also discuss the applicability and utility of each of these methods.

Keywords: Clustering, topic modelling, COVID-19, business research, word co-occurrence, word cloud.

Introduction

The outbreak of the coronavirus pandemic impacted almost all aspects of our daily lives. COVID-19 is a severe respiratory disorder that was first identified in Wuhan, China (Hui *et al.*, 2020; Kucharski *et al.*, 2020). Early symptoms of COVID-19 include fatigue, a high fever, and a dry cough. Additionally, joint pain, a sore throat, and a poor sense of smell and taste are common. Finally, severe pneumonia and a variety of other cardiovascular complications would occur during the disease's course. The UN World Health Organization (WHO), on 11 March 2020, declared COVID-19 a global pandemic (WHO, 2020). Since the outbreak of the disease, the world has suffered from its multiple aftershocks. More than 134 million people were infected with COVID-19 at the time of writing, and more than 2.91 million people had been reported to have died from COVID-19-related causes (JHU CSSE, 2021).

Governments across countries took measures to stifle the virus spread and imposed various restrictions. This impacted all business processes severely. Economic activity in every region of the world was disturbed (Chudik *et al.*, 2020; Ibn-Mohammed *et al.*, 2021; UNCTAD, 2020; World Economic Forum, 2020b; WTO, 2020). Businesses faced financial difficulties and reduced their manufacturing capacity. As a result, joblessness and underemployment have been increasing (Bofinger *et al.*, 2020).

Additionally, government and corporate debt have increased, resulting in financial instabilities that extended the COVID-19 recovery period (Donthu and Gustafsson, 2020). Closures of borders and lockdowns have disrupted global trade (Gruszczynski, 2020; Ibn-Mohammed et al., 2021; OECD, 2020; UNCTAD, 2020; World Economic Forum, 2020b; WTO, 2020). The global economy faced significant challenges in 2020, and its recovery in 2021 remains uncertain due to the evolving nature of the COVID-19 pandemic. As we approach mid-2021, the journey toward economic stabilization is complex and contingent upon various factors including ongoing efforts to control the pandemic, the effectiveness of governmental responses, and the pace of vaccination campaigns (Evenett, 2020; SDG Knowledge Hub, 2021). The COVID-19 crisis has wreaked havoc on supply chains, affecting consumers, business owners, and the overall world economy (Ivanov, 2020). Globalization increased the complexity and interdependence of supply chains, making them more susceptible to disruption caused by COVID-19. Supply chains and sectoral activities had to be reshaped in order to maintain visibility, agility, and productivity (Barman et al., 2021; Grida et al., 2020; Guan et al., 2020; Ivanov, 2020; PricewaterhouseCoopers, 2020b; Sharma et al., 2020a; Sharma et al., 2020b; World Economic Forum, 2020a).

COVID-19 has also influenced shopping behaviour (Hakim et al., 2021; Laguna et al., 2020; Mehta et al., 2020; Sheth, 2020). The demand for essential goods such as household goods, dairy products, and medical care increased, providing sellers and service providers with additional opportunities to serve consumers in their homes (Addo et al., 2020; Hakim et al., 2021; Juaneda-Ayensa et al., 2016; Kapoor et al., 2020). Market sentiment changed on a microscale. Due to the scarcity of goods and services, buyers had to reassess their purchasing habits and requirements, placing a premium on essentials. A rise in demand for basic goods, panic shopping, and customer demand changes coupled with industrial shutdowns have severely affected the global production system (Ivanov, 2020). Grocery and convenience stores struggled to keep up with rising demand as consumers stockpiled supplies in anticipation of extended lockdowns, movement restrictions, and supply shortages (Addo et al., 2020).

Many service-related businesses closed, and the ones running incurred severe losses (Garvey and Carnovale, 2020). Sectors such as hospitality and tourism collapsed as a result of social isolation, border controls, quarantine restrictions, and fear of virus spread. Tourism ceased in March 2020, with international travel bans affecting more than 90% of the world's population (Altuntas and Gok, 2021; Davahli et al., 2020; Grech *et al.*, 2020; Kaushal and Srivastava, 2021; Moreno-Luna *et al.*, 2021; Sigala, 2020). However, service sectors such as the information technology industry clearly enjoyed growth during COVID-19, as it was able to switch to the work-from-home model easily (Alashhab *et al.*, 2020; Evans, 2020; Evenett, 2020; PricewaterhouseCoopers, 2020a; Vargo *et al.*, 2021). Even the education industry felt tremors during the initial phase of the pandemic. However, increased digitalization aided educational institutions in their transition to distance education (Dhawan, 2020; Fairlie and Loyalka, 2020; World Bank, 2021). Fortunately, there are a variety of contemporary tools available to facilitate the process of distance learning. However, certain critical components of the learning process, such as assessment, laboratory work, personality development, and psychological support, can be difficult to accomplish through digital education (Batra *et al.*, 2021; García and Weiss, 2020; The Lancet, 2020; Rashid and Yadav, 2020; Son *et al.*, 2020, p. 15; Teräs *et al.*, 2020).

In the backdrop of COVID-19 affecting all spheres of business, it is essential to study how businesses are responding to these evolving challenges. While business owners realigned their priorities to address long-standing concerns such as strategic planning, organizational effectiveness, business continuity planning, and potential threats, the pandemic put their resilience to the test as they attempted to pave the way towards recovery (Ivanov, 2020). This study analyzed a corpus of COVID-19-related business articles to gain insight into business research trends to help business owners and researchers determine the impact of the pandemic and help understand future business trends. By clustering and topic modelling of business research trends, we extracted implicit knowledge from research corpora. The research will assist industries, businesses, and researchers in better understanding business research trends and aligning with future opportunities while also understanding the corresponding threats.

Literature Review

Text mining and data analysis should be increasingly used to extract implicit knowledge from the published research literature (Antons *et al.*, 2020). With the growth of content from journals, social media, and business press releases, as well as scientific articles and discourse, knowledge extraction from literature will become increasingly difficult in the future. Digitization efforts in nearly every business domain would increase the volume and variety of unstructured data. Applying out-of-date techniques, such as manual selection and classification (Antons *et al.*, 2016), to research documents containing an increasing amount of unstructured data is already out of scope. Therefore, we require novel and automated techniques to deal with the data and problems of the 21st century.

Due to the increasing volume of publications on COVID-19, text mining and natural language processing models are the only feasible options for extracting useful insights from published research literature, social media data, business press releases, etc. These methods are widely used in computer linguistics, patent analysis, idea mining, etc. (Antons *et al.*, 2019; Choi *et al.*, 2013; Thorleuchter and Van den Poel, 2015; Thorleuchter *et al.*, 2010; Tseng *et al.*, 2007), but their application in the field of business literature is rare. There is an urgent need to apply these methods in business domains to help industries and businesses use the extracted knowledge to better understand business opportunities and the corresponding threats. There are a few studies focused on business-related literature, but they use manual methods for data collection and analysis (Antons *et al.*, 2016). These methods have the advantage of expert involvement and hence provide good insights even from a small dataset. However, these methods are inapplicable in today's environment, given the sheer volume and diversity of literature associated with COVID-19. Other methods which are common for literature analysis are bibliographic and citation analysis. Bibliometric analysis is a method used for examining the evolution of research domains, topics, and authors by examining a set of published research papers (Ferreira *et al.*, 2016; Muñoz-Leiva *et al.*, 2012). There are many bibliographic studies on COVID-19 (Dehghanbanadaki *et al.*, 2020; ElHawary *et al.*, 2020; Hossain, 2020; Mao *et al.*, 2020; Wang and Tian, 2021; Zhang and Shaw, 2020; Zyoud and Al-Jabi, 2020); however, only a few bibliometric and citation analysis studies have assessed COVID-19's impact on businesses (Donthu and Gustafsson, 2020; He and Harris, 2020; Nasir *et al.*, 2020; Verma and Gustafsson, 2020). These studies have various shortcomings: for example, they rely on small datasets, and they require manual input from experts for data collection (using Web of Science or Scopus word-based search), cleaning data (manually removing duplicates and checking for the language of paper), and selection of data (scope of paper, type of paper, and research direction of paper).

In view of the various shortcomings of manual classification of research articles, we attempted to develop an automated prototype for literature analysis. In this research, we present an unsupervised *t*-distributed stochastic neighbour embedding (*t*-SNE) *k*-means clustering technique to identify current business research trends. After clustering of the literature, we implement topic modelling on each cluster using latent Dirichlet allocation (LDA). This is done to identify the keywords in each cluster. Furthermore, co-word analysis is implemented by using the abstract text of clustered literature. This provides an overview of the relationships between keywords in the abstract text. Finally, we provide a word cloud of the abstract text as well as a world cloud from the keywords obtained through topic modelling. This helps us visualize the most frequent terms from the research corpus.

Research Methodology Article Selection

We used the COVID-19 Open Research Dataset (CORD-19) for our study (Lu Wang *et al.*, 2020). CORD-19's rich collection of metadata and structured full-text papers is intended to aid in the implementation of text analysis and knowledge discovery systems. CORD-19 is a freely available resource for researchers all over the world that contains a large selection of academic papers on COVID-19. The dataset contains articles from bioRxiv, medRxiv, PubMed, Elsevier, Springer, and WHO's COVID-19 Database (Lu Wang *et al.*, 2020). We used the dataset released on 1 March 2021 (CORD-19, 2021), including the metadata file, the parsed data file, and also the cord-embedding file.

This dataset consists mostly of papers from the medical field (around 90%); hence, it is necessary to filter out business-related papers. We searched for business-related terms in titles and abstract texts using the "metadata.csv" file from the CORD-19 dataset. Then, the associated full texts were selected from the dataset. We tested various search keywords to automatically get the business-related papers. The noteworthy search keywords used are "management" and "business". The search for the "management" keyword filtered 35,005 articles, while the search result for "business" filtered 3,779 articles. On checking the results from both searches, we found out that articles with the "management" keyword were mostly from the medical field, whereas those with the "business" keyword were a combination of business and other fields. Hence, we decided to use the "business" keyword. After getting the 3,779 articles from the initial search, we checked the language of all the selected research papers (through code) and retained only English-language papers in our dataset. The final dataset was reduced to 3,363 articles. This dataset is many times larger than the manual dataset prepared for bibliographic and citation-based studies discussed earlier. All the subsequent analyses were performed on these selected articles.

Text pre-processing

Once we obtained the 3,363 articles, we removed the stop words. In addition, we also removed custom stop words such as "doi", "preprint", "copyright", "peer", "reviewed", "org", "https", "et", "al", "author", "figure", "rights", "reserved", "permission", "used", "using", "biorxiv", "medrxiv", "license", "fig", "fig.", "al.", "Elsevier", "PMC", "CZI", "www", and "springer". These words appear frequently in the corpora under study and hence need to be removed. Once the stop words were removed, we parsed the text from the selected articles. After this step, we applied SPECTER embedding to the data (Cohan *et al.*, 2020). We used the SPECTER model to learn scientific paper representations, which is based on a transformer language model. This model is preferred because it achieves significant improvements over a variety of baselines. After changing the embeddings to SPECTER embeddings, we get a dataset with dimensions of (3363,768). See Figure 1 for entire research process.

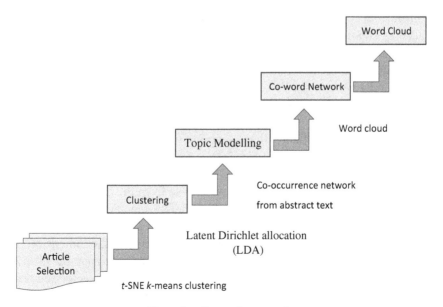

Figure 1. Research approach.

Clustering

Clustering, or cluster analysis in some cases, is a type of unsupervised machine learning task. Clustering automatically groups similar data together (Adamyan *et al.*, 2020; Wenliang *et al.*, 2005). In contrast to supervised learning algorithms, clustering algorithms simply interpret the input data and search for naturally occurring groups or clusters in a feature space. When there is no class to predict and the instances must be divided into natural groups, clustering techniques are used. Clustering can be useful as a data analysis activity for pattern or knowledge discovery, which is when you want to learn more about the problem domain. Although many clustering-specific quantitative measures exist, evaluating identified clusters is subjective and may require the assistance of a domain expert (Adamyan *et al.*, 2020; Baker and McCallum, 1998; Čolović *et al.*, 2016; Šubelj *et al.*, 2016; Wenliang *et al.*, 2005).

For our research, we combined t-SNE and k- means clustering (Haraty *et al.*, 2015; Linderman and Steinerberger, 2017). We began by reducing the dimensionality of each feature vector and clustering similar research articles in the plane with two dimensions using t-SNE. By attempting to keep similar and dissimilar instances apart, the t-SNE algorithm reduces the dimensionality. Then, for the k-means clustering, we plotted distortion against various k values in order to find the k value for which the distortion decreases are negligible. This demonstrates the optimal number of clusters. This is known as the "elbow method" in k-means clustering for determining the desired number of clusters. We can see in Figure 2 that the k values between 10 and 20 are ideal. After that, the reduction in distortion is not noticeable. To keep things simple, we use $k = 20$. In the next step, to decrease the dimensionality of the input data, we use principal component analysis (PCA). PCA is a linear algebraic technique used to create a dataset consistent with the learning model or algorithm when data are being prepared (Ding and He, 2004). Reducing the dimensionality to fewer variables helps in simplifying the model and improves performance when predicting new data (i.e., removes noise from the data). Our vectorized data had a dimension of (3,363,768) before the application of PCA. We used a variance of 95% for PCA, and the dimensions of the data were reduced to (3,363,300). We can see a good reduction in the dimension of the data without losing much information as a high variance of 95% is applied. We used the k-means clustering algorithm on this vectorized text to group similar articles. The k-means method classifies each vector by

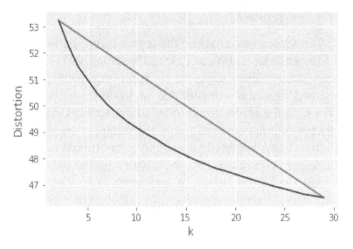

Figure 2. Elbow method.

computing the mean distance to a randomly chosen centroid, and the centroids are revised sequentially.

In the third and last step, we used the *t*-SNE clusters with *k*-means as our labels to get the final clustering results.

Topic modelling using latent Dirichlet allocation

After clustering the literature, we find the most important words in each cluster. The articles were clustered using *k*-means, but the important topics in each cluster need to be identified. We used topic modelling to determine the most important words in each cluster. This will help clarify the types of papers included in each cluster. We used the LDA algorithm to decide the topics for each cluster (Antons *et al.*, 2019; Asmussen and Møller, 2019; Blei *et al.*, 2003; Brust *et al.*, 2017; Davahli *et al.*, 2020; Maier *et al.*, 2018). However, it does not generate topic labels, and they must be manually identified. LDA is a generative model that elucidates why certain components of data are similar. LDA is a widely used probabilistic text modelling technique, especially in natural language processing and statistical machine learning applications. Additionally, LDA has a number of advantages over related techniques such as latent semantic indexing (LSI) and probabilistic semantic indexing (pLSI), which were among the first topic modelling algorithms (Blei *et al.*, 2003).

Co-occurrence networks

We used VOSviewer to analyze the connections between keywords extracted from abstract texts (van Eck and Waltman, 2011). We generated a two-dimensional map of keyword co-occurrence networks (adjectives and nouns) and used this network file in VOSviewer. We checked for keywords only in the abstract text to avoid unnecessary data congestion. When two keywords appear in the same abstract, they are said to co-occur. The similarity of two keywords is roughly proportional to their distance from one another. As a result, keywords with a higher co-occurrence rate are more likely to be discovered in conjunction (Andersen *et al.*, 2020; Mao *et al.*, 2020; Martinez-Perez *et al.*, 2020; Verma and Gustafsson, 2020).

Word cloud creation

As the final step in our visualization process, we employ a word cloud. A "word cloud" is a graphical representation of the frequency of occurrence of particular words. The bigger the term in the word cloud image, the more frequently it occurs in the analyzed text (Atenstaedt, 2017; Depaolo and Wilkinson, 2014). Word clouds are gaining popularity as a clear and simple technique for determining the focus of written material. They have been used to visualize the content of research papers in a variety of fields, including medicine, business, and education.

Results

We identified the business research trends during COVID-19. Our research can help students, researchers, academic leaders, journal editors, business practitioners, and policymakers discover trends in business research during COVID-19. Our experiments are designed to evaluate various techniques for identifying business research trends. We discuss the results for all the methods implemented in this section. We also evaluate the usability and applicability of these methods based on our analysis:

- unsupervised *t*-SNE *k*-means clustering to identify business research paper clusters,
- LDA topic modelling to get the keywords from each cluster,

- co-occurrence networks to understand connections between various research themes,
- word clouds to understand the most important words in the corpus,
- checking the accuracy of our clustering approach using supervised methods.

Cluster analysis

Figures 3 and 4 illustrate the results of t-SNE without labels and t-SNE with k-means labels, respectively. While t-SNE performed admirably in terms of dimensionality reduction, k-means improves understanding by labelling clusters. The labelled plot illustrates the organization of the papers. It's interesting to note that despite their independence, t-SNE clustering and k-means clustering concurred on clusters. The positioning of each paper was determined by t-SNE, and k-means clustering was applied for labelling each cluster. k-means labelled the clusters where many papers were clustered by t-SNE. This demonstrates that the literature has been properly clustered by using both t-SNE and k-means.

Many clusters are concentrated in a particular area, demonstrating a good clustering result. Cluster numbers 1, 4, 6, 8, etc., are highly concentrated, implying that the literature in these clusters belongs to very close research themes or domains. Similarly, a few clusters, such as cluster numbers 0, 4, 14, etc., are spread over a long distance, indicating multidisciplinary research themes. Other clusters fall between these two extreme scenarios. One of the interesting insights from these clustering results is that many clusters have more than one research theme. This is primarily because business research is highly multidisciplinary. Another important observation is that a few clusters are large compared to other clusters. This indicates that certain research domains have received more attention compared to other research domains during COVID-19. Overall, the results of clustering are highly satisfying. The fact that even an unsupervised method is performing well in identifying research themes is a great indication of the applicability of the method to our research question.

In the next step, we delved deeper into research trends, identified cluster-related topics, and analyzed the keywords extracted from each cluster using LDA. By categorizing topics, we can gain a better understanding of research trends. This can aid in the comprehension and differentiation of research trends, the identification of research gaps, and the understanding of the dynamics of business research on COVID-19. Thus, developing a profile associated with specific topics can aid in sharpening the overall understanding in the field of business research.

Topic modelling analysis

From a total of 3,363 business-related articles and 20 clusters, our LDA model identified 457 topics. Table 1 displays 457 topics clustered roughly into the various management themes. There were several prominent research themes and subthemes identified from the clustered topics. Some of the clusters, such as 2, 3, and 5, point dominantly in a particular research direction; however, we noted that many clusters, such as 0, 2, and 14, had multiple research themes. We restricted the table to just one

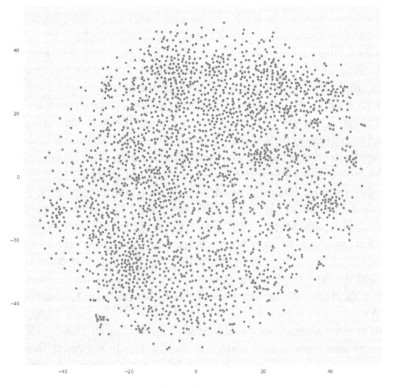

Figure 3.   *t*-SNE clustering.

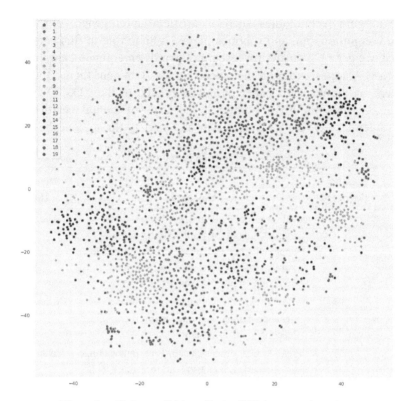

Figure 4. (Color available online) *t*-SNE *k*-means clustering.

dominant research theme to avoid unnecessary confusion. For many clusters, it was quite difficult to tag just one cluster; nonetheless, we tagged them with one significant research theme.

The analysis is not surprising given the change COVID-19 had brought to the world. Significant research trends in each cluster, such as "Technology", "Healthcare", "Economy", "Finance", "Supply Chain", "Education", "Travel and Tourism", "Trade", "Mental Health", "Emerging Technology", "Energy Sector", "Policy", "Workplace and Employee", and "Strategic Decision Making", were captured using topic modelling. A maximum number of 28 keywords were obtained for cluster number 13, and a minimum of 14 keywords were obtained from cluster number 1. A significant trend towards emerging technology research signifies the rapid shift that happened due to COVID-19. Emerging technologies were critical in responding to COVID-19's global emergency.

Emerging technologies such as artificial intelligence, blockchain, cloud computing, 5G, and robotics played a huge role in this pandemic. Hence, we get a big cluster for research towards emerging technology and business. Also, as expected, healthcare is the dominant theme for many clusters, as the research paper corpus is related to the COVID-19 pandemic. Another important finding is the issue of mental health during the pandemic. COVID-19 caused fear and anxiety throughout the world.

Table 1. Topic modelling results.

Cluster	Number of keywords	Keywords	Dominant theme
0	26	covid, use, model, datum, prediction, news, market, sentiment, online, user, quality, approach, increase, need, process, target, size, public, information, medical, machine, rate, detection, new, risk, research	Technology
1	14	health, disease, pandemic, hospital, model, distance, family, medium, covid, food, time, leadership, disaster, new	Healthcare
2	23	digital, model, process, team, firm, innovation, study, market, management, research, global, organization, company, mode, tourism, brand, knowledge, agile, publish, experience, article, share, small	Technology
3	20	health, lockdown, covid, case, country, policy, community, social, distance, worker, pandemic, safe, medium, public, sale, department, time, healthcare, consequence, unprecedented	Healthcare
4	27	market, food, consumer, study, online, restaurant, measure, engagement, organization, safety, datum, people, research, economy, shop, social, use, user, news, search, concern, covid, hotel, city, change, medium, behaviour	Economy
5	25	patient, health, care, state, datum, worker, public, guidance, pandemic, home, science, provide, challenge, review, use, study, improve, management, cost, evidence, year, time, reduction, intervention, trial	Healthcare

Table 1. (*Continued*)

Cluster	Number of keywords	Keywords	Dominant theme
6	27	economic, policy, covid, investment, bank, market, risk, financial, trade, crisis, international, China, estate, real, value, use, indicator, model, issue, education, test, change, stress, key, European, member, union	Finance
7	20	business, pandemic, supply, covid, import, waste, trade, sars, wildlife, crisis, household, record, coronavirus, management, affect, firm, epidemic, stock, food, economic	Supply chain
8	20	online, learn, virtual, education, team, program, platform, simulation, communication, use, interaction, curriculum, health, research, student, home, account, design, process, flexible	Education
9	22	urban, area, energy, tourism, public, disaster, business, farm, model, food, time, price, wildlife, crisis, hotel, law, covid, base, industry, need, century, family	Travel and tourism
10	19	covid, patient, test, disease, pandemic, use, datum, case, state, country, knowledge, sample, people, antibody, shutdown, positive, successful, curve, detection	Healthcare
11	22	firm, covid, shock, study, risk, program, trade, small, company, loan, search, uncertainty, use, cycle, policy, activity, tax, measure, model, provide, safety, economic	Trade
12	24	covid, pandemic, study, health, participant, mental, knowledge, food, practice, psychological, depression, high, consumption, crisis, trauma, significant, associate, violence, religious, product, survey, work, promote, social	Mental health

(*Continued*)

Table 1. (*Continued*)

Cluster	Number of keywords	Keywords	Dominant theme
13	28	process, technology, information, use, blockchain, model, digital, approach, big, health, network, cloud, application, plan, ecosystem, datum, user, actor, problem, key, platform, result, behaviour, technique, experience, local, event, theoretical	Emerging technology
14	22	traffic, pandemic, business, lockdown, concentration, covid, health, air, operation, ship, service, period, emission, country, site, policy, decrease, energy, sector, act, run, action	Energy sector
15	25	model, datum, case, covid, growth, policy, risk, county, mobility, transmission, infection, location, traffic, foot, test, restaurant, diffusion, rural, urban, work, shop, community, reproductive, limitation, npi	Policy
16	24	pandemic, covid, crisis, research, study, service, paper, policy, environment, employee, firm, argue, information, education, development, social, dynamic, growth, individual, community, university, work, remote, overcome	Workplace and employee
17	27	network, study, paper, strategic, technology, maintenance, food, recycle, industry, production, customer, datum, supply, chain, shock, relationship, time, firm, financial, small, market, plan, contingency, performance, corporate, enterprise, integrate	Strategic decision making
18	22	pandemic, business, covid, article, new, small, travel, need, school, policy, withdrawal, health, company, live, work, economic, change, operation, education, industry, firm, state	Education
19	20	patient, mask, use, practice, care, covid, blood, report, orthopaedic, pandemic, article, trauma, screen, donor, product, supply, service, surgical, dental, design	Healthcare

This led to various psychosocial and mental health issues that have a direct impact on all types of businesses.

Co-occurrence network analysis

Clustering identified the related literature. LDA topic modelling assisted in obtaining keywords; however, it did not assist in obtaining relationships and connections between keywords. We used co-occurrence analysis to identify popular topics and their connections, which can be used to monitor and track the evolution of business research trends during COVID-19. Co-occurrence analysis was used to identify emerging research directions and popular topics. A network map of co-occurrences was constructed using the abstract texts from all the included studies. We focused on the connections from the word "business" in Figure 5 because we are interested in relationships and the direction of keyword connections. Thus, co-occurrence analysis provides additional knowledge for identifying and

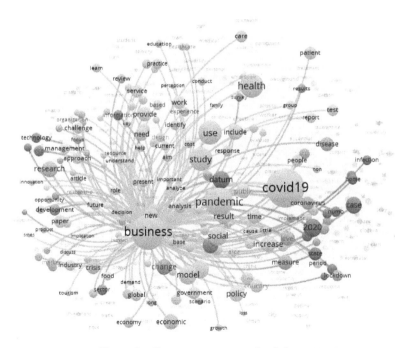

Figure 5. Co-occurrence network of abstract text.

visualizing the business research trends. The connections with the word "business" represent most of the themes and research trends, as shown in Figure 5.

Word cloud analysis

A word cloud was created using the abstract texts; the most frequently used terms include "business", "use", "result", "covid19", and "pandemic" (see Fig. 6). Similarly, a word cloud generated using topic modelling keywords shows that the terms "covid", "pandemic", "use", "model", and "health" were more frequently used (see Fig. 7). This analysis does not appear to contain a great deal of information about business research trends. However, we included word cloud analysis to demonstrate the variety of methods available for identifying research trends.

Classification analysis

Despite being arbitrary, the data are now "labelled" after performing *k*-means. As a result, we can now examine the generalizability of the clustering via supervised learning. If *k*-means had successfully identified the labels and grouped the data correctly, a classifier could be trained to predict the expected cluster. We divided the total of 3,363 articles into 2,690

Figure 6. Word cloud from topic modelling terms.

Figure 7. Word cloud from topic abstract text.

Table 2. SGD classifier results.

Measure	Training set (%)	Testing set (%)
Accuracy	79.37	69.09
Precision	80.82	71.05
Recall	79.05	68.55
F1 Score	79.76	69.17

(80%) for training and 763 (20%) for testing. We used the stochastic gradient descent (SGD) classifier for testing our clustering algorithm. The SGD classifier's output for the training and testing sets is illustrated in Table 2.

Finally, we computed the overall dataset's mean cross-validation value. We were able to achieve a mean cross-validation value of 82.22%, indicating the high performance of our clustering algorithm.

Discussion

The research presented in this chapter is an empirical study that used k-means clustering, LDA topic modelling, co-occurrence network analysis, and word cloud visualization to identify business research trends. We used a subset of the CORD-19 corpus, which consists of thousands of research articles. We looked at a variety of methods for identifying business research trends. Our approach is highly efficient, as indicated by the high accuracy values obtained. We also repeated the experiments multiple times to ensure that there were no mistakes and that our findings are reproducible. We are of the view that our clustering, topic modelling, and network representation from abstract texts are helpful in getting insights that can be used by researchers and businesses. We are, however, not satisfied with the results of the word clouds, and we will try to modify our algorithm to enhance the usefulness of the word clouds.

We would like to incorporate a few useful additions in future research. To begin, we hope to put our model to the test on business articles from a variety of domains and topics. We also plan to create our own corpus in the future, which will offer us greater flexibility in our approach towards our research question. Although our findings show high accuracy, we believe that more experiments on a larger dataset, focusing specifically on business research articles, should be conducted to confirm our findings. In the future, we would like to perform supervised classification of research articles. The main constraint of this approach is how to automatically identify the classes or labels for the classification model. Given the scope and volume of research publications, we believe that we should concentrate our efforts on automatic methods using machine learning, deep learning, and other data analysis techniques.

Conclusion

In this chapter, we presented a technique focused on identifying business research trends during the COVID-19 pandemic. Our clustering, topic modelling, and co-word network mapping techniques perform well in identifying research literature groups, identifying keywords in each cluster, and finding relationships between key terms in the abstracts. Using a supervised classifier, we tested the accuracy of our unsupervised clustering model and found it to be 82.22% accurate.

References

Adamyan, L., Efimov, K., Chen, C. Y., and Härdle, W. K. (2020). Adaptive weights clustering of research papers. *Digital Finance*, 2(3), 169–187. https://doi.org/10.1007/s42521-020-00017-z.

Addo, P. C., Jiaming, F., Kulbo, N. B., and Liangqiang, L. (2020). COVID-19: Fear appeal favoring purchase behavior towards personal protective equipment. *The Service Industries Journal*, 40(7–8), 471–490. https://doi.org/10.1080/02642069.2020.1751823.

Alashhab, Z. R., Anbar, M., Singh, M. M., Leau, Y.-B., Al-Sai, Z. A., and Abu Alhayja'a, S. (2020). Impact of coronavirus pandemic crisis on technologies and cloud computing applications. *Journal of Electronic Science and Technology*, 100059. https://doi.org/10.1016/j.jnlest.2020.100059.

Altuntas, F., and Gok, M. S. (2021). The effect of COVID-19 pandemic on domestic tourism: A DEMATEL method analysis on quarantine decisions. *International Journal of Hospitality Management*, 92, 102719. https://doi.org/10.1016/j.ijhm.2020.102719.

Andersen, N., Bramness, J. G., and Lund, I. O. (2020). The emerging COVID-19 research: Dynamic and regularly updated science maps and analyses. *BMC Medical Informatics and Decision Making*, 20(1), 309. https://doi.org/10.1186/s12911-020-01321-9.

Antons, D., Kleer, R., and Salge, T. O. (2016). Mapping the topic landscape of JPIM, 1984–2013: In search of hidden structures and development trajectories. *Journal of Product Innovation Management*, 33(6), 726–749. https://doi.org/10.1111/jpim.12300.

Antons, D., Joshi, A. M., and Salge, T. O. (2019). Content, contribution, and knowledge consumption: Uncovering hidden topic structure and rhetorical signals in scientific texts. *Journal of Management*, 45(7), 3035–3076. https://doi.org/10.1177/0149206318774619.

Antons, D., Grünwald, E., Cichy, P., and Salge, T. O. (2020). The application of text mining methods in innovation research: Current state, evolution patterns, and development priorities. *R&D Management*, 50(3), 329–351. https://doi.org/10.1111/radm.12408.

Asmussen, C. B., and Møller, C. (2019). Smart literature review: A practical topic modelling approach to exploratory literature review. *Journal of Big Data*, 6(1), 93. https://doi.org/10.1186/s40537-019-0255-7.

Atenstaedt, R. (2017). Word cloud analysis of the BJGP: 5 years on. *The British Journal of General Practice*, 67(658), 231–232. https://doi.org/10.3399/bjgp17X690833.

Baker, L. D., and McCallum, A. K. (1998). Distributional clustering of words for text classification. *Proceedings of the 21st Annual International ACM SIGIR Conference on Research and Development in Information Retrieval* (pp. 96–103). https://doi.org/10.1145/290941.290970.

Barman, A., Das, R., and De, P. K. (2021). Impact of COVID-19 in food supply chain: Disruptions and recovery strategy. *Current Research in Behavioral Sciences*, 2, 100017. https://doi.org/10.1016/j.crbeha.2021.100017.

Batra, K., Sharma, M., Batra, R., Singh, T. P., and Schvaneveldt, N. (2021). Assessing the psychological impact of COVID-19 among college students: An evidence of 15 countries. *Healthcare*, 9(2). https://doi.org/10.3390/healthcare9020222.

Blei, D. M., Ng, A. Y., and Jordan, M. I. (2003). Latent Dirichlet allocation. *The Journal of Machine Learning Research*, 3, 993–1022.

Bofinger, P., Dullien, S., Felbermayr, G., Fuest, C., Hüther, M., Südekum, J., and Weder di Mauro, B. (2020). Economic implications of the corona crisis and economic policy measures. *Wirtschaftsdienst (Hamburg, Germany: 1949)*, 100(4), 259–265. https://doi.org/10.1007/s10273-020-2628-0.

Brust, L., Breidbach, C. F., Antons, D., and Salge, T. O. (2017, December). Service-dominant logic and information systems research: a review and analysis using topic modeling. In ICIS. *International Conference on Information Systems, South Korea*, 38(1), 1–12.

Choi, S., Kim, H., Yoon, J., Kim, K., and Lee, J. Y. (2013). An SAO-based text-mining approach for technology roadmapping using patent information: An SAO-based text-mining approach for technology roadmapping. *R&D Management*, 43(1), 52–74. https://doi.org/10.1111/j.1467-9310.2012.00702.x.

Chudik, A., Mohaddes, K., Pesaran, M. H., Raissi, M., and Rebucci, A. (2020, October 19). Economic consequences of Covid-19: A counterfactual multi-country analysis. *VoxEU.Org*. https://voxeu.org/article/economic-consequences-covid-19-multi-country-analysis.

Cohan, A., Feldman, S., Beltagy, I., Downey, D., and Weld, D. S. (2020). SPECTER: Document-level representation learning using citation-informed transformers. *ArXiv*: 2004.07180 [Cs]. http://arxiv.org/abs/2004.07180.

Čolović, Z. K., Beran, I. M., and Raguž, I. V. (2016). The impact of clustering on the business performance of Croatian SMHEs. *Economic Research-Ekonomska Istraživanja*, 29(1), 904–913. https://doi.org/10.1080/1331677X.2016.1204101.

CORD-19. (2021). CORD-19 historical releases. https://ai2-semanticscholar-cord-19.s3-us-west-2.amazonaws.com/historical_releases.html.

Davahli, M. R., Karwowski, W., Sonmez, S., and Apostolopoulos, Y. (2020). The hospitality industry in the face of the COVID-19 pandemic: Current topics and research methods. *International Journal of Environmental Research and Public Health*, 17(20). https://doi.org/10.3390/ijerph17207366.

Dehghanbanadaki, H., Seif, F., Vahidi, Y., Razi, F., Hashemi, E., Khoshmirsafa, M., and Aazami, H. (2020). Bibliometric analysis of global scientific research on coronavirus (COVID-19). *Medical Journal of the Islamic Republic of Iran*, 34, 51. https://doi.org/10.34171/mjiri.34.51.

Depaolo, C., and Wilkinson, K. (2014). Get your head into the clouds: Using word clouds for analyzing qualitative assessment data. *TechTrends*, 58, 38–44. https://doi.org/10.1007/s11528-014-0750-9.

Dhawan, S. (2020). Online learning: A panacea in the time of COVID-19 crisis. *Journal of Educational Technology Systems*, 49(1), 5–22. https://doi.org/10.1177/0047239520934018.

Ding, C., and He, X. (2004). K-means clustering via principal component analysis. In *21st International Conference on Machine Learning — ICML'04* (p. 29). https://doi.org/10.1145/1015330.1015408.

Donthu, N., and Gustafsson, A. (2020). Effects of COVID-19 on business and research. *Journal of Business Research*, 117, 284–289. https://doi.org/10.1016/j.jbusres.2020.06.008.

ElHawary, H., Salimi, A., Diab, N., and Smith, L. (2020). Bibliometric analysis of early COVID-19 research: The top 50 cited papers. *Infectious Diseases: Research and Treatment*, 13, 1178633720962935. https://doi.org/10.1177/1178633720962935.

Evans, C. (2020). The coronavirus crisis and the technology sector. *Business Economics*, 55(4), 253–266. https://doi.org/10.1057/s11369-020-00191-3.

Evenett, S. J. (2020). Sicken thy neighbour: The initial trade policy response to COVID-19. *The World Economy*, 43(4), 828–839. https://doi.org/10.1111/twec.12954.

Fairlie, R., and Loyalka, P. (2020). Schooling and Covid-19: Lessons from recent research on EdTech. *npj Science of Learning*, 5(1), 1–2. https://doi.org/10.1038/s41539-020-00072-6.

Ferreira, J. J. M., Fernandes, C. I., and Ratten, V. (2016). A co-citation bibliometric analysis of strategic management research. *Scientometrics*, 109(1), 1–32. https://doi.org/10.1007/s11192-016-2008-0.

García, E., and Weiss, E. (2020). COVID-19 and student performance, equity, and U.S. education policy: Lessons from pre-pandemic research to inform relief, recovery, and rebuilding. https://www.epi.org/publication/the-consequences-of-the-covid-19-pandemic-for-education-performance-and-equity-in-the-united-states-what-can-we-learn-from-pre-pandemic-research-to-inform-relief-recovery-and-rebuilding/.

Garvey, M. D., and Carnovale, S. (2020). The rippled newsvendor: A new inventory framework for modeling supply chain risk severity in the presence of risk propagation. *International Journal of Production Economics*, 228, 107752. https://doi.org/10.1016/j.ijpe.2020.107752.

Grech, V., Grech, P., and Fabri, S. (2020). A risk balancing act — Tourism competition using health leverage in the COVID-19 era. *The International Journal of Risk & Safety in Medicine*, 31(3), 121–130. https://doi.org/10.3233/JRS-200042.

Grida, M., Mohamed, R., and Zaied, A. N. H. (2020). Evaluate the impact of COVID-19 prevention policies on supply chain aspects under uncertainty. *Transportation Research Interdisciplinary Perspectives*, 8, 100240. https://doi.org/10.1016/j.trip.2020.100240.

Gruszczynski, L. (2020). The COVID-19 pandemic and international trade: Temporary turbulence or paradigm shift? *European Journal of Risk Regulation*, 11, 337–342. https://doi.org/10.1017/err.2020.29.

Guan, D., Wang, D., Hallegatte, S., Davis, S. J., Huo, J., Li, S., Bai, Y., Lei, T., Xue, Q., Coffman, D., Cheng, D., Chen, P., Liang, X., Xu, B., Lu, X., Wang, S., Hubacek, K., and Gong, P. (2020). Global supply-chain effects of COVID-19 control measures. *Nature Human Behaviour*, 4(6), 577–587. https://doi.org/10.1038/s41562-020-0896-8.

Hakim, M. P., Zanetta, L. D., and da Cunha, D. T. (2021). Should I stay, or should I go? Consumers' perceived risk and intention to visit restaurants during the COVID-19 pandemic in Brazil. *Food Research International*, 141, 110152. https://doi.org/10.1016/j.foodres.2021.110152.

Haraty, R. A., Dimishkieh, M., and Masud, M. (2015). An enhanced k-means clustering algorithm for pattern discovery in healthcare data. *International Journal of Distributed Sensor Networks*, 11(6), 615740. https://doi.org/10.1155/2015/615740.

He, H., and Harris, L. (2020). The impact of Covid-19 pandemic on corporate social responsibility and marketing philosophy. *Journal of Business Research*, 116, 176–182. https://doi.org/10.1016/j.jbusres.2020.05.030.

Hossain, M. M. (2020). Current status of global research on novel coronavirus disease (COVID-19): A bibliometric analysis and knowledge mapping. *F1000Research*, 9, 374. https://doi.org/10.12688/f1000research.23690.1.

Hui, D. S., I Azhar, E., Madani, T. A., Ntoumi, F., Kock, R., Dar, O., Ippolito, G., Mchugh, T. D., Memish, Z. A., Drosten, C., Zumla, A., and Petersen, E. (2020). The continuing 2019-nCoV epidemic threat of novel coronaviruses to global health—The latest 2019 novel coronavirus outbreak in Wuhan, China. *International Journal of Infectious Diseases: IJID: Official Publication of the International Society for Infectious Diseases*, 91, 264–266. https://doi.org/10.1016/j.ijid.2020.01.009.

Ibn-Mohammed, T., Mustapha, K. B., Godsell, J., Adamu, Z., Babatunde, K. A., Akintade, D. D., Acquaye, A., Fujii, H., Ndiaye, M. M., Yamoah, F. A., and Koh, S. C. L. (2021). A critical analysis of the impacts of COVID-19 on the global economy and ecosystems and opportunities for circular economy strategies. *Resources, Conservation, and Recycling*, 164, 105169. https://doi.org/10.1016/j.resconrec.2020.105169.

Ivanov, D. (2020). Predicting the impacts of epidemic outbreaks on global supply chains: A simulation-based analysis on the coronavirus outbreak (COVID-19/SARS-CoV-2) case. *Transportation Research Part E: Logistics and Transportation Review*, 136, 101922. https://doi.org/10.1016/j.tre.2020.101922.

JHU CSSE. (2021). Johns Hopkins University CSSE. Johns Hopkins Coronavirus Resource Center. https://coronavirus.jhu.edu/map.html.

Juaneda-Ayensa, E., Mosquera, A., and Sierra Murillo, Y. (2016). Omnichannel customer behavior: Key drivers of technology acceptance and use and their effects on purchase intention. *Frontiers in Psychology*, 7, 1117. https://doi.org/10.3389/fpsyg.2016.01117.

Kapoor, A., Guha, S., Kanti Das, M., Goswami, K. C., and Yadav, R. (2020). Digital healthcare: The only solution for better healthcare during COVID-19 pandemic? *Indian Heart Journal*, 72(2), 61–64. https://doi.org/10.1016/j.ihj.2020.04.001.

Kaushal, V., and Srivastava, S. (2021). Hospitality and tourism industry amid COVID-19 pandemic: Perspectives on challenges and learnings from India. *International Journal of Hospitality Management*, 92, 102707. https://doi.org/10.1016/j.ijhm.2020.102707.

Kucharski, A. J., Russell, T. W., Diamond, C., Liu, Y., Edmunds, J., Funk, S., Eggo, R. M., and Centre for Mathematical Modelling of Infectious Diseases COVID-19 Working Group. (2020). Early dynamics of transmission and control of COVID-19: A mathematical modelling study. *The Lancet. Infectious Diseases*, 20(5), 553–558. https://doi.org/10.1016/S1473-3099(20)30144-4.

Laguna, L., Fiszman, S., Puerta, P., Chaya, C., and Tárrega, A. (2020). The impact of COVID-19 lockdown on food priorities. Results from a preliminary study using social media and an online survey with Spanish consumers. *Food Quality and Preference*, 86, 104028. https://doi.org/10.1016/j.foodqual.2020.104028.

Linderman, G., and Steinerberger, S. (2017). Clustering with t-SNE, provably. *SIAM Journal on Mathematics of Data Science*, 1. https://doi.org/10.1137/18M1216134.

Lu Wang, L., Lo, K., Chandrasekhar, Y., Reas, R., Yang, J., Eide, D., Funk, K., Kinney, R., Liu, Z., Merrill, W., Mooney, P., Murdick, D., Rishi, D., Sheehan, J., Shen, Z., Stilson, B., Wade, A. D., Wang, K., Wilhelm, C., Xie, B., Raymond, D., Weld, D. S., Etzioni, O., and Kohlmeier, S. (2020). CORD-19: The covid-19 open research dataset. *ArXiv*. https://www.ncbi.nlm.nih.gov/pmc/articles/PMC7251955/.

Maier, D., Waldherr, A., Miltner, P., Wiedemann, G., Niekler, A., Keinert, A., Pfetsch, B., Heyer, G., Reber, U., Häussler, T., Schmid-Petri, H., and Adam, S. (2018). Applying LDA topic modeling in communication research: Toward a valid and reliable methodology. *Communication Methods and Measures*, 12(2–3), 93–118. https://doi.org/10.1080/19312458.2018.1430754.

Mao, X., Guo, L., Fu, P., and Xiang, C. (2020). The status and trends of coronavirus research: A global bibliometric and visualized analysis. *Medicine*, 99, e20137. https://doi.org/10.1097/MD.0000000000020137.

Martinez-Perez, C., Alvarez-Peregrina, C., Villa-Collar, C., and Sánchez-Tena, M. Á. (2020). Citation network analysis of the novel coronavirus disease 2019 (COVID-19). *International Journal of Environmental Research and Public Health*, 17(20). https://doi.org/10.3390/ijerph17207690.

Mehta, S., Saxena, T., and Purohit, N. (2020). The new consumer behaviour paradigm amid COVID-19: Permanent or transient? *Journal of Health Management*, 22(2), 291–301. https://doi.org/10.1177/0972063420940834.

Moreno-Luna, L., Robina-Ramírez, R., Sánchez, M. S.-O., and Castro-Serrano, J. (2021). Tourism and sustainability in times of COVID-19: The case of Spain. *International Journal of Environmental Research and Public Health*, 18(4). https://doi.org/10.3390/ijerph18041859.

Muñoz-Leiva, F., Viedma-del-Jesús, M. I., Sánchez-Fernández, J., and López-Herrera, A. G. (2012). An application of co-word analysis and bibliometric maps for detecting the most highlighting themes in the consumer behaviour research from a longitudinal perspective. *Quality & Quantity*, 46(4), 1077–1095. https://doi.org/10.1007/s11135-011-9565-3.

Nasir, A., Shaukat, K., Hameed, I. A., Luo, S., Alam, T. M., and Iqbal, F. (2020). A bibliometric analysis of corona pandemic in social sciences: A review of influential aspects and conceptual structure. *IEEE Access*, 8, 133377–133402. https://doi.org/10.1109/ACCESS.2020.3008733.

OECD. (2020). COVID-19 and international trade: Issues and actions. *OECD*. http://www.oecd.org/coronavirus/policy-responses/covid-19-and-international-trade- issues-and-actions-494da2fa/.

PricewaterhouseCoopers. (2020a). COVID-19 and the technology industry. *PwC*. https://www.pwc.com/us/en/library/covid-19/coronavirus-technology-impact.html.

PricewaterhouseCoopers. (2020b). COVID-19: Operations and supply chain disruption. *PwC*. https://www.pwc.com/us/en/library/covid-19/supply-chain.html.

Rashid, S., and Yadav, S. S. (2020). Impact of covid-19 pandemic on higher education and research. *Indian Journal of Human Development*, 14(2), 340–343. https://doi.org/10.1177/0973703020946700.

SDG Knowledge Hub. (2021). WTO highlights linkages between trade policy and COVID-19 vaccine value chain. https://sdg.iisd.org:443/news/wto-highlights-linkages-between-trade-policy-and-covid-19-vaccine-value-chain/.

Sharma, A., Adhikary, A., and Borah, S. B. (2020a). Covid-19's impact on supply chain decisions: Strategic insights from NASDAQ 100 firms using Twitter data. *Journal of Business Research*, 117, 443–449. https://doi.org/10.1016/j.jbusres.2020.05.035.

Sharma, A., Gupta, P., and Jha, R. (2020b). COVID-19: Impact on health supply chain and lessons to be learnt. *Journal of Health Management*, 22(2), 248–261. https://doi.org/10.1177/0972063420935653.

Sheth, J. (2020). Impact of covid-19 on consumer behavior: Will the old habits return or die? *Journal of Business Research*, 117, 280–283. https://doi.org/10.1016/j.jbusres.2020.05.059.

Sigala, M. (2020). Tourism and COVID-19: Impacts and implications for advancing and resetting industry and research. *Journal of Business Research*, 117, 312–321. https://doi.org/10.1016/j.jbusres.2020.06.015.

Son, C., Hegde, S., Smith, A., Wang, X., and Sasangohar, F. (2020). Effects of COVID-19 on college students' mental health in the United States: Interview survey study. *Journal of Medical Internet Research*, 22(9). https://doi.org/10.2196/21279.

Šubelj, L., van Eck, N. J., and Waltman, L. (2016). Clustering scientific publications based on citation relations: A systematic comparison of different methods. *PLOS One*, 11(4), e0154404. https://doi.org/10.1371/journal.pone.0154404.

Teräs, M., Suoranta, J., Teräs, H., and Curcher, M. (2020). Post-covid-19 education and education technology 'solutionism': A seller's market. *Postdigital Science and Education*, 2(3), 863–878. https://doi.org/10.1007/s42438-020-00164-x.

The Lancet. (2020). Research and higher education in the time of COVID-19. *The Lancet*, 396(10251), 583. https://doi.org/10.1016/S0140-6736(20)31818-3.

Thorleuchter, D., and Van den Poel, D. (2015). Idea mining for web-based weak signal detection. *Futures*, 66, 25–34. https://doi.org/10.1016/j.futures.2014.12.007.

Thorleuchter, D., den Poel, D. V., and Prinzie, A. (2010). Mining ideas from textual information. *Expert Systems with Applications*, 37(10), 7182–7188. https://doi.org/10.1016/j.eswa.2010.04.013.

Tseng, Y.-H., Lin, C.-J., and Lin, Y.-I. (2007). Text mining techniques for patent analysis. *Information Processing & Management*, 43(5), 1216–1247. https://doi.org/10.1016/j.ipm.2006.11.011.

UNCTAD. (2020). *Impact of the COVID-19 Pandemic on Trade and Development*. UNITED NATIONS. https://unctad.org/system/files/official-document/osg2020d1_en.pdf.

van Eck, N. J., and Waltman, L. (2011). Text mining and visualization using VOSviewer. *ISSI Newsletter*, 7–56.

Vargo, D., Zhu, L., Benwell, B., and Yan, Z. (2021). Digital technology use during COVID-19 pandemic: A rapid review. *Human Behavior and Emerging Technologies*, 3(1), 13–24. https://doi.org/10.1002/hbe2.242.

Verma, S., and Gustafsson, A. (2020). Investigating the emerging COVID-19 research trends in the field of business and management: A bibliometric analysis approach. *Journal of Business Research*, 118, 253–261. https://doi.org/10.1016/j.jbusres.2020.06.057.

Wang, P., and Tian, D. (2021). Bibliometric analysis of global scientific research on COVID-19. *Journal of Biosafety and Biosecurity*, 3(1), 4–9. https://doi.org/10.1016/j.jobb.2020.12.002.

Wenliang, C., Xingzhi, C., Huizhen, W., Jingbo, Z., and Tianshun, Y. (2005). Automatic word clustering for text categorization using global information. In Myaeng, S. H., Zhou, M., Wong, K.-F. and Zhang, H.-J. (eds.) *Information Retrieval Technology* (pp. 1–11). Springer, Berlin Heidelberg. https://doi.org/10.1007/978-3-540-31871-2_1.

WHO. (2020, March 11). WHO Director-General's opening remarks at the media briefing on COVID-19—11 March 2020. https://www.who.int/director-general/speeches/detail/who-director-general-s-opening-remarks-at-the-media-briefing-on-covid-19---11-march-2020.

World Bank. (2021). The changing role of teachers and technologies amidst the COVID 19 pandemic. https://blogs.worldbank.org/education/changing-role-teachers-and-technologies-amidst-covid-19-pandemic-key-findings-cross.

World Economic Forum. (2020a). The ongoing impact of COVID-19 on global supply chains. *World Economic Forum*. https://www.weforum.org/agenda/2020/06/ongoing-impact-covid-19-global-supply-chains/.

World Economic Forum. (2020b). How COVID-19 has affected trade, in 8 charts. *World Economic Forum*. https://www.weforum.org/agenda/2020/11/how-covid-19-has-reshuffled-international-trade/.

WTO. (2020). COVID-19 and world trade. https://www.wto.org/english/tratop_e/covid19_e/covid19_e.htm.

Zhang, H., and Shaw, R. (2020). Identifying research trends and gaps in the context of COVID-19. *International Journal of Environmental Research and Public Health*, 17(10), 3370. https://doi.org/10.3390/ijerph17103370.

Zyoud, S. H., and Al-Jabi, S. W. (2020). Mapping the situation of research on coronavirus disease-19 (COVID-19): A preliminary bibliometric analysis during the early stage of the outbreak. *BMC Infectious Diseases*, 20(1), 561. https://doi.org/10.1186/s12879-020-05293-z.

Chapter 23

Resilience of Street Food Vendors of Lucknow during COVID-19 Pandemic

Shatrughna Ojha[*,‡], Vandana Dubey[*,§], and Claire Buisson[†,¶]

[*]*Amity School of Engineering and Technology,
Amity University, Lucknow, Uttar Pradesh, India*
[†]*HEC Paris, Paris, France*
[‡]*shatrughna1ojha@gmail.com*
[§]*vandanashuklaec05@gmail.com*
[¶]*klaire.buisson@yahoo.fr*

Abstract

Street food vending provides employment opportunities as well as easily accessible foods to millions of people across the world. Street food vending is among the general choices of migrants from rural areas, as the overhead is low as compared to setting up a permanent registered business. They have a large share in the unorganized sector of any developing country's economy. Although many studies are available with basic information on street food vendors and food safety, very few have emphasized the need to understand how their income is interrelated with their personal and perceptual factors. Therefore, understanding their personal prospects and needs is crucial to providing them with a conducive vending environment in which to run their business. A detailed and intriguing analysis of the personal, social, and economic factors affecting the business of street food vending during COVID-19 in Lucknow is presented with the help of suitable visualizations and tables. The study also represents the resilience of street food vendors of Lucknow during COVID-19 as they were hit the hardest economically but not personally. A brief analysis of the relationships among the various personal and economic aspects has also been added to the study. Data collection was done by conducting a primary survey in 10 different areas of Lucknow using random and purposive sampling approaches, and the number of samples collected was 90, with a response rate of 0.84. Some of the key findings of this study include a consistent change in income with the level of confidence of the street food vendors in their individual future and that of their family or children.

Keywords: Street food vendors, future, Lucknow, family, income.

Introduction

Street food vendors are an integral part of the unorganized sector of the Indian economy. Street food vendors sell ready-to-eat food, beverages, or both, and they can have a permanent food stall or a mobile vending cart. It has been observed that most of the street food vendors are usually migrants; they come from rural backgrounds in the hope of having a better lifestyle in the cities (refer A11, B1, and B2 in Appendix). They provide easy and low-cost food to thousands of people in a city. Moreover, the street food vending business provides a way to become self-employable, and it also has the ability to create employment opportunities. Hence, understanding the impacts of COVID-19 on the everyday lives of street food vendors is crucial to comprehending their needs and limitations, which can help policymakers come up with better comprehensive plans to improve the lives of street food vendors. While there are numerous existing reports based on the basic information of street food vendors across countries, very few of them have emphasized the interconnections among the various personal (Hemsley-Brown *et al.*, 2016) and social factors. This chapter is more focused on the psychological, economic, and social factors affecting the business of street food vendors with the rise of the COVID-19 pandemic and also on the resilience of street food vendors during one of the toughest phases of their lives. The hygiene and food safety issues have been discussed in depth in various reports; however, the personal aspirations of street food vendors have not been given enough emphasis. Therefore, we took this opportunity to understand the relationships among their different perceptual factors, along with their personal factors.

Literature Review

Kotwal *et al.* (2018) have discussed the challenges posed by the huge number of street food vendors in regulating this part of the informal sector. They have also emphasized the lack of attention given to the registration and licensing of street food vendors by the local municipal authorities as well as the food safety departments of the respective states. As per their sample report, 82.5% of street food vendors in Delhi belonged to rural areas of other states, which is quite consistent with our sample report (refer A11, B1, and B2 in Appendix) for the Lucknow region. As per their report, street food vendors in both rural and urban areas scored low on hygiene-related issues. The use of gloves, caps, and aprons was rare; however, the vendors maintained the appropriate size of their hair and trimmed their nails. Chakraborty and Koley (2018) have taken samples of the street vendors in Jamshedpur and emphasized the basic problems they faced in their daily business. They have discussed the importance of accepting their business as part of the mainstream, as they add to the values and spirit of any city. Consistent with Kotwal *et al.* (2018) and our report, Chakraborty and Koley (2018) have also noted that most of the street vendors are unskilled and less educated migrants from rural areas who come to cities in the hope of having a better lifestyle. They earn less and live in poor safety conditions at their workplaces. Kumar (2015) has studied the perception of street food vendors about the quality, adulteration, freshness, preparation, and safety of food in Lucknow.

Scope and Methodology

In this study, we have investigated the impacts of COVID-19 on the lives of street food vendors in Lucknow and how their course of future is interrelated with their thought process. Also, our purpose was to inspect an underresearched topic pertaining to building an interrelation between COVID-19 and the socioeconomic changes in the lives of street food vendors. We needed qualitative as well as quantitative data to have an overall perspective on the conditions of street food vendors. The initial set of questionnaires was more quantitative; therefore, the questionnaire was revised thrice before its finalization. Initially, the response rate was low, but it was observed that the response rate increased drastically by inculcating an empathetic surveying style (Leake, 2019), while assuring the vendors about the fair use of their data for educational purposes.

The lack of adequate secondary data available about the targeted group motivated us to collect primary data by conducting a survey across 10 different locations (Figure 1) in Lucknow: Munshi Pulia, Polytechnic Chauraha, Malhaur, Bhootnath Market, Burlington Chauraha, Hazratganj, Alambagh, Charbagh, Aminabad, and 1090 Chauraha. The data were collected between 31 January 2021 and 25 February 2021. We selected only those stalls that:

(a) sold only the items featured in the undermentioned types,
(b) didn't sell any tobacco products.
   i. Type I: Tea Stalls, Bread and Butter, Packaged Snacks, etc.;
   ii. Type II: Puri Sabji, Chawal Daal, Chhole, Pakode, and Bati Chokha;
   iii. Type III: Veg Kebab Rolls, Veg Kebab Parathas, and Veg Biryani;
   iv. Type IV: Chaat Shop, Pani Puri Shop, Bhel Puri Shop, etc.;
   v. Type V: Chinese Foods, Momos, and Continental Fast Foods;
   vi. Type VI: Soya Chaap Stalls and Veg Tandoori;
   vii. Type VII: Egg Rolls, Chicken Rolls, Kaleji Roll, and Non-veg Biryani.

The survey was based on purposive sampling (Palinkas *et al.*, 2015) and random sampling. The survey was conducted by reaching out to the vendors personally and asking the questions from a set of 37 subjective and objective questions. The questionnaire was prepared using Google Forms, and it took approximately 20 minute to record a single response.

The sample size was 90, and the response rate was approximately 0.84.

Due to COVID-19, a significant number of street food vendors discontinued their business, and as a result, the survey sample was smaller in size. Moreover, the number of qualitative questions could be increased to enhance the comprehensibility of their personal as well as professional situations. Most of the street food vendors in Lucknow have not registered their businesses (Chandra, 2017) and hence were wary of being asked about their licence to run their businesses during the survey.

Therefore, the questionnaire had to be prepared in such a manner that we could take the vendors into confidence so as to avoid any misunderstanding about the survey's purpose.

The data collected through the survey were then analyzed using certain Python programming language libraries, including Pandas, Numpy, and Matplotlib. Tools such as Seaborn and Folium were also used for visualizations of the analyzed data.

Basic Observations

As mentioned in the methodology, the response rate of the street food vendors in the survey was 0.84, but the full participation rate was 0.59. Among the types of shops, Type I was recorded to be abundantly available during the survey, whereas Type VII was observed to be the least available on the streets. Type VII included primarily nonvegetarian dishes, such as Chicken Biryani and Mutton Kebab, and due to a surge in anti-COVID-19 precautions, the vendors opined that customers generally avoided nonvegetarian foods. The vegetarian shops contributed 86% of the total participation, and the other 14% were nonvegetarian shops. Out of the 90 samples, only two vendors were women, and the rest were men; the mean age of the vendors was 32.27 years, and the median age was 30 years. The average income of the street food vendors in Lucknow had declined by 34.35% from Rs. 1,639 to Rs. 1,076.40 (see Table C in Appendix). The average number of people living together with the vendors from their respective families was observed to be 4; however, the vendors mostly lived alone in Lucknow. Around 32% of the vendors had been in the street food vending business for more than 10 years, whereas 24% had been operating for less than one year (see Table A in Appendix).

During the lockdown phases in India in 2020, due to COVID-19, almost 50% of the street food vendors had moved back to their respective villages or hometowns. And interestingly, 98% of the street food vendors recorded that they didn't get infected with COVID-19 to their knowledge, and 95% of them denied any news of COVID-19 infection from their respective families or relatives. Also, 82.25% of them were wearing a mask, and 83.60% of the street food vendors said that they had followed the norms of home quarantine during the lockdown period (see Table B in Appendix). However, only 14.51% of the street food vendors had implemented the new sanitary norms in accordance with the WHO guidelines for prevention of COVID-19 (WHO Advice for Public, 2020).

The street food vendors were primarily concerned about protecting themselves and their families from COVID-19. Their next major concerns were staying in good health, earning money, and finding food and daily supplies for their respective families. They were least concerned about not being able to meet their relatives. The other concerns noted were continuing their children's education and not knowing when the spread of COVID-19 would be mitigated. It was also observed that the types of customers who visited before the pandemic generally consisted of Indian tourists, foreign tourists, and random travellers, along with the general public. However, after the pandemic, there was a decline in the number of both kinds of tourists. After the rise of the COVID-19 pandemic, 44% of the street food vendors were optimistic, 10% were unaffected, 16% had no idea, and 30% were pessimistic about their personal future. Conversely, 54% of the street food vendors were optimistic, 20% were unaffected, 12% had no idea, and 14% were pessimistic about their family's future. It was observed that most of the street food vendors were confident about setting up a better future for their respective families.

Discussions and Key Findings

Figure 1 depicts the concentration of street food vendors among the surveyed areas in Lucknow along the metro line. The areas such as Munshipulia, Bhootnath, and 1090 Chauraha had a high concentration of street food vendors, whereas the thickly populated regions such as Aminabad and Polytechnic Chauraha had a lesser number of vendors. As mentioned above, the number of street food vendors decreased after the COVID-19 lockdowns in India since most of the vendors were migrants and many of them didn't return to the city after the lockdown period (PRS India, 2020) was over.

As per the analysis, on average, married street food vendors earned less than unmarried street food vendors (Figure 2). It was observed that 59% of the surveyed vendors were married, 38% vendors were unmarried, and 3% were widowed (see A8 in Appendix). Before COVID-19, the average daily income of married street vendors was approximately Rs. 1,184, whereas the average daily income of unmarried vendors was approximately Rs. 2,717. During the pandemic, the average income of married vendors decreased by almost 25%, whereas the average income of unmarried vendors decreased by almost 44%. It was also observed that

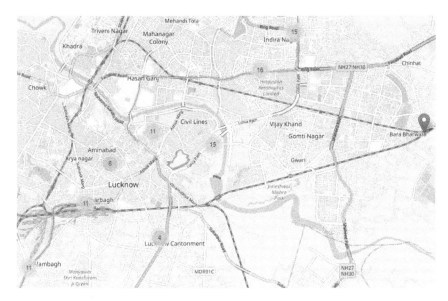

Figure 1. Number of samples taken from different locations in Lucknow.

	Average daily income before?		Average daily income now?	
	mean	median	mean	median
Marital Status				
Married	1183.823529	600.0	880.882353	350.0
Unmarried	2717.647059	2000.0	1503.470588	1300.0
Widow	250.000000	250.0	110.000000	110.0

Figure 2. Interrelations between marital status and average income before and after COVID-19.

most of the unmarried vendors, among married and unmarried vendors, were new to the business of street food vending, and hence, the share of other sources of income for unmarried vendors decreased after the COVID-19 pandemic (Figure 3).

Astonishingly, it was observed that there were some interrelations between optimism for future prospects and their average daily income (see Figures 4 and 5). There was consistency in the average daily income

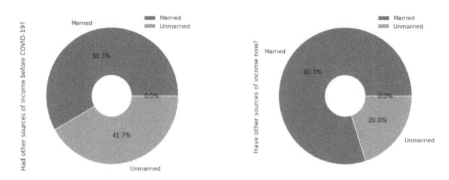

Figure 3. Marital status and other sources of income before and after the COVID-19 pandemic.

How confident are you about your future after COVID-19?	Average daily income before?	Average daily income now?	Change %
Equally	1830.000000	1240.000000	32.240437
Less	1226.470588	582.882353	52.474820
More	1988.636364	1530.454545	23.040000
No Idea	1466.666667	661.111111	54.924242

Figure 4. Interrelation between confidence about personal future and average income before and after COVID-19.

How confident are you for your children or family or both after COVID-19?	Average daily income before?	Average daily income now?	Change %
Equally	1785.000000	830.000000	53.501401
Less	1683.333333	756.555556	55.056106
More	1801.785714	1382.857143	23.250743
No Idea	583.333333	316.666667	45.714286

Figure 5. Interrelation between confidence about family's future and average income before and after COVID-19.

before and after the COVID-19 pandemic with the level of confidence in their individual future prospects (see Table C in Appendix). The vendors who were more confident about their future were earning the highest on average, whereas those who were least confident about their future were earning the least on average. It was true for both their personal future prospects and their family's future prospects. Another intriguing point noted was that, after COVID-19, the percentage decrease in the average daily income of the street food vendors who were more confident about their future was the lowest — approximately 23%, and the percentage decrease in the average daily income of the street food vendors who were least confident about their future was the highest — approximately 54% (see Figures 4 and 5).

Moreover, among the food vendors who were optimistic about their personal future, 95.45% were also optimistic about their family's future, and 4.55% were unaffected about their family's future (see Figure 6). Among the people who were pessimistic about their individual future prospects, 47.06% were pessimistic, 23.53% were optimistic, 23.53% were unaffected, and 5.88% had no idea about their family's future prospects.

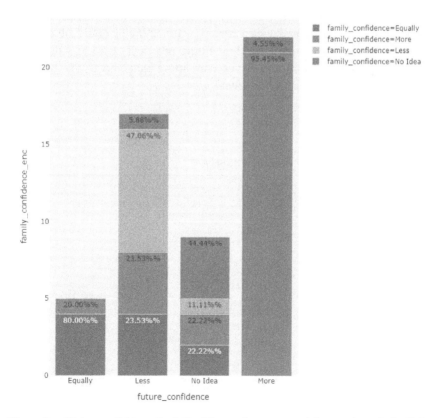

Figure 6. (Color available online) Confidence about personal future vis-a-vis family's future of street food vendors.

Conclusion

The COVID-19 pandemic has hit the street food vendors in Lucknow economically the hardest, as they observed a significant decline in their average daily incomes after the pandemic. However, as per the survey report, they were least affected by the infection personally and socially. Almost 98% of them were safe from COVID-19 infection, and most of them termed it a "rich man's disease" in their remarks during the survey. The street food vendors in Lucknow generally have their homes in the slum areas of Lucknow, and it was even intriguing to the local authorities in Lucknow as to how the slum areas were the least affected by the COVID-19 pandemic (Times of India, 2020).

It was also noted that there were some relationship between one's confidence about his future and his daily income. One reason behind this could be that the people who are earning less tend to be pessimistic about their future prospects, and vice versa. The other factor could be that the people who are confident about their future prospects tend to work positively for a better future and hence earn more than those who are less confident about their future prospects.

Appendix

Table A

A1	Total samples	90
A2	Response rate	0.80
A3	Full participation rate	0.59
A4	Type of shops	
	TYPE I	25
	TYPE II	19
	TYPE III	10
	TYPE IV	09
	TYPE V	09
	TYPE VI	05
	TYPE VII	04
	Total answered	81

Table A. (*Continued*)

A5	Category	
	Vegetarian	43
	Non vegetarian	07
	Total answered	50
A6	Places	
	Bhootnath	16
	1090 Chauraha	15
	Hazratganj	11
	Charbagh	11
	Alambagh	11
	Munshipulia	15
	Polytechnic Chauraha	04
	Aminabad	04
	Burlington Chauraha	02
	Malhaur	01
	Total answered	90
A7	Religion	
	Hindu	59
	Muslim	13
	Total answered	72
A8	Marital status	
	Married	43
	Unmarried	28
	Widowed	02
	Total answered	73
A9	Gender	
	Male	88
	Female	02
	Total answered	90

(*Continued*)

Table A. (*Continued*)

A10	Age	
	Mean	32.27
	Median	30
	Mode	40
	Total answered	73
A11	Type of house in Lucknow	
	Permanent	22
	Rent	40
	Homeless	01
	Total answered	63
A12	Number of people living together from family in Lucknow	
	Mean	04.08
	Median	04
	Mode	01
	Total answered	63
A13	Time spent in vending at the particular location	
	More than 10 year	20
	Between 3 year to 10 year	17
	Between 1 year to 3 year	10
	Less than 1 year	15
	Total answered	62

Table B

B1	Stayed in Lucknow during the lockdown period?	
	Yes	31
	No	31
	Total answered	62

Table B. (*Continued*)

B2	Moved to another place during the lockdown period?	
	Yes	32
	No	29
	Total answered	61
B3	Did you get infected with COVID-19?	
	Yes	61
	No	60
	Choose not to tell	01
	Total answered	62
B4	Did anyone in your family get infected with COVID-19?	
	Yes	01
	No	59
	I don't know	01
	Choose not to tell	01
	Total answered	62
B5	Did you follow home quarantine rules during the lockdown period?	
	Yes	51
	No	10
	Total answered	61
B6	Do you wear a mask?	
	Yes	51
	No	07
	Sometimes	04
	Total answered	62
B7	Do you avoid close contact with people?	
	Yes	42
	No	08
	Sometimes	12
	Total answered	62

(*Continued*)

Table B. (*Continued*)

B8	Do you personally follow proper sanitary rules?	
	Yes	41
	No	11
	Sometimes	10
	Total answered	62
B9	Have you implemented the new sanitary norms at your stall?	
	Yes	09
	No	53
	Total answered	62

Table C

C1	Major concerns of street food vendors during lockdown (priority-wise)	
	Protecting your family from the COVID-19	56
	Protecting yourself from the COVID-19	56
	Finding food and daily supply	44
	Staying in good health	43
	Earning Money	42
	Not knowing how long it will last	25
	Continuing your children's education	14
	Avoid fighting and quarrelling with family inside home	09
	Not being able to meet with the extended family	03
C4	Types of customers before COVID-19 pandemic	
	Students	51
	Office staff	50
	Mix of several	48
	Families	46
	Indian tourists	38
	Foreign tourists	18
	Travellers	06
	Celebrities	01

Table C. (*Continued*)

C5	Types of customers now	
	Mix of several	48
	Students	48
	Office staff	46
	Families	42
	Indian tourists	28
	Foreign tourists	07
	Travellers	07
	Nearby shopkeepers	01
C6	Average daily income before COVID-19 pandemic	
	Mean	Rs 1639.00
C7	Average daily income now	
	Mean	Rs 1076.40
C8	How confident are you about your future after COVID-19?	
	More (Optimistic)	22
	Equally (Unaffected)	05
	No Idea	08
	Less (Pessimistic)	15
	Total answered	50
C9	How confident are you about the future of your family after COVID-19?	
	More (Optimistic)	27
	Equally (Unaffected)	10
	No Ideas	06
	Less (Pessimistic)	07
	Total answered	50

References

Chakraborty, P., and Koley, S. (2018). Socio-economic view on street vendors: A study of a daily market at Jamshedpur. *Journal of Advanced Research in Humanities and Social Sciences*, 5(1), 14–20. https://doi.org/10.24321/2349.2872.201804.

Chandra, V. (2017, April 2). Lucknow has not even one licensed street vendor. *The Times of India*. https://timesofindia.indiatimes.com/city/lucknow/city-has-not-even-one-licensed-street-vendor/articleshow/57968302.cms.

Google Forms. (n.d.). Google forms: Free online surveys for personal use. Retrieved 31 January 2021 from https://www.google.com/forms/about/.

Hemsley-Brown, J., and Oplatka, I. (2016). Personal influences on consumer behaviour. *Higher Education Consumer Choice*, 44–64. https://doi.org/10.1007/978-1-137-49720-8_3.

Investopedia. (n.d.). How simple random samples work. https://www.investopedia.com/terms/s/simple-random-sample.asp.

Kotwal, V., and Satya, P. S. (2018). Food safety & hygiene practices among urban and rural street food vendors: A comparative study in and around Delhi, India. *International Journal of Current Research*, 10(02), 65500–65506. https://www.journalcra.com/sites/default/files/issue-pdf/28943.pdf.

Kumar, R. (2015). Study on perception of street food vendors about food safety in Lucknow. *South Asian Journal of Food Technology and Environment*, 1(2), 136–139. https://doi.org/10.46370/sajfte.2015.v01i02.06.

Kumar, R. (2016). Study on understanding about food hygiene among street food vendors in Lucknow, Uttar Pradesh. *South Asian Journal of Food Technology and Environment*, 2(3 & 4), 452–457. https://doi.org/10.46370/sajfte.2016.v02i03and04.05.

Leake, E. (2019). Empathy as research methodology. *Handbook of Research Methods in Health Social Sciences*, 237–252. https://doi.org/10.1007/978-981-10-5251-4_65.

Palinkas, L. A., Horwitz, S. M., Green, C. A., Wisdom, J. P., Duan, N., and Hoagwood, K. (2013). Purposeful sampling for qualitative data collection and analysis in mixed method implementation research. *Administration and Policy in Mental Health and Mental Health Services Research*, 42(5), 533–544. https://doi.org/10.1007/s10488-013-0528-y.

The Times of India. (n.d.). Less Covid-19 cases in Lucknow slums puzzle doctors. https://timesofindia.indiatimes.com/city/lucknow/less-covid-19-cases-in-lucknow-slums-puzzle-doctors/articleshow/79514744.cms.

World Health Organization. (n.d.). Advice for the public. https://www.who.int/emergencies/diseases/novel-coronavirus-2019/advice-for-public.

© 2025 World Scientific Publishing Company
https://doi.org/10.1142/9789811292101_0024

Chapter 24

Exploring the Impact of Organizational Culture on Employee Performance

Saloni Devi* and Garima Kohli†

The Business School, University of Jammu, Jammu, India
*saloneepadyar@gmail.com
†garima.kohli5@gmail.com

Abstract

COVID-19 pandemic had hit humankind in the most atrocious manner, bringing about notable health and lifestyle changes. The world was at a crossroads, and India was facing a humanitarian crisis. As we move past this crisis and begin to enter a new normal, organizations are facing new challenges and realities. An organization's culture will make or break its ability to be resilient and rebound, following the pandemic crisis. This study aims to provide a comprehensive understanding of the relationship between organizational culture and employee performance under the situation of COVID-19 and handling the new normal. This study is an individual empirical attempt to provide evidences of the relationship between the concepts. Further, the data collection was done by sending a self-administered Google Form to the working employees of the Jammu region of the union territory of Jammu and Kashmir. Convenient sampling technique was used to select the participants, and a total of 166 respondents filled out the Google Form. The findings accomplished the objective of the current study. The model was devised on the basis of a literature review and revealed that there is a positive relationship between organizational culture and employee performance. Furthermore, this study is important and timely, as it provides an immense contribution to the field in the post-COVID-19 situation, providing insights and enhancing scholars' and practitioners' understanding of how organizational culture improves employee performance. Lastly, the study also tries to provide an insight into practical and theoretical implications for organizations and employees, which will facilitate further strategy formulation in the post-COVID-19 situation.

Keywords: Work culture, COVID-19, employee performance, innovation, training, adaptability and coordination.

Introduction

The COVID-19 pandemic has caused destruction around the world and in India. Because of worldwide connectivity, every nation will be impacted by the destruction caused by this pandemic. Probably, by the time when this pandemic finishes, we will most likely observe another world, a new world order, and new social standards with far-reaching economic and social consequences. When the COVID-19 outbreak began spreading around the world, thousands of people started facing rigorous health issues, and the death rates increased. The best way to stop the spread of this pandemic was to stop all social and monetary activities in the infected nations for an uncertain time frame. This drove numerous nations to force total lockdown across the globe. In such a situation, all business units and activities across all industries were totally halted. This lockdown affected different segments to varying degrees. The pandemic has caused tremendous disturbances in business organizations, which will take a very long time to recover if everything goes well.

To control the spread of this infection during the pandemic, numerous preventive measures were proposed by health organizations, which have brought tremendous changes to our societal, cultural, and behavioural well-being. Social distancing, wearing mass when in public spaces, effective hand washing, use of sanitizers, and avoiding mass get-together places, such as theatres, schools/universities, shopping centres, and worship places. All these norms have become an essential part of every individual's life (Bavel *et al.*, 2020).

This distraction has probably led to the perpetual shut-down of numerous business organizations, incapable of bearing the monetary losses and disturbances brought about by this pandemic. To get over such losses, some organizations and individuals engaged in administrative jobs are trying to run their workplaces in the work from home (WFH) mode. Organizations are attempting to cope with the economic turmoil caused by COVID-19 by implementing troublesome but innovative techniques by means of the WFH concept.

The WFH concept was driven by the practice of social distancing, which was the need of the hour for corporates and other sectors to keep alive an effective working environment for employees. It should provide a place from where the individuals can perform their duties from home through the utilization of several advanced technologies. After the pandemic, business patterns will be completely changed, and most of the activities of trade and business will be carried out through digital applications. With the advent of emerging technologies, such as artificial intelligence and analytics, the functioning of all organizations has changed the way companies used to perform their work and operations in a business. In order to maintain the functioning of the businesses and corporate organizations, during the prevailing pandemic period, employees were compelled to work from home. Each activity has its advantages and disadvantages; the same is the case with the acceptance of the WFH initiative. If, from one aspect, this pandemic has affected the economy, trade, and business organizations in a harmful manner, on the other side, it has also forced the companies and business organizations to adopt digital technologies to perform their operations effectively in a timely manner. WFH has been an optimistic change for a majority of the individuals, as it keeps them productive while helping them in maintaining a balanced work life. It is not only all about maintaining a work–life balance, but also about facing all the difficulties confidently and efficiently as the situation demands. Thus, this concept, though helpful in the pandemic situation, is accompanied by some disadvantages as well. This emergency has forced all bosses, employees, and HR consultants to revamp, reorganize, and replan the most suitable practices that need to be followed for the success of their organizations.

Adjusting to this changed situation has an enormous effect on the working environment of employees. This work culture has a huge impact on our homes, working environments, and day-to-day lives. Numerous workers across the globe working in different enterprises are scared of becoming unemployed as the new normal demands new innovative techniques and strategies to deal with an uncertain future (Watkin, 2020). Thus, it is anticipated that, with the passage of time, WFH will become a culture that every organization will adopt. It is foreseen to cause important changes in how individuals work, shop, live, play, communicate, and work across each organization (Merriman, 2020).

The COVID-19 pandemic has had an enormous effect on the behavioural patterns while working from home, but this concept was a great initiative in the present time, keeping in mind the health, safety, security, and welfare of every individual. It is therefore the need of the hour for every organization to rapidly put resources into implementing a strong digital platform (Sharma, 2020). There are an ample number of digital platforms, such as Google Docs, Cisco WebEx, Zoom, and Skype, available for normal communication and interaction between all the employees and employers working from home, which have made life easier. The industries and business organizations may be officially equipped to respond to the rapid adjustments; however, it is also equally essential to psychologically adopt this new culture.

This pandemic has and will have a considerable effect on our behaviour, well-being, ways of living, habits, traditions, customs, and culture as a whole (Huen, 2020). It's an ideal opportunity to invite in the latest cultural changes and adjust our ways of living with these cultural changes as we are adopting a new work culture (Gautam, 2020).

The work culture of any business organization is derived from its strategic objectives and ethics. In creating a dynamic and productive work culture, both employers and employees act as lubricants for the organization. An employee, before choosing any job, usually investigates the work environment of the particular organization so that he can adjust himself to that culture, which will further help him in performing his duties and responsibilities and maintaining cordial relations with the management as well as other employees.

Organizational culture and organizational practices coincide, which further affects the value of the socioeconomic factors created by the firms. The study conducted by Schein (2006) highlights that a vibrant corporate culture is very important for an organization, which enables the firm to adopt a supervisory approach to solving complex issues so as to achieve the estimated level of performance. The culture of an organization is also affected by the system of the organization; though it has diverse backgrounds, it can adhere to universal ethics and ways of living (Robbins and Sanghi, 2007). These ethics, values, beliefs, and standards have a great impact on the overall productivity, performance, and stability of the firm (Stewart, 2010). The standards of workers impact the continuous achievement of goals and the administration of organizational culture, which leads them to attain profitable results. Further, to improve the efficiency and productivity of employees, there is a great impact of job performance on organizational culture. Though the standards, beliefs, ethics, and values of an organization can exhibit diverse cultures, they have a great influence on the management of employees. If the culture in an organization is good, it permits the effectual and competent administration of workers and employees. The universal goal of effective utilization of resources in such a cultural climate helps in the affirmative growth of the organization. The commitment of the employees to working efficiently as a group helps in enhancing their performance, which brings stability to the organization.

Further, in this context, Shahzad *et al.* (2013) stated that organizational culture is the main ingredient for the performance and survival of the organization, which further brings laurels and successes to the organization. Thus, a sound organizational culture is like a heart in the body. Employee performance can only be achieved if there is a sound and stable organizational culture, which leads to the overall development of the organization. The reliability of the employees depends on their understanding and responsiveness to the culture, which enhances the performance of the organization (Brooks, 2006). An increase in profitability and efficiency leads to employee responsibility and dedication to standards, morals, and values, which helps in developing the culture as a whole. The structure of the organization is dependent on an effective cultural environment that develops a strong learning atmosphere in the organization. All these factors help in improving the performance of employees by developing an effective culture in an organization. Understanding the requirements of employees in the present time of the pandemic gives management the chance to enable their workers to set up an encouraging and supportive work culture, which may bring about a greater number of employees exhibiting the motivation and enthusiasm to work from home. This may result in greater job satisfaction and thus improve the performance of employees, which leads to greater effectiveness in employees by achieving maximum output at minimum cost. These factors lead to maintaining better relationship and the building of a sense of commitment in employees when there exists a supportive organizational work culture. Therefore, it is essential for the organization to know the importance of incorporating tolerance, trust, and cooperation upheld by a strong mechanical framework to ensure soundness and digital advancement in this hard time of the pandemic (Bajaj, 2020). Thus, the main aim of this

Figure 1. Proposed model.

chapter is to explore the impact of organizational culture on employee performance amid the COVID-19 situation as shown in Figure 1.

Theoretical Framework and Hypothesis Development

Organizational culture encourages employees to proactively participate in team affairs and value team goals, which helps build collective confidence and generate a sense of community to achieve collaboration. Organizational culture plays a primary function in modelling the behaviour and performance of the firm through the collective efforts of the individual members of the organization. According to Deal and Kennedy (1982), performance management is the responsibility of top management. Consequently, managers make deliberate efforts towards developing a performance-driven organizational culture. Subsequently, Bennett *et al.* (1994) explained that the success of an organization depends on an effective alignment of strategy, structure, and culture. Further, Cooper *et al.* (2001) provided empirical evidence in support of the influence of organizational culture on performance and also argued that culture acts as a stabilizer of individual behaviour. In addition, Giberson *et al.* (2009) emphasized that organizational culture is an integrating force that pulls organizational behaviour in the direction desired by management. Furthermore, O'Reilly and Chatman (1996) stressed the functional perspective of organizational culture and viewed it as a means of social control by which behaviour and beliefs are determined and shaped. Empirical evidence positively linking organizational culture with firm performance has been reported by Peters and Waterman (1982), Deal and Kennedy (1982), and Denison and Mishra (1995). Scholars arguing in support of an affirmative link between organizational culture and performance maintain that a strong culture is necessary for superior performance because it enhances consistency in organizational performance efforts. Consequently, organizational culture's impact on performance is influenced by its alignment with strategy, structure, and other supportive organizational resources.

Culture is considered strong when a majority of organizational members share common values and beliefs promoted by the leaders of the organization (Deal and Kennedy, 1982). Thus, on the basis of the reviewed literature, researchers advance the argument that organizational culture supports the implementation of strategy and creates a defence against competitive imitation, thereby leading to superior performance outcomes. From the above discussion, the following hypotheses are framed.

Organisational culture and employee performance

In all corporate sectors and business establishments, the culture of the organization is considered to be one of the important elements that can help gain a competitive advantage and remains the same in the future, which further affects the behaviour of employees, on the one hand, and the performance of the organization as a whole, either positively or adversely, on the other (Bogdanowicz, 2014). The growth of the organization is the outcome of employees' hard work: those organizations that give importance to their employees, and those employees help in maintaining good customer relationships, so as to develop a brand image for their products, which leads to attaining maximum profits for the organization at minimum costs. This, in turn, leads to increased productivity and performance of the employees and the organization as a whole (Timothy and Lerzan, 2015). Thus, it is because of the supportive organizational culture that has value for employees, which brings maximum gain and thus enhances their performance, that an organization becomes successful. Hence, there exists a positive relationship between the culture of the organization and employees' performance, with different authors stating that culture is a very important component of work performance that leads to the achievement of organizational success (Shahzad *et al.*, 2013). Thus, in order to create a positive work culture, it is necessary for the organization to remove all the negative attributes that affect employee performance.

HI: There exists a positive relationship between organizational culture and employee performance.

Coordination and employee performance

Coordination and trust are interlinked, and organizational performance can be achieved if there exists cordial cooperation, trust, and coordination among employees (Lehtimäki, 1996). From the viewpoint of Barney and Hansen (1994), to achieve organizational growth and performance, trust is considered the major motivator that is built through coordination among the employees. Although there are various reasons that affect the work culture, workplace, and work schedule of any organization, coordination plays a major role by acting as a balancing rod (Ronen *et al.*, 2007). Thus, if there is coordination between employees, it will lead to trust and cooperation, which in turn give rise to better organizational performance. With trust and coordination, performance can be enhanced through a strong communication channel. Further, Arnaud and Schminke (2007) highlighted in their study that the arrangement of each component in an organization ought to feasibly influence the performance directly. It is only because of coordination that all the components within and outside the organization can become interlinked with each other. Therefore, cooperation leads to coordination, i.e., maintaining norms and standards inside and outside the organization and encouraging cordial relations, which helps in improving performance and trust among the employees. It is only through coordination that employee performance can be improved.

H2: There exists a positive relation between coordination and employee performance.

Training and employee performance

Training in this digital environment is considered an essential vehicle for improving the performance and productivity of employees. Performance is the most important, multifaceted dimension that has a strong association with strategic objectives and thus aims to accomplish organizational goals (Mwita, 2000). Improved performance basically means the potential of the organization to accomplish its most desired outcomes proficiently and viably at the minimum cost. Reduced performance leads to inefficient training provided to the employees working in the organization and thus affects the overall growth of the workers and the organization (Muhammad, 2009). Various researchers (Colombo and Stanca, 2008; Sepulveda, 2005; Konings and Vanormelingen, 2009), in their research, stated that for the attainment of goals and overall objectives of an organization, training and development play an essential role, which results in improving the performance, productivity, and profitability of the firm. Without imparting training to the employees, an organization cannot survive; therefore, they act as an instrument which bridges the gap and helps in boosting the employees' performance. A study conducted by Swart *et al.* (2005) highlighted that providing specific training to workers helps in improving their capabilities, skills, and knowledge, which helps in boosting their overall performance. Thus, from the above studies, it is concluded that training is necessary for improving the performance of employees.

H3: Training positively leads to employee performance.

Innovation and employee performance

Employees are of huge significance in modernization and advancement methods and thus affect the innovative performance of the corporate culture. All types of natural and environmental stress are faced by the organizations as they have to answer to the changing needs and requirements of customers (Tidd and Bessant, 2009). Like never before, digitally innovative, practical, and profitable concepts are being promoted at the present time (Galbraith, 1982). The performance of the workers has a huge impact on the innovation of the latest techniques, which further helps in improving the growth and performance of the organization (Huiskamp *et al.*, 2008). Thus, it is presumed that digital advancement is a significant method to overcome all the difficulties that come in the way of a digitally shifting work culture. Workers play a vital role in bringing the latest innovative techniques and thus impact the development and performance of the organization. Subsequently, organizations need to pursue innovation to remain spirited and increase the compensation of employees to keep them engaged. A study conducted by Brockman and Morgan (2003) found that both innovation and performance are directly related to each other. Further, Camisón and Villar-López (2014) also highlighted that innovative concepts and ideas in an organization helps in improving the monetary benefits of the employees. Likewise, Gunday and Alpkan (2011) discovered that any organization's innovative ideas help in improving the growth and performance of its employees. Therefore, on the whole, it was observed by Bowen *et al.* (2010) that there is a direct relationship between innovation and the performance of the employees, and the study supports the following fourth hypothesis as well.

H4: Innovation positively leads to employee performance.

Adaptability and employee performance

Organizational work culture provides guidance to its employees to act in response to the changing circumstances that take place through a mutual comprehension of steps and systems (Chatman *et al.*, 2014; Schein, 2010). According to research conducted by Patrickson (1987) and Thach and Woodman (1994), changes in the old techniques and adapting to the digitally advanced technologies and procedures in the work culture help employees in improving their skills to perform the task assigned effectively and efficiently. In today's digital platform, an organization considers adaptability the chief component of their working environment and will appoint people according to their innovative skills, who are imaginative and inventive, and are ready to face challenges. Adaptive organizations comprehend that recruiting intelligent people will lead to the reliability of adaptive behaviour among employees and thus enhance the capability of the organization to continue to exist, and this leads to an improvement in overall performance of the employees (Ployhart and Turner, 2014). Adaptability is considered the main component for the survival of any organization in the present time and for responding to the changing needs of the organizational culture (Aldrich and Ruef, 2006; Katz and Kahn, 1966). By giving direction and common implications to its individuals on what to value and their behaviour, work culture assists the organizations in planning, recognizing, and reacting to the changing needs of the organization. Thus, adaptability helps in meeting the changing needs of the employees, which leads to growth and survival and thus improves the overall performance of the employees (Gelfand *et al.*, 2012; Hartnell *et al.*, 2011; Kotrba *et al.*, 2012).

H5: Adaptability positively leads to employee performance.

Research Design and Methodology

This research is evaluative in nature. It evaluates the relationship between organizational culture and employee performance. The following steps have been taken to make this research more objective and accurate.

Sample design and data collection

The population for the study comprised 200 working employees of the Jammu province of the Union Territory of Jammu & Kashmir, India. The convenient sampling technique was used to collect the data. All 200 employees were contacted through their email IDs, and research information was generated through Google Forms during the lockdown. Out of 200, only 166 participated in the survey, resulting in a response rate of 83%.

Results

A two-step approach of structural equation modelling (SEM) using AMOS was applied, as suggested by Anderson and Gerbing (1988). CFA was conducted in step one to assess the proposed measurement model fit and construct validity, while step two aimed at developing and estimating the structural model for testing the significance of the theoretical relationship.

Measurement validation

After the survey, the collected data were used to assess scale-level reliability and validity. To evaluate the internal consistency among the items, Cronbach's alpha was calculated. Scale reliability was also assessed through a composite reliability measure and the average variance extracted (AVE). The results of the scale-level reliability and validity assessment are summarized in Table 1. All factor loadings were highly significant, indicating the good quality of the measurement items. Cronbach's alpha and composite reliability were all above the conventional cut-off limit (>0.7), and AVE was more than 0.5.

Impact of organizational culture on employee performance

SEM was used to assess the impact of organizational culture on employee performance (Figure 2). The path traced between organizational culture and employee performance is significant and positive (SRW = 0.52, p = 0.001). The reason might be that organizational culture enhances employees' ability to develop new ideas and also makes them think outside the box.

Table 1. Results of scale-level reliability and validity assessment.

Construct	Standardized loadings	Average variance extracted	Bentler–Bonnet coefficient delta	Composite reliability	Cronbach's alpha
Organizational culture		0.874	0.978	0.982	0.860
Coordination	0.874				
Training	0.993				
Innovation	0.682				
Adaptability	0.949				
Employee performance		0.639	0.943	0.988	0.793
Ep 10	0.943				
Ep 8	0.553				
Ep 6	0.500				
Ep 7	0.563				

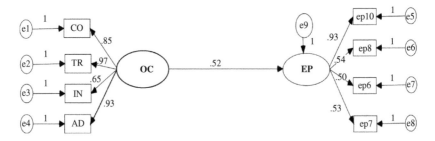

Figure 2. Model 1.

Notes: OC = Organisational Culture (Predictor), EP = Employee Performance (Outcome), CO = Coordination, TR = Training, IN = Innovation, AD = Adaptability, ee6 to ee10 = Manifest variables.

It has been observed that organizational culture induces empathy, consideration, and support for employees, which help them overcome the fear of facing the status quo, leading to better performance and creativity. Further, the values of various model fitness indices are GFI = 0.867, AGFI =

0.899, CFI = 0.907, and RMSEA = 0.043, which reflect good model fit and acceptance of hypothesis 1.

Dimension-wise impact of organizational culture on employee performance

In the second model, we examined the dimension-wise impact of organizational culture, i.e., cooperation, training, innovation, and adaptability, on employee performance. The goodness-of-fit indices for structural model 2 (Figure 3) (GFI = 0.990, AGFI = 0.948, NFI = 0.928, CFI = 0.964, RMR = 0.018, and RMSEA = 0.062) are also well within the generally accepted limits, indicating a good fit.

Impact of coordination on employee performance

This path traced a positive impact of coordination on employee performance (SRW = 0.57, $p < 0.001$). The reason may be that through coordination, a leader encourages employees to achieve more than they would based solely on their own self-interest. This shows that coordination is necessary among different teams and employees to ensure that everyone can openly and honestly share their grievances, successes, and challenges.

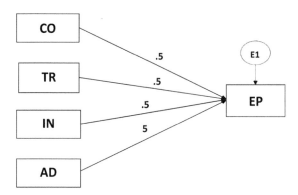

Figure 3. Model 2.

Notes: CO = Coordination, TR = Training, IN = Innovation, AD = Adaptability, EP = Employee Performance.

Further, in the present situation of the pandemic, coordination among employees encourages one-on-one coaching and establishes a support network and mentoring system.

Impact of training on employee performance

Training has a significant impact on employee performance (SRW = 0.56, $p < 0.001$). The rationale behind this is that through training, leaders and employees develop digital and cognitive capabilities, their social and emotional skills are enhanced, and they cultivate resilience and adaptability. The culture of introducing training initiatives, specifically in response to the COVID-19 pandemic, is prevalent among organizations. Further, pandemic training, such as educating employees about remote work policies, training about hardware and software related to WFH, and health and safety measures, boosts employee performance and strengthens companies for future disruptions.

Impact of innovation on employee performance

There is a significant and positive impact of innovation on employee performance (SRW = 0.50, $p < 0.001$). It has been observed that through innovation, leaders pay attention to the employees' development needs and delegate work projects in a manner that stimulates a high level of creativity. Further, technology plays an important role in determining the success of new ways of working. In the present situation, integrating digital workplaces into the culture of any company is not primarily a matter of innovation or technology. Rather, it depends on how well the company culture is maintained and what possibilities are offered for social interaction between employees. Therefore, the global outbreak of COVID-19 presents a significant problem. However, amid its volatility, uncertainty, complexity, and ambiguity lie hidden opportunities for learning, reinvention, and evolution at the individual, organizational, and societal levels.

Impact of adaptability on employee performance

This path shows a significant influence of adaptability on employee performance (SRW = 0.58, $p < 0.001$). The reason behind this is that through adaptation, employees will need to come to grips with new technologies and new ways of working in a home environment, where they may need to deal with a number of distractions and conflicting responsibilities, including children studying from home, a working spouse, and other elements. Alongside the personal adjustments, their working style, habits, and behaviours will need to adapt. Retaining or adapting a personal daily/routine work culture will be important for boosting employee performance.

Discussion

The purpose of this study is to assess the impact of organizational culture on employee performance and the dimension-wise impact of organizational culture, i.e., cooperation, training, innovation, and adaptability, on employee performance. This study has several important findings. The results demonstrated that organizational culture is positively related to employee performance, and the same follows for the lockdown situation. This finding of the study revealed that employees are prone to remain loyal and rely strongly on organizational culture to perform better in a new work frontier. The leader uses symbols and emotional appeals to focus group members' efforts, thus encouraging them to achieve more than they would based solely on their own self-interest. During these times of change, when almost from one day to the next, the workforce needs to shift the manner in which it works, organizational culture will come under strain. Individuals and teams are working for the first time at home and are physically separated. Training is the initial focus for organizations to ensure their businesses can successfully navigate this new world. Both technical and emotional training are critically important in the present situation to consider their impact on employees' performance. Through innovation, leaders can pay attention to the employees' developmental needs and delegate work projects in a manner that stimulates learning experiences. Leaders can give employees prudence to satisfy their developmental needs and act accordingly; in turn, employees can devote more time to their work due to enhanced feelings of discretion and the provision of enriched opportunities to test their work capabilities. Thus, employees are stimulated to achieve high levels of creativity and innovation. Through adaptations, organizations provide assistance to employees who are not used to working from home and consider creating a support network, for example, by assigning a remote working champion per business unit to help colleagues understand how best to work from home within the context of their roles. As home working environments open the door to personal devices and applications being used to distribute corporate assets and information, employees need guidance and advice ahead of time. Thus, the COVID-19 isolation measures have abruptly changed our ways of working. The rapid shift to remote working is a cause of significant anxiety among the workforce. It is going to put many company cultures to the test. The right culture, i.e., a culture that embraces change, recognizes the new challenges facing employees and encourages them to take the initiative, do things differently, and can more effectively support this shift, easing the transition and driving productivity.

Managerial Implications

1. The decision-making process should be driven by the cultural values of the organization, and it should be visible in the actions of all.
2. Leaders should take concrete and visible steps that can have a positive ripple effect as they flow through your organization.
3. Provide guided steps to adapt new ways of working to gain success during prolonged WFH and encourage employees to collaborate and share creative problem-solving techniques.
4. Considering employees' well-being, organization should partner with doctors/hospitals and specialists to support them and provide online consultation and guidance.
5. Physical, emotional, financial, and social well-being should be focussed on to help improve employee productivity while working from home.

Limitations of the Study

1. The data were collected from Jammu only, so the study lacks generalized results.
2. A proper list of employees was not available. Therefore, the convenience sampling technique was applied.
3. The study is cross-sectional in nature.

Conclusion

The situation created by COVID-19 has shaken up the socio-cultural framework of society and organizational work culture. A new normal has emerged, with the primary focus on safeguarding against the highly infectious pandemic. Now, facemasks, hand gloves, sanitizers, and physical distancing have become integral parts of life. Moreover, every coin has two sides; the same is the case with the pandemic situation: it has both opportunities and challenges. With the changed organizational culture, employees are empowered to work remotely based on their convenient flexible working hours. However, in the long term, remote working may also increase physiological stress, dilute work–life boundaries, create communication gaps among team members, and lead to a lack of interpersonal relationships, concern over job security, and diminished organizational culture. Further, the new normal will create new ways of living for the survival of human beings. Moreover, to drive profitable growth, successful organizations need to adapt themselves to enhanced uses of cutting-edge technologies and invest efforts in enhancing employees' experiences. Therefore, employees may need significant training, coordination, innovation, and adaptability to accept the newer ways of working. Thus, successful organizations should invest maximum efforts to safeguard organizational culture and should be people-centric to boost employee performance.

References

Aldrich, H., and Ruef, M. (2006). *Organizations Evolving*, 2nd edn. Sage, London.

Anderson, J. C., and Gerbing, D. W. (1988). Structural equation modeling in practice: A review and recommended two-step approach. *Psychological Bulletin*, 103(3), 411–423.

Arnaud, Anke, and Marshall Schminke (2007). Ethical work climate: A weather report and forecast. *Managing Social and Ethical Issues in Organization*, pp. 181–227. Information Age Publishing, Greenwich.

Bajaj, S. (2020). COVID-19: Building a crisis-resistant organizational culture and technology core. *People Matters*. 22 April 2020. www.peoplematters global.com/article/culture/covid-19-building-a-crisis-resistantorganizational-culture-and-technology-core-25406.

Barney, J. B., and Hansen, M. H. (1994). Trustworthiness as a source of competitive advantage. *Strategic Management Journal*, 15, 175–190.

Bavel, J. J. *et al.* (2020). Using social and behavioural science to support COVID-19 pandemic response. *Nature Human Behaviour*, 2020. 30 April 2020. https://doi.org/10.1038/s41562-020-0884-z. Accessed 15 May 2020.

Bennett, R. H., Fadil, P. A., and Greenwood, R. T. (1994). Cultural alignment in response to strategic organizational change: New considerations for a change: New considerations for a change framework. *Journal of Managerial Issues*, 6, 474–490.

Bogdanowicz, M. (2014). Organizational culture as a source of competitive advantage: A case study of telecommunication company in Poland. *International Journal of Contemporary Management*, 13(3), 53–66. Available at: http://www.ejournals.eu/ijcm/2014/13(3)/art/5227print.

Bowen, F. E., Rostami, M., and Steel, P. (2010). Timing is everything: A meta-analysis of the relationships between organisational performance and innovation. *Journal of Business Research*, 63(11), 1179–1185.

Brockman, B, K., and Morgan, R. M. (2003). The role of existing knowledge in new product innovativeness and performance. *Decision Sciences*, 34(2), 385–419.

Brooks, I. (2006). *Organizational Behavior: Individuals, Groups and Organization*. Pearson Education Limited, Essex.

Camison, C., and Villar-Lopez, A. (2014). Organizational innovation as an enabler of technological innovation capabilities and firm performance. *Journal of Business Research*, 67(1), 2891–2902.

Chatman, A. *et al.* (2014). Parsing organizational culture: How the norm for adaptability influences the relationship between culture consensus and financial performance in high-technology firms. *Journal of Organizational Behavior*, 35(6), 785–808. doi: 10.1002/job.1928.

Colombo, E., and Stanca, L. (2008). The impact of training on productivity: Evidence from a large panel of firms. *International Journal of Manpower*, 35(8), doi: 10.1108/IJM-08-2012-0121. Available at SSRN.

Cooper, L. C., Cartwright, S., and Earley, C. P. (2001). *The International Handbook of Organizational Culture and Climate*, 1st edn. Wiley, Hoboken, NJ.

Deal, T. E., and Kennedy, A. A. (1982). *Corporate Cultures: The Rites and Rituals of Corporate Life*. Addison-Wesley, Reading, MA.

Denison, D. R., and Mishra, A. K. (1995). Towards a theory of organizational culture and effectiveness. *Organization Science*, 6, 204–223.

Galbraith, J. R. (1982). Designing the innovating organization. *Organizational Dynamics*, 10(3), 4–25.

Gautam, A. (2020). Post-Covid: Transformation in work culture. https://timesofindia.indiatimes.com/. 6 May 2020. timesofindia.indiatimes.com/readersblog/post-covid-19-impact-on-working-culture/postcovid-transformation-in-work-culture-18804/. Accessed 14 May 2020.

Gelfand, M. J., Leslie, L. M., Keller, K., and de Dreu, C. (2012). Conflict cultures in organizations: How leaders shape conflict cultures and their organizational-level consequences. *Journal of Applied Psychology*, 97, 1131–1147. doi: 10.1037/a0029993.

Giberson, T. R., Resick, C. J., Dickson, M. W., Mitchelson, J. K., Randall, K. R., and Clark, M. A. (2009). Leadership and organizational culture: Linking CEO characteristics to cultural values. *Journal of Business Psychology*, 24, 123–137.

Gunday, G., and Alpkan, L. (2011): Effects of innovation types on firm performance. *International Journal of Production Economics*, 133(2), 662–676

Hartnell, C. A., Ou, A. Y., and Kinicki, A. (2011). Organizational culture and organizational effectiveness: A meta-analytic investigation of the competing values framework's theoretical suppositions. *Journal of Applied Psychology*, 96, 677–694. doi: 10.1037/a0021987.

Huen, B. (2020). COVID-19: Here's How One Pandemic Will Change Our Lives, Forever. https://www.zdnet.com/. 3 April 2020. www.zdnet.com/article/covid-19-how-one-pandemic-will-change-our-lives-forever/. Accessed 11 May 2020.

Huiskamp, R., de Jong, T., and Den Hoedt, M. C. B. (2008). HRM en innovative werkgedrag: Een verkenning. TNO rapport, Hoofddorp.

Katz, D., and Kahn, R. L. (1966). *The Social Psychology of Organizations*. Wiley, New York.

Konings, J., and Vanormelingen, S. (2009). The Impact of Training on Productivity and Wages: Firm Level Evidence, Discussion Paper No. 244. Available at SSRN.

Kotrba, L. M., Gillespie, M. A., Schmidt, A. M., Smerek, R. E., Ritchie, S. A., and Denison, D. R. (2012). Do consistent corporate cultures have better business performance? *Exploring the Interaction Effects. Human Relations*, 65, 241–262. doi: 10.1177/0018726711426352.

Lehtimäki, Hanna (1996). Coordination through Social Networks. University of Tampere. Series A1, Studies 43.

Merriman, M. (2020). Beyond COVID-19: How a crisis shifts cultural and societal behaviors. www.ey.com, www.ey.com/en_gl/advisory/beyond-covid-19-how-a-crisis-shifts-culturaland-societal-behaviors. Accessed 8 May 2020.

Mohamad, A. A., Lo M. and La M. K. (2009). Human resource practices and organizational performance. Incentives as moderator. *Journal of Academic Research in Economics*, 1(2), 229–244.

Mwita, J. I. (2000). Performance management model. A system- based approach to system quality. *The International Journal of Public Sector Management*, 13(1), 19–12.

O'Reilly, C., and Chatman, J. (1996). Culture as a social control: Corporations, cults and commitment. In Staw, B. M., and Cummings, L. L. (eds.) *Research in Organizational Behaviour. An Annual Series of Analytical Essays and Critical Reviews*, Vol. 18. JAI Press, Greenwich, CT, pp. 157–200.

Patrickson, M. (1987). Adaptation by employees to new technology. *Journal of Occupational Psychology*, 59, 1–11.

Peters, T. J., and Waterman, H. R. (1982). *In Search of Excellence: Lessons from America's Best-Run Companies*. Harper & Row, New York, NY.

Ployhart, R. E., and Turner, S. F. (2014). Organizational adaptability. In Chan, D. (ed.) *Individual Adaptability to Changes at Work: New Directions in Research*. Routledge, New York, pp. 73–91.

Robbins, S. P., and Sanghi, S. (2007). *Organizational Behavior*. Pearson Education, New Delhi.

Ronen, S., Friedman, S., and (Hilla) Ben-Asher, H. (2007). Flexible working arrangements: Societal forces and implementation. In *Managing Social and Ethical Issues in Organization*. Information Age Publishing, Greenwich, pp. 3–51.

Schein, E. H. (2006). *Organizational Culture and Leadership*, Vol. 356. John Wiley & Sons. Retrieved from https://scholar.google.com/scholar?hl=en&as_sdt=0%2C5&q=Schein%2C+E.+H.+%282006%29.+Organizational+culture+and+leadership+%28Vol.+356%29.+John+Wiley+%26+Sons.&btnG=.

Schein, E. H. (2010). *Organizational Culture and Leadership*, 4th edn. Jossey-Bass, San Francisco.

Sepulveda, F. (2005). Training and productivity: Evidence for US manufacturing industries. Available at SSRN.

Shahzad, F., Iqbal, Z., and Gulzar, M. (2013). Impact of organizational culture on employees job performance: An empirical study of software houses in Pakistan. *Journal of Business Studies Quarterly*, 5(2), 56–64. Retrieved from http://jbsq.org/wpcontent/uploads/2013/12/December_2013_4.pdf.

Sharma, A. (2020). Looking at the workplace post lockdown. People Matters, 24 April 2020. www.peoplematters.in/article/c-suite/looking-at-the-workplace-post-lockdown-25432. Accessed 15 May 2020.

Stewart, D. (2010). Growing the Corporate Culture, obtained from https://www.wachovia.com/foundation/v/index.jsp?vgnextoid=ab411f07760aa110VgnVCM1000004b0d1872RCRD&vgnextfmt=default on April, 23, 2012.

Swart, J., Mann, C., Brown, S., and Price, A. (2005). *Human Resource Development: Strategy and Tactics*. Elsevier Butterworth-Heinemann Publications, Oxford, UK.

Thach, L., and Woodman, R. W. (1994). Organizational change and information technology: Managing on the edge of cyberspace. *Organizational Dynamics*, 23(1), 30–46.

Tidd, J., and Bessant, J. (2009). *Managing Innovation: Integrating Technological, Market and Organizational Change*, 4th edn. John Wiley, Chichester.

Timothy K., and Lerzan A. (2015). Why managers should care about employees loyalty. http://hiring.monster.com/hr/hr-best-practices/workforce-management/employee-performancemanagement/why-loyalty-matters.aspx2015.

Watkin, J. (2020). The Future Cultural Transformation Through & Beyond COVID-19. Total Telecom. 12 May 2020. www.totaltele.com/505888/THE-FUTURE-Cultural-Transformation-Through-Beyond-COVID-19. Accessed 17 May 2020.

Chapter 25

Mindfulness Practices and Their Essentiality for Teachers

Pooja Deshmukh

Institute of Management and Research,
MGM University, Aurangabad, India
pooja.deshmukh@mgmiom.org

Abstract

Every human has a desire to be a successful individual in life. However, is it possible to acquire victory without encountering obstacles? I guess the answer is no. Why would we spend hours together getting annoyed about things only to finally end up with nothing? Our workplace is a fast-paced, annoying environment. The teaching environment is likewise, and no longer an exception to it. Being a facilitator, one has to play diverse roles, including those of a motivator, mentor, and guide, and one has to continually strive to become a superior version of oneself. The teacher must have a great awareness of the current needs, considering the pandemic era and online teaching practices. In addition, they must have the best of high-quality reinforcement qualities, which can motivate students to learn new things. These countless anticipated requirements create process dissatisfaction, job fatigue, and burnout, and they decrease occupational commitment. Various research studies have proved that if one can practice mindfulness, it can lead to better outcomes at work and even for oneself. This is an attempt to evaluate whether or not mindfulness practices enhance teaching quality and reduce perceived stress.

Keywords: Stressful environment, workplace, teachers mindfulness, teaching quality.

Introduction

In this globalized world, each company and every sector expects more fruitful results from their employees. Our salaries not only satisfy our basic, simple needs but also pay all our expenses, allow us to purchase luxury products, assist in times of medical emergencies, and even give our lives meaning. The policies and procedures, which can be obligatory to observe within the primary, secondary, and tertiary sectors, are the same as those within the quaternary sector. There were days when the teacher was the role model of the classroom, and students used to obey the instructions and pieces of advice of the teachers; however, the teaching world has transformed dramatically. Indeed, we are no longer in the age of *Guru–Shish Parampara*. We have to accept the realities of the changed scenario. A teaching career in the globalized world has become more hectic and tiresome, considering the expectations of all the stakeholders.

Teachers are also subject to numerous pressures similar to their counterparts in other professions. We often experience similar job stress as that which arises as a result of performing responsibilities in various industries. Nowadays, the teaching profession has also become similar to other professions due to field-specific expectations (workload, reputation, duty hours, etc.). Similarly, there are pressures from different stakeholders (parents, regulatory bodies, and the outside world).

A person who focuses on several complicated tasks at once may become exhausted, confused, and unproductive. So far, the pandemic era has added more obligations and difficulties to the regular practices of teachers. On the other side of the coin, the mind wanders and worries about what will happen in the next moment due to the threat posed by COVID-19. Teachers are exhausted by the constantly changing status of schools and colleges and by the fact that they have to work from home. Moreover, it is challenging to maintain equilibrium between the lockdowns and routine life. The constant lockdowns made the task more difficult not only for teachers but also students. One of the biggest challenges ever is making students understand the subject, and it has become more difficult now because of online teaching. More stressful is when the teacher is being evaluated based on the results of the students, despite their varying understanding capacities.

Sometimes, we clutter our minds by thinking about what to make for dinner, thinking about shopping, worrying over a pending deadline, or worrying about the future in general. Many things compete for our attention, which causes us to lose focus. How to handle these circumstances and maintain mental peace is a great challenge ahead. Being aware of the state of our mind helps us focus, which leads to increased productivity. The aim is not to exhaust one's mind of all ideas but to become more aware of our surroundings and our feelings at the moment, along with our surroundings.

Literature Review

The impact of mindfulness training interventions on managing job-related stress in the teaching profession was studied by Milne in his research in 2019.

Based on the findings of their study, Luken and Sammons (2016) point out that mindfulness practice reduces the mental exhaustion of teachers and healthcare professionals.

McLean and Connor (2015), in their paper, have concluded that teaching is a critical process; it's related to mental ability and highly impacts the well-being of teachers. They have pointed out further that it is a profession characterized by high risk.

The research by Elder *et al.* (2014) finds that due to long working hours and expectations from the school, teachers face significant anxiety levels.

Franco *et al.* (2010), based on their study on the effects of a mindfulness programme on a group of students in the first year of compulsory secondary education in three public schools, concluded that teachers experience severe stress due to work, as it is related to psychological issues.

According to a study by Brackett *et al.* (2010), consistent teacher programmes can enhance emotional regulation and result in positive outcomes. The study examined the relationship between emotion-regulation ability (ERA) and job satisfaction and burnout among teachers.

Gold *et al.* (2010) indicated that one can derive benefits from practising mindfulness. It reduces mental trauma, and one can easily achieve individual and organizational aims. Additionally, it enables us to meet the demands better.

Gause and Coholic (2010), in their paper, stated that mindfulness practices are helpful in understanding the true self and realities. Individuals will be able to open up to themselves and others through these processes, giving them happier and meaningful lives.

The paper by Gold *et al.* (2010) has clearly stated that mindfulness programmes have typically been developed and designed for the students but not for the teachers, even though they are significant for the latter.

The **research question** was framed as follows: can mindfulness practices help teachers reduce their stress levels and enhance teaching quality?

Objectives of the Study

The study aims:

1. to explore the question 'What is mindfulness?' and its historical perspectives;
2. to examine the significance of mindfulness practices in enhancing the quality of teaching;
3. to study how mindfulness practices are helpful in achieving well-being and stress reduction.

Research Methodology

The research is based on secondary data and is therefore qualitative in nature. The purpose of the study is to understand the importance of mindfulness practices. The literature, consisting of leading scholarly articles and websites, provided secondary data for this study.

The Ancient Concept of Mindfulness

Humankind has adopted mindfulness techniques since the Buddhist era. '*Sati*' means mindfulness in ancient Greek (conscious attention). *Sati* practice has been accepted thoughtfully and adapted throughout its journey up to the present day. On the one hand, this made it more appealing to a broad audience; on the other hand, it meant that it lost a lot of its basis in the process.

The context and depth of the entire Buddhist practice are considered the means of understanding oneself and achieving mental serenity and well-being. If an action is not appropriate, it will not lead to perfection. Utmost perseverance and dedication are required to develop these skills and qualities. These characteristics will also contribute to mental stability and a strong sense of tranquillity. Ancient beliefs accepted in every society have always influenced knowledge development, especially in psychology, and Indian history is a rich source of knowledge (Shamasundar, 2008).

Mindfulness is an umbrella term that includes a number of practices. Nonetheless, the purpose of all practices is to observe your feelings and mindset. Though it is not necessary to go back in time to comprehend the ancient applications of mindfulness, even a basic understanding can lead to various life changes. The following are a few examples.

Day Intention: Meeting new people every day, juggling many responsibilities that aren't necessarily related to our profession, and possibly encountering pointless conflicts such as unexpected incidents will add to our stress levels. However, you can make a habit of planning things well in advance, and if you start a day by deciding what to do, it will be easier to arrange the necessary tasks. Considering those primary motivations, one can establish this connection between material and nonmaterial things. The aim of starting the day with a positive mindset might help you focus on duties without becoming disheartened.

Be Satisfied in Your Stomach: The food we eat for breakfast, lunch, or dinner should provide us with mental and emotional satisfaction. The food should not be taken with the intention of filling our stomachs. We often get distracted for many reasons, such as watching television, discussing with family members, or planning for any event. While doing so, we never realize that what we are eating only fills our stomach, but we will not feel the satisfaction of eating the food. Mindful eating is a sign of being in the now. We can sense and feel what we eat, and we can taste it with each bite. It's a signal that our brain receives which conveys taste, satisfaction, and fullness. Rather than criticizing, mindful eating necessitates being aware.

Exercise: It is always beneficial to remain physically fit. If we are always active, we usually achieve better results with less energy. If we are in good health, our brains work more quickly. Physical strength can help us avoid ailments, such as heart disease, stroke, diabetes, and other diseases caused by obesity, lower blood pressure, prevent depression, and improve our appearance. Health and mindfulness are inseparably linked. Exercise aids in the development of a strong memory as well as constructive thinking. Regular exercise helps us lower blood pressure, anxiety, and depression. A person can work uninterrupted for the entire day and become more productive.

Mindfulness Reduces Stress and Improves Quality

To take on the responsibility of being a teacher, one must have a reasonable determination to do so. Teachers benefit from mindfulness because it improves their fundamental self and wellness, helps them comprehend student needs and perspectives, and sets them up to be more productive. Insight, kindness, and empathy are just a few of the good qualities cultivated via mindfulness practice. Understanding the positive and negative effects of the job is beneficial. When the environment is happy, it connects with the pupils, allowing them to reach their full potential.

If teachers are self-aware, they may communicate more effectively, manage problems, create a sound teaching–learning environment, and assist students in deepening their relationships. The bond between teacher and student will be stronger if the teacher acts kindly. Self-awareness is the ability to recognize and perceive oneself as a unique individual. Mental stability makes a person productive and enthusiastic, capable of building strength, and able to find areas for progress. In the classroom, emotions can help create a healthy environment.

Emotional intelligence and mental stability help improve the quality of teaching and whatever work we undertake. We will always find pleasure in what we do, and we not only become more productive but result-oriented also. Such adjustments provide a wonderful sense of fulfilment and a sense of satisfaction and admiration among colleagues. It gives us the added benefit of leaving for the day feeling fulfilled, accomplished, and satisfied.

Mindfulness practice not only helps us forget about negativity, but it also teaches us how to use the mind effectively to choose the thoughts that lead to positive outcomes. Mindfulness also enhances cognitive function and helps us concentrate better, lowering our stress, anxiety, and depression.

Conclusion

There are a number of situations that are extremely uncertain. We don't know what will happen, how long this system will last, or how things will look tomorrow. One thing we do know, however, is that worrying about them is not going to change the result. This research concluded the importance of mindfulness practices and their benefits concerning improving teaching quality and preserving well-being. According to the study, mindfulness practice improves teaching–learning quality, while also lowering instructors' stress and anxiety levels. Learning to tolerate uncertainty is an important part of developing healthy adaptive skills that we then want to inculcate in our students.

References

Brackett, M. A., Palomera, R., Mojsa-Kaja, J., Reyes, M. R., and Salovey, P. (2010). Emotion-regulation ability, burnout, and job satisfaction among British secondary-school teachers. *Psychology in the Schools*, 47(4), 406–417.

Broderick, P. C., *et al.* Evaluating the quality of mindfulness instruction delivered in school settings: Development and validation of a teacher quality observational rating scale. https://link.springer.com/article/10.1007/s12671-018-0944-x.

de Carvalho, J. S., *et al.* (2021). Effects of a mindfulness-based intervention for teachers: A study on teacher and student outcomes. https://link.springer.com/article/10.1007/s12671-021-01635-3.

Elder, C., Nidich, S., Moriarty, F., and Nidich, R. (2014). Effect of transcendental meditation on employee stress, depression, and burnout: A randomized controlled study. *The Permanente Journal*, 18(1), 19–30.

Flook, L., Goldberg, S. B., Pinger, L., Bonus, K., and Davidson, R. J. (2021). Mindfulness for teachers: A pilot study to assess effects on stress, burnout and teaching efficacy. Published: 22 April 2021.

Franco, C., Mañas, I., Cangas, A. J., and Gallego, J. (2010). The applications of mindfulness with students of secondary school: Results on the academic performance, self-concept and anxiety. In *Knowledge Management, Information Systems, E-Learning, and Sustainability Research: Third World Summit on the Knowledge Society, WSKS 2010, Corfu, Greece, September 22-24, 2010. Proceedings, Part I 3* (pp. 83–97). Springer, Berlin Heidelberg.

Gause, R. and Coholic, D. (2010). Mindfulness-based practices as a holistic philosophy and method. *Currents: Scholarship in the Human Services*, 9(2).

Gold, E., Smith, A., Hopper, I., Herne, D., Tansey, G., and Hulland, C. (2010). Mindfulness based stress reduction (MBSR) for primary school teachers. *Journal of Child and Family Studies*, 19(2), 184–189.

https://buddho.org/mindfulness-according-to-the-buddha/?gclid=Cj0KCQjwpBh DvARIsAF1_BU1erV9xfMtUUAMj-lAnB2zpArHA9Gm_v2XxWqWAzA-riWxgjR2a7Ts0aAkDuEALw_wcB.

https://openforest.net/ancient-origins-mindfulness/.

https://www.universalclass.com/articles/business/the-basics-of-mindfulness-in-the-workplace.htm.

Luken, M. and Sammons, A. (2016). Systematic review of mindfulness practice for reducing job burnout. *The American Journal of Occupational Therapy*, 70(2), 7002250020p1–7002250020p10.

McLean, L. and Connor, C. M. (2015). Depressive symptoms in third-grade teachers: Relations to classroom quality and student achievement. *Child Development*, *86*(3), 945–954.

Milne, K. (2029). Stress and teacher burnout: The impact of mindfulness strategies. *Culminating Projects in Education Administration and Leadership*. 66. https://repository.stcloudstate.edu/edad_etds/66.

Shamasundar, C. (2008). Relevance of ancient Indian wisdom to modern mental health — A few examples. *Indian Journal of Psychiatry*, 50(2). April-June 2008.

Chapter 26

Women Faculty and Increased Working Hours due to COVID-19 in Higher Educational Institutions: An Empirical Analysis

Rizwana Rafiq* and Mir Insha Farooq†

*Central University of Kashmir, Ganderbal,
Jammu & Kashmir, India*
*drrizwanarafiq17@gmail.com
†insha_dms@cukashmir.ac.in

Abstract

The COVID-19 pandemic has disproportionately affected working women, particularly in the valley of Jammu and Kashmir, where they already faced challenges due to the abrogation of Article 370. Before the pandemic, women performed 75% of the care economy work, three times more than men. The pandemic has increased the burden of the care economy on women by 30% and has taken a toll on their work-life balance.

A study was conducted to investigate whether COVID-19 increased the workload of women faculty in higher educational institutions in the Kashmir region. The study found that women faculty spent more hours on childcare and official work after COVID-19. The work-life balance satisfaction was low for working women faculties both with and without children.

The paired *t*-test was applied to check the pre- and post-COVID-19 workload of female faculty. The results showed that female faculty spent more time on household and childcare after COVID-19. Their husbands' contribution towards care increased slightly after COVID-19. The time spent on official work increased significantly after COVID-19.

The study has implications for policymakers and academicians. Policymakers can formulate reasonable policies to relieve women of workload, help them manage time effectively, and achieve work-life balance satisfaction. Academicians can conduct further research to identify relationships between extended work hours and the career advancements of women at the workplace.

Keywords: COVID-19, women faculty, higher education, work-life balance

Introduction

The spread of the COVID-19 pandemic in early 2020 forced authorities to close down almost all the major economic sectors across the globe, exerting an outsized impact on working women, especially working mothers. The erstwhile state of Jammu and Kashmir (J&K) was no exception to this; the people of the valley were already facing a number of glitches in almost all sectors much before the outbreak of COVID-19 due to the abrogation of Article 370 in August 2019. However, the educational institutions were the worst hit due to closure and communication blockades, and now, the outbreak of the pandemic has further compounded the difficulties faced by the faculty, especially the female faculty in the valley. The pandemic has taken a disproportionate toll on working women in every profession, and they are certainly facing the greater brunt of the community and economic consequences of this outbreak. In India, the pandemic has increased the burden of the care economy on women in terms of time by 30% (Anu *et al.*, 2020). However, across the globe, without exception, women contributed nearly three-quarters of the care economy prior to the outbreak of COVID-19, which is 3.2 times more than men (Charmes, 2019), and 606 million working-age women perform full-time care-economy work, against 41 million men (ILO, 2020). Many emerging studies argue that the current situation of the pandemic will lead to the equalization of several aspects of gender equality, as male counterparts have increased their contributions towards childcare and household work (Schulte, 2020); however, whether this will be applicable to this part of the world as well, where women are performing 99% of the unpaid care work, is a debatable matter.

Literature Review

Extended work hours, work–life balance satisfaction, and gender gap

Women who are responsible for most of the household assignments not only need to fulfil their professional expectations but also have to manage them without compromising their personal life expectations, which increases the focus on working women's work–life balance. The major concern in society and business organizations nowadays is the effect of manifold roles on the health and well-being of working women and their repercussions on work and family performance stability. The absence of balance between professional and personal lives is associated with a decrease in productivity, an increased rate of absenteeism, lower work satisfaction, and low general well-being (Georgellis *et al.*, 2012; Chang *et al.*, 2010). The topic of work–life balance satisfaction among working women has gained considerable attention nowadays globally, where both males and females equally share financial responsibilities for the well-being of their families. Hence, it becomes equally imperative to recognize how women balance their professional as well as personal lives. In this modified scenario, females mostly abide by the twofold burden of paid employment and unpaid care work (MacDonald *et al.*, 2005). As a result, the gender gap in work–life balance satisfaction has attracted significant scholarly attention (Chung and Van der Lippe, 2018). Moreover, scholars find that the number of work hours per week, the quantity and frequency of overtime required, obstinate work schedules, obstructive supervisors, and an unreceptive organizational culture increase the probability that female employees will experience conflict between their personal as well as professional roles.

COVID-19 has surely increased the working hours of female faculty, as they perform both personal as well as professional duties from home. However, the closing of laboratories and libraries and a lack of research work have restricted their competencies, placing an additional burden on their mental well-being. The current situation has uncovered numerous inadequacies and inequities in the workforce market, which is just one facet of human work. However, the major consequences of COVID-19 were on personal work due to extended chores and childcare resulting from the closure of crèches and schools. Prior to COVID-19, women were performing three times as much unpaid care and domiciliary work as men globally. Additional work hours have taken away personal time from women. The greater work hours and work pressure lead to fatigue, anxiety, and many other adverse psycho-physiological consequences that eventually have a negative impact on personal as well as professional commitments (White *et al.*, 2003).

Methodology

This study's primary objective is to investigate whether COVID-19 has increased the workload of women faculty in higher educational institutions in the Kashmir region. Therefore, the current study intends to fulfil the following objectives:

- to assess the difference between the perceptions of women assistant professors in higher education in the Kashmir region with regard to the working hours spent by them before and after COVID-19;
- to find out whether there is any difference in the perceptions of sample respondents with regard to the working hours spent by their husbands' before and after COVID-19;
- to ascertain the work–life balance satisfaction among female assistant professors in sample institutions;
- to examine the effect of demographic factors on the aforementioned issues.

Research design

This study is an exploration wherein the intent is to identify whether women working in educational institutions are subject to high working hours, including both at work and at home, primarily due to COVID-19. The study employed a mixed methodology, utilizing both qualitative and quantitative approaches.

Data collection

Data were collected from both primary and secondary sources. Primary data were collected through a questionnaire circulated via the online mode using Google Forms. A link to the questionnaire was shared with all the principals of the colleges and the registrars of all the universities across the Kashmir region. Secondary data were collected through journals, books, newspapers, various internet portals, etc.

Sampling

The sampling technique used for the current study includes non-probability sampling, combing convenience and snowball sampling. To begin with, an official email was forwarded to various heads of the colleges and universities, in which we requested data from their female assistant professors. A total of 250 questionnaires were distributed online to female faculty across the various colleges and universities in the Kashmir region. Out of those, only 41 responses were received.

Results and Discussion

Descriptive statistics, using frequency, percentages, mean, and standard deviation, for how much total number of hours female faculty spend on childcare and official work both before and after COVID-19 were calculated. The findings revealed that out of the 41 faculties, 61% represented those from colleges, with the majority of them (nearly 59%) being less than 34 years of age. Moreover, 73.2% had children, with 36.6% of them having at least one child. Further, 41.5% had children within the age group of 0–5 years. An increased workload was felt among various women faculty in Kashmir. The total average working hours for female faculty have gone up from 14.75 hours before COVID-19 to 19.68 hours after it. Further, the analysis reflected that the work–life balance mean is low for working women faculties both with and without children: M (with children) = 2.26 and M (without children) = 2.46; SD (with children) = 0.85525 and SD (without children) = 0.49212.

Hypotheses testing

The paired t-test was applied to check the pre- and post-COVID-19 workload of female faculty, primarily on childcare, then on official working hours, and finally on the total amount of work. The results are described as follows:

H1: Pre-COVID-19 and post-COVID-19 hours spent on household and childcare by female faculty: The results depicted the average number of hours spent by female faculty on household and childcare before the pandemic, with M = 7.9512 and SD = 3.97461, whereas there was a drastic increase in the average number of hours spent after the start of the pandemic, with M = 11.1707 and SD = 5.40788. On average, female faculty felt that they were spending more time on care after COVID-19; $t(40) = -6.295, p < 0.05$.

H2: Pre-COVID-19 and post-COVID-19 hours spent on household and childcare by husbands: The results reflected the average number of hours spent by female faculty's husbands on household and childcare before the pandemic, with M = 3.9512 and SD = 3.88556, whereas the results showed a slight increase in the average number of hours spent after the start of the pandemic, with M = 5.561 and SD = 4.75420. On average, female faculty opined that their husband's contribution towards care has increased after COVID-19, $t(40) = -4.158, p < 0.05$.

H3: Pre-COVID-19 and post-COVID-19 hours spent on official work by female faculty: The analysis of the data revealed the average number of hours spent by female faculty on official work before the pandemic, with M = 6.8049 and SD = 0.92789, whereas the results showed a significant increase in the average number of hours spent after the start of the pandemic, with M = 8.5122 and SD = 4.08119. On average, the time spent on official work has increased after COVID-19; $t(40) = -2.670, p < 0.05$.

Implication and Limitation

This study is significant for policymakers and academicians. Policymakers can make use of this study to formulate reasonable policies so that a particular gender (women) is relieved of their workload, able to manage time effectively, and achieves work–life balance satisfaction. For academicians, further research can be carried out to identify relationships between extended work hours and the career advancements of women at the workplace.

One of the limitations of this study is that the data were collected during the pandemic, due to which online data collection was preferred. The online response rate was very low, which limits the generalizability of this study. Also, this study primarily focussed on working hours in determining workload; hence, when citing this study or using the findings, careful consideration needs to be given. Also, the number of hours of domiciliary work contributed by husbands should be understood from a female perspective.

Conclusion and Suggestions

The primary objective of this study was to investigate whether COVID-19 has increased the workload of women working in higher educational institutions. The findings revealed that most of the childcare and domiciliary treatment, especially associated with COVID-19, falls more on women than their male counterparts. Further, a work–life balance satisfaction analysis revealed that working women with children find balancing work and family more difficult, especially during the pandemic. The extended working hours are making it difficult to maintain balance.

Therefore, while drafting working hour guidelines, higher educational authorities need to consider the extra work hours women put into the care economy. There should also be therapy classes and counselling to relieve women's stress caused by unbalanced work and personal lives. Higher education should come up with fixed working hours as the post-COVID-19 adoption of e-systems has made employees' availability 24/7 compulsory. The study also endorses the idea that universities and colleges should prioritize support for female faculty who are seeking to establish their professional identities.

References

Chang, A., McDonald, P., and Burton, P. (2010). Methodological choices in work-life balance research 1987 to 2006: A critical review. *The International Journal of Human Resource Management*, 21(13), 2381–2413.

Charmes, J. (2019). The unpaid care work and the labour market. An analysis of time use data based on the latest world compilation of time-use surveys. Working Paper, December 19, 2019.

Chung, H. and Van der Lippe, T. (2018). Flexible working, work–life balance, and gender equality: Introduction. *Social Indicators Research*, 151(2), 365–381.

Georgellis, Y., Lange, T., and Tabvuma, V. (2012). The impact of life events on job satisfaction. *Journal of Vocational Behavior*, 80(2), 464–473.

International Labour Organization. (2020). Unpaid care work and motherhood employment penalty widen gender gaps. February 5, 2020.

Kim, H. (2017). Investigating the effects of work-family spillovers, gender, and formal mentoring on career goal of managers. *International Journal of Manpower*, 38(8), 1065–1085.

MacDonald, M., Phipps, S., and Lethbridge, L. (2005). Taking its toll: The influence of paid and unpaid work on women's well-being. *Feminist Economics*, 11(1), 63–94.

Madgavkar, A., White, O., Krishnan, M., Mahajan, D., and Azcue, X. (2020). COVID-19 and gender equality: Countering the regressive effects. *McKinsey & Company*, July 15, 2020.

Rangarajan, R. (2018). A study on work life balance of working women with special reference Chennai city. *International Journal of Creative Research Thoughts (IJCRT)*, 6(2). April 2018. ISSN: 2320-2882.

Schulte, B. (2020, May 21). Interview by Terry Gross. National Public Radio. Retrieved from https://www.npr.org/2020/05/21/860091230/pandemic-makes-evident-grotesque-gender-inequality-in-household-work.

White, M., Hill, S., McGovern, P., Mills, C., and Smeaton, D. (2003). High-performance' management practices, working hours and work–life balance. *British Journal of Industrial Relations*, 41(2), 175–195.

Chapter 27

Analyzing Business and Functional Areas of 'Didi Ki Rasoi': A JEEViKA Initiative

Mrinal Keshri* and Yash Kumar[†]

Development Management Institute (DMI), Patna
*mrinalkeshri444@gmail.com
[†]yash.kumar1494@gmail.com

Abstract

Didi Ki Rasoi, a JEEViKA initiative, is a prime example of grassroot empowerment. Enterprising women in self-help groups (SHGs) chart a path to prosperity. Think of a situation where resources are not sufficient. Vulnerability exists in terms of lack of education, cultural and religious discrimination, overpopulation, unemployment, and corruption, and you belong to the marginalized sections of society. Irrespective of circumstances, these women have the courage to do something new and their way of life is appreciable. JEEViKA aims to enhance the social and economic empowerment of the rural poor in Bihar. It has come up with different livelihood projects. Didi Ki Rasoi is one of them, and it focuses on the financial and economic inclusion and capitalization of poor women through collaborative frameworks.

It is a collective enterprise where a village organization (VO) enters into contract with a group of women from SHGs. These women are owners of canteens for a contractual period. This chapter captures the business and functional areas of two different Didi Ki Rasoi: Vaishali and Buxar. It is interesting to note that the enterprise follows a decentralized model of intervention. In short, it follows 'keep it simple and small' (KISS). In the first phase of this pilot project, five government hospitals, namely, the Sadar Hospitals of Vaishali, Shivar, Buxar, Gaya, and a sub-divisional hospital, are selected for this project, where the role of Didi Ki Rasoi is to provide a regular healthy diet to admitted patients. Bhawish and Himmat are the names of the respective VOs in Vaishali and Buxar. They signed memoranda of understanding (MoUs) with hospitals. It is important to note that space, electricity, and water are provided by the State Health Society, Bihar. Didi Ki Rasoi is an open cafeteria, which means normal customers can also visit. It also supplies food to government institutions.

Kudumbashree is JEEViKA's consultant for this non-farm project and, as a resource person, provides guidelines for the identification of premises and selection. They also organize training for identified members and finalize members who will operate the canteen. The canteen or café industry is highly competitive, with private vendors already present in the market. In order to achieve customer segmentation, Didi Ki Rasoi is being positioned as a provider of homely food, which includes hygiene and quality as key components. There are a few managerial issues when it comes to finance and operations. Although these women are good enough to sustain this enterprise, it's necessary to compete in the local market. JEEViKA has provided a consultant or canteen manager for a particular tenure to tackle managerial issues. These women aren't professional cooks or chiefs. Their capacity is limited. Therefore, a head cook could be hired for the initial 3–6 months for smooth operations.

The capital structure of this collective enterprise is as follows: 80% of profit will be kept as retention money for the different activities of the business; owners may be given up to 15% of profit; and 1% of profit may be given to respective VOs after one year. Each owner has a share of Rs. 20,000 in this enterprise. There is a provision of paying interest at up to 12% annually; however, in this case, it is 0% for a deposit of up to Rs. 20,000. As of now, VOs are not fully functional, but JEEViKA will soon completely handover this enterprise to VOs. This is a suitable example of 'withdrawal from community-based intervention.'

Safety becomes a critical issue as women work in the kitchen. It has been observed that minor as well as major accidents have occurred in the past few months. Health/Life insurance will be provided on time. Food safety and quality assurance are a must. Customer feedback is necessary because their customers also includes patients.

For example, a diabetes patient is not supposed to eat rice because he has to take care of carbohydrate intake to manage his blood glucose levels, whereas the hospital dietary is common for all patients. Inventory management is also a crucial task, as demand is not easily estimated in most cases. Hence, to increase profit, preparing day-wise menus is an alternative solution for the optimal utilization of resources. It also helps in pre-cooking preparation, reducing serving time, and reducing food wastage. Working in public institutions, a few women also faced sexual harassment at the workplace. Usually, the canteens close at around 09:30 pm. Returning home late night becomes a challenge for them.

Last but not least, although hospital patients definitely provide a permanent source of revenue to make business more sustainable, timely payment remains a key issue, which can be easily found at both locations.

Keywords: Didi Ki Rasoi, JEEViKA initiative, grassroot empowerment, community based organisations, financial inclusion, customer segmentation, sustainable business

The Organization: 'Didi Ki Rasoi'

Genesis and growth

The Bihar Transformative Development Project (BTDP) intervenes with a focus on marginalized communities, such as the SCs, STs, minorities, extremely backward castes (EBC), and other backward castes (OBC) (World Bank Group, 2016). The BTDP project is expected to cover around 60 lakh (6 million) poor families spread over 300 blocks across 32 districts of Bihar. Its four themes or programmes include institution and capacity building, social development, microfinance, and livelihoods.

'Didi Ki Rasoi,' or canteen, aims to diversify and enhance household income by setting up community-based organizations (CBOs). Women workforce participation rate has rapidly increased over the past few years in Bihar. The reason behind this is the self-help groups (SHGs) of JEEViKA. SHGs have significantly improved the lives of women in terms of literacy rate, child marriages, spousal violence, financial inclusion, body mass index (BMI), and household decisions. The SHGs are widely viewed by the government of Bihar as ideal platforms for efficient targeting and delivery of various social welfare programs and have shown promise in delivering long-term behaviour change critical to achieving higher outcomes in the areas of health, nutrition, and sanitation. Its prime example is alcohol prohibition in Bihar.

Quality food at reasonable rates has been a challenge at government institutions, such as hospitals, district collectorates, and the judiciary. Didi Ki Rasoi is emerging as a potential collective enterprise to serve hygienic and quality food. As of now, it is operating at two locations: Vaishali and Buxar. JEEViKA is planning to replicate this model in the future to eradicate poverty and provide sustainable livelihoods in non-farm sectors. The first Didi Ki Rasoi started on 10 October 2018 at Sadar Hospital, Hajipur, in the Vaishali district of Bihar. Initially, they were involved in counter selling. Around two months post-intervention, the Health Society and Didi Ki Rasoi came together for a formal MoU (Figure A1, Annexure A).

The second Didi Ki Rasoi was inaugurated on 28 February 2019 at Himmat village organization (VO) in Buxar. Hajipur's women were trained in Kerala, and Buxar's women (Didi) were trained in Buxar. Kudumbashree is JEEViKA's consultant for this non-farm project and, as a resource organisation, provides guidelines for identification of premises and selection. They also organize training for identified members and finalize the members who will operate the canteen. Detailed information about the different activities involved in establishing the canteen and training outline is provided in Tables A1 and A2 in Annexure A. Figure 1 shows bottom to top approach of establishing a canteen. The café

Figure 1. Process leading up to the inauguration of a Didi Ki Rasoi.

was modelled after the Adheba Institute of Food Research and Hospitality Management (AIFHRM), which is formed under Kudumbashree as a hospitality management and training group. It aims not only at revolutionizing the hospitality sector in the state but also local economic development by providing gainful employment to poor women from Kudumbashree families. It has been managing the cafes for over 10 years and has worked with multiple government departments as well.

In the first phase of this pilot project, five government hospitals, namely, Sadar Hospitals of Vaishali, Shivar, Buxar, and Gaya, and a sub-divisional hospital, are selected for this project, where the role of Didi Ki Rasoi is to provide a regular healthy diet to admitted patients.

Vision, mission, and objectives

Vision

JEEViKA has the vision to become a leading contributor to the process of livelihood promotion among the rural poor in the Madhya Bharat region by the year 2015.

Objectives

The objective of this initiative is to create an ecosystem where good food can be made available at fair prices, while also creating livelihoods for the community.

Institution's objectives:

- Hygienic canteens maintained on the institution's premises.
- High-quality food made available to officers, staff, visitors, etc.

JEEViKA objectives:

- Entrepreneurs would emerge from the community who would gain the skill of operating at high quality.
- Canteens would act as a source of employment for community members.

Organizational structure

Didi Ki Rasoi is registered as a collective firm in the name of its VO, or cluster-level federation (CLF). For example, Vaishali's Didi Ki Rasoi is registered as 'Bhawish Didi Ki Rasoi,' where 'Bhawish' is the name of its VO. Women of this VO are the primary stakeholders of the enterprise. This is done so because the names of enterprises must not be similar. Usually, Didi Ki Rasoi does not prominently show its VO's name. Vaishali's canteen has nine women as employees. There are stakeholders as well as shareholders of this enterprise. The locality of the women is also considered before employing them since the distance between the canteen and the women's homes must not exceed 8 km. Bhawish and Himmat are the names of Hajipur canteen and Buxar canteen, respectively. In the coming days, their respective VOs will be responsible for monitoring them. At the same moment, the VOs will be involved in decision-making activities, including the withdrawal of poorly performing employees, infrastructure development, capacity building, profit sharing, and its expansion. Right now, the VOs are not very vibrant and active, but this must be developed as part of institution building.

Membership distribution and spread ownership of collective

Since it is a collective enterprise which is solely owned by a VO, this enterprise comes under the group ownership (all owners) model of canteens, where all JEEViKA members involved in the canteen would invest an equal amount of equity and hence have equal ownership. Vaishali's canteen has employed nine women, and they are also owners. Four of them have an equity share of Rs. 20,000. Others are supposed to pay the respective amounts soon.

Profit sharing mechanism: All members would get an equal share in the profit (up to 15% in the case of Buxar), with a certain percentage earmarked for investment back into the business.

Functional Area-Wise Study

Procurement and field operations

Bihar, with its plentiful regular assets of fertile soil, plenteous water, deferred atmosphere, and rich social and historical legacy, is a standout for its most interesting conditions in India. As much as 79% of Bihar's population is dependent on agriculture. It produces different types of food grains, fruits, vegetables, spices, and flowers. Agriculture is the major occupation in the state. Therefore, it supports the collective enterprise of Didi Ki Rasoi, which acts as a backward linkage. Vaishali comes under **agro-climatic zone I** (Northern West). It receives an average rainfall of 120 cm (approx.). The soil pH varies from 6.5 to 8.4. March–June is the summer season, with an average temperature of 35–40 degrees Celsius. Usually, two types of soil are found in this zone: sandy loam and loam. The major fruit crops grown in this zone are mangoes, guavas, litchis, bananas, and so forth, and in between these major yields, minor yields of Makhana, pineapple, and betelvine are additionally grown. The agricultural cropping pattern is dominated by cereals. The major cropping sequences of the different zones are as follows: Rice–Wheat, Rice–Rai, Rice–Sweet Potato, Rice–Maize (Rabi), Maize–Wheat, Maize–Sweet Potato, Maize–Rai, Rice–Lentil, Rice–Linseed (Agriculture Department of Bihar, n.d.). The rice–wheat cropping system occupies more than 70% of the gross cropped area.

Cooking is an art which is inherent in most women in India. The concept of a collective enterprise goes beyond profit maximization. The VOs have to monitor and involve themselves in decision-making processes. This requires a productive human resource, which is easily available in a country like India, where delicious cuisine includes a variety of items or products. It is a possibility that this business model will be replicated in all districts of Bihar in the coming days. Once it is done, we can have various collective enterprises running simultaneously. For example, one enterprise will produce and supply napkins or serviettes. Other materials, such as spices, frozen vegetables, and milk, will also be procured from similar collective enterprises of women. This will be the **value chain model** of the enterprise.

As of now, they have three different vendors for procurement. 'Ghar Sansar' supplies cereals, including rice, pulses, and spices. Two other vendors supply milk and liquefied petroleum gas (LPG) cylinders. Ghar Sansar is selected after the announcement of a tender offer. 'Prince Provisional Store' is the vendor for cereals in Buxar. The selection is done on the basis of the cost and quality of cereals. For example, there is a formal Memorandum of Understanding between 'Bhawish JEEViKA Mahila Gram Sangathan' and Ghar Sansar. Usually, the enterprise procures cereals for the next 15 days based on the demand during the previous 15 days from Ghar Sanasar. Didi Ki Rasoi procures on credit and pays the previous bills at the time of the next purchase. Quality assurance (QA)/quality control (QC) is performed by women and the manager of the enterprise before keeping it in store. Local transports, such as mini-carrier trucks and autos, are used to carry these items. Perishable items, such as milk, vegetables, and curd, are purchased on a daily basis based on the demand on the previous day.

Production/Operation functions

Bihar is known for its healthy food items. The cities in Bihar are still small, and their culture influences their diet. Regular meals include rice, pulses, vegetables, and roti. Apart from these items, Bihar is also known for *Litti Choka* (meshed potato), *Sattu* (gram drink), and *Petta* (Bagiya). Didi Ki Rasoi has its own cultural food segment. Most of these items are frequently consumed, and they are achieved through internationally claimed layout and technology. Workforce allocation is done after considering an individual's capacity and skills. The location provides a permanent source of revenue for the business, as hospital patients are their regular customers, and food menu for the patients (Table B1, Annexure B) is decided in the MoU between the Health Society, Bihar, and the respective VO of Didi Ki Rasoi. The Health Society pays different prices to these two enterprises, as hospital dietary requirements also vary. Profits made are 3.22% and 5.92% for Bhawish Didi Ki Rasoi, Hajipur, and Himmat Didi Ki Rasoi, Buxar, respectively. For counter sales, they provide a variety of food items. The food menu is influenced by the culture at the location. The price is also reasonably low as compared to the market price. Hence, they have a competitive advantage. The reason behind operating at low prices is the availability of space, water, and electricity, which are provided free of cost by the Health Society. There seems to be cross-subsidization, as the profit margin is relatively low for hospital dietary.

The canteens have kitchen planning guidelines with access standards, as their layout and kitchen equipment satisfy internationally set standards (Figure C1, Annexure C). Didi Ki Rasoi has been provided with a computer (e-PoS) for all billing and reporting. The CFM has to ensure that proper entries are being made. Each canteen has a billing manager to manage the e-PoS, reconcile books, etc. Each canteen has hired a canteen manager, a consultant hired by JEEViKA (SPMU). The canteen manager's role involves guiding the women (*Didis*) for a period of time to achieve capacity building for them. Didi Ki Rasoi is in an introductory phase, and it's impossible to exactly determine demand. As of now, they consider the previous week's demand to estimate the demand for the current week. Inventory is managed manually, but, hopefully, they'll transition to using inventory management software in the coming days. Since it is a collective enterprise where each woman is an owner as well as a staff member, distribution of work is required in order to achieve smooth operation of the business. They mutually distribute work, which interchanged every week. It provides each woman the opportunity to improve her efficiency in any kind of job. Monitoring and accountability become important in such kind of intervention where there is a scarcity of resources, such as MIS, quality workforce, professionals, and revenue. These resources are important because the market is competitive and they have to sustain themselves while competing against private outlets. In order to achieve transparency and avoid complaints, each woman has a predefined role for a week. They mutually decide their works, such as procurement, serving food on the table, store (inventory) management, cooking food, and accounting (Table D1, Annexure D).

The *Didis* believe that they are good at cooking and procurement of raw materials, but education becomes a barrier. Work such as accounting, inventory management, and serving food on tables requires skills. Mrs. Rinku Devi believes, 'we are in [a] learning phase. We don't have much idea about these woks but we're trying our best to overcome these issues.' Mrs. Sanju Devi says, 'I try my best to tackle such issues because they hamper our business. My focus is on learning. I become happy when I learn something new.' Briefly, these women don't have proper educational qualifications as hotel management professionals, and capacity building requires time as they've started from scratch.

Markets and marketing

Sadar Hospitals are located in the districts of Bihar, where the cities or towns may or may not have big food franchises, such as Domino's Pizza, Kentucky Fried Chicken (KFC), McDonald's, and Haldiram. Nonetheless, restaurants, hotels, small cafes, and *dhabas* are easily available. Each of them has its own market segment.

The restaurant or canteen business is a highly competitive market. Hence, Didi Ki Rasoi is a price taker instead of a price setter, but there is a permanent source of revenue in this business. First, an MoU between the Health Society and VO is signed, in which it is agreed that it can also obtain revenue as an open cafeteria. Accommodation, water, and electricity are provided by the Health Society. Therefore, operating costs are low. They are also establishing other institutional tie-ups. Hajipur canteen supplied food during the general election of 2019 in Hajipur and earned Rs. 8,63,537 as sales from such a tie-up. Other sources of income are the District Project Coordinate Unit (DPCU) and training centres of JEEViKA. Hence, market segments are consciously chosen by the enterprise for specific reasons.

Didi Ki Rasoi became operational in October 2018 and February 2019 at Hajipur and Buxar, respectively. It's a pilot project of JEEViKA under the label of non-farm interventions. Hence, both enterprises are in the introductory phase (launch) of the business life cycle. During this phase, sales are low but slowly increasing. They are constantly improving customer segmentation in order to achieve comparative advantages and value propositions. Expectedly, revenue is low and initial start-up costs are high, as enterprises are prone to incur losses in this phase. Hence, the cash flow during the launch phase is also negative.

Since the market segment of the restaurant and food industry is highly competitive, Didi Ki Rasoi have some unique selling propositions (USPs) to sustain in the market. Restaurant chains such as KFC, McDonald's, Café Coffee Day (CCD), and Domino's Pizza have different USPs. Usually, customers' perceptions of these fast-food restaurants are different from those of conventional restaurants. They serve special food items in terms of taste, recipe, and hospitality. KFC is known for its fried chicken recipe, which is the world's largest fast-food chicken chain. McDonald's is known for its hamburgers. CCD is known for being India's favourite hangout for coffee and conversations. In the same fashion, Didi Ki Rasoi is being positioned as a provider of homemade food, which includes hygiene and quality as key components. It is located at government hospitals. Based on feedback from different sources, we have the following concluding facts. Very often, people avoid eating on hospital premises because they have preconceived notions about it. At the same moment, customers have alternative options available on the market. Directly competing in the market might be a bad idea for the enterprise, as a predefined source of income (dietary in hospital) is available in this case. Hence, market segmentation and positioning are going to play vital role in the long term. Homely food is the best option as its unique selling point (USP), which matches its brand name, Didi Ki

Rasoi. It'll also help with brand positioning. Customers perceive homely food as hygienic and quality food. In the upcoming days, when Didi Ki Rasoi becomes a sustainable business model, it may also deliver food via online food delivery applications, such as Swiggy, Zomato, and Foodpanda. Hajipur canteen has recently developed a feedback mechanism. It received a certificate of service satisfaction from the hospital authority. The customer wouldn't get the feeling that those foods are being served by a different unit. For the customer, it is only a single brand: Didi Ki Rasoi.

Human resources management

An orientation would be conducted in the groups around the proposed canteen area. The distance between Sadar Hospital and the women's locality must not exceed 8 km. The theme of discussion is centred around the following facts. The canteen has to become a self-sustaining profit-making enterprise. All canteens would be serving inpatients at the prevailing rates of the hospital, while the canteen would be free to set its own rates for all other customers. Interested candidates would be mobilized based on the eligibility criteria. Such candidates are supposed to fill out Form 2A (Table E1, Annexure E), and an initial evaluation will be done based on this form. The process flow for human resource (HR) planning and recruitment is illustrated in Figure 2.

The previous paragraph covered the orientation and mobilization of a particular community. The next stage is to check the background and shortlist candidates. It involves the following points:

1. must be a member of an SHG HH under JEEViKA, and the SHG must be at least one year old;
2. must have an attendance of at least 60% in their respective SHGs;

Figure 2. Process for identification of entrepreneurs.

3. must have taken loan from their respective SHG, with 70% loan repayment percentage as per the repayment schedule;
4. needs to be literate and adept at handling finances;
5. prior experience of running a small *dhaba*/café/restaurant would be given preference;
6. willing and able to undergo training programmes and exposure visits;
7. willing to contribute their own investment;
8. willing to work as needed for canteen operation at the canteen premises.

Once the process is done, qualified candidates are evaluated on the basis of Form 2B during the interview (Table E2, Annexure E). The CLF/VO may invite the BPM of the concerned block to be part of the selection process. The recommendations of ACs/CCs will be considered before announcing the final shortlist. CLF/VO would conduct a second round of interviews with all shortlisted candidates. The CLF/VO may choose to invite the DPM of the concerned district, the project manager — non-farm, or any others to be part of the interview panel, along with the nominated interview panel members of the CLF/VO.

A skill training (residential or non-residential) programme for 10–15 days would be conducted by Kudumbashree RPs, supported by a local resource person and staff, on various recipes, quality standards, hospitality, restaurant management, and interaction with customers. Hajipur's women were given non-residential training in Kerala, whereas Buxar's women were given residential training at a restaurant named 'Raj Rasoi,' which is located in Buxar Market. The broad topics covered include:

- communication with customers,
- accounting and bookkeeping,
- techniques of bulk cooking and preparation of traditional cuisines of Bihar,
- maintenance of cleanliness and hygiene,
- group behaviour,
- crisis management,
- use of occupational safety gear,
- waste management,
- techniques of purchasing raw materials,
- business promotion.

All these topics are vital. Hospitality, accounts, and safety are key major topics which are delivered in a very effective manner.

It is worth noting that the number of people would be lower if the size of the canteen were smaller. Also, the salary has to meet the minimum wage criteria prescribed by the state.

Salary is directly sent to the bank account of each woman and additional staff. They also hire helpers in cases of sudden demand. *Didis* or owners can take leave on their meeting day of SHGs. Hence, leave days range from 4 to 5. They've mutually decided that there would be absenteeism of just one owner on a particular meeting day. The canteen operates 365 days a year. As there is no provision for leave on Saturday or Sunday, they take leave successively (one person at a time). A detailed salary plan can be seen in Table F1 in Annexure F.

Finance and accounts

Fixed costs in a canteen are those that don't change (or change rarely), such as costs of obtaining food licences and certification (Partnership Deed, Health Trade Licence, Eating House License, GST Number, FSSAI Licence, and Pollution Certificate), insurance, salaries, and kitchen equipment. Fixed costs are easier to budget for when opening a canteen because they don't fluctuate much each month. Variable costs of a canteen include labour, food, transportation, and marketing. Variable costs are harder to predict when opening a canteen because they vary according to customer demand or output. However, after several months, it is easily known what to expect each month. The budget allocation is up to Rs. 24 lakh (2.4 million) per canteen (unit cost in guidelines). It is to be noted that this is the maximum limit, and the actual budget is released based on requirements and the business plan. This is a one-time grant given to a Didi Ki Rasoi. A rational structure of investment in various assets for setting up a canteen is provided in Tables 1 and 2. It must be noted that the actual amount may vary depending on location, estimated footfall, requirements for kitchen equipment and employees, and other resources.

Hence, if we allocate a budget for a canteen, which includes the total fixed cost and operating expenses, it becomes Rs. 2,162,767. The estimated budget (Table G1, Annexure G) was Rs. 2,239,032 in the case of Buxar; however, only Rs. 1,200,000 (approx.) has been

Table 1. Investments in various fixed assets.

Fixed cost			
Fixed assets (kitchen) — A			
Description	Nos.	Unit cost (Rs.)	Total cost (Rs.)
Bain-marie	1	50,000	50,000
Working table	3	20,000	60,000
Cooking range (3 Bunner)	1	30,000	30,000
Bulk cooking range	1	30,000	30,000
Dish rack	1	25,000	25,000
Sink for dishwash	1	30,000	30,000
Refrigerator	1	20,000	20,000
Mixer	1	5,000	5,000
Wet grinder	1	60,000	60,000
Kitchen vessels	Lump sum	50,000	50,000
Tea pantry counter	Lump sum	50,000	50,000
Juice counter	Lump sum	35,000	35,000
Food service cutleries and crockeries	Lump sum	1,00,000	1,00,000
Total			**5,45,000**
Fixed assets (service area) — B			
Description	Nos	Unit cost (Rs.)	Cost (Rs.)
Tables	12	10,000	120,000
Chairs	46	1,000	46,000
Service trolley	1	30,000	30,000
Clearance trolley	1	20,000	20,000
Side table	1	12,500	12,500
Cash counter	1	25,000	25,000
Billing machine	1	30,000	30,000
Total			**2,83,500**
Total capital expenditure (A + B)			8,28,500
Pre-operative expenses — C			
Description	Nos	Unit cost (Rs.)	Cost (Rs.)
Building refurbishment*	Lump sum	1,00,000	1,00,000
Uniform (@ 3 sets for all people)	15	2,000	90,000
Signboards/glow sign	Lump sum	50,000	50,000

Table 1. (Continued)

	Fixed cost		
	Lump sum	30,000	30,000
			2,70,000
...-operative expense			2,70,000
Total fixed cost (A + B + C)			10,98,500

Table 2. Operating expenses.

Description	Operating expense (indicative)		
	Unit cost	Number/Unit	Monthly cost (Rs.)
Tentative salaries/month (actual salaries & no. of employee will be fixed by concerned nodal VO/CLF)			
Member salaries	10,000	8	80,000
Waiters	4,000	4	16,000
Cleaners	4,000	2	8,000
Accountant & billing	8,000	2	16,000
Additional operating expense/month			
Marketing	3,000	Lump sum/month	3,000
Transportation	3,000	Lump sum/month	3,000
Others*	20,000	Lump sum/month	20,000
Annual maintenance			
Auditor	30,000	Lump sum	
Licence(s) renewal	20,000	Lump sum	
Insurance	100,000	Lump sum	
Total annual maintenance	150,000		
Annual maintenance split into monthly cost			12,500
Raw material			5,51,012
Total monthly operating expense (working capital)			7,09,512
Total operating expense (working capital for 45 days)			10,64,267

allocated till date. This results in the unavailability of the kit, chimney, uniforms, refrigerator, wet grinder, juice counter, etc., hindering the smooth operation of the canteen. The situation at the Hajipur canteen is better as compared to that at the Buxar canteen, as it received a fund of Rs. 1,800,000 (approx.) in two phases. A major challenge, which is common to both enterprises, is maintaining working capital or operating expenses. Government departments are major stakeholders in Didi Ki Rasoi. Untimely payment becomes an issue as well as a threat to business in the case of any violations of the terms and conditions mentioned in the MoU between the Health Society and Didi Ki Rasoi. The respective hospital is expected to pay the amount for the dietary within 30 days of the submission of the bill. However, it is found that payment is constantly delayed, and there is no provision to charge a certain amount of interest (the time value of money) if payment is delayed. This is something which must be included in MoUs in the future. Keeping such a large amount of money out of business (unavailability) is a serious issue which hampers the business financially in the long run.

The financial health of Didi Ki Rasoi, Hajipur, is summarized in Table 3.

It is found that April sales are highest because it supplied food to government officials during the general election of 2019; however, it's on credit. Taking a close look at the 'Paid' column, we can see that most cells are filled with Rs. 0. The cash reserve from December to May is critical because the estimated working capital is Rs. 10,64,267.

Table 3. Sales analysis for Hajipur canteen.

Month	Total sales (Rs.)	Cash sales (Rs.)	Credit (Rs.)	Paid (Rs.)	Cash reserve (Rs.)
October	50,049	38,460	11,589	0	909,512
November	102,372	57,363	45,009	3,600	709,512
December	238,582	62,836	175,746	10,800	523,512
January	221,692	47,332	174,360	51,458	287,512
February	188,413	31,103	157,310	0	351,755
March	305,124	38,314	266,810	0	179,311
April	721,274	28,213	693,061	0	180,882
May	390,064	3,657	389,307	0	97,575

Figure 3. (Color available online) Financial health of Didi Ki Rasoi, Hajipur.

Table 4. Sales analysis for Buxar canteen.

Month	Total sales (Rs.)	Cash sales (Rs.)	Credit (Rs.)	Cash reserve (Rs.)
March	116,732	93,857	36,555	4,149
April	109,201	79,551	29,650	9,095
May	176,554	83,254	93,300	12,949.5

From the graph shown in Figure 3, it is found that the cash reserve has sharply declined because of delays in payment from respective departments. Cash or counter sales are also very low as compared to total sales.

The financial health of Didi Ki Rasoi, Buxar is summarized in Table 4.

This canteen is in its early introductory phase, but the cash reserve or working capital is very low. One can imagine the difficulties that plague this canteen. It is operating on daily earnings and credit from suppliers (Figure 4). Because of lower operating expenses, salaries for the women often get delayed.

In the case of profit, 80% will be kept as retention money for the business for different activities, the owners may be given up to 15% of profit, and 1% of profit may be given to the respective VO after one year. Each owner has a share of Rs. 20,000 in this enterprise. There is a provision for paying interest up to 12% annually, although, in this case, it is 0%.

As of now, they are not using any accounting software. They maintain a ledger, and data are entered in a predefined format in MS Excel by an accountant. It is further used for submitting monthly reports. Tax compliance mechanisms follow government rules, i.e., 5% GST (includes both CGST and SGST). They have their own unique GST number.

Figure 4. (Color available online) Financial health of Didi Ki Rasoi, Buxar.

Table 5. BEP in sales, Bhawish Didi Ki Rasoi.

Parameters	Amount (Rs.)
Sales	2,217,570
Variable cost	1,420,471
Contribution	797,099
Contribution margin ratio	**0.36**
Fixed cost	
Assets	1,098,500
Salary paid till date	718,666
Total fixed cost	1,817,166
BEP in Sales	**5,055,448**

Breakeven point in sales

The breakeven point (BEP), or breakeven level, represents the sales amount in revenue (sales) terms, which is required to cover the total costs, consisting of both fixed and variable costs, of operating a Didi Ki Rasoi. The total profit at the breakeven point is zero. Hence, sales lower than the BEP will result in losses after considering all the costs.

Table 5 shows the BEP sales analysis until May 2019 for the Hajipur canteen.

Sales lower than the BEP will result in losses after considering all the costs, which are due to a high fixed cost.

Table 6 shows the BEP sales analysis until May 2019 for the Buxar canteen.

The negative contribution margin ratio of this canteen indicates that its variable costs and expenses exceed its sales. In other words, if sales increase in the same proportion as in the past, it will experience larger losses.

Table 6. BEP in sales, Himmat Didi Ki Rasoi.

Parameters	Amount (Rs.)
Sales	402,487
Variable cost	505,493
Contribution	−103,006
Contribution margin ratio	**−0.26**
Fixed cost	
Assets	1,098,500
Salary paid till date	201,000
Total fixed cost	**1,299,500**

Profitability analysis

Didi Ki Rasoi is most concerned about its profitability, as it is in its introductory (launch) phase, and the initial investment is high. Hence, financial ratios hold significant importance. One of the most frequently used tools for financial ratio analysis is profitability ratios, which are used to determine a canteen's bottom line and its returns to its investors. Profitability ratios show a canteen's overall efficiency and performance. This section presents the details only for the Hajipur canteen. Buxar canteen is excluded as its CMR is already negative.

Gross Profit Margin = (Revenue − Costs of Goods Sold)/
  Revenue × 100%
  = (Rs. 2,217,570 − Rs. 1,420,471)/(Rs. 2,217,570)
    × 100%
  = **35.94%**

Net Profit Margin = PAT/Revenue × 100%
  = (757,244.05)/(2,217,570) × 100%
  = **34.15%**

Monthly sales turnover and receivables

Credit sales are a major challenge, as discussed in the previous section. A simple line graph is shown in Figures 5 and 6 for both canteens to highlight the serious financial trouble (for further details, see Tables G2 and G3 in Annexure G). Counter sales are just a fraction of sales, which

Figure 5. (Color available online) Monthly sales turnover and receivables, Vaishali.

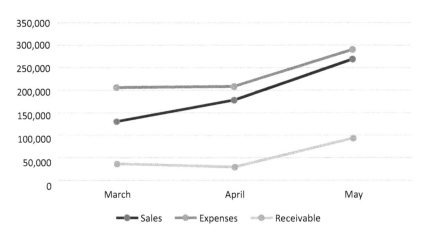

Figure 6. (Color available online) Monthly sales turnover and receivables, Buxar.

is the gap between the sales curve and the receivables. Hospital patients are regular customers. Supplying food during a training & capacity-building programme is supplementary. In the month of April, Didi Ki Rasoi operated at an economy of scale. Expenses also include fixed costs together with other costs, including those of raw materials and overheads, and their value can't be zero. Certain expenses are always fixed. The gap between sales and expenses shows that they registered the largest profit in April, but Didi Ki Rasoi hasn't received the amount from different government departments. The maximum sales are on credit.

Buxar's canteen is in the introductory phase as they are just four months old. The expense curve is still above sales, which shows that it is still operating at a loss.

Further, dependence on a single bulk consumer is extremely risky, and the canteen needs to spread its risk and ensure that not more than 50% of its sales revenue comes from a single bulk consumer, such as a hospital. Therefore, the functioning of the payment system needs to be ensured; otherwise, the entire system will collapse. This is applicable to all businesses. Hence, effective management of credit on both purchases and sales is the key differentiator between success and failure.

Any delayed sale realization not only puts additional financial costs (cost of working capital in terms of interest), it can also bring down the entire business. So, if any cost is based on cash sale basis, the same cost cannot and will not withstand credit sales, as the cost will be much higher, with no limit on the upper end. Hence, the business may need to be reassessed in terms of its expenses and hence the pricing of its products.

Governance and Decision-Making

Board-level participation and decision-making process

If the partners in the partnership firm demand uninterrupted operation, the decision regarding keeping the canteen open is made by the Joint Vigilance Board of Women's Organization. According to the rules, a two-thirds majority of the board of directors is required for the decision to be valid for such decision partners.

In the event of a dispute among owners, the first party, the block unit, or the district coordination unit, and in the case of complaints over quality, the first party will be the JEEViKA women's VO. It can be removed, and according to need, a new owner can be appointed once she pays Rs. 20,000 to the enterprise as a deposit.

The selected VO would work as a nodal VO, and funds would be managed by the respective VO. Monitoring is ensured by the Community Based Organisations for purchases, products, staff, Regular availability of products, regular updating of accounts, and regular payment to the workers on a monthly basis. All the partner members have the right to take care of day-to-day work and activities. It is necessary that the signing of any contract letter, document, etc., be done after authorization from the VO. It can be signed by the selected member on behalf of the partnership. Salaries can be paid to the employees on the basis of the decision of the partners of the partnership firm, and on the basis of the decision of the VO, incentive money as per the profits in the business will be decided.

Member participation in GB and decision-making process

It is mandatory to attend the monthly meetings of the VO. One owner has to attend. If there are any administrative issues related to the canteen, they can be raised by any owner (staff) in the monthly VO meetings.

Delegation of powers and managerial decision-making

If any woman (owner) wants to resign from this job, then she has to provide one month's notice to the other owners and the VO.

In the case of the death of a member, her contract would not be invalidated. Her nominee may receive the profits and dividends. Once a deposit is made by an owner, there is no provision to use the amount for personal use during the contractual period.

Owners (staff) are supposed to analyze and update the availability and cost of raw materials. They are expected to provide the exact same hospital dietary, but they have the freedom to decide food items for counter sales. Any institution or organization can approach Didi Ki Rasoi to supply food because there is no such restriction/limitation on operation or production. Quality food, hygiene, and nutrition are key parameters, which are the responsibility of the owners. Any official from JEEViKA (BPIU and DPCU) and VO can occasionally visit for inspection or audit.

There is provision for purchasing raw materials collectively in groups as per guidelines, except perishable items. Proper maintenance of documents for any transaction as well as inventory is compulsory.

If any owner withdraws her contract, then her deposit will be returned, and the dividend will be decided by the canteen's VO.

Training and capacity building of board members

Kudumbashree-NRO is identified as the resource agency by the World Bank, which helps JEEViKA roll out the canteens at different locations.

JEEViKA may enter into a formal MoU with a technical agency to develop standard operating procedures and protocols, capacity building modules, and handholding systems for canteen/cafe enterprises.

In addition to the technical agency, JEEViKA would allow for the hiring of local RPs by nodal CLF/VO from relevant districts, who would have the local market intelligence and experience of running a canteen. This person would support the resource agency and the canteen in their day-to-day operations.

Strategic Issues/Challenges and Coping Mechanisms

Competitive posture of the enterprise, and its competitive strategies

- **The menu:** A good balanced menu plays a critical role in a canteen. It must not contain too many or too few items. The customer segment depends on many factors, such as culture, locality, and economy. The next question is whether the items are appropriately priced? Food costing is a need of the hour. Too large a menu means longer kitchen order ticket (KOT) times. If a canteen has too many different dishes cooking at the same time and not enough of the same items in the same pans, more time is consumed in producing orders. Each table takes longer to serve. A day-wise menu can solve the problem (Table H2, Annexure H). A demand estimate would be made. Preparations prior to cooking of food according to the day would also reduce production and automatically reduce serving time. Bulk production also increases profitability.
- **Customer service:** Customers' expectations and perceptions are factors which define customer satisfaction. A happy customer means he had a nice experience, and possibility is that he may visit the canteen frequently. Hospitality matters a lot. It includes dedication to customers' well-being.
- **A unique selling point:** *Didis* are not professional cooks. They are in their learning phase. Since the market segment of the restaurant and food industry is highly competitive, Didi Ki Rasoi should have some USPs to sustain itself in the market. Didi Ki Rasoi is being positioned as a provider of homemade food, which includes hygiene and quality as key components. **Homely food is the best option as its USP, which matches its brand name: Didi Ki Rasoi. It'll also help in brand positioning.**

- **Management and capital:** Inventory Management, working capital (irregular payment from different departments), bulk procurement to increase profitability and earn a few USPs, accessibility and transparency of e-PoS, and unity of command are a few major issues, and Didi Ki Rasoi is constantly trying to tackle these issues.

Value chain analysis

PESTLE analysis (Figure 7) is a framework used to analyze and monitor macro-environment factors that impact a Didi Ki Rasoi.

SWOT analysis (Figure 8) is a strategic planning technique used to identify strengths, weaknesses, opportunities, and threats related to this collective enterprise.

Government policy and regulatory environment

The Food Safety and Standards Authority of India License (FSSAI) is one of the most important licences required to open a canteen and is obtained

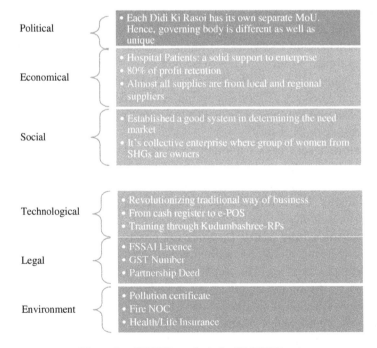

Figure 7. PESTEL analysis for Didi Ki Rasoi.

Figure 8. SWOT analysis for Didi Ki Rasoi.

from the FSSAI because this licence reassures the customers that the food of a particular restaurant affirms to the food safety standards of India (The Restaurant Times, n.d.). As part of the licence, a unique 14-digit registration number is given to the canteen. The following documents are required for the FSSAI license:

- ID and address proofs
- Valid email ID
- Phone number
- Affidavit
- Declaration of food safety management plan
- Kitchen layout plan
- List of food categories
- Water testing report from ISI-approved facility
- No objection certificate (NOC) from the owner or the partner (VO, in this case)
- Medical certificates of employees

Local civil authorities, such as the state's municipal corporation or the health department, provide a health/trade licence with the imperative that public health must be given supreme importance.

The Eating House License is provided by the Licensing Police Commissioner (LPC) of the city where the canteen would be opened. The canteen has to submit the following documents in order to receive the licence, and the approximate cost required is Rs. 300 for three years:

- NOC from the landlord.
- Site plan containing details of the size of eating house.
- Photographs of the place.
- Residence proof of the applicant.
- An affidavit on a stamp paper of Rs. 10 duly attested by Notary Public.
- Fire NOC if the seating capacity of the eating house is 50 or more.
- Undertaking with regard to amusement activities.
- Undertaking regarding the installations of CCTV cameras with 30 days recording facility.

These are the few major licences which need to be obtained for small or large canteen operations. A few additional certificates and licences are also required depending on the size of the operation (Table I1, Annexure I).

Our Learnings from the Study of the Organization

Development is a multi-dimensional approach where the success of an intervention also depends on its stakeholders. One may have an innovative business plan that can be easily jotted down on paper. However, its execution or implementation could be difficult. When an intervention is discussed, there are many assumptions, and many real-life scenarios are neglected. At this point in time, we can say that 'poka-yoke' is still a major key to success in any community-based intervention. It is perfectly said that there is a huge difference between growth and development. We're more interested in holistic development, where a business plan includes an action plan as an essential road map that guides an enterprise towards its summit.

Didi Ki Rasoi, a JEEViKA initiative, is definitely an appreciable non-farm project. It's a pilot project. We visited both the canteens, which were inaugurated on 10 October 2018 and 28 February 2019 in Vaishali and Buxar, respectively. There is an MoU among the owners, CBOs, and government hospitals. It is found that if proper clauses aren't mentioned, it will lead to jeopardy. Therefore, before any intervention, it is necessary to also consider ground realities. For example, everyone knows that government departments have a delayed or untimely payment mechanism. Because of this, they are failing to maintain working capital. The budget adds a roadmap towards the goals and objectives of any enterprise, which will measure success, even in terms of community empowerment. It's high time to diversify the risk portfolio because hospital patients are bulk as well as regular customers of Didi Ki Rasoi. Location also plays a crucial role. In this case, we can say, 'a hospital isn't a good place to hangout.' A conservative mindset is always there. What we could do is have a venue nearby the hospital so that food could be served to patients as well as customers.

There are many things which are usually not shown on records. This has advantages as well as disadvantages. In short, nothing is better than something. Truthfulness and integrity are required at each and every stage of intervention. The plan and its execution should align in the right way. Deviation and distorted outcomes can cause vulnerabilities because a community's sentiments are also associated with development professions. It's not because we work without looking for profit. Empowering the community or society at large is our legitimate goal. Once this is accomplished, withdrawal from community-based intervention is also vital. We must do this honestly. We've realized these facts in the past two months. We've gone through business models, partnership deeds, various MoUs, the role of JEEViKA, and Kudumbashree.

Building a team is also essential in the development sector. We may not have a talented workforce for these community-based interventions, but an effective team is still required. Here, women are owners, but they don't have much idea about the different business and functional areas of an enterprise. Capacity building isn't an overnight process. It's slow and steady by nature. That's why it is said that overnight development leads to destruction or catastrophe. We must also analyze the factors of market expertise, target customers, and operational results to make the right things happen. We are investing ample resources, money, and time. It becomes necessary to observe proper execution so that we are armed with the abilities to take action and generate desired results.

Last but not least, continuous improvement should be the ultimate approach to tackling challenges. Mistakes may happen in the absence of resources, but continuous improvement is the only solution. In other words, perseverance is the medicine to cure the disease called failure. Sales and cash flow become essential in order to maintain the working capital at Didi Ki Rasoi. This can only be solved by acquiring expert market knowledge of the problem and the size of the opportunity. For example, a niche market or customer segment has been identified, which involves supplying prisoners in the central jail. It wasn't planned early, but the idea became inculcated over time. In this last section of this work, we would also like to talk about the value chain of a business, which can be developed over a period of time. Suppose we set up Didi Ki Rasoi in all the main districts of Bihar. We can work on strengthening the backchain of the enterprise. For example, women in SHGs will produce napkins and supply them. Other groups of women can produce spices, oil, chopped vegetables, and packaging bags. This shows how we could create additional enterprises consecutively. Innovation is the mother of all success. In order to have such value chain modelling, we must have cutting-edge technologies. We can incorporate artificial intelligence, blockchain technology, and market-trend predictors, where the theory of bounded rationality must not be distorted.

Case study: Enterprising women of SHGs chart a path to prosperity

From a rural homemaker to a successful entrepreneur and trusted businesswoman, for many women in the area, the story of Sanju Devi of Kamarpur (Buxar) is an inspiring tale of how women in rural India can change their lives given the slightest of opportunities.

Sanju Devi of Kamarpur village of Buxar district (Figure 9), Bihar, is happy and proud about her newly established collective enterprise, 'Himmat Didi Ki Rasoi,' which has a capacity to serve and supply food to customers as well as patients of Sadar Hospital, Buxar. This has become possible after six skilful women (including her) agreed to join the canteen as owners back in February 2019: 'My husband, Mr. Guru Charan Singh, works as vehicle driver in a private firm in Mumbai, which is about 1614 km from her house and he visits Kamarpur twice a year.'

Before joining Didi Ki Rasoi as a means of livelihood, Sanju Devi's quality of life was uncertain. She and her family lived in a small house.

Figure 9. Sanju Devi (second from right) and her colleagues in their canteen, discussing key issues with BPM to run smooth operation of Himmat Didi Ki Rasoi.

She has two *bigha* of land; however, floods and drought were major issues for crop failure. Even this piece of land is scattered. They used to cultivate wheat and paddy, which require ample amounts of water. She was not getting the right price in return for her efforts, as there were no irrigation facilities or governmental support. She knows sewing, and she attended a beautician course, but her village doesn't provide demand for her skills. Her family had no other permanent means of livelihood, except her husband's job. The income from all sources was just enough for household expenses, such as oil, spices, medicines, and the education of children.

Opportunity knocks

Sanju, a homemaker (Figure 10), helped her family on the farm and took care of her two children. As the secretary of her SHG, she had additional responsibilities. During a SHG council meeting in 2019, Sanju heard about an income generation project to be implemented in her district. She knew about JEEViKA and BRLPS, and she was directly involved with the organization. Chandrashekar Patel, area coordinator, and Sanjay, community coordinator, visited the SHG and delivered information. Didi Ki Rasoi

Figure 10. Sanju Devi at Didi Ki Rasoi.

seemed like a revenue recurring business model, as women would be owners of this collective enterprise. She learned that they were on the lookout for businesses to work as owners to provide quality food to hospital patients as well as customers. Seeing an opportunity to supplement their income, Sanju's family supported her decision to enrol in the project.

Trained to catalyze

Sanju and the other 24 participants were trained in technical methods to reduce costs and risks associated with the firm. Training was provided for six days by a team of Kudumbashree RPs, and six women got selected. Major segments of the training focused on hospitality, serving food, the importance of uniforms, and cooking tips. Himmat Didi Ki Rasoi was inaugurated on 28 February 2019. 'Now for anything related to cooking, my friends or family members seek my advice,' she adds with a laugh.

Himmat Didi Ki Rasoi

As of now, women have learned a lot from running their collective enterprise. She has motivated the other women to coordinate their collective enterprise. 'Serving food to patients is just like blessings for me as they undergo treatment and duty is god; work is worship.' Persuading women to attend meetings and making them listen and implement her advice was an uphill battle. But when they observed that they had a better profit than they previously had, they slowly began accepting her advice. She is a challenge acceptor in her real life. She doesn't panic if her work extends well into the night. She always welcomes guests irrespective of her mood because she completely understands the difference between personal life and professional life. She takes care of the functional department and tries to learn new skills required for managing the canteen. Sanju gained popularity not only in her village but in nearby villages as well.

Today, she has reached a stage of self-sufficiency: 'I feel good. I can cook different dishes. I don't have any problem. I am happy and I have dignified life.'

Annexure A

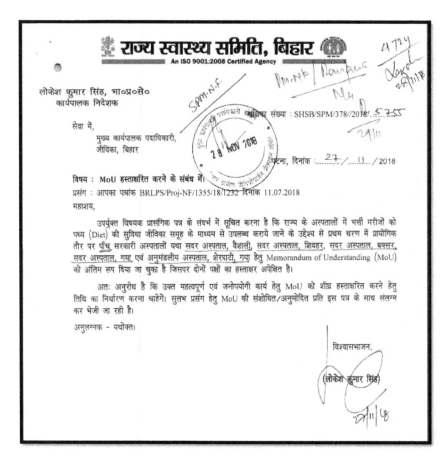

Figure A1. Photo of the memorandum of understanding (MoU) between the Health Society and JEEViKA (BRLPs).

Table A1. Activities sheet for the establishment of Didi Ki Rasoi.

Activities	Responsibility	Support
Meeting with the concerned manager	YP-NF	
Premises identification & selection		
Visit by Kudumbashree[14] team to premises	Kudumbashree-RP	
Sharing of floor design to premises	Kudumbashree-RP	YP-NF
Final refurbishment of location	District administration	
Member identification & selection		
Identification of members	BPIU	DPCU
Identification of nodal CBOs	BPIU	DPCU
Interview of selected members	BPIU	YP-NF
Organizing training of identified members	Kudumbashree	YP-NF
Finalizing members who would operate canteen	Kudumbashree	BPIU
Purchasing of equipment & other branding items		
List of equipment shared to district team	Kudumbashree- RP	
Meeting with nodal VO/CLF for quotation procurement	BPIU	YP-NF
Quotations sought from the market	BPIU	
Vendors finalized based on quotation	BPIU	
Orders placed with all vendors	BPIU	
Equipment received	BPIU	
Fund release		
SOP approval	YP-NF	
Fund release to the concerned district	YP-NF	SPM/ PM-NF18
Fund release to the concerned CBOs	DPCU	
Canteen operations		
Equipment testing and inventory listing	YP-NF	
Identification and liaison with local vendors	DPCU	
Finalizing billing assistant	DPCU	
Hiring of consultant	YP-NF	
Inauguration of canteen		

Table A2. Items required for training.

Sl. No.	Items	
1	Stationery (notepads, pens, pencil, sketch pens)	
2	Apron	For all selected members
3	Chart paper	For group activities
4	Marker	For group activities
5	Projector	
6	Laptop	
7	Internet connectivity	
8	Raw materials for food preparation	

Food items to be made during training: Samosa, idli & sambhar, and puri bhaji.

Equipment and their count required to prepare the above items:

- Large *kadhai* (pan) for frying samosas and cooking bhaji: 2;
- Chakla (base) and Belan (roller): 2;
- Idli steamer (12 idlis at a time): 1;
- Large cooker: 1;
- Basic utensils for making the food items.

Annexure B

Table B1. Food costs for hospital dietary.

	Schedule: Hospital Dietary Services			
	Sadar Hospital, Hajipur			
Sl. No.	Menu	Unit/pic	Rate/pic/kg	Price
Breakfast				
1	Bread	6	1	6
2	Egg	1	5	5
3	Milk	200	38	7.6
4	Fruits	1	3	3
Lunch				
1	Roti	2 pic	2.5	5
2	Rice	125 g	5	5
3	Daal	50 g	5	5

(*Continued*)

Table B1. (*Continued*)

Schedule: Hospital Dietary Services
Sadar Hospital, Hajipur

Sl. No.	Menu	Unit/pic	Rate/pic/kg	Price
4	Sabji	100 g	5	5
5	Dahi	50 g	4	4
Snacks				
1	Biscuit	2 pic	1	2
2	Tea	50 ml	3	3
Dinner				
1	Roti	4	2.5	10
2	Daal	50 g	5	5
3	Sabji	100 g	5	5
Total				70.6
Additional cost				
1	Labour cost	20–30%		14.12
2	Fuel cost	10–12%		7.06
3	Management cost	0		0
4	GST	5%	5% of 100	5
Gross total				**96.78***

Note: Price of raw materials vary. Health Society pays Rs. 100 per patient per day. Revenue benefit: 3.22%.

Schedule: Hospital Dietary Services
Sadar Hospital, Buxar

Sl. No.	Menu	Unit/pic	Rate/pic/kg	Price
Breakfast				
1	Bread	6	0.56	3.36
2	Egg	1	4.83	4.83
3	Milk	200	40	8
4	Fruits	1	3.75	3.75
Lunch				
1	Rice	125 g	4.25	4.25
2	Daal	50 g	5	5
3	Sabji	100 g	5	5
4	Dahi	50 g	4.5	4.5
Snacks				
1	Biscuit	2 pic	0.33	0.66
2	Tea	50 ml	3	3

Table B1. (*Continued*)

Schedule: Hospital Dietary Services
Sadar Hospital, Hajipur

Sl. No.	Menu	Unit/pic	Rate/pic/kg	Price
Dinner				
1	Roti	4	2.5	10
2	Daal	50 g	5	5
3	Sabji	100 g	5	5
Total				62.35
Additional cost				
1	Labour cost	20–30%		13.47
2	Fuel cost	10–12%		6.74
3	Management cost	0		0
4	GST	5%	5% of 98.3	4.91
Gross total				**92.48**

Note: Price of raw materials vary. Health Society pays Rs. 100 per patient per day. Revenue benefit: 5.92%.

Annexure C

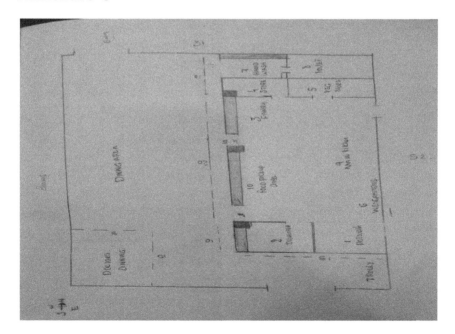

Figure C1. Floor design: Buxar, Sherghati, and Sheikhpura.

Note: This layout is for the design and construction of canteen in Buxar. A similar layout will be used for the canteens in Sherghati and Sheikhpura.

Annexure D

Table D1. Duty plan for the week.

	Didi Ki Rasoi, Sadar Hospital, Buxar				
	Duty plan for the week				
	Kitchen team	**Food service team**	**Housekeeping team**	**Store**	**Finance/ Billing**
Monday	Priyanka, Sanju, Devanti, Munnamoti, Mehgraj	Chandmunni+ Manorma+ Indu	Priyanka+ Sanju	Devanti+ Munnamoti	Rajkumar+ Nisha+ Priyanka
Tuesday	Devanti, Munnamoti, Chandmunni, Manorma, Meghraj	Priyanka, Sanju, Indu	Chandmunni+ Manorma	Sanju+ Meghraj	Rajkumar+ Nisha+ Sanju
Wednesday	Priyanka, Meghraj, Sanju, Manorma	Devanti+ Chandmuni+ Indu	Manorma+ Chandmunni	Manorma +Nisha	Rajkumar+ Nisha+ Manorma
Thursday	Chandmunni, Devanti, Munaamoti, Meghraj	Manorma, Priyanka	Devanti, Sanju	Meghraj+ Priyanka	Rajkumar+ Nisha+ Devanti
Friday	Priyanka, Sanju, Devanti, Munnamoti, Mehgraj	Chandmunni+ Manorma+ Indu	Munnamoti+ Priyanka	Chandmunni+ Meghraj	Rajkumar+ Nisha+ Chandmunni
Saturday	Manorma, Chandmunni, Meghraj, Munnamoti	Priyanka, Sanju, Indu	Chandmunni+ Manorma	Devanti+ Munnamoti	Rajkumar+ Nisha+ Munnamoti
Sunday	Devanti, Munnamoti, Chandmunni, Manorma, Meghraj	Chandmunni+ Manorma+ Indu	Priyanka+ Sanju	Devanti+ Munnamoti	Rajkumar+ Nisha+ Priyanka

Annexure E

Table E1. Form 2A: Café canteen — Applicant grading sheet @ CBO.

Name of Applicant: **Name of SHG:**

Sl. No.	Criteria	Scoring	Max. marks	Marks obtained
1	Education	Blow 8th Grade	0	
		8th–12th	1	
		Graduate	2	
2	Attendance in weekly meeting (to be verified by SHG OB members)	<50%	0	
		60–70%	1	
		>70%	2	
3	Loan amount taken from SHG (as per cash book/meeting minutes of SHG)	<Rs. 30,000	0	
		= Rs. 30,000	1	
		>Rs. 30,000	2	
4	Loan repayment by the member (to be verified by SHG OB members)	<60%	0	
		60–70%	1	
		>70%	2	
5	Has the member ever been part of canteen operations or owner of a canteen	0 years	0	
		1 year	1	
		>1 year	2	
Total marks			10	

Signature of VO OB Members   Signature of CM

Table E2. Form 2B: Café Canteen-Interview Grading Sheet @CBO

Name of Applicant: **Name of SHG:**

Sl. No.	Criteria	Score (/10)	Remarks
1	Experience		Does the candidate have cooking knowledge? Have they ever worked in a canteen, or owned a canteen? etc.

(Continued)

Table E2. (Continued)

Sl. No.	Criteria	Score (/10)	Remarks
2	Work commitment		Enough family support and general wherewithal to work in the canteen. Is it safe and viable for them to travel for work every day?
3	Financial health		Should have a strong repayment record within groups and with the bank. What is the capacity of the household to bear a risk?
4	Entrepreneurial ability		Can be judged by asking if the member has tried to do any entrepreneurial activity in the past. How do they plan to manage the risks? is someone in their family an entrepreneur? What are their motivations to join the canteen?
5	Passion		Passion to work, become an entrepreneur, and be open to learning

It is to be noted that a group needs to be formed based on their individual and family consent and cohesiveness of the members than by compulsion or force. Hence interested women from different Jeevika SHG near the proposed sites for the cafe can be motivated to form a team for the café unit.

Annexure F

Table F1. Bhawish Didi Ki Rasoi: Salary for the month of January 2019.

Sr. No.	Employee name	Designation	Salary	Total days in month	Present days	Absent days	Final salary days	Salary per day	Gross salary	Advance	Final salary
1	Shobha Devi	Cook	8,000	31	29	2	31	258	8,000		8,000
2	Rita Devi	Cook	8,000	31	29	2	31	258	8,000		8,000
3	Sangita Devi	Cook	8,000	31	29	2	31	258	8,000		8,000
4	Rinku Devi	Cook	8,000	31	26	5	30	258	7,740		7,740
5	Sharmila Devi	Cook	8,000	31	29	2	31	258	8,000		8,000
6	Ranju Devi	Cook	8,000	31	30	1	30	258	8,000		8,000
7	Sarila Devi	Cook	8,000	31	30	1	30	258	8,000		8,000

Table F1. (Continued)

Sr. No.	Employee name	Designation	Salary	Total days in month	Present days	Absent days	Final salary days	Salary per day	Gross salary	Advance	Final salary
8	Asha Devi	Cook	8,000	31	27	4	31	258	8,000		8,000
9	Mala Devi	Cook	8,000	31	29	2	31	258	8,000		8,000
10	Vinita Kumari	Cashier	9,000	31	29	2	31	300	9,000		9,000
11	Manish Kumar	Helper	8,000	31	6	25	6	258	1,548		1,548
12	Shankar Kumar	Helper	8,000	31	3	28	3	258	774	2700	−1,926
13	Dhanesh Rai	Head Cook	9,000	31	7	24	7	300	2,100	6500	−4,400
	Total								85,162		75,962

Annexure G

Table G1. Tentative canteen set-up cost, Buxar.

Sl. No.	Head	Amount (Rs.)
1	Fixed cost	1,186,484
2	Operating cost	849,000
3	Misc.	203,548
	Total canteen set-up cost (Lumpsum)	22,39,032

Table G2. Monthly sales turnover and receivables (in Rs.), Didi Ki Rasoi, Vaishali.

Month	Sales	Expenses	Receivable
October	50,049	154,442	11,589
November	102,372	185,841	45,009
December	238,582	239,353	175,746
January	221,692	194,775	174,360
February	188,413	228,799	157,310
March	305,124	256,946	266,810
April	721,274	517,662	693,061
May	390,064	361,319	366,321

Table G3. Monthly sales turnover and receivables (in Rs.), Didi Ki Rasoi, Buxar.

Month	Sales	Expenses	Receivable
March	130,412	205,858	36,555
April	177,967	208,429	29,650
May	268,931	290,259	93,300

Annexure H

Table H1. Himmat Didi Ki Rasoi, Sadar Hospital, Buxar.

\multicolumn{4}{c}{Breakfast: 07:30 AM to 11:30 AM}			
Sattu Paratha	Rs. 10/piece	Puri Sabji	Rs. 25/plate
Aloo Paratha	Rs. 10/piece	Kachori Chola	Rs. 30/plate
Bread Omlet	Rs. 15/piece	Chola Bhatura	Rs. 30/plate
Sandwich	Rs. 20/piece	Tea	Rs. 7/cup
Coffee	Rs. 10/cup	Sudha Lassi (MRP)	Rs. 10/pack
Lunch: 11:30 AM to 04:00 PM			
Plain Thali[20]	Rs. 50/dish	Roti Sabji[21]	Rs. 40/plate
Paneer Sabji	Rs. 40/plate	Plain Sabji	Rs. 15/plate
Chicken rice	Rs. 100/plate	Chicken	Rs. 40/piece
Egg curry	Rs. 15/piece	Egg curry Rice	Rs. 50/plate
Khichidi	Rs. 25/plate	Pulse	Rs. 15/plate
Pulse fry	Rs. 30/plate		
Evening snacks 4:00 PM to 7:00 PM			
Pyaj pakoda		Samosa	
Paneer pakoda		Chana pakoda	
Aloo pakoda		Bread pakoda	
Litti Chokha	Rs. 7/piece	Ghee litti chokha	Rs. 10/piece

Table H2. Himmat Didi Ki Rasoi, Sadar Hospital, Buxar.

	Food menu (day-wise)						
	Monday	Tuesday	Wednesday	Thursday	Friday	Saturday	Sunday
Breakfast	Chola Bhatura	Sattu Paratha	Kachori-Chola	Aloo Paratha	Puri Bhaji	Litti Chokha	Bread Omelette

Table H2. (Continued)

	Food menu (day-wise)						
	Monday	Tuesday	Wednesday	Thursday	Friday	Saturday	Sunday
Lunch	Veg/Non-veg Thali	Veg Thali	Veg/Non-veg Thali	Veg Thali	Veg/Non-veg Thali	Veg Thali	Veg/Non-veg Thali
Evening snacks	Pakoda (aloo/onion), Samosa	Sabudana vada, Samosa	Uttapam, Dosa, Samosa	Bread Pakoda, Paneer Pakora Samosa	Samosa, Cutlet, Dosa	Samosa, Khasta Kachori	Veg/Non-veg Noodles, Sandwich
Dinner	Veg/Non-veg Thali	Veg Thali	Veg/Non-veg Thali	Veg Thali	Veg/Non-veg Thali	Veg Thali	Veg/Non-veg Thali

Annexure I

A detailed list would be prepared based on the scale of operations of the canteen, as all licences would not be required for small operations, while additional licences may be required for larger operations.

Table I1. Licence and certification checklist (indicative).

Sl. No.	Item	Y/N
1	Partnership seed	
2	Health trade licence	
3	Eating house licence	
4	GST number	
5	FSSAI licence	
6	NOC from fire department	
7	Pollution certificate	
8	Certificate of environmental clearance	
9	Signage licence	
10	Insurance	

References

Agriculture Department of Bihar. (n.d.). Department of Agriculture Govt. of Bihar. Retrieved 10 June 2019 from Krishi Bihar: http://krishi.bih.nic.in/Introduction.htm.

The Restaurant Times. (n.d.). Complete List of All the Licenses Required to Open a Restaurant In India. Retrieved from The Restaurant Times: https://www.posist.com/restaurant-times/resources/licenses-required-to-open-a-restaurant.html.

World Bank Group. (2016). India — Bihar Transformative Development Project. World Bank, Washington, D.C.

Chapter 28

A Digital Transformation Toolkit to Formulate CXO Office Strategy Overcoming Disruptions, Including the COVID-19 Pandemic

Ashutosh Dubey* and Arif Khan[†]

National Payments Corporation of India, Mumbai, Maharashtra, India
*ashutosh.dubey@npci.org.in
†arif.khan@npci.org.in

Abstract

Over the ages, it has been reiterated that crises often result in great global experiments which are likely to induce enduring mass adoption of digital tools, digitization of processes, and even digitization of behaviour. The adoption of technology and transformation practices at this scale could not be seen without disruptions, as organizations, governments, regulators, and even normal people were sceptical about their impact on productivity and work behaviour. This research proposes a digital transformation (DX) which aims to be friendly to chief transformation officers (CXOs) and act as a risk-aware decision-making framework for organizations and decision-makers. It is ideal for organizations to design and revamp their digital transformation strategies. It includes the most salient information regarding approaches and practices in DX identified by experts around the world and observed in various organizations to deliver an exhaustive resource of information. A DX toolkit lists the phases and key activities as part of a CXO's office strategy. The different phases identified in the toolkit are performing background assessment and formulating project management, problem identification and analysis, identification of key areas for DX, identification of the priority areas for DX, identification of operational and financial risks, compliance evaluation and positioning of a DX charter, formulation of a DX strategy and governance design, identification of tool and technology selection, teams, and roles, implementation of strategies, deploying tools and technology, monitoring the performance against defined key performance indicators, and incorporating feedback to consider other priority items. This toolkit provides CXOs and their teams with different roles in tech transformation, from enablers to thought leaders to programme leaders. COVID-19 has emerged as an opportunity for CXOs to take the reins and drive a more transformative overhaul of their organizations' technology and business processes.

Keywords: COVID-19, digital transformation, innovation, technology, digital workforce, toolkit.

Introduction

COVID-19 has swept across the world, leaving a trail of economic and social damage in its wake. Forward-thinking organizations have already started to plan for post-COVID-19 circumstances (Wade, 2020). The current study makes a reasonable attempt to lay emphasis on digital transformation (DX) measures which lay a strong foundation for a DX strategy in organizations regarding the way they work, behave, and operate. The world has simply never faced a crisis like this one before and never felt so closely knit in solving the problem while using DX to the best. Digital forces are reshaping every industry, company, country, and government across the world (Yokoi, 2020). The pandemic has played the role of a catalyst in the journey of DX. The transformation helps in formulating an innovative, successful, and adaptable strategy for what to do next and assessing how an organization should evolve to extract the most value from digital technologies, businesses, and market models (Desk, 2020).

The current research is based on best practices and possible ways to keep up with the upcoming digital disruption in the post-COVID-19 world. Thus, COVID-19 is considered a pandemic and an event of digital disruption. The digitization of products, services, and business processes ensures the entry of disruptive and innovative players to deliver the expected value and experience for the products and services without having to reinvent the value chain and drive changes in customer behaviour. DX will enable the organization to analyze opportunities and threats and help in developing customized defensive and aggressive strategies to bring about a competitive advantage and strengthen the foundation of that organization to withstand the wave of digital disruption (Bonnet, 2020). This will enable organizations to learn about the different values which they are bringing into the ecosystem and their drivers of competitive differentiation. Further, this will help organizations identify ways or approaches to digitizing existing business models, products, and value chains. A good transformation will enable organizations sense changes in the environment, analyze data effectively, and execute rapidly at an effective pace so that organizations can fail and scale quickly as needed. Also, it enables organizations to learn and discover the key behaviours and core competencies required to be an effective digital transformation team in an era of continuous change and digital disruption (Reis, 2018).

Another important question arises about how the organization will react to the digital tools and technologies that have emerged because of the pandemic and the situations resulting from them. This will definitely play a critical role in the DX journey that the organization adopts. However, it can be felt that some organizations will be 'digital accelerators,' whereas some will be 'digital laggards' (Indriastuti, 2020). This pandemic resulted in a surge in the development and usage of new digital technologies. Now, even for work and socialization, there is a requirement for technology. Video conferencing solutions are now mainstream for work and fun. Mobile applications, software providers, and technology service providers have to ensure the availability of their businesses online 24×7 and perform work anytime from anywhere (Aralelemath, 2021). With the new norms of social distancing and restrictions to physical presence beyond a certain limit, new digital forms of tools supporting meetings, workplaces, and entertainment are being developed. With access to cheaper smart devices and infrastructure, organizations across the world have become accustomed to living, working, and socializing with technology. This causes a digital disruption and demands special attention from organizations around the world to transform themselves into digitally savvy organizations (Bonnet, 2020).

Literature Review

Understanding the digital disruption

Digital disruptors do not replicate the value chains and operational models of traditional companies. They focus on the use of digital business models to minimize costs, enhance customer experiences, and extend scale through their products or services. The COVID-19 pandemic is an example of a disruption that can force all sectors to think about the adoption of a transformation strategy and lay down a roadmap to keep themselves relevant among their competitors. Mature companies can act like disruptors themselves by enhancing three forms of value, namely cost, experience, and platform, to create their own digital business models and offerings (Indriastuti, 2020). One of the primary reasons why transformation programmes falter in times of disruption, such as COVID-19, is because organizations lack a clear understanding of their operational business model(s) and the strategic directions required to create value for their customers.

Table 1 shows how the pandemic resulted in digital disruption through specific inducements.

Table 1. Disruption parameters and its key drivers.

Parameters	Disruption	Key drivers
Technology	• Technologies with disruption potential include blockchain, artificial intelligence, edge computing, robotics, intelligent assistance, IoT, and virtual and augmented realities.	• 24×7 service requirements • Hyperpersonalization • Open APIs • Platformization
Customer behaviour	• Preference for contactless systems with less human intervention	• User experience • Demand for continuous assistance
Business ecosystem	• Pay per use as a revenue model • Customer intentions towards more freebies and a freemium approach	• Competitors evolving their business models • Customers compare realizable values for every service and products

Table 1. (*Continued*)

Parameters	Disruption	Key drivers
Research and innovation	• Evolution of technology-driven business models, where technology provides differentiator services	• Aggressive strategies by competitors • Market demand and fulfilment of existing gaps
Regulatory intervention	• Regulations regarding the privacy and use of data. • Capping pricing for essential services • Variation in the tax regime	• Customers focus on their privacy and are ready to switch if it gets compromised. • Tweaking of regulations by online platforms resulted in an added advantage over traditional players

Pillars of digital transformation (DX)

A digital transformation strategy builds bridges between the current state, i.e., during COVID-19, and the desired long-term plan for an organization, and this strategy has to work around six major pillars (Newman, 2018), as detailed in Table 2.

Digital transformation toolkit

DX is a strategy that is not about disruption or technology. It relies on people, customers, value and its drivers, optimization, rapid capitalization of resources in the organization through intelligent systems, hyperaware use of technologies, and insights derived from the ecosystem (Benlian, 2015). Companies, governments, regulators, and even start-ups should seize this opportunity to enhance operations and be ready for any other future crises of such sort (Rabra, 2020). Either one has to act now or live to regret it, as there is a unique opportunity to initiate the transformation journey as part of behaviour and actions in the way they operate or run the business. This research proposes a DX toolkit which aims to be user-friendly and act as a risk-aware, decision-making toolkit for all organizations and other decision-makers from anywhere in the world, considering the design and deployment of a digital transformation roadmap. It aims to present the most salient information related to approaches and the world's best practices on DX identified by various

Table 2. Pillars of digital transformation, impact of the pandemic, and the future.

Pillars for DX	Impact of pandemic	Future expectations
Customer	• Customers as a dynamic network. They believe in engaging with environmental, social, and even governance-related matters • Customers are the key influencers. They can influence taking up or giving up services or products to others	• Marketing to inspire purchase, loyalty, and advocacy • Reciprocal value flows • Economies of (customer) value • Listening to customer expectations
Competitors	• Blurred distinctions between partners and rivals • A few dominant competitors per category	• Platforms with partners who exchange value • Winner-takes-all due to network effects
Data	• Data are continuously generated everywhere • Data turned into valuable information • Unstructured data increase, which are highly usable and valuable • Data as a tool for optimizing business processes	• Data as value only if they connect across silos • Data as an asset for value creation • Data-specific roles as keys to the future digital strategy of the organization
Innovation	• Decisions after testing and validation • Organizations looking to retain their edge • They increase non-tariff barriers to R&D and intellectual property • Extreme automation and exploration of new technologies which are resilient and reliable	• Innovation as a challenge to solve the right problem • Focus on minimum viable prototypes and iterations before final launch • Quick feedback and fast delivery with a holistic overview of requirements with respect to the ecosystem, competition, and suggestions from the product & marketing team
Values	• Focus on design and usability in product development with contactless, ensuring safety, and keeping the customer informed about actions	• Stay ahead of the curve with hyperawareness about the market, ecosystem, and regulations

Table 2. (*Continued*)

Pillars for DX	Impact of pandemic	Future expectations
	• Unleash the upcoming opportunity for customer value	• Evaluation of changes and implement the means to create next business or lead to expansion • Paranoid about offerings and agile in changing business and market models
Digital skill-sets	• The pandemic leads to a transformation of approaches to work, mobility, and flexible working models. • Acceleration in alternative work delivery models as well as employment constructs. • The emergence of digital platforms	• The roles of the future would be built on a triad of domain/functional, digital, and professional skills • Organizations may reflect the digital talent base, focus on reskilling and leveraging the adjustment between work from the office and work from anywhere to build a pervasive digital skill foundation that can work and provide support from anywhere • Focus on team building, nonverbal communications, and virtual behaviour will increase

experts around the world rather than serve as an exhaustive resource. The toolkit is developed in order to serve as a fact-based and neutral guide. This chapter does not recommend or discourage the adoption of DX practices, nor does it endorse the best-suited technology or platform for implementation. The DX toolkit provides high-level guidance and information for:

1. organizations which are evaluating how to drive digital transformation,
2. CXOs of organizations and DX evangelists.

The toolkit talks about 12 different sections and their roles in the DX strategy roadmap, adoption, and implementation. They are described in Table 3.

Table 3. DX toolkit: Activities.

Activity	Key tasks	Performed by
Background assessment and project management	• List the institution's current high priorities and strategic goals related to digital transformation • Identify the institution's constraints that could influence digital transformation • Analyze existing research agenda related to digital transformation • Analyze in-house knowledge, experience, and expertise	CXO and its team
Problem identification and analysis	• List the major industry-specific conditions, issues, and limitations that could affect the usefulness or desirability of digital transformation • Start by identifying the problems that digital transformation could address, examining how viable and feasible it is in addressing these problems and the viability of alternative approaches	CXO and digital business analyst
Identify the key areas for digital transformation	• List the important existing and future forces, trends, market participants, and services necessary to consider for digital transformation • Identify the valuable or important areas to address with ranks on a scale of 1–10. A score of 1 indicates the problem is minimally valuable to address, and a score of 10 indicates it is extremely valuable to address	CXO and its team
Identify the priority area for digital transformation	• Once scores are assigned to the problems and areas to be tackled under digital transformation are identified, the area which scores the most will be considered a priority, while management has the leeway to prioritize other areas as well • Compute the feasibility and suitability of solving each of the problems identified above. A score of 1 for feasibility indicates digital transformation would be very difficult to implement for this problem, and a score of 10 indicates it would likely be very easy to implement. A score of 1 for suitability indicates digital transformation would solve very little of the problem, and a score of 10 indicates it would likely be very effective in solving the problem	CEO, CXOs

Table 3. (*Continued*)

Activity	Key tasks	Performed by
Identification of operational and financial risks	• List the key risks associated with the problem statement and the key areas identified	Digital business analyst and risk team
Compliance evaluation and digital transformation charter	• Engage with the compliance team to evaluate the changes and the cost of transformation for the identified areas • Develop a digital transformation charter with procedural guidelines in the given area, the expected changes and system operating procedures, and associated SLAs.	Digital business analyst
Strategy and governance design	• Decision-makers should conduct their own research and fully evaluate business processes, technology solutions, and providers • Evaluate if there is sufficient skill set availability and expertise to support the digital transformation plan • User engagement and consultation are critical for effective strategy design; evaluate how users can be engaged as early as feasible in the digital transformation process • Engage end users to be consulted on the digital transformation concept and provide input to the design and testing process • Evaluate the solution requirements required for usability, user interfaces, identity, privacy, and security • Documentation of a user guide or FAQs for various classifications of participants, with educational resources and background information on how to successfully participate in the digital transformation roadmap. It may be a tool implementation, process documentation standardization, new product line, etc.	CXO and its team
Tool and technology selection	• Identify the trade-offs, pros, and cons associated with various technology options • Evaluate the interoperability with existing systems and IT infrastructure • Evaluate the process and technology deployed and tested in the organization	CXO and its team

(*Continued*)

Table 3. (*Continued*)

Activity	Key tasks	Performed by
Team and role identification	• Identify the key resources which have defined skill sets associated with the problem areas identified and key digital skill sets, not limited to UI-UX, full stack development, data analytics, and business analysis • Engage with partners who can help in bridging the missing skill sets required for the digital transformation plan	CXO and HR
Implement strategy and deploy tools and technology	• Document the milestones and key deliverables at the end of a definite period. • As part of the digital transformation roadmap, if a new SOP is in practice, it will be informed to all and given time to share feedback • If a tool is rolled out, user guidelines and a demo need to be planned before rollout • Users will also be told about the key performance indicators (KPIs) and key expectations of the solution as part of the roadmap • Deploy the technology solution, monitor the usage, and compute the difference in productivity, experience, ease, and engagement with respect to the previous	CXO team
Monitor the performance against defined KPIs	• Framework for the identification of KPIs for the strategy has to be laid down before deployment and will be monitored from day 1 • Evaluation of milestones of KPIs at periodic intervals	CXO team
Incorporate feedback and take other priority items	• Incorporate feedback from the users and bring about changes if acceptable to the strategy • If definite success is achieved in the identified areas, the other areas can be looked up	CXO and its team

The toolkit is shown in Figure 1.

Innovation leaders will be looking for intuitive ways to upgrade, modernize, and make their systems resilient. This toolkit may become a source for them to devise their strategies for the same. Technology is likely to be at the forefront of their minds and play a great role in DX (Hess *et al.*, 2016).

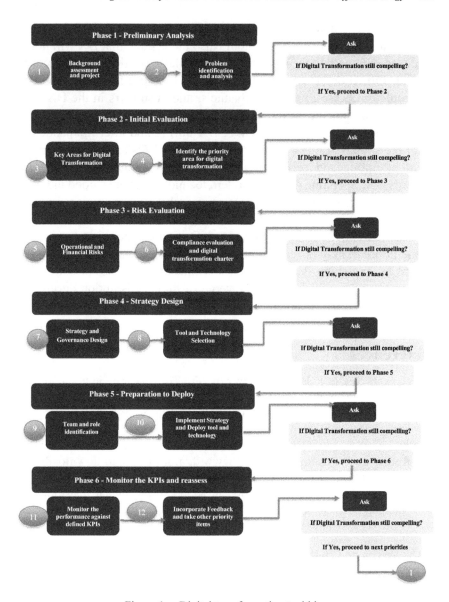

Figure 1. Digital transformation tool kit.

Conclusion and Future Research Agenda

It is important to realize that DX is necessary. During pandemic times, we can see that the adoption of digitization helps accelerate the speed of pandemic relief measures, such as supply chains, information exchange, education, engagement between working teams, and vaccine information sharing and development. One should also understand that DX will not be achieved only with tools; it's a mindset that plays a critical role in successful transformation. The toolkit proposed for DX specifies the importance of people, processes, products, channels, and customers in the DX journey. Also, define the strategies, key activities, and an implementation framework to smooth the journey of DX during and after the pandemic. With the proposed toolkit, it is expected that CXOs and senior management of public and private organizations will adopt the correct path towards DX. Spending on IT or modern technology is not a good indicator of how an organization is transforming. The transformation emerges within. It may include the effects of modern-day tools, communication approaches, skill availability, and the definition of operating procedures. In the future, it may provide the DX scores for the organization using this toolkit by analyzing the organization within the same sector and across different sectors, which are in the verge of digital disruption during and after the COVID-19 pandemic.

References

Aralelemath, S. (2021, January). Power of Zero Trust Security in the Journey of Digital Transformation. Retrieved from BusinessWorld: http://www.businessworld.in/article/Power-Of-Zero-Trust-Security-In-The-Journey-Of-Digital-Transformation/29-01-2021-371184/.

Benlian, C. M. (2015). Digital transformation strategies. *CATCHWORD*. Retrieved from https://www.dga.or.th/upload/download/file_cd634d3f094a12a6e57730d750e75c6f.pdf.

Bonnet, D. (2020, July). A revolution in adoption, but digital transformation challenges awai. Retrieved from IMD: https://www.imd.org/research-knowledge/articles/A-revolution-in-adoption-but-digital-transformation-challenges-await/.

Desk, C. (2020, October). Covid-19 Speeding up Digital Transformation, Shows Study. Retrieved from CXOtoday: https://www.cxotoday.com/news-analysis/covid-19-speeding-up-digital-transformation-shows-study/.

Hess, T., Matt, C., Benlian, A., and Wiesböck, F. (2016). Options for formulating a digital transformation strategy. *MIS Quarterly Executive*, 15(2), 123–139.

Indriastuti, M. (2020). Impact of Covid-19 on digital transformation and sustainability in small and medium enterprises (SMEs): A conceptual framework. Advances in Intelligent Systems and Computing, Vol. 1194.

Newman, D. (2018, May). Understanding The Six Pillars of Digital Transformation Beyond Tech. Retrieved from Forbes: https://www.forbes.com/sites/danielnewman/2018/05/21/understanding-the-six-pillars-of-digital-transformation-beyond-tech/?sh=c8ab6603f3b3.

Rabra, S. (2020, June). COVID-19: The perfect storm for digital acceleration. Retrieved from KPMG: https://home.kpmg/in/en/home/insights/2020/05/covid-19-the-perfect-storm-for-digital-acceleration.html.

Reis, J. C. (2018). Digital transformation: a literature review and guidelines for future research. *Trends and Advances in Information Systems and Technologies*, 411–421.

Wade, M. R. (2020, May). Scenario planning for a post-COVID-19 world. Retrieved from IMD: https://www.imd.org/research-knowledge/reports/scenario-planning-for-a-post-covid-19-world.

Yokoi, T. (2020, June). Beyond the Covid-19 hackathons: Matchathons. Retrieved from Forbes: https://www.forbes.com/sites/tomokoyokoi/2020/06/10/beyond-the-covid-19-hackathons-matchathons/?sh=6b5c25ea1fbd.

© 2025 World Scientific Publishing Company
https://doi.org/10.1142/9789811292101_0029

Chapter 29

Impact of Online Reputation on Neobank Adoption during COVID-19

Puneett Bhatnagr[*,‡], Anupama Rajesh[*,§], and Richa Misra[†,¶]

[*]*Amity International Business School,
Noida, Uttar Pradesh, India*

[†]*Jaipuria Institute of Management,
Noida, Uttar Pradesh, India*

[‡]*puneett.bhatnagr@gmail.com*

[§]*anupamar@amity.edu*

[¶]*richa.misra@jaipuria.ac.in*

Abstract

Easy accessibility of the internet on multiple smart devices has resulted in increased online product adoption. The COVID-19 lockdowns promoted internet usage by consumers across the globe, which made their search for goods and products online, and they preferred to buy or transact financial products online while reviewing and assessing them. A new generation of alternative challenger banks, known as 'neobanks,' arose due to expanded internet and mobile penetration. Currently a part of fintech companies, being digital-only banks, and a reasonably new concept, neobanks face challenges in how users, especially in India, can accept and use the new technology. Online ratings and reviews play an essential role in increasing product adoption. Previous studies on variables such as online ratings and reviews have been significant in improving adoption in other industries. This study proposes a conceptual model based on the UTAUT-3 technology adoption model while adding additional variables such as online ratings and reviews to assess the impact of online reputation on technology adoption. The study involved conducting an online survey for 460 participants across the Delhi NCR region. The study has found that variables such as performance expectancy, social influence, and personal innovativeness are highly significant, in addition to online ratings and reviews, in adopting neobank services. This study will further contribute to extending the literature around neobanking technology adoption, which is currently unavailable, and will help fintech managers establish neobank plans and focus on online reputation by assessing inline ratings and reviews before introducing new financial products into the online market.

Keywords: Online reputation, Neobanking, UTAUT-3, SMART-PLS, structural equation modelling (SEM), intention to use, India.

Introduction

COVID-19 has expedited the digitalization of everything, from education to foodstuffs, and it will certainly be a significant turning point in terms of loans, insurance, and microservices, but more so for fintech adoption (INC 42, 2021). COVID-19 also accelerated the shift to digital, with segments of the population adopting digital technologies and contactless payments faster than experts had predicted (Accenture, 2021). Taking advantage of increased internet and smartphone penetration, a new wave of alternative challenger banks has emerged. These are what we call today 'neobanks.'

As the term suggests, this new form of banking disrupts the financial services industry in various ways. Neobanks are alternative challenger banks that offer banking services exclusively online (Infomineo, 2021). In other words, these fintech firms do not have a physical presence in brick-and-mortar branches. This means that all neobank business is conducted only through digital means, such as mobile apps and online platforms. Neobanks have been attracting new customers at a mesmerizing rate. In the UK alone, they have almost tripled the number of customers in 2019, going from 7.7 million in 2018 to nearly 20 million in 2019, according to Accenture, recording a growth rate of 150%, outpacing that of traditional banks. According to an AT Kearney report, neobanks in Europe attracted more than 15 million new customers in 2011–2019. Their customer base is expected to reach 85 million by 2023 (Infomineo, 2021).

The popularity of neobanks has resulted in a decline in branch banking over the past few years. Financial companies were forced to start changing their networks as a result. The global COVID-19 crisis did not start the trend, but it has certainly exacerbated it (Accenture, 2021).

Banks need to compete for customers in both physical and digital environments (Bankbound, 2021). Offering digital facilities that need fewer employees and fewer physical branches will save neobanks much money in running costs. Customers would also benefit from banking services' ease, frequency, and accessibility around the clock. Although COVID-19 has increased the demand for digital banking services, customers' increasing desire for digitization is unique.

Customers often look for other consumers' online feedback in a digital marketplace before making a buying decision. According to studies, consumers depend heavily on online feedback before making a buying decision (Teo, 2003; Kim, 2007, 2011) since online reviews have an oblique product experience. Consumers use online feedback to find content, evaluate options, and reduce purchase risk and expense (Park and Lee 2009; Mudambi and Schuff 2010). However, electronic word-of-mouth (eWoM) can be supplied by family, friends, or collaborators. Moreover, eWoM can become tainted because it has contributions from individuals who don't use their real names, resulting in a weakening of its message and a dilution of its persuasive effect. Since online reviews provide users with a fair gauge of quality details and possible dangers associated with buying a product, their perceived reputation is critical (Kiecker and Cowles, 2002).

Financial organizations must feature prominently because 82% of people choose to study online before making a purchasing decision, and online reviews are an essential aspect of successful offsite SEO. To improve adoption and consumer service, they should remain a top priority.

According to Fan and Fuel (2016), 94% of online consumers read feedback before making a purchase decision. According to the Spiegel Research Centre (2017), 95% of shoppers read product feedback before making a purchase. According to BrightLocal (2017) research, 97% of users use ratings to find local facilities. Consumers read ratings for restaurants and cafes 60% of the time, B&Bs 40% of the time, and emergency care 33% of the time. According to Small Business Trends (2017), 83% of job seekers use online reviews to help them decide which employers to apply to, and 84% of patients use online reviews to assess doctors before signing in. Since online reviews are generally perceived as having a high degree of credibility and trustworthiness, customers generally return to such sources of information regarding any products and services they would like to explore further (Filieri and McLeay, 2014; Filieri, 2015). As long as customers perceive such an information source as comprehensive, credible, updated, and relevant, they are more likely to have positive attitudes towards and perceive the platform (Mathwick and Mosteller, 2017). Furthermore, online ratings give customers direct visual clues about the product's quality and performance, which, in turn, saves the customers' time and efforts, unlike qualitative online reviews, which require much more time to read and analyze. Online ratings also enable customers to specify a limited number of options to be considered, which allows them to appraise the shopping process more simply (Filieri, 2015).

Neobanks, on the other hand, have not taken off as well in India as they had hoped. The following goals are intended to be met through this research. First, this study identifies critical determinants that can be used to forecast neobank adoption using the UTAUT-3 model. As indicated earlier, most studies on technology and banking adoption have relied on TAM and UTAUT, which are incapable, insufficient, or incapacitated in explaining or accounting for the dynamism in users' behaviour towards technology and its adoption. This study addresses this gap, as it is modelled on the UTAUT-3 model, which is predicted to assess 68% predictability for consumer adoption as per earlier studies.

As part of this study, we would also review the impact of online review and rating factors on the customer experience, which also influence adoption of banks, which can then support neobanks to further increase and predict adoption by creating an integrated model of UTAUT-3 combining online review and rating factors. Moreover, none of the earlier studies has investigated the impact of UTAUT-3, online reviews, and online ratings as constructs on the usage/adoption of neobanks. This chapter provides a condensed model to better understand actual neobank consumer behaviour by examining customer-specific variables that affect technology adoption and usage among Indian neobank customers. Given the high level of customer engagement in the online service context, which necessitates active participation, customer characteristics are critical (Lovelock and Wirtz, 2004).

A summary of the literature on banking technology adoption is presented in the following section. We suggest a model of customers' intentions to use neobanks and the testing of theories that go with it. This is followed by sections in which we go into the research methods and discuss the results of the scientific data analysis. The chapter ends with a review of the study's shortcomings and managerial consequences.

Literature Review

A financial institution is one of the service industries heavily affected by information technology's evolution in developing digital financial systems. The introduction of disruptive technology in human progress is due to the users' immense interconnections (Patwardhan, 2017). Over the years, many have refined the TAM model, which further defined the UTAUT model (Davis *et al.*, 2003; Brown and Venkatesh, 2005).

Research has found that behaviour attitude is important for users behavioural usage and intention. Several types of research have confirmed the utility of the UTAUT model.

UTAUT2 was an extension of UTAUT, which had other factors: hedonic motivation (H.M.), price value (P.V.), and habit (H.B.). Variance in behavioural purpose and technological use in UTAUT2 has significantly increased (Chang, 2012). Venkatesh *et al.* (2012) extended UTAUT by integrating it into banking using three additional exogenous structures: H.B., H.M., and P.V., and four exogenous constructions from UTAUT (Farooq, 2017). UTAUT has been expanded into UTAUT2, which offers significant changes in the specified behavioural purpose variation between 56% and 74% and use behaviour between 40% and 52%. H.M. applies the pleasure of consumers to new technology (Owusu Kwateng, 2018). Price value is for a person who can withstand the economic shifts in new technologies due to knowledge (Paulo *et al.*, 2018). The variable habit illustrates how people already use technologies (Hussain *et al.*, 2018).

Previous empirical and theoretical tests have demonstrated UTAUT2 under different conditions, such as in internet banking (Alalwan, 2017; Morosan and DeFranco, 2016), online shopping, and information and communication technology (ICT) (Chipeva, 2018); however, UTAUT-3 has still not been evaluated for neobanks. To address the gap and review the literature relevant to technology adoption, this study further builds on the UTAUT-3 model.

In this analysis, the UTAUT-3 model was chosen as a conceptual model due to its 66% explanatory potential to foresee technology adoption. Due to its strength and simplicity, the extended UTAUT-2 model (UTAUT-3) is studied to explain adoption in this research.

This research explores the adoption and usage of neobanking services in India during COVID-19 times by evaluating the UTAUT-3 model (Farooq, 2019). All independent variables were hypothesized to determine behavioural intention adoption (BIA) and behaviour usage (BIU).

Online reputation management

Online reputation management (ORM) is a set of techniques for monitoring and improving an entity's public image on the internet (companies, products, and institutions). ORM experts strive to reduce the negative impact of information about a person or company while maximizing the positive material to increase trustworthiness. ORM experts strive to reduce the negative impact of information about a person or company while maximizing the positive material to increase trustworthiness, due to massive Internet related data published every day (Rodríguez-Vidal *et al.*, 2020).

Despite difficulties in reading user reviews, written customer feedback remains one of the most valuable sources of intelligence for both users and marketers. User comments have a more significant influence on buying decisions and perceived trustworthiness than star scores (Tsang and Prendergast, 2009). Similarly, it was found that, while users looked at star ratings to help them make choices, they still read and applied knowledge from written feedback (Chevalier and Mayzlin, 2006).

To find out what other people had to say about products and services before buying, 86% of internet users look online (Zhu and Zhang 2010). It is just as essential to provide an honest opinion of something when purchasing it to get a good deal (Senecal and Nantel, 2004; Dellarocas *et al.*, 2007). Regarding the body of literature on online feedback, users look for reliable and trustworthy information and are willing to include it when evaluating a product. The study by Leskovec *et al.* (2007) found that 'eWoM is valuable in fortifying ads,' maybe even more so in a market where players' attitudes can flip from negative to positive and back again to negative, particularly in games-based markets. Finally, this body of study details how beneficial ratings are to online transactions.

Both buyers and advertisers will learn from the abundance of knowledge available in online reviews: it allows consumers to make decisions while also providing helpful input to the marketer. However, it is possible to gather insights from customers' ratings, with both advertisers and customers unable to make sense of the abundance of online feedback. A one-star ranking may be dependent on star ratings, for example. Such an award given a five-star ranking has no uniformity (for example, in how customers express it).

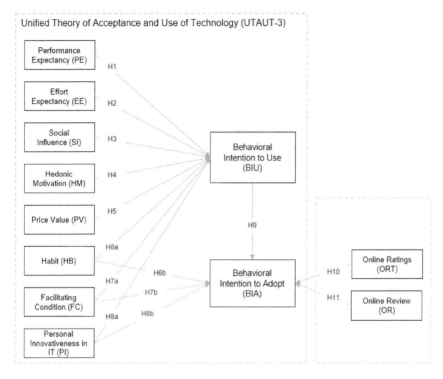

Figure 1. Neobank conceptual model.

Except in the best case, the product might not meet all the buyer's expectations, but this does not dissuade them from writing a negative review (or vice versa). That is, in general, people don't approach them methodically.

After a detailed literature review, we have found that online ratings and reviews have been researched in detail across all the industry sectors but not in neobanks. Being a digital-only bank, a study on their online ratings and reviews will help with adoption. Hence, this study proposes a conceptual model (Figure 1).

Research Hypothesis

Performance expectancy (P.E.)

Performance expectancy refers to a user's belief that using technologies can help them achieve work success gains (Venkatesh *et al.*, 2003). In previous research, P.E. was the best intent marker of technology acceptance (Duyck *et al.*, 2008). Referring to earlier banking research, P.E. has been found to be a significant contributor to adoption. Hence, building on the context of neobanks, this study expects the following:

H1: P.E. influences the intention to adopt neobanks.

Effort expectancy (E.E.)

Effort expectancy would most certainly equate technology with ease of use (Venkatesh *et al.*, 2003). It's similar to the previous TAM model's supposed ease of use. E.E. has been studied widely in banking studies and is a strong predictor. Even if prospective customers feel that an interface is functional, at the same time, they may consider the system to be too complex to use. The advantages of efficiency outweigh the potential of using technology (Davis, 1989). This study expects the following:

H2: E.E. influences the intention to adopt neobanks.

Social influence (S.I.)

Social influence also influences user intention towards technology acceptance as a significant predictor. It is considered essential by others to believe they should use the new technology. We believe that the decision to use neobanks impacts social power, as family members, coworkers, and others can impact neobank usage.

S.I. has been studied widely in banking studies and is a strong predictor.

H3: S.I. influences the intention to adopt neobanks.

Hedonic motivation (H.M.)

Hedonic motivation is the degree to which customers feel that using an I.S. method is entertaining, leading to hedonic motivation (Venkatesh *et al.*, 2012). Many are users who initially developed these programmes to be predominantly task-oriented. Hence, adoption was initially based on personal values and practical matters (Thong *et al.*, 2006). When designers discovered that users used the device to accomplish assignments and be amused, they modified their design philosophy. I.S. marked by playfulness, amusement value, and pleasure were first inferred. Then, excited curiosity is the non-utilitarian use of I.S. (Dwivedi *et al.*, 2015). Venkatesh *et al.* (2012) found these connections in existing adoption models, which motivated the scholarly community to change and incorporate structures that tapped into hedonic motivation (Kim *et al.*, 2008a). In this study, we hypothesize the following:

H4: H.M. influences the intention to adopt neobanks.

Price value (P.V.)

The consumer context of the UTAUT2 model necessitated the addition of a new construction related to the monetary cost of new technology usage. As a result, P.V. was described by Venkatesh *et al.* (2012) as "customers' cognitive trade-off between both the perceived advantages of the applications and the financial expense of using them."

H5: P.V. influences the intention to adopt neobanks.

Habit (H.B.)

The UTAUT2 model was conceptualized by Venkatesh *et al.* (2012) by integrating the habit notion that non-task-setting automatic activities affect actions. Specifically, they included 'Habit,' which mirrors how people perform habits due to repetition (Venkatesh *et al.*, 2012), which is created once a level of behaviour has been repeated (Orbell *et al.*, 2001). For a variety of models, H.B. was distinguished from behaviour (Khalifa and Liu, 2007) but proved to be a predictor of behavioural intentions (Pavlou and Fygenson, 2006) and has subsequently been validated as a predictor of continuous use of ICT (Lankton *et al.*, 2010).

H6a: H.B. influences the intention to use neobanks.
H6b: H.B. influences the intention to adopt neobanks.

Facilitating condition (F.C.)

The degree to which an individual thinks the mechanism can be used by organizational and technical infrastructure is described by F.C. (Venkatesh *et al.*, 2003). While Tam *et al.* (2018) did not find any evidence that F.C. has an essential role in influencing mobile application usage, neobanks, being digital-only banks, do get accessed through mobile apps. Hence, it is predicted that F.C. in the context of neobanks will have a significant influence.

H7a: F.C. influences the intention to use neobanks.
H7b: F.C. influences the intention to adopt neobanks.

Personal innovativeness (P.I.)

New information technologies represent innovations to reach customers. Technology acceptance research has its roots in the literature on innovation diffusion (Yi *et al.*, 2006). Personal innovativeness in the domain of information technology (PIIT) was described by Agarwal and Prasad (1998) as 'the capacity of a person to try out any new information technology' in the sense of technology.

H8a: P.I. influences the intention to use neobanks.
H8b: P.I. influences the intention to adopt neobanks.

Behavioural intention to adopt (BIA)

The intention is a conscious provocation or tendency to engage in a specific behaviour execution, manifested as a commitment to act in a specific, specified manner (Ajzen, 1991). According to the planned behaviour principle, there are three mutually distinct reasons for adopting particular behaviour or changing behaviour: attitude towards behaviour, subjective standard for behaviour, and assumed behavioural controls (Ajzen, 1991). Besides, UTAUT describes purpose as the result of technology's perceived success, commitment, and social impact. Moreover, motive is characterized as the subjective likelihood of a person's action or behaviour (Venkatesh *et al.*, 2003). The desire to adopt technologies over time is described as a behavioural goal (Ajzen, 1991). As a result, the ability and self-prediction to use technology differ from behaviour purpose. We define behavioural purpose as the desire to follow a new behaviour (Ajzen, 1991). The purpose is also a well-known proxy for behaviour or adoption (Ajzen, 1991).

Behavioural intention to use (BIU)

There is clear evidence in the literature that users and non-users have different expectations of any emerging technology's success and risk, influencing their potential adoption plans. In research on internet banking use conducted by Ozdemir *et al.* (2008), the results showed perceptual variations between adopters who viewed internet banking as more user-friendly, efficient, and less dangerous than non-adopters. As a result, this study hypothesizes the following:

H9: Intention to use influences the intention to adopt neobanking.

Online review (ORE)

Reviews written by consumers are known as eWoM since they are written online (Filieri, 2015). When buyers buy goods or consider alternatives online, feedback becomes increasingly regarded as an essential and necessary tool (Huang *et al.*, 2015). Therefore, online reviews' vital influence has continuously been discovered to suggest the product which the prospective user plans to follow if they have read online reviews (Cheung *et al.*, 2008). Using the results of the study conducted by Elwalda *et al.* (2016), which discovered a clear and optimistic association between features that consumers speak about while leaving online consumer feedback and online store visits, we may suggest the hypothesis as follows:

H10: Online review influences the intention to adopt neobanks.

Online rating (ORT)

Online consumers' ratings are a feature synonymous with online reviews. According to Filieri (2015, p. 1264), this definition is regarded as 'an alternative way of describing crowd opinion' and reflects reviewers' average appraisal of a product's or a service's multiple features. Additionally, consumers have the option of ranking their purchases on a numerical scale, using a five- or seven-point Likert scale. Overall reviews of goods or service providers may be captured depending on various characteristics using such scores. These goods and services are measured by prior consumers and scored on their respective values, such as consistency, price, accuracy, and delivery time (King *et al.*, 2014). As a result, consumers' checkout experiences are more straightforward and transparent, leading to customers becoming more likely to use neobanks. Thus, we have the following hypothesis:

H11: Online rating influences the intention to adopt neobanks.

Measurement Scale

The behaviour scale has previously been tested on various technology types, such as mobile phones, smartphones, and internet technologies. For example, Danielson *et al.* studied the UTAUT2 model and adapted the assessment to different contexts. Assessment questions remained survey questions were created after detailed literature review. Factors such as P.E., E.E., SI, H.B., F.C., and P.I. are all accounted for using three-item scales. Furthermore, two elements, price value and hedonic motivation, were included on two measurement scales, as given by Venkatesh *et al.* (2017). As Hani *et al.* (2013) recommended, we followed survey measurements on a seven-point Likert scale based on the participant responses, ranging from 'strongly disagree' (1) to 'strongly agree' (7).

Data Collection

Respondents were polled using a sample population which included individuals (18 years or older) from across India. The respondents remained classified into two categories in this sample: users and non-users who said they had online banking accounts. Two trained experts validated the survey instrument. Academic experts analyzed the instrument's validity and measurement scale based on the consistency of comprehension, wording, and form (Boateng *et al.*, 2018). The sample size is calculated according to the desired accuracy, confidence level, and approximate percentage of the specified population. With 95% acceptance rate, 385 responses were selected which were higher then the minimum requirement based on previous researches. The method adopted in this study was found to adequately satisfy the recommended minimum of standard distributions (5:1) in the sample size/ratio of parameters to be calculated (Bentler and Chou, 1987), with almost all loads exceeding 0.70 (Guadagnoli and Velicer, 1988). Detailed demographics and descriptive information about the respondents are included in Table 1. However, no noteworthy differences were discovered in the answer modes in the demographics of saved and discarded answers. The survey results are also summarized in Table 1.

Table 1. Demographic details.

Demographic	Characteristic	Frequency	Percent (%)
Gender	Female	218	47.4%
	Male	242	52.6%
Age	18 – 25	170	37.0%
	26 – 35	166	36.1%
	56 years and above	50	10.9%
	46 – 55	42	9.1%
	36 – 45	32	7.0%
Education	Bachelors	256	55.7%
	Masters's	117	25.4%
	Post Graduate	46	10.10%
	High School	36	7.8%
	PhD	5	1.1%
Occupation	Student (college / University)	146	31.7%
	Executive / Manager	77	16.7%
	Professional	64	13.9%
	Computer Technical Engineering	40	8.7%
	Academic / Teacher	39	8.5%
	Self-employed / Own company	29	6.3%
	Clerical / Administrative	26	5.7%
	Homemaker	17	3.7%
	Unemployed, Looking for work	12	2.6%
	Retried	10	2.2%
Income	50,000 to 75,000	206	44.8%
	75,000 to 1 Lac	96	20.9%
	Less than 50,000	90	19.6%
	Greater than 1 Lac	68	14.8%

(*Continued*)

Table 1. (*Continued*)

Demographic	Characteristic	Frequency	Percent (%)
Experience	More than 2 years	292	63.5%
	Up to 1 year	124	27.0%
	1 to 2 year	44	9.6%
Online Financial Users	Daily	187	40.7%
	Once a month	135	29.3%
	Once in 2 month	64	13.9%
	Weekly	47	10.2%
	Never	27	5.9%

A pilot study was held with a modified questionnaire among 40 customers (Saunders *et al.*, 2007).

A questionnaire that used Google Forms was sent to 700 recipients, and 96% of the emails were answered in November and December 2020. Secured data collection techniques, which are known to be easier to use, ubiquitous, and safer (Rayhan *et al.*, 2013), were adopted. Cochran's formula was used to quantify the scale and nature of populations for which it was appropriate (Cochran, Table 1 — Survey respondents).

Empirical Estimation

Based on the recommendations of Ringle (2012) and Sarstedt (2012), the study performed data analysis using the estimation model for validity and reliability evaluation. As a result, we conducted hypothesis testing using the partial least-squares structural equation model (PLS-SEM) (Hair *et al.*, 2017). As per Hair *et al.* (2017), SmartPLS-3 was helpful in PLS analysis, as it is widely applied in the information technology field (Chin *et al.*, 2003).

Research Review and Findings

Measurement analysis

The measurement model, as suggested by Hair (2017), is tested to assess the durability of data structures, such as Cronbach's alphas with composite reliability. Accuracy measures are used to calculate the distinguishing factor loadings. Item properties are present in all systems when it comes to psychometric properties. The results are summarized in Table 2.

The measurement model outcomes show that the conceptual model has good internal accuracy and ensures the durability of the predictor and convergent and discriminant validity. Our proposed model is statistically significant and evaluates a suitable fundamental model.

Structural model

As it has been mentioned, this study uses a structural equation modelling methodology based on variance and PLS-SEM. To perform all theoretical calculations related to the structural model's evaluation, the up-to-date edition of Smart-PLS-3.3.3 was utilized. As part of the model structure analysis, all hypothesized path coefficients were scrutinized for the degree of path sensitivity (beta) and path bias and *t*-values for relationship significance. Figure 2 shows a complete overview of the model's findings.

Figure 2 shows that all eight UTAUT-3 constructs, namely P.E., E.E., SI, P.V., H.B., F.C., H.M., and P.I., account for 76.9% of BIU variance ($R^2 = 0.769$) for neobanking services.

Table 2. Measurement model.

Constructs	α	CR	AVE
PE	0.760	0.762	0.519
EE	0.869	0.867	0.689
FC	0.839	0.840	0.637
HB	0.823	0.823	0.609
HM	0.798	0.798	0.664
PI	0.864	0.862	0.679
PV	0.840	0.860	0.759
SI	0.794	0.794	0.564
BIA	0.852	0.856	0.666
BIU	0.846	0.848	0.650
ORE	0.838	0.838	0.722
ORT	0.902	0.903	0.823

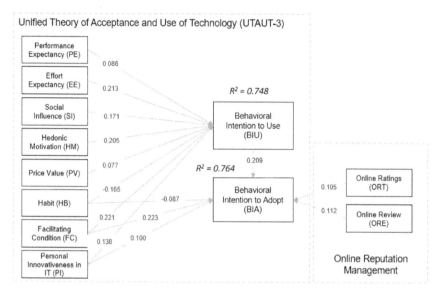

Figure 2. UTAUT-3 constructs.

As a result, the conceptual model describes 63.3% of the total variation, according to the final R^2 results. According to Hair et al. (2017), a model may be graded as weak, moderate, or significant based on the R^2 values of 0.19, 0.33, or 0.67, respectively. This analysis's theoretical model has a high explanatory capacity ($R^2 = 0.633$) for understanding neobanking acceptance, consumer behaviour, and subsequent suggestions based on these parameters. The findings were also similar to previous experiments using a similar contemplative measurement scale (Nair et al., 2015; Venkatesh et al., 2012).

Goodness of fit measurements

The calculation of PLS-SEM under SmartPLS currently does not support the calculation of goodness of fit (GoF). Hence, R^2 values are calculated using standard formulae for GoF (GoF = $\sqrt{(AVE \times R^2)}$) (Wetzels et al., 2009). The values of the GoF index are listed in Table 3. Considering the recommendations of Henseler (2016), Table 3 suggests a substantial GoF value of 70.9%.

Table 3. GoF model.

Constructs	AVE	R^2
PE	0.519	—
EE	0.689	—
FC	0.637	—
HB	0.609	—
HM	0.664	—
PI	0.679	—
PV	0.759	—
SI	0.564	—
ORE	0.722	—
ORT	0.823	—
BIU	0.650	0.748
BIA	0.666	0.764
Average of constructs	0.665	0.756
Average × R^2		0.503
GoF = (AVE × R^2)		**0.709**

Hypotheses Results

The relationship between all the variables was comparatively meaningful, with the aim of usage and adoption at the $p < 0.01$ significance level, as per the hypothesis. Table 4 gives a quick overview of the hypotheses.

Research Contributions and Implications

Practical implications

This research brings a new conceptual model to light about customers' intent to adopt and utilize neobanks. This research has discovered that online ratings and reviews influence customers' intentions. The study encourages financial administrators to leverage the internet and their customer base to conduct or seek customer feedback online. Customers should be surveyed to better understand their banking needs so that products can be developed that help them fulfil their needs. Global lockdowns

Table 4. Hypothesis relationship.

Hypotheses		Beta	Error	t-values	Decision
H1	PE -> BIU	0.086	0.031	2.715	Accepted
H2	EE -> BIU	0.213	0.043	5.004	Accepted
H3	SI -> BIU	0.171	0.052	3.341	Accepted
H4	HM -> BIU	0.205	0.033	6.155	Accepted
H5	PV -> BIU	0.077	0.028	2.768	Accepted
H6a	HB -> BIA	−0.165	0.027	6.096	Accepted
H6b	HB -> BIU	−0.087	0.027	3.110	Accepted
H7a	FC -> BIA	0.221	0.048	4.682	Accepted
H7b	FC -> BIU	0.223	0.051	4.442	Accepted
H8a	PI -> BIA	0.138	0.031	4.444	Accepted
H8b	PI -> BIU	0.100	0.029	3.399	Accepted
H9a	BIU -> BIA	0.209	0.048	4.331	Accepted
H10	ORE -> BIA	0.105	0.031	3.431	Accepted
H11	ORT -> BIA	0.112	0.030	3.774	Accepted

have forced users to access banks online, and focus by banking managers on online ratings and reviews will increase adoption. Second, personal innovativeness also played a key role in user intention in adopting neobanking, according to the study results. Advertising relevant to this new technology to the user could result in a favourable impact. Personal characteristics should be given increased consideration by policymakers and their marketing strategies and by staff members. The third recommendation is based on characteristics related to either the use of technology or the internet (i.e., online ratings and reviews). Online ratings and reviews could influence users' intentions to adopt neobanking. As opinions on social websites and blogs may be crucial for marketing adoption, customer understanding is key. The more rewarding a neobanking website would be, the more likely users are to use and recommend neobanks.

Managerial implications

The results of the study have huge implications for India's banking regulators. The COVID-19 situation has moved banks to focus on digitalization.

Neobanking strategies should be planned and developed by the bank's management. It is possible to mount marketing campaigns aimed at online ratings and reviews, emphasizing the speed, convenience, and security of neobanking. To provide a secure, safe, constant, and reliable neobank, rules must be made to support online customers' financial behaviour. There are numerous benefits in publishing easy-to-understand guidelines about neobanking on the banks' websites.

Theoretical implications

We created an original conceptual model that incorporates elements from two well-known theoretical models, UTAUT-3 and ORM, in theory development. When compared to other studies that looked at users' intentions to follow neobanking, ours has a higher explanatory power of 78.3% than that of Rahi *et al*. (2018) but a lower explanatory power of 6.64% than that of Rahi *et al*. (2018). Identifying online banking (i.e., content details, website design, and webpage characteristics) is critical, particularly in a financial setting. The findings revealed that a positive relationship between users' intentions to use and their intentions to adopt is more stable. Finally, the proposed model contributes significantly to the emerging banking literature, especially in creative and online digital banking.

Limitations and Future Research

While our research builds on the current body of expertise, it is essential to note some of the challenges we faced. The advanced model blends UTAUT-3 intentions and online review and rating with the perceptions of bank protection to predict users' future intentions. We cannot claim that our complex model fully describes future intentions of neobanking adoption. Thus, more development of this recently created technology is required in the current model, and a new technology adoption model is required. However, certain things may be amplified by the use of moderator variables, such as age and gender. Future studies are predicted to focus on how the integrated model can apply constructs to various cultural settings and during COVID-19 times.

Conclusion

This chapter's primary goal is to create a conceptual model that integrates UTAUT-3 with online review and rating to forecast and clarify consumer intent in adopting and using neobanks. The findings suggest that the proposed model has a high degree of predictive capacity and robustness in forecasting customers' ability to adopt neobanks. We contribute to the body of knowledge by providing an online analysis and ranking that moderates the impact among users' intentions to adopt and use neobanks. The moderating effect of online reviews and ratings showed that, while their effects are more robust, the favourable association between a user's intention to adopt and the user's intention to use is more stable. The findings showed that innovativeness is an essential factor in determining a user's decision to use neobanking. As a result, managers should concentrate on innovative features to boost user interest in neobanking adoption. Theoretically, this research lays the groundwork for further refining individual adoption models and enriching the literature by incorporating novel elements, especially in banking adoption.

References

Accenture. (2021). https://www.accenture.com/_acnmedia/PDF-145/Accenture-Banking-Top-Trends-2021-SIBOS-Transcript.pdf.

Agarwal, R., and Prasad, J. (1998). A conceptual and operational definition of personal innovativeness in the domain of information technology. *Information Systems Research: ISR*, 9(2), 204–215.

Ajzen, I. (1991). The theory of planned behavior. *Organizational Behavior and Human Decision Processes*, 50(2), 179–211. doi: 10.1016/0749-5978(91)90020-t.

Alalwan, A. A., Rana, N. P., Dwivedi, Y. K., and Algharabat, R. (2017). Social media in marketing: A review and analysis of the existing literature. *Telematics and Informatics*, 34(7), 1177–1190.

Bentler, P. M., and Chou, C.-P. (1987). Practical issues in structural modeling. *Sociological Methods & Research*, 16(1), 78–117.

Bhalla, K. (2021, January 13). From Super Apps to Neobanking — The Fintech Trends to Watch Out for in 2021. Inc42 Media. https://inc42.com/buzz/from-super-apps-to-neobanking-the-fintech-trends-to-watch-out-for-in-2021/.

BrightLocal. (2017). https://www.brightlocal.com/learn/local-consumer-review-survey/#q1.

Bronner, F., and de Hoog, R. (2010). Vacationers and eWOM: Who posts, and why, where, and what? *Journal of Travel Research*, 50(1), 15–26. doi: 10.1177/0047287509355324.

Brown, S. A., and Venkatesh, V. (2005). Model of adoption of technology in households: A baseline model test and extension incorporating household life cycle. *MIS Quarterly*, 29(3), 399.

Chang, C.-C., Chuang, S.-C., Cheng, Y.-H., and Huang, T.-Y. (2011). The compromise effect in choosing for others. *Journal of Behavioral Decision Making*, 25(2), 109–122. doi: 10.1002/bdm.720.

Chen, Y., and Xie, J. (2005). Third-party product review and firm marketing strategy. *Marketing Science*, 24(2), 218–240. doi: 10.1287/mksc.1040.0089.

Cheung, C. M. K., Lee, M. K. O., and Rabjohn, N. (2008). The impact of electronic word-of-mouth. *Internet Research*, 18(3), 229–247. doi: 10.1108/10662240810883290.

Chevalier, J. A., and Mayzlin, D. (2006). The effect of word of mouth on sales: Online book reviews. *Journal of Marketing Research*, 43(3), 345–354. doi: 10.1509/jmkr.43.3.345.

Chin, W. W., Marcolin, B. L., and Newsted, P. R. (2003). A partial least squares latent variable modeling approach for measuring interaction effects: Results from a Monte Carlo simulation study and an electronic-mail emotion/adoption study. *Information Systems Research*, 14(2), 189–217.

Chipeva, P. et al. (2018). Digital divide at individual level: Evidence for Eastern and Western European countries. *Government Information Quarterly*, 35(3), 460–479.

Cochran, W. G. (1977). *Sampling Techniques*, 3rd edn. John Wiley & Sons, Nashville, TN.

D.B. (2019). Why positive reviews are so valuable to small businesses. Smallbiztrends. https://smallbiztrends.com/2017/04/importance-of-online-reviews.html.

Davis, F. D. (1989). Perceived usefulness, perceived ease of use, and user acceptance of information technology. *MIS Quarterly*, 13(3), 319.

Dellarocas, C., Zhang, X. (Michael), and Awad, N. F. (2007). Exploring the value of online product reviews in forecasting sales: The case of motion pictures. *Journal of Interactive Marketing*, 21(4), 23–45. doi: 10.1002/dir.20087.

Duyck, W., Vanderelst, D., Desmet, T., and Hartsuiker, R. J. (2008). The frequency effect in second-language visual word recognition. *Psychonomic Bulletin & Review*, 15(4), 850–855. doi: 10.3758/pbr.15.4.850.

Dwivedi, Y. K., Kapoor, K. K., and Chen, H. (2015). Social media marketing and advertising. *The Marketing Review*, 15(3), 289–309. doi: 10.1362/146934715x14441363377999.

Elwalda, A., Lü, K., and Ali, M. (2016). Perceived derived attributes of online customer reviews. *Computers in Human Behavior*, 56, 306–319. doi: 10.1016/j.chb.2015.11.051.

Farooq, M. S. and Radovic-Markovic, M. (2017). Modeling entrepreneurial education and entrepreneurial skills as antecedents of intention towards entrepreneurial behaviour in single mothers: A PLS-SEM approach. *Entrepreneurship: Types, Current Trends and Future Perspectives*, Presented at the *5th International Conference "Employment, Education and Entrepreneurship"* (EEE 2016). Faculty of Business Economics and Entrepreneurship, University of Belgrade, Belgrade, Serbia, pp. 198–216.

Fan and Fuel. (2016). https://fanandfuel.com/no-online-customer-reviews-means-big-problems-2017/.

Filieri, R. (2015). What makes online reviews helpful? A diagnosticity-adoption framework to explain informational and normative influences in e-WOM. *Journal of Business Research*, 68(6), 1261–1270. doi: 10.1016/j.jbusres.2014.11.006.

Filieri, R., and McLeay, F. (2013). E-WOM and accommodation. *Journal of Travel Research*, 53(1), 44–57. doi: 10.1177/0047287513481274.

Guadagnoli, E., and Velicer, W. F. (1988). Relation of sample size to the stability of component patterns. *Psychological Bulletin*, 103(2), 265–275.

Gunasinghe, A., Hamid, J. A., Khatibi, A., and Azam, S. M. F. (2019). The adequacy of UTAUT-3 in interpreting academician's adoption to e-learning in higher education environments. *Interactive Technology and Smart Education*, 17(1), 86–106. doi: 10.1108/itse-05-2019-0020.

Hair, J. F., Risher, J. J., Sarstedt, M., and Ringle, C. M. (2019). When to use and how to report the results of PLS-SEM. *European Business Review*, 31(1), 2–24.

Henseler, J., Hubona, G., and Ray, P. A. (2016). Using PLS path modeling in new technology research: Updated guidelines. *Industrial Management & Data Systems*, 116(1), 2–20. https://doi.org/10.1108/IMDS-09-2015-0382.

Hong, S., Thong, J. Y. L., and Tam, K. Y. (2006). Understanding continued information technology usage behavior: A comparison of three models in the context of mobile internet. *Decision Support Systems*, 42(3), 1819–1834. doi: 10.1016/j.dss.2006.03.009.

How Online Reviews Influence Sales — The Medill IMC Spiegel Research Center. (2020). Spiegel. https://spiegel.medill.northwestern.edu/online-reviews/.

Huang, J., Baptista, J., and Newell, S. (2015). Communicational ambidexterity as a new capability to manage social media communication within organizations. *The Journal of Strategic Information Systems*, 24(2), 49–64. doi: 10.1016/j.jsis.2015.03.002.

Hussain, S. et al. (2018). Consumers' online information adoption behaviour: Motives and antecedents of electronic word of mouth communications. *Computers in Human Behavior*, 80, 22–32.

Infomineo. (2021, January 5). Neo-banks: Taking the challenge to a well-established banking sector. https://infomineo.com/neo-banks-taking-the-challenge-to-a-well-established-banking-sector/.

Khalifa, M., and Liu, V. (2007). Online consumer retention: Contingent effects of online shopping habit and online shopping experience. *European Journal of Information Systems*, 16(6), 780– 792. doi: 10.1057/palgrave.ejis.3000711.

Kiecker, P., and Cowles, D. (2002). Interpersonal communication and personal influence on the internet: A framework for examining online word-of-mouth. *Journal of Euromarketing*, 11(2), 71–88. doi: 10.1300/j037v11n02_04.

Kim, D.-Y., Park, J., and Morrison, A. M. (2008). A model of traveller acceptance of mobile technology. *International Journal of Tourism Research*, 10(5), 393–407. doi: 10.1002/jtr.669.

King, R. A., Racherla, P., and Bush, V. D. (2014). What we know and don't know about online word-of-mouth: A review and synthesis of the literature. *Journal of Interactive Marketing*, 28(3), 167–183. doi: 10.1016/j.intmar.2014.02.001.

Kwateng, K. O., Atiemo, K. A. O., and Appiah, C. (2019). Acceptance and use of mobile banking: An application of UTAUT2. *Journal of Enterprise Information Management*, 32(1), 118–151.

Lankton, N. K., Wilson, E. V., and Mao, E. (2010). Antecedents and determinants of information technology habit. *Information & Management*, 47(5-6), 300–307. doi: 10.1016/j.im.2010.06.004.

Leskovec, J., Adamic, L. A., and Huberman, B. A. (2006). The dynamics of viral marketing. In *Proceedings of the 7th ACM Conference on Electronic Commerce — E.C. '06*. doi: 10.1145/1134707.1134732.

Lo, A. S., and Yao, S. S. (2019). What makes hotel online reviews credible? *International Journal of Contemporary Hospitality Management*, 31(1), 41–60.

Lovelock, C., and Wirtz, J. (2004). *Services Marketing: People, Technology, Strategy*, 7th edn. ISBN: 978-0-13-610721-7.

Ludwig, S., de Ruyter, K., Friedman, M., Brüggen, E., Wetzels, M. and Pfann, G. (2013). More than words: The influence of affective content and linguistic style matches in online reviews on conversion rates. *Journal of Marketing*, 77(1), 87–103. doi: 10.1509/jm.11.0560.

Mathwick, C., and Mosteller, J. (2016). Online reviewer engagement. *Journal of Service Research*, 20(2), 204–218. doi: 10.1177/1094670516682088.

Moran, G., and Muzellec, L. (2014). eWOM credibility on social networking sites: A framework. *Journal of Marketing Communications*, 23(2), 149–161. doi: 10.1080/13527266.2014.969756.

Morosan, C., and DeFranco, A. (2016). Co-creating value in hotels using mobile devices: A conceptual model with empirical validation. *International Journal of Hospitality Management*, 52, 131–142.

Mudambi, S. M., and Schuff, D. (2010). Research note: What makes a helpful online review? A study of customer reviews on Amazon.com. *MIS Quarterly*, 34(1), 185. doi: 10.2307/20721420.

Nair, P. K., Ali, F., and Leong, L. C. (2015). Factors affecting acceptance & use of ReWIND: Validating the extended unified theory of acceptance and use of technology. *Interactive Technology and Smart Education*, 12(3), 183–201.

Ooley, A. (2020, October 23). Why Online Reviews are so Vital to Banks and Credit Unions. Bankbound. https://www.bankbound.com/blog/online-reviews-vital-banks-credit-unions/.

Orbell, S., Blair, C., Sherlock, K., and Conner, M. (2001). The theory of planned behavior and ecstasy use: Roles for habit and perceived control over taking versus obtaining substances. *Journal of Applied Social Psychology*, 31(1), 31–47. doi: 10.1111/j.1559-1816.2001.tb02480.x.

Ozdemir, M. E., Cilingir, I. U., Ilhan, G., Yildiz, E., and Ohanoglu, K. (2018). The effect of the systematic birth preparation program on fear of vaginal delivery and quality of life. *Archives of Gynecology and Obstetrics*, 298, 561–565. doi: 10.1007/s00404-018-4835-0.

Park, C., and Lee, T. M. (2009). Information direction, website reputation and eWOM effect: A moderating role of product type. *Journal of Business Research*, 62(1), 61–67. doi: 10.1016/j.jbusres.2007.11.017.

Park, D.-H., Lee, J., and Han, I. (2007). The effect of online consumer reviews on consumer purchasing intention: The moderating role of involvement. *International Journal of Electronic Commerce*, 11(4), 125–148. doi: 10.2753/jec1086-4415110405.

Patwardhan, A. (2018). Financial inclusion in the digital age. *Handbook of Blockchain, Digital Finance, and Inclusion*, Vol. 1, pp. 57–89.

Paulo, M. M., Rita, P., Oliveira, T., and Moro, S. (2018). Understanding mobile augmented reality adoption in a consumer context. *Journal of Hospitality and Tourism Technology*, 9(1), doi: 10.1108/JHTT-01-2017-0006.

Pavlou, P. A., and Fygenson, M. (2006). Understanding and predicting electronic commerce adoption: An extension of the theory of planned behavior. *MIS Quarterly*, 30(1), 115. doi: 10.2307/25148720.

Pavlou, P. A., and Gefen, D. (2004). Building effective online marketplaces with institution-based trust. *Information Systems Research*, 15(1), 37–59. doi: 10.1287/isre.1040.0015.

Qiu, L., Pang, J., and Lim, K. H. (2012). Effects of conflicting aggregated rating on eWOM review credibility and diagnosticity: The moderating role of review valence. *Decision Support Systems*, 54(1), 631–643. doi: 10.1016/j.dss.2012.08.020.

Rahi, S., and Ghani, M. A. (2018). The role of UTAUT, DOI, perceived technology security and game elements in internet banking adoption. *World Journal of Science, Technology and Sustainable Development*, 15(4), 338–356.

Rayhan, R. U., Zheng, Y., Uddin, E., Timbol, C., Adewuyi, O., and Baraniuk, J. N. (2013). Administer and collect medical questionnaires with Google Documents: A simple, safe, and free system. *Applied Medical Informatics*, 33(3/2013), 12–21.

Rodríguez-Vidal, J., Gonzalo, J., Plaza, L., and Sánchez, H. A. (2019). Automatic detection of influencers in social networks: Authority versus domain signals. *Journal of the Association for Information Science and Technology*. doi: 10.1002/asi.24156.

Roy, S. K., Shekhar, V., Lassar, W. M., and Chen, T. (2018). Customer engagement behaviors: The role of service convenience, fairness and quality. *Journal of Retailing and Consumer Services*, 44, 293–304. doi: 10.1016/j.jretconser.2018.07.018.

Sarstedt, M., Ringle, C. M., and Hair, J. F. (2017). Partial least squares structural equation modeling. *Handbook of Market Research*, pp. 1–40. doi: 10.1007/978-3-319-05542-8_15-1.

Saunders, M., Lewis, P., and Thornhill, A. (2007). *Research Methods for Business Students*, 4th edn. Prentice Hall, London.

Senecal, S., and Nantel, J. (2004). The influence of online product recommendations on consumers' online choices. *Journal of Retailing*, 80(2), 159–169. doi: 10.1016/j.jretai.2004.04.001.

Team, M. (2020, June 25). Neobanking 2.0: Global Deep Dive 2020 — Report By. MEDICI. https://gomedici.com/neobanking-2-0-global-deep-dive-2020-report-by-medici.

Tsang, A. S. L., and Prendergast, G. (2009). Does culture affect evaluation expressions? *European Journal of Marketing*, 43(5/6), 686–707. doi: 10.1108/03090560910947007.

Venkatesh, V., and Agarwal, R. (2006). Turning visitors into customers: A usability-centric perspective on purchase behavior in electronic channels. *Management Science*, 52(3), 367–382. doi: 10.1287/mnsc.1050.0442.

Venkatesh, V. et al. (2003). User acceptance of information technology: Toward a unified view. *MIS Quarterly: Management Information Systems*, 27(3), 425.

Venkatesh, V., Thong, J. Y. L., and Xu, X. (2012). Consumer acceptance and use of information technology: Extending the unified theory of acceptance and use of technology. *MIS Quarterly*, 36(1), 157.

Xie, J., Sreenivasan, S., Korniss, G., Zhang, W., Lim, C., and Szymanski, B. K. (2011). Social consensus through the influence of committed minorities. *Physical Review E*, 84(1). doi: 10.1103/physreve.84.011130.

Xu, H. (2018). Social interactions in large networks: A game theoretic approach. *International Economic Review*, 59(1), 257–284. doi: 10.1111/iere.12269.

Yi, M. Y., Jackson, J. D., Park, J. S., and Probst, J. C. (2006). Understanding information technology acceptance by individual professionals: Toward an integrative view. *Information & Management*, 43(3), 350–363. doi: 10.1016/j.im.2005.08.006.

Zhu, F., and Zhang, X. (Michael). (2010). Impact of online consumer reviews on sales: The moderating role of product and consumer characteristics. *Journal of Marketing*, 74(2), 133–148. doi: 10.1509/jmkg.74.2.133.

Chapter 30

Technological Developments and Innovations to Drive the Post-COVID-19 World Economy

Shyam Sundar Panigrahi

TATA Consultancy Services, Mumbai, India
sspanigrahi7@gmail.com

Abstract

The novel coronavirus has just highlighted the value of digital preparedness and Industry 4.0-driven technologies that helped businesses across the globe be functional even during these unprecedented times. In the past, as was the case with the Spanish flu pandemic that broke out in the 1920s, it was witnessed that these kinds of pandemics could wreak havoc and disrupt supply chains, thereby rendering businesses functionless. However, this pandemic demonstrated that organizations and businesses could stay relevant and be fully operational even in these uncertain times by adopting new technologies and refining the ones already in use. 'Necessity is the mother of all inventions,' and this pandemic proved to be the ultimate catalyst for digital transformation that will greatly accelerate several major trends that were already well underway before the pandemic (Banafa, 2020). The global lockdown has forced industries to adopt remote working, something that was already there but was never adopted on a larger scale. Work from home thereby helped in the large-scale adoption of cloud computing and virtualization. Predictive analytics driven by artificial intelligence (AI) and deep learning have also been refined in this COVID-19 era to promote e-commerce and online business. AI, virtual reality (VR), 3D printing, the Internet of Things (IoT), and cloud computing are some of the technologies that were always touted to disrupt the entire industrial scenario and hence were regarded as Industry 4.0 technologies. Despite this, in the pre-COVID-19 era, there were industries that were hesitant to adopt them on a large scale for their operations. However, in this pandemic era, there has been large-scale adoption of these technologies, and after COVID-19, this trend is likely to continue. In this chapter, we discuss the world economy post COVID-19 from a technological perspective that could benefit businesses.

Keywords: Cloud computing, deep learning, artificial intelligence, virtualization, virtual reality, 3D printing, Internet of Things, predictive analytics.

Introduction

The COVID-19 pandemic has left an everlasting mark in human history and has completely changed the lifestyles of people and business firms around the world. The pandemic has not only forced people to adopt newer norms, such as work from home (WFH) and maintaining hygiene, but has also made it obligatory for companies around the world to come up with new innovative ideas to continue their operations without disruption. The companies were made to rethink and restructure their entire business models in a really short duration to cope with the pandemic, and that required an agile backbone. Businesses around the globe embraced the challenge and redesigned their models by adopting new-age technologies and remaining agile in this ever-changing world. Technology is the backbone of all successful businesses, and some of the innovations that could kick-start the new era of human civilization post pandemic are artificial intelligence (AI), virtual reality (VR), 3D printing, cloud computing, (Figure 1) and the list could just keep getting longer. This article will touch upon some of these technologies and how they can change the shape of the world post pandemic.

Figure 1. Industry 4.0 technologies.
Note: Some niche technologies transforming businesses.

Artificial intelligence

AI is simply the simulation of the human brain that could be achieved by implementing various complex neural network algorithms. It gives machines and software the ability to think and make smart decisions on their own. Knowingly or unknowingly, we have been using AI for a very long time. The mobile assistive services, such as Siri and Google Assistant, on our smartphones are typical examples where AI is used; apart from this, AI also powers the chatbots used in various apps and websites. Surprisingly enough, AI also powers the search recommendations on Netflix and other streaming services. It is also a key force driving e-commerce platforms, such as Amazon and Flipkart, and is also powering autonomous vehicles, which could be a trend in the future.

In this current pandemic scenario, AI has been used in ways that were never thought of before. AI-powered cameras are used to identify whether a person is wearing a mask and maintaining a minimum physical distance. AI helps in developing vaccines and treatments at a much faster rate than usual and is also helpful for clinical trials during the development of vaccines (Vaishya *et al.*, 2020). This technology helps in developing predictive mathematical models that can analyze COVID-19 clusters (often referred to as COVID-19 hotspots) and, based on the data, forecast which areas could potentially be under threat of rising COVID-19 cases, so that preventive measures could be taken before the situation in that area goes out of control. This clearly illustrates the importance of AI in the medical sector in the present scenario. Work is in progress to enable AI bots to perform surgeries and operations, and a prototype robot named 'Da Vinci' already has a successful surgery under its belt. At this alarming pace, AI could not only perform surgeries but also other critical medical tasks with little or no human intervention. Companies such as Google and Uber have already begun testing AI-powered electric autonomous vehicles. With an attempt by countries around the world to bring pollution levels down, electric vehicles could possibly dominate the automobile sector by the next decade, and an autonomous version of these green vehicles could be the cherry on top. Some other areas where the role of AI could be expanded in a post-COVID-19 world are:

Operations and Supply Chain: AI has always played a major role in warehouse management, inward–outward material movement trackers, and inventory control, right from the turn of the new millennium. However, its share in this area is expected to increase by leaps and bounds in the post-COVID-19 era. AI and blockchain have the potential to create unprecedented visibility across the supply chain for all stakeholders, from manufacturers to distributors, retailers, and even end customers (Balakrishna, 2020). AI helps speed up logistics and fulfilment, thereby helping businesses.

Online Businesses and E-commerce: Customers' purchasing behaviours and patterns are likely to change post pandemic. In the past, at least before the outbreak of the pandemic, consumers preferred to buy products and necessary commodities by going to shopping malls and retail stores. E-commerce had its fair share of success in the pre-COVID-19 world; however, the global lockdown during the pandemic outbreak had forced people to do shopping completely online and even buy the smallest of things online. This was evident from the fact that Amazon's sales soared during the peak lockdown period. The e-commerce firm's sales surged 40% for the three months ending 30 June 2020 to $88.9 billion (£67.9 billion) (BBC News, 2020). AI and cloud computing are the backbone of any online business. AI helps predict consumer behaviour and buying patterns, thereby helping retailers fill up their stocks. With consumer behaviour changing after COVID-19, it is expected that AI will keep growing in importance in the retail and e-commerce sectors.

Banking Sector: AI helps in enhancing the security levels of the banking sector. Biometrics, such as fingerprint scan and iris scan, have already started replacing the traditional PIN and password approach to accessing confidential details. These biometrics (particularly the iris scanners) are classic examples of real-time gadgets in which the Internet of Things (IoT), AI, and cloud computing can all be integrated together. AI also helps banks with fraud detection through complex AI-powered encryption algorithms that are very difficult to crack. With paperless and contactless transactions being promoted during the COVID-19 lockdown, it becomes even more critical to safeguard the banking and transaction details of customers, and this is when AI-powered security features will get their time to shine. AI also helps in implementing 'know your customer' (KYC), which is a middle-office service, thereby providing a great cost-saving opportunity to banks. Banks, such as ICICI Bank and Citibank, have already started implementing AI in their mobile applications, and this trend of adoption of AI in the banking sector is likely to grow in the future as well, thereby fuelling the post-COVID-19 banking scenario across the world.

3D printing

3D printing has proven to be a game changer ever since the technology was adopted for the widespread manufacturing of commercial goods. 3D printing is an additive manufacturing technique for creating 3D objects (made of thermoplastic polymers that are durable) from a digital file. This digital file could be an AutoCAD or similar CAD file, which is used to design the object, and this design is then fed into a 3D printer to fabricate the object of the requisite shape and dimension. There are many 3D printing techniques, such as fused deposition modelling (FDM), stereolithography, and selective laser sintering (SLA). Each method has its own merits, demerits, and industrial use cases. The FDM method is easy to work with and is quite inexpensive; however, models made out of it lack detail and are not very fine. On the other hand, the SLA method can make 3D objects with great precision but, in turn, increases the manufacturing cost.

Today, 3D printers are used to make consumer goods, artificial organs, small yachts, aircraft engines, etc., and this is a never-ending list. 3D printing has its fair share of advantages over traditional subtractive manufacturing techniques, as it helps industries produce customizable goods in large volumes at a lower price, thereby creating a win-win scenario for both the customer and the industry. 3D printing also reduces the carbon footprint during manufacturing and improves productivity on shop floors.

During the COVID-19 pandemic, the medical sector fully harnessed the potential of this marvellous technology. The digital versatility and quick prototyping of 3D printing empower a swift mobilization of the technology and hence a rapid response to emergencies (Choong *et al.*, 2020). With the pandemic on the rise, there was a requirement to increase the production of necessary medical equipment, including PPE kits, face masks, testing kits, and other necessary medical accessories. However, with global supply chains disrupted, this was an uphill task. More and more manufacturers started adopting the technology to manufacture the necessary medical equipment.

The success story of 3D printing is not limited to the medical sector. Its ripple effects could be felt in other industries as well. With global supply chains fragmented and largely broken down due to the pandemic, manufacturing companies are increasingly adopting this technology to usher in a new era of manufacturing, with shortened and drastically simpler supply chain linkages. This technology will play an important role in boosting the economy after COVID-19.

Cloud computing

The on-demand delivery of computing resources (such as storage, memory, and processing) over the internet is called cloud computing. Knowingly or unknowingly, people around the world have been using the cloud for a long time. Google Drive, OneDrive, and other storage services that can be accessed via the internet are classic examples of cloud storage services. Mail services (e.g., Gmail and Outlook), online apps (e.g., Google apps, which include the likes of Google Sheets and Google Docs, and Office 365 online apps, such as MS Word Online), and many more are services provisioned to consumers via the cloud, and this type of service model is called 'software as a service' (SaaS) model, wherein software developed by the cloud provider is provisioned to customers on a pay-to-use basis. Apart from SaaS, there are two more cloud service models as well: infrastructure as a service (IaaS) and platform as a service (PaaS). In IaaS, the entire virtual machine (VM) is provisioned to customers, and they can decide on which operating system (OS) to use and which software to install. In simple words, in IaaS, the customer is in charge of the entire VM; however, it is important to note that the actual cloud infrastructure resides in the data centres of the service provider, and only VMs are provisioned to the user on a pay-to-use basis. In the PaaS model, the entire platform for development is provisioned to the users (generally, the developers). In this service model, the cloud infrastructure, just like in the other two service models, resides in the service provider's data centres, and the service provider takes care of the maintenance and security of the VMs. The service provider installs the OS and necessary software for development so that the developers and programmers can just focus on writing the codes and developing the software and not worry about the security and maintenance aspects of the VMs.

People and organizations alike have been leveraging the benefits offered by the cloud for a long time; however, a spike in cloud usage was reported during the COVID-19 lockdown. Cloud computing proved to be a lifeline for businesses during these unprecedented times. With remote working becoming the new norm in the IT industry, it was important to safeguard the sensitive data of clients. To ensure business continuity, the IT workforce was provided with laptops and desktops with preinstalled VMs (a use case of cloud computing) to enable safe remote working. Organizations increasingly adopted cloud computing during the pandemic and are now seeing its benefits over traditional methods. Cloud platforms can help deploy new digital customer experiences in days rather than months and can support analytics that would be uneconomical or simply impossible with traditional technology platforms (McKinsey, 2020). Cloud computing helped by providing greater flexibility, helping with faster deployment of apps, and reducing operational costs.

During the COVID-19 lockdown, the demand for streaming services grew exponentially. Streaming services provide multimedia content streamed over the internet using a cloud backbone. The leading content streaming service Netflix has added 10.1 million new paid subscribers as people stayed home, as the company reported net earnings of $720 million over $6.15 billion in revenue for its second quarter (the April–June 2020 period) (ET BrandEquity, 2020). With India under lockdown due to the pandemic, Google-owned YouTube saw a 20.5% surge in its subscriber base in the country (Business Standard, 2020). Social media platforms, such as Instagram, Facebook, and Snapchat, also reported an increase in their user base during the lockdown.

E-commerce applications (e.g., Amazon, Flipkart), banking applications, and various other mobile applications have a cloud-based backbone. After COVID-19, it is expected that the user base for these cloud applications will stay strong. As far as companies and businesses are concerned, it is highly unlikely that they will revert to their usual pre-COVID-19 operational ways. It is likely that a post-COVID-19 hybrid, i.e., a hybrid working model (which includes remote working for certain days in a week), could be adopted by companies if they find it sustainable for their business models.

Virtual reality

VR is a technology in which the user's perception of reality is completely based on virtual or digital information that creates a simulated virtual environment around the user that is very immersive. VR could be implemented using VR caves, VR holographic projectors, or VR helmets. This revolutionary technology is finding its use cases in areas such as gaming, education and research, virtual training and recruitment, and the travel industry. In the game console industry, VR technology is used by the likes of Sony's PlayStation, Nintendo, and Microsoft. The use of VR in the gaming industry creates a fully immersive gaming environment, which is something that is appreciated by game enthusiasts. These days, VR is used by athletes and sportspersons to create realistic simulations that help them iron out their weaknesses in an effective way. VR is finding its application in the military to prepare soldiers for a war-like situation by creating VR simulations. Another one of its uses includes treating post-traumatic stress disorder (PTSD) in soldiers who have returned from combat and need help adjusting to normal life situations; this is known as virtual reality exposure therapy (VRET) (FDM, 2020). The use of VR in the field of education is something that is highly appreciated by scientists, teachers, and students alike. Scientific studies have shown that students are likely to remember and grasp the concepts easily when they engage themselves in presentations and group discussions and take part in a simulated experience created by VR. Some use cases of VR in the field of education are as follows:

1. Google Expeditions is a VR app that could assist students in learning geography and help them visit different geographical places virtually.
2. VR apps, such as Unimersiv, help students go back in time and get a look and feel of ancient empires and cultures virtually. Such an enriching experience could be useful to make learners appreciate and remember historical events of great significance.
3. The Sites 3D VR app could help people and students see historical places and monuments in a manner as if they are physically present there. This is possible because of the immersive experience created by the VR app and the surround-sound system integrated with the app.

From the above discussion, it is clear that VR has applications in various fields. However, with the pandemic wreaking havoc, the adoption of this technology increased exponentially. With people stuck at their homes during lockdown, various clubs and organizations started leveraging the technology to help people socialize despite sitting in the comfort of their homes. The tourism and hospitality industries were hit hard during the pandemic. Nonetheless, the pandemic did not deter the aspirations of people to see new places thanks to the VR technology provisioned to them by companies using the technology. Startups such as Jaunt VR, YouVisit, and Berlin-based Inne.io leveraged the technology to provide virtual tourism. With the psychological health of children impacted due to COVID-19 restrictions and lockdown, more and more schools started using this technology to create a playful learning environment virtually without having to open the schools. Companies such as Microsoft, Google, and a few other start-ups provided financial and technical support to schools to acquire and use the technology.

The demand for VR technology grew during COVID-19, and with the demand likely to increase after the pandemic as well, it is expected that more companies will invest in the technology to serve the needs of their customers. Moreover, with an increase in competition, the prices of VR gear and equipment will go down. Currently, price is one of the constraints that prevents people from buying VR gear, but this scenario is likely to change post-COVID-19. Market competition and R&D could make VR gear cheaper and more affordable for the masses. VR has enormous potential in various fields, and with it, the possibilities are endless.

Conclusion

The COVID-19 pandemic has left a mark in human history, and it will be remembered for decades to come, not solely for the bad reasons, but also for the ways it has changed the lifestyles of people and forced businesses to change the way they operate by adopting niche technologies. Today, there is nothing like a 'non-tech' company, as every company across all business domains has been using or has started using technology to sail through the tough times. Industry 4.0 technologies, including AI, cloud computing, VR, and blockchain, have a great role to play in shaping the future of human civilization, and the massive adoption of these technologies has accelerated R&D efforts to improve these technologies even further. The pandemic may have hampered the growth trajectory for a brief moment, but it has shown our resilience to get past any difficult situation. 'Necessity is the mother of all inventions,' and the massive adoption of technology during these unprecedented times has justified this saying. The future of human civilization post pandemic is certainly bright, and a lot of credit has to go to the technologies and gadgets that have made our lives a lot simpler and will continue to do so in the future as well.

References

Balakrishna, D. R. (2020, August 18). The expanding role of AI in a post-covid world. AI Business. https://aibusiness.com/author.asp?section_id=796&doc_id=763264.

Banafa, A. (2020, June 8). 8 Key Tech Trends in a Post-COVID-19 World. OpenMindBBVA. https://www.bbvaopenmind.com/en/technology/digital-world/8-key-tech-trends-in-a-post-covid-19-world/.

BBC News. (2020, July 30). Amazon, Facebook and Apple thriving in lockdown. https://www.bbc.com/news/business-53602596.

Business Standard News. (2020, April 21). YouTube sees surge in subscriber base, views due to Covid-19 lockdown. https://www.business-standard.com/article/technology/youtube-sees-surge-in-subscriber-base-views-due-to-covid-19-lockdown-120042100710_1.html.

Choong, Y. Y. C., Tan, H. W., Patel, D. C., Choong, W. T. N., Chen, C.-H., Low, H. Y., Tan, M. J., Patel, C. D., and Chua, C. K. (2020, August 12). The global rise of 3D printing during the COVID-19 pandemic. *Nature Reviews Materials*, 5, 637–639. https://www.nature.com/articles/s41578-020-00234-3.

ETBrandEquity. (2020, July 17). Covid-19: Netflix adds 10 million new paid subscribers as people stay home. https://brandequity.economictimes.indiatimes.com/news/media/covid-19-netflix-adds-10-million-new-paid-subscribers-as-people-stay-home/77023929.

FDM. (2020, April 10). Exciting Uses for Virtual Reality. https://www.fdmgroup.com/5-exciting-uses-for-virtual-reality/.

Formlabs. (n.d.). Stereolithography (SLA) 3D Printing. Guide to Stereolithography (SLA) 3D Printing. https://formlabs.com/blog/ultimate-guide-to-stereolithography-sla-3d-printing/.

Fu, A. (2017). 7 Different Types of Cloud Computing Structures. Uniprint. https://www.uniprint.net/en/7-types-cloud-computing-structures/.

Huguen, P. (2018). What is VR? The devices and apps that turn real world virtual. *NBC News Mach*. https://www.nbcnews.com/mach/science/what-vr-devices-apps-turn-real-world-virtual-ncna857001.

McKinsey. (2020, July 21). Three actions CEOs can take to get value from cloud computing. *McKinsey Digital Quarterly*. https://www.mckinsey.com/business-functions/mckinsey-digital/our-insights/three-actions-ceos-can-take-to-get-value-from-cloud-computing.

Vaishya, R., Javaid, M., Kahn, I. H., and Haleem, A. (2020). Artificial intelligence (AI) applications for Covid-19 pandemic. *Diabetes & Metabolic Syndrome: Clinical Research & Reviews*. 17(3), 337–339. https://www.sciencedirect.com/science/article/pii/S1871402120300771.

© 2025 World Scientific Publishing Company
https://doi.org/10.1142/9789811292101_0031

Chapter 31

Agri-Tech Start-ups in India: Present Status and Future Scope in Reference to COVID-19

Supriya Singh* and Alka Lalhall†

*Department of Management Sciences,
Mahatma Gandhi Central University,
Motihari, Bihar, India*
*supiya_munnu13@rediffmail.com
†alkalahall12@gmail.com

Abstract

Start-ups play a key role in promoting innovation in a society. Agri-technology start-ups are offering sustainable solutions across the agricultural value chain. These start-ups, with their innovations, have come to the aid of stressed farmers and have given a significant impetus to the COVID-19-hit agricultural sector. A new wave of entrepreneurs and start-ups is leading the way in disrupting the agriculture sector in India for a better future. The time has come to enunciate agricultural strategies with innovations. In this regard, this chapter is a descriptive analysis and review of the status of agri-tech start-ups in India. The chapter aims to highlight the push agri-tech start-ups have rendered towards the agricultural ecosystem. Despite COVID-19, the agriculture sector of India has perseveringly marked growth in its GDP. This chapter deliberates the technological intervention brought about by agri-tech start-ups. It outlines the present status of agri-tech start-ups, focusing on their growth and sectorial presence. It also elaborates on the role of agri-tech start-ups in the survival of the agricultural sector during the COVID-19 pandemic. The opportunities brought about by these start-ups backed by government schemes and the challenges faced by them during and after the COVID-19 crisis are also outlined. The inferences from this study will be helpful in designing policy interventions for ensuring the sustainability of agri-tech start-ups during and after the pandemic.

Keywords: Start-ups, agri-tech start-ups, agri-start-ups, agribusiness, precision farming, geographic information systems, digital technology.

Introduction

The Indian agricultural sector has gone through a major transformation in recent years, from struggling for survival to becoming commercially viable. It has realized the status of self- sufficiency in production and has gradually become an export hub for food grains (Singh, 2019). Agriculture and allied activities are the mainstays of the Indian economy. It is viewed as one of the most significant contributors to economic growth and income generation in India (Himani, 2014; Pattanayak and Mallick, 2017). COVID-19 has impacted lives and livelihoods across the globe, and India is no exception. The prolonged lockdown with severe restrictions disrupted supply chains in almost all major sectors and deterred economic growth. Agriculture and allied activities, however, emerged as the only hope with 3.4% GDP growth (Economic Survey, 2020). As per the National Statistical Office (NSO), the GDP growth in agriculture increased from 2.4% in the financial year 2019 to 4% in the financial year 2020 (Dev and Sengupta, 2020).

The current crisis has been an eye-opener to several opportunities arising in different sectors. During lockdown, agriculture has already demonstrated its potential to revive the pandemic-hit economy through different types of innovations and reforms. There is remarkable development in every sector of agriculture due to the presence of productive and updated technologies. Agri-start-ups are emerging as one of the major technology-based innovations in the field of Indian agriculture. As a result of this, young and budding entrepreneurs in the country are engaging in technology-driven agri-start-ups. These agri-start-ups are predicted to account for a significant increase in employment opportunities (Sharma, 2019). Agri-start-ups are the key reason for innovation-based development in the agriculture and agribusiness sectors. Agri-tech is the use of modern technologies and their application to the agricultural sector. It aims at enhancing production and revenue efficiently by making use of any applications, practices, products, and/or services that enhance any aspect of the agricultural process, be it an input function or the output received (Anand and Raj, 2019).

Agri-tech start-ups during the COVID-19 pandemic have accelerated the growth of the rural economy. According to a report by NASSCOM (2019), there was an annual growth of 25% in start-ups, amounting to 450 agri-tech start-ups in the country. In the financial year 2019, $29.8 crore ($298 million) was generated from agri-tech start-ups, which was more than 300% in comparison to last year (Sharma, 2019). Acknowledging the potential of impetus given by agri-tech start-ups to agriculture, the Government of India has been focussing on initiating various policies related to finance and technology to promote and support these agri-start-ups in the country. The aftershocks from this pandemic need great government support, which also demands synergetic integration between industry, banks, and government agencies (OECD, 2020). The Government of India, with its start-up-friendly policy, has backed up incubator ecosystems over the past several years to promote an entrepreneurship ecosystem in the country.

This chapter highlights the importance and growth of agri-tech start-ups. Globally, COVID-19 has shaken up the world economy, and this crisis has left countries gasping for immediate solutions for their economy. In this backdrop, this study aims to shed some light on agri-tech start-ups that are working tediously in changing the face of Indian agriculture by providing farmers with low-cost farming solutions; connecting farmers to market accessibility, which is one of the biggest problems faced by them; equipping farmers with the right tools to grade, assort, and even transport their produce; and empowering farmers and ensuring that they receive a remunerative price for their produce. This chapter also deliberates on the agri-tech subsectors in the Indian start-up ecosystem, such as big data analytics, supply chain/market-linked models, FaaS, and IoT-enabled, engineering-led innovations. We focus on the constraints and opportunities for new start-ups in agriculture development in India. The specific objectives of the study are to elaborate on the role of agri-start-ups in the current scenario (COVID-19) with already available innovative technologies, to know the strategies adopted by start-ups for survival and sustainability, and also to identify the role of the government's financial support during the COVID-19 crisis.

Agri-Tech Start-ups: Present Status

Starting with the onset of the internet era in 1995 in India, the start-up ecosystem gained pace. The incorporation of Technology Development and Information Company of India in 1988 marked the beginning of a new era of technology-driven start-ups. Over the past decades, a number of product start-ups and now service start-ups have emerged. Until July 2020, more than 34,000 start-ups were registered with the Department of Promotion of Industry and Internal Trade. Currently, only about 6,400 start-ups are funded (IVCA, 2020). It is estimated that there are close to 1,100 agri-start-ups and another 800 or more food and beverage start-ups in India. An upsurge in internet usage, increase in smartphone penetration, the emergence of start-ups, and various government initiatives in rural areas are facilitating technology adoption in the farm sector (Ganguly, 2018). The rural start-up ecosystem needs to be strengthened and facilitated by the government by including it in rural development programmes.

Many agri-tech start-ups in India are mainly in the marketplace segment, where e-commerce companies provide fresh and organic fruits and vegetables procured directly from farmers. Over the past years, many start-ups have come up with the aim of providing innovative and sustainable solutions for farmers' problems. Start-ups have provided solutions such as biogas plants, solar-powered cold storage, fencing and water pumping, weather prediction, spraying machines, seed drills, and vertical farming, thereby enabling farmers to engage in precision farming (Sachitanand, 2018). Agri-techs have the potential to address several challenges faced by the sector and, subsequently, change the face of Indian agriculture. Technology intervention has been specifically beneficial to agricultural value chains. Although technology solutions for most issues in agriculture are available, the challenge is for the solutions to reach every farmer on a larger scale, and agri-tech caters to this specific problem.

Agri-Tech Start-ups and COVID-19

Agri-start-ups have played a critical role in combating the economic fallout of COVID-19. They need to be made ready to adjust and adapt to a new normal with better cash flow management and revenue streams. However, the challenges and opportunities for agri-start-ups due to COVID-19 are yet to be understood. Start-ups in their seed phase are the most vulnerable because they usually arrange funds from personal investors, friends, and banks, given that institutional funding agencies are not ready to invest (Kessler, 2020). These start-ups are likely to be affected adversely and deserve special attention, as they are in a sensitive and fragile stage of their business lifecycle (Baker *et al.*, 2020). Even with the resilient crisis-management strategies that start-ups are adopting at individual levels, better coping mechanisms and government-initiated policy frameworks to redesign, rework, or reinvent the technologies and protocols in a post-COVID-19 scenario are required, thereby creating the paradigm for a new normal within a minimum response time. However, empirical understanding of the functioning and challenges of agri-start-ups is virtually absent in India.

Sectoral Presence of Agri-Tech Start-ups in India

India has made a strong name for itself in the global startup community. India ranks among the top five countries in the world in terms of the number of start-ups founded. Every ninth agri- tech start up in the world is from India. Start-ups are providing the missing link in the agri value chain and delivering efficient products, technologies, and services to farmers. In a bid to double farmers' income by 2022, the Government of India is continuously looking for ways to boost agricultural production, food processing, and marketing avenues through the integration of the latest technologies and innovations, thus creating a huge scope for food and agri-tech start-ups in the country (Balaji, 2018). Start-ups working on farm automation, weather forecasting, drone use, online vegetable marketing, smart poultry and dairy ventures, and other technology-driven, powerful solutions are set to revolutionize the agriculture sector (Chauhan, 2020).

It is estimated that India houses 7,200–7,700 start-ups, creating more than 85,000 employment opportunities. Start-ups in India were projected to grow to more than 11,500 by 2020, with job creation from these entrepreneurs reaching 250,000–300,000 by 2020 (NASSCOM, 2018; FICCI, 2018). Agriculture is one of the important pillars of the Indian economy. According to a report from FICCI (2018), about 54% of the Indian population depends directly on agriculture, and it accounts for around 17.3% of GDP. Although agriculture in India has majorly seen a steady growth in the past few years, not much has been done to encourage young, fresh, and unique innovative ideas in the sector. It was only in 2007 that the era of start-ups saw a boost and things started to change. Young entrepreneurs are now quitting their jobs in the IT sector and MNCs to establish their own start-ups. These young entrepreneurs are now beginning to realize that investing in agriculture is one of the very few safe and profitable businesses (MahyCo, 2018). Agriculture is a crucial sector of our economy, and the demand for agricultural products is never expected to reduce. There is a new wave of budding entrepreneurs and emerging start-ups in the country that are leading the way in disrupting the agriculture sector in the country and setting a new innovative technological ecosystem. They want to deploy technology in this sector and bring about reforms in the sector. Agri-tech start-ups globally are prevalent in agricultural biotechnology, online farm-to-consumer, farm management software, sensing and IoT, robotics, mechanization equipment, novel farming systems, food safety, traceability, etc. (Saiz-Rubio and MásOrcID, 2020). In 2016, global agri-tech investment stood at $3.23 billion. India has continued to retain its position among the top six countries in the world, with the highest number of deals in agricultural technology. Indian agri-tech start-up firms contributed around 9% of global investment, or approximately $313 million, which was raised by 53 start-ups in 2016. This increased to $10.1 billion in 2017, spanning 994 deals from 1,487 investors, marking a 29% year-on-year (YoY) growth. Out of this, $2.6 billion went into agri-tech alone (Pahwa, 2020). Nationally, the focus of agri-tech start-ups hovers around certain key subsectors, which are listed in Table 1.

Table 1. Key subsectors for agri-start-ups.

Subsectors	Key areas for start-ups
Supply chain	• E-distributor • Listing platform • Marketplace
Infrastructure	• Growing systems & components • Aquaponics • Hydroponics • Drip irrigation
Finance	• Payments • Revenue sharing • Lending
Farm data and analytics	• Integrated platform • Remote sensing • Software platforms • Farm mapping • Farm management solution • Field operations
Information platform	• Information dissemination

Increasing Number of Agri-Tech Start-ups

Many agri-tech start-ups in India have come up in the past few years to address the problems of Indian agriculture, such as supply chain management, the use of outdated equipment, and improper infrastructure.

These agri-tech start-ups have the potential to change the face of the Indian agriculture sector and eventually raise farmers' incomes. According to NAASCOM, a total of 366 agri-based start-ups have come up from 2013 to 2017. The perusal of the data presented in Figure 1 revealed that the year 2015 saw the maximum number of start-ups (117) getting started. It was followed by 2016, which also presented a good number of start-ups (109) getting started to answer the concerns associated with Indian agriculture. It is to be noted that more than 50% of the start-ups got started in 2015 and 2016.

With more than 350 agri-tech start-ups in India, many are now targeting breakeven point as investors show continuous interest in further rounds of funding. According to NASSCOM, more than half (59%) of the investor funding rounds that took place from 2013 to 2017 were focussed on number of 38 start-ups in seed stage. It was followed by early-stage start-ups, which occupied 32% of the investor funding rounds. A small percentage of 9% of the funding rounds was covered by the start-ups in the growth stage. It was concluded that more than 90% of funding was focused on seed-stage and early-stage start-ups, which increases focus on quality and scaling up.

Key Indian States Focusing on Agri-Tech Start-ups

Looking at the geographical distribution, Karnataka and Maharashtra together account for almost 50% of the total agri-tech start-ups opened in

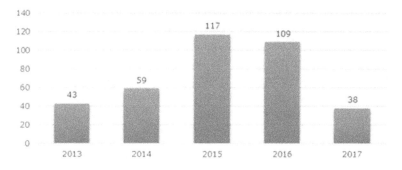

Figure 1. Number of agritech startups (2013–2017).
Source: Traxcn Data; NASSCOM, 2018.

2013–2017. As we have learned earlier from the analysis of the Indian start-up ecosystem, Bengaluru (Karnataka) is one of the established start-up ecosystem hubs in India, along with Mumbai and Delhi & NCR.

Opportunities for Agri-Tech Start-ups

Agri-tech start-ups are also leveraging technology in market linkages, such as retail, B2C and B2B marketplaces, and digital agronomy platforms. Agri-tech start-ups were able to address the input challenges of agriculture in India from the very beginning. They are also a source of correct information, techniques, and efficiencies for farmers, both for pre-harvest applications and post-harvest use cases (Modgil, 2017). The government has already initiated attractive incentive offers, including easy loans, insurance schemes, and tax benefits for farmers-cum-entrepreneurs. Developing entrepreneurs in agriculture can immensely benefit the Indian economy by reducing the burden on agriculture, generating employment opportunities for rural youth, reducing the need for migration from rural to urban areas, thereby reducing pressure on urban cities, and increasing individual and national incomes. They are empowering farmers by providing correct and timely information, techniques, and efficiencies to farmers both for pre- and post-harvest applications.

Indian agriculture has the potential to be a global export hub. Although the pandemic has caused a decrease of 27.7% in the export of major agri-products from India, there are unseen opportunities lying within this sector, as India is the second-largest global producer (Economic Survey, 2020). The recent European Union's decision to ease the rules for the import of fruits and vegetables from India is very encouraging. According to a market intelligence report by APEDA, many countries, including Iran, Russia, Afghanistan, Egypt, the Philippines, and Indonesia, have placed fresh orders for export commodities such as Indian black tea, fruits and vegetables, rice, and wheat, which indicates the magnitude of opportunities available for agri-start-ups in the international market. However, to ease the export process, there is still a need for robust infrastructural support, stringent quality control measures, and other reforms, such as single-window clearance, which will be beneficial for global outreach and facilitate the business environment for agri-start-ups in the international market. Some innovative agripreneurs have embraced value-added agri-products by providing agri-tech services, the rental business of farm equipment, agri/eco-tourism, processed forest-based products, and organic products, which have added significantly higher entrepreneurial income for agripreneurs (Iyer, 2020).

Opportunities in Food-Tech Agri-Start-ups

B2C food-tech is targeted at consumers and may concern plant-based (meatless) meals, novel distribution systems, or nutrition-based tech. Industrial food tech is a subsegment of food tech that focuses on addressing the fundamental business models and B2B pain points within the food industry. The related companies include innovators in novel processing and packaging technology and new/functional ingredients that have improved nutritional, labelling, or formulation characteristics (Table 2).

Some of the key accelerators and incubators for the agri-tech sector in India are listed in Table 3.

Table 2. Food-tech and agri-tech business opportunities.

Typology	Characteristics
Ag(ri)-tech start-ups are disrupting agriculture. They come up with solutions to improve farming output and quality using drones, sensors, and farm management software.	Farm management software Start-ups are assisting farmers in managing, organizing, and optimizing all the tasks on their farms. Drones & Robots Start-ups provide farmers with robots and drones. These tools are used to collect data or directly to perform human tasks. Urban and Novel Farms Start-ups developing urban farms to reduce the distance between production and consumption or developing new-generation farms to increase yields, quality, and sustainability.
Ag(ri)-tech is also about new farm products, next-generation farms, and urban farming	Agriculture Marketplaces Start-ups working on B2B e-commerce marketplaces for farmers (with products ranging from seeds to equipment.) Ag-Biotech Research and development-oriented start-ups with a focus on living systems and organisms for agriculture and food. Precision Farming Precision agriculture, satellite farming, or site-specific crop management is a farming management concept based on observing, measuring, and responding to inter- and intra-field variability in crops.
Food-science start-ups develop new food products,	Future Foods Start-ups working on breakthrough food products, mostly to replace those currently in use with more sustainable and healthier alternatives.

(Continued)

Table 2. (*Continued*)

Typology	Characteristics
answering the need for more transparency, health, and environmental concerns. Products range from market innovations to radical disruptions using revolutionary ingredients.	**Meal Substitutes** Start-ups reinvent the meal. Their bars, drinks, or powders replace the traditional meal with highly nutritious alternatives. **Packaging** Start-ups develop smarter and more sustainable food and beverage packaging. **Product Innovation** Start-ups work on already well-established ingredients on the market (such as chocolate or baby food). The innovation is either in the product itself, the transparency of its composition, the means of distribution, or greater customization of the products. **Drinks** Start-ups work on new forms of drinks, to promote new ingredients, or a healthier lifestyle. **Appliances and Cookware** Start-ups develop a new generation of appliances or cookware. They provide improved technology, new distribution channels, or more personalization.

Table 3. Some key accelerators and incubators for the agri-tech sector.

AGRI UDAAN	AGRI UDAAN is India's first food & agribusiness accelerator organized by NAARM, a-IDEA, IIM-A, and CIIE in partnership with Caspian Impact Investment and supported by DST. The programme focuses on catalyzing the scale-up stage of food & agribusiness start-ups through rigorous mentoring, industry networking, and investor pitching. The impact of AGRI UDAAN includes 200 agribusiness start-ups applying for the accelerator program, 40 start-ups being mentored, end-to-end capacity building for 8 start-ups in their value chain, and 3 out of 8 start-ups mentored receiving a total of funding worth Rs. ~2.5 crore. Focus areas include sustainable inputs, precision/smart agriculture, innovative food technology, and supply chain technology. Some shortlisted incubatees from this cohort are Gen Agritech, Delmos Research Pvt Ltd, Agricx, Intello Labs, Smoodies, Jivabhumi, Yukti Harvest, RF Wave technologies, Odaku, Growyi, etc.

Table 3. (*Continued*)

Centre for Innovation Incubation and Entrepreneurship (CIIE)	CIIE is a collective of interventions in the space of innovation-driven entrepreneurship in India. It has its genesis at the Centre for Innovation Incubation and Entrepreneurship ('Centre'), IIM Ahmedabad — an academic centre focussed on research in innovation and entrepreneurship. CIIE continues to support the research and learning undertaken by the Centre. The impact of CIIE includes 500 ventures trained, incubated, or accelerated, 3,000 jobs generated, 100 start-ups seed-funded, and many more. It has launched a food and agribusiness accelerator in partnership with a-IDEA — the business incubator at the National Academy of Agricultural Research Management (NAARM).
a-IDEA (Association for Innovation Development of Entrepreneurship in Agriculture)	a-IDEA is a technology business incubator (TBI) hosted by ICAR — National Academy of Agricultural Research Management, Hyderabad (ICAR-NAARM) and the Department of Science & Technology, Govt. of India (DST, GOI). a-IDEA has been housed at the Centre for Agri-Innovation at ICAR-NAARM to foster innovation and entrepreneurship in agriculture in India. a-IDEA aims to help entrepreneurs ideate, incubate, and accelerate their innovative early-stage start-ups that are scalable to become competitive food and agri-business ventures through capacity building, mentoring, networking, and advisory support.
International Crops Research Institute for the Semi-Arid Tropics (ICRISAT)	In December 2002, the International Crops Research Institute for the Semi-Arid Tropics (ICRISAT), a non-profit organization, joined forces with DST, an Indian government agency, to develop an agribusiness incubator (ABI) at ICRISAT. The incubator is supported by DST's National Science and Technology Entrepreneurship Development Board, which promotes the development and commercialization of indigenous technologies by providing financial assistance through public–private partnerships. ICRISAT launched the Innovation Hub (iHub) to support agri-tech entrepreneurs, scientists, and technology experts, so that they can collaborate to innovate cutting-edge ideas across the whole agriculture value chain.
T-Hub	T-Hub is a unique public–private partnership between the government of Telangana, three academic institutes, IIIT-H, ISB, and the National Law University, Nalsar, and key private sector leaders. These entities have come together with a clear

(*Continued*)

Table 3. (Continued)	
	vision to create an innovation ecosystem centred around Hyderabad, leveraging the city's traditional strengths in technology, education, and entrepreneurship, as well as its position as a preferred destination for multiple national and international businesses across sectors. T-Hub is designed to support technology-related start-ups, and its mission is to catalyze the creation of one of the tightest and most vibrant entrepreneur communities in the world in order to encourage and fuel more start-up success stories in India.
Agri-Tech Start-up Accelerator CIE, Hyderabad	IIIT-Hyderabad and the National Institute of Agricultural Extension Management (MANAGE) have signed an MOU to start an agri-tech start-up accelerator programme. This programme will identify, support, and facilitate idea-stage enterprises using the latest technologies and innovations to solve agriculture-specific issues faced in India.

Source: NASSCOM (2018b) and FICCI (2018).

Post-COVID-19 Government Initiatives

The Government of India decided to boost and strengthen the start-up ecosystem in the country and help India become a nation of job creators rather than job seekers during the current economic crisis. The government, through various initiatives and policies, aims to empower start-ups to grow through innovation and design and to accelerate the spread of the start-up movement. According to the Ministry of Agriculture and Farmer's Welfare, there have been 234 more start-ups in the agriculture and allied sectors with a sum of Rs. 24.58 crore under a central scheme funded in the past fiscal year. The government is promoting innovation and agripreneurship by providing financial support and nurturing the incubation ecosystem under the Rashtriya Krishi Vikas Yojana — Remunerative Approaches for Agriculture and Allied Sectors Rejuvenation (RKVY-RAFTAAR). A total of 346 start-ups in the agriculture and allied sectors are being funded with a sum of Rs. 36.71 crore in this phase. These agri-start-up entrepreneurs are being trained for two months at 29 Agri-Business Incubation (ABI) centres across India, thus addressing agripreneurship, income generation, and unemployment in rural ecosystems.

Policy intervention by the Government of India

PM Modi's government has set an aim to double the average farmer's income by 2022. With 157.35 million hectares, India holds the second-largest agricultural land area in the world. There is a huge investment opportunity in agricultural infrastructure, such as irrigation facilities, warehousing, and cold storage (Balaji, 2018). New schemes, such as Paramparagat Krishi Vikas Yojana, Pradhanmantri Gram Sinchai Yojana, and Sansad Adarsh Gram Yojana, have been initiated with a view to elevating the status of the farmers (Table 4). There is a huge marketing

Table 4. Government interventions for agri-start-ups and the agribusiness sector in India.

Government interventions	Objectives
Pradhan Mantri Fasal Bima Yojana (PMFB)	The Pradhan Mantri Fasal Bima Yogana was introduced on 14 January 2016 with a aim of reducing agricultural distress and farmers' welfare. This scheme provides financial support to farmers for crop losses. It covers rabi, kharif, horticultural, and commercial crops. 'Farm Guide' is a data-driven tech start-up's attempt to bring all stakeholders in agriculture on to a digital platform, thus working towards achieving PMFB in India.
Paramparagat Krishi Vikas Yojana (PKVY)	It is a traditional farming improvement programme launched in April 2015 to support and promote organic farming and improve soil health. This scheme encourages farmers to adopt eco-friendly concepts of cultivation and reduce their reliance on fertilizers and agricultural chemicals to increase yields.
Zero Budget Natural farming (ZBNF)	It is a set of farming methods and also a grassroots peasant movement. This scheme was announced by the current Finance Minister Nirmala Sitharaman to reduce the costs of production for farmers and thereby double their incomes. The word 'budget' refers to credit and expenses; thus, the term 'zero budget' means not using any credit and not spending any money on inputs. 'Natural farming' means farming with natural materials and without chemicals.
Startup India	Start-up India is an initiative of the Government of India. The campaign was first announced by the Indian Prime Minister, Narendra Modi, during his speech on 15 August 2015. Through this initiative, the government plans to empower start-up ventures to boost entrepreneurship, economic growth, and employment across India.

(*Continued*)

Table 4. (*Continued*)

Government interventions	Objectives
Atal Innovation Mission	Atal Innovation Mission (AIM) is Government of India's flagship initiative launched in 2016 to create and promote a culture of innovation and entrepreneurship across the length and breadth of the country.
Make in India	Make in India is an initiative launched in 2014 by the Government of India to encourage companies to manufacture in India and incentivize dedicated investments in manufacturing.
Digital India	Digital India is a campaign launched by the Government of India in 2015 in order to ensure that the government's services are made available to citizens electronically through improved online infrastructure, and by increasing internet connectivity, or making the country digitally empowered in the field of technology.

opportunity in the organized marketing structure for agro produce, facilities for transportation and storage, microfinance, and the marketing of superior technology to give timely information to farmers and agripreneurs. India houses 7200–7700 start-ups, creating more than 85,000 employment opportunities. In the year 2017, $53 million was poured into agri-tech start-ups through more than 17 deals. Agri-tech start-ups are bringing innovation into the farming space in areas such as storage, improving the supply chain, quality seed procurement, increased production logistics, and distribution (Nair, 2018). Indian agri-tech start-ups have received 300% more funding in the first six months of 2019 than the total funding received in 2018. Agri-tech companies raised $248 million until June 2019, which was only $73 million in 2018, according to NASSCOM. 'Farmers and Agritech start-ups in India have evolved rapidly over the past few years due to digital penetration and funding, majorly driving the growth in this sector,' says the report. New areas in the agri-tech sector, such as market linkage, digital agriculture, better access to inputs, farming as a service (FaaS), and financing, are attracting more and more stakeholders to connect with this new trend in agriculture. Indian agri-tech companies are also focussing on Southeast Asia, Europe, Africa, and South America (Sharma, 2019). Multiple enabling policies have been implemented to support start-ups, their early take-off, and successful operations (Startup India, 2019). Start-up India, Atal Innovation Mission, New Generation Innovation and Entrepreneurship Development Centre, Make in India, and Digital India are some of the flagship programmes of the Government of India aimed at creating and supporting the start-up ecosystem in the country. The on-ground impact and intervention of these schemes could be empirically tested by future research.

Challenges for Agri-Start-ups Ecosystem in India

Dutia (2014), in his article on challenges and opportunities for agri-tech start-ups, elaborated on the following challenges:

1. **Small and fragmented landholding size:** Small landholdings by farmers don't allow mechanization of their farms to be cost-effective.
2. **Returns for the investors:** Agri-tech is a long-term business which requires patience from investors before generating returns.
3. **Talent retention:** Agri-tech start-ups and enterprises are finding it hard to retain technical talent working in this sector.
4. **Long gestation period:** Farmers as well as small investors will take time to develop full trust in agri-tech technologies, which might affect investors' interest.
5. **Technology affordability:** Farmers' incomes are still a concern in major parts of India, making it hard for them to afford agriculture technologies.
6. **Economic slowdown due to pandemic:** One of the major challenges is the ongoing economic crisis, as this has impacted several start-ups in their early stages. COVID-19 has had devastating effects on the survival and sustainability of agri-start-ups because of a sudden erosion of value. There are only a few start-ups that would be able to survive if this current crisis continues beyond six months to a year. However, there are many start-ups that are trying to sail through this crisis by adopting measures such as reducing their staff strength, minimizing operational costs, postponing new market entries, modifying technologies as per current needs, and reducing working hours.
7. **Skill adaptability:** Making farmers adapt to the required skills for working on these technologies requires a lot of effort.

8. **Acquisition of agri-tech companies:** In India, there are a very few agri-tech start-ups, which are being acquired by large businesses and thus hindering them from scaling up their levels. Global success stories, such as Blue River and Climate Crop, were acquired by John Degree and Monsanto, respectively.

Way Forward

Agripreneurship and thrust for agri-tech start-ups are the need of the hour for the Indian economy. COVID-19 has had devastating effects on the survival and sustainability of almost all sectors, but the one sector that has been doing unexpectedly well in the country is agriculture. The reports of the Economic Survey (2020) have highlighted a contraction of 23.9% in the national GDP for the quarter ending in June 2020; however, optimistically, agriculture has been the only sector to have recorded growth. The recent RBI estimates indicated that the agriculture sector in 2019–2020 recorded a real GVA growth of 4%t due to record food grain production, which has accounted for 15.2% of the economic growth, and this is a new record for the agriculture sector in India. The current crisis offers a great opportunity for agricultural transformation with enablers such as agri-start-ups, academia, corporates, and government collaboration through smart incentives and easy regulation.

The agri-start-up ecosystem can be seen as a ray of hope for the Indian economy amidst this global crisis. These start-ups are growing at a fast pace, providing innovative technological solutions, and creating employment opportunities. The government needs to develop targeted policies and procedures, thereby creating investment opportunities. Further, there needs to be a push towards establishing end-to-end programmes, from piloting to developing business consortia, providing holistic research and development solutions, and leveraging networks and innovation support schemes with a shift towards a knowledge- and innovation-based economy. The government can provide capital access and market access support through the creation of separate fast-tracked agri-start-up funds, easy term loans/debt funding, or collateral-free loans to replenish their working capital, and assets to unlock the potential of start-ups at this crucial juncture. India currently shelters more than 450 agri-tech start-ups, and the sector is growing at a rate of 25% YoY. Digital transformation and the start-up ecosystem are playing a vital role for bringing new innovation to this sector. In the past five years, more than five global agri-tech companies have started in India, and many agri-start-ups are focusing specifically on market linkage, digital agriculture, better access to inputs, and financing; these technological mechanisms are enabling local farmers to become sustainable and profit-yielding agripreneurs. Overall, the COVID-19 pandemic has negatively impacted the majority of sectors, while agriculture and its allied sectors have experienced renewed thrust, as they remain the backbone of the Indian economy. The revival of the pandemic-hit Indian economy is being shouldered by these agri-tech start-ups. They are effectively and continuously headed towards realizing the objectives of a self-reliant India and the vision of '*Aatma Nirbhar Bharat*.'

References

Aishwarya Chauhan, N. S. (2020). Agro entrepreneurship. *Kurushetra*, 56–60.
Anandaraja, N., Sivabalan, K. C., and Lalson, M. T. (2019). Changing scenarios and career ambitions of Agricos: A Study from Kerala state, India. *Labour*, 5, 07–81.
Anand, A., and Raj, S. (2019). Agritech Start-ups: A Ray of Hope in Indian Agriculture. National Institute of Agricultural Extension Management (MANAGE), Hyderabad.
Ayyappan, S., Kataktalware, M. A., and Letha Devi, G. (2019). Agri Start-ups for Smart Farming.
Baker, S., Bloom, N., Davis, S., Terry, S., Baldwin, R., di Mauro, B. W., Pugsley, B. *et al.* (2020). Start-ups and Employment Following the COVID-19 Pandemic: A Calculator. https://voxeu.org/article/startup-employment-calculator-covid-19.
Baruah, S. B., Dutta, A., and Guha, R. (2020). COVID-19: Implications of entrepreneurship in North-East India. *AMC Indian Journal of Entrepreneurship*, 3(4), 34–45.
Bhooshan, N., and Kumar, A. (2020). How did agri-start-ups fare during the COVID-19 pandemic? *Economic & Political Weekly*, 55(50), 13.
Deshmukh, S., and Raj, S. (2021). Dawn of the AgriStart-ups in India.
Dev, S. M., and Sengupta, R. (2020). Impact of Covid-19 on the Indian Economy: An Interim Assessment. Indira Gandhi Institute of Development Research, Mumbai.
Dutia, S. G. (2014). AgTech challenges and opportunities for sustainable growth. 9(12), 161–193.
Gupta, S. K., Kumar, R., Limbalkar, O. M., Palaparthi, D., and Divte, P. R. (2019). Drones for future agriculture. *Agriculture & Food: e-Newsletter*, 16.

Himani. (2014). An analysis of agriculture sector in Indian economy. *Journal of Humanities and Social Science*, 19(1), 47–54.

Iyer, D. A. (2020). New horizons of agri-entrepreneurship and agro MSMEs. *Kurushetra*, 70–74.

Jennifer, B. (2020). Assessment of COVID-19's Impact on Small and Medium-sized Enterprises: Implications from China. Testimony, 10 March, 2020.

Kessler, B. (2020). COVID-19 Impact: MostVulnerable Are Start-ups in the Early Phase (seed). Startup Spider, 18 March. https://www.start-upspider.com/assets/files/EN_Tips&Tricks4Start-ups_COVID19_StartupImpact.pdf.

Mittal, R., and Singh, S. R. (2019). Agri incubation centre's: A new way of agripreneurship development. *Annals of Horticulture*, 12(2), 126–129.

Mani, M., Sheera, V. P., and Narwal, K. P. Incubation through agri-business. *Business Management and Social Innovations*, 191.

Maurya, V. K. (2020). Agri-export start-ups: Changing the career of Indian agriculture. *Biotica Research Today*, 2(12), 1295–1297.

Modgil, S. (2017, December 29). Startup Watchlist: 12 Indian Agritech Start-ups To Watch Out For In 2018. Retrieved from https://inc42.com/features/watchlist-agritech-start-ups-2018/.

oecd.org. (2020). A systemic resilience approach to dealing with Covid-19 and future shocks. OECD.

Pahwa, A. (2020, September 8). How agritech start-ups are changing the face of Indian agriculture. Retrieved from EY.com: https://www.ey.com/en_in/start-ups/how-agritech-start-ups-are-changing-the-face-of-indian-agriculture.

Pattanayak, U., and Mallick, M. (2017). Agricultural Production and Economic Growth in India: An Econometric Analysis. Research Gate Publication, V(3). Retrieved from https://www.researchgate.net/publication/330213062_Agricultural_Production_and_Economic_Growth_in_India_An_Econometric_Analysis.

Saiz-Rubio, V., and MásOrcID, F. R. (2020). From Smart Farming towards Agriculture 5.0. Agronomy.

Sah, V. A Study on Agri Start-Ups in India.

Sharma, S. (2019, August 26). Indian agritech start-ups to generate 90 lakh jobs, see 300% increase in funding. Retrieved March 2020, from Financial Express: https://www.financialexpress.com/industry/sme/indian-agritech-start-ups-to-generate-90-lakh-jobs-see-300-increase-in-funding/1686336/.

Singh, R. B. (2019). Agricultural Transformation — A Roadmap to New India. National Academy of Agricultural Sciences New Delhi, New Delhi.

Srinivas, K., Gerard, M., Singh, V., Gupta, M., Soam, S. K., Arunachalam, A., and Datt, S. (2018). AGRIM Agri-Start-ups: Reflection of ICAR Technologies in Market.

Swarnam, T. P., and Velmurugan, A. (2020). Prospects for entrepreneurship development in integrated farming systems: Island perspective. *Journal of the Andaman Science Association*, 25(1), 9–14.

Index

A

adaptability, 63, 242–244, 332, 340, 342–345, 347–348, 350, 475
adaptation, 56, 81, 83, 120, 127, 139–141, 143, 145, 147, 149, 151, 153, 155, 157, 159, 161, 277, 344–345, 350
agility, 83–84, 111, 155, 254, 260, 264, 273, 289

B

banking, 80, 152, 426–432, 434–436, 439–444, 447, 449, 454–455, 457
bibliometric, 257, 291, 308–314
Bihar, 213, 369–372, 374–377, 380, 396, 410, 461

C

childcare, 361–363, 365–367
children, 19–20, 130, 155, 181, 316, 320, 328, 345, 361, 365, 367, 397, 459
China, 2, 18, 20, 25, 42, 96, 99, 101, 112, 116, 118, 130, 138–140, 158, 161, 164, 172, 287–288, 301, 310, 478

cluster, 90–91, 93–94, 144, 158, 160, 287–314, 374, 453
covid, 1–9, 11, 13, 15–21, 23–29, 33, 35–39, 41–49, 51, 53, 55–56, 58, 63–64, 67–77, 79–80, 83–85, 87–109, 111–404
cultural, 20, 47, 49, 57, 64, 80, 94, 116, 175, 209, 256, 277, 332, 334–335, 346, 348–349, 351, 369, 375–376, 443, 461–465, 471–473, 476–478

E

ecosystem, 120, 122, 124, 264, 302, 310, 373, 413–416, 461, 463–464, 468, 472, 475–476
educational, 99, 149, 154, 231, 272, 309, 318, 361–362, 364, 367, 377, 419
effective, 6, 49, 56–58, 61, 65, 100, 106, 122, 127, 129–130, 132–133, 135–137, 150, 152, 202, 204, 210, 217, 223–236, 241–242, 251, 256, 282, 285, 289–290, 333, 335–336, 346, 348–349, 358, 362, 366, 381, 389, 395, 413, 418–419, 448, 458, 475, 477

emerging, 24, 29, 36, 68, 76, 104–105, 122, 124, 157–158, 160–161, 166, 171, 196–197, 202, 209–210, 256–257, 288, 299–300, 302–303, 307, 313, 333, 362, 372, 434, 443, 462, 466
emotional, 6, 21, 127, 130, 138, 154, 282, 344–346, 355, 357–358
empathy, 75, 206–207, 209–210, 330, 342, 358
employment, 42, 98, 124–125, 202–203, 286, 288, 315–316, 363, 367, 369, 373, 417, 446, 462, 465, 468, 472–474, 477
enterprises, 143, 253, 285, 333, 374–376, 378, 384, 391, 396, 422, 472, 475, 478
entrepreneurs, 113–115, 117, 120–123, 125–127, 223, 256, 285, 373, 379, 446, 461–463, 465–466, 468, 471–475, 477–478
entrepreneurship, 113–115, 117, 120, 122–123, 125–127, 256, 446, 463, 471–475, 477–478
environmental, 16, 19–21, 43, 53, 77, 90, 213–217, 220, 223–226, 261, 308, 312, 314, 339, 409, 416, 470

F
Facebook, 149, 153, 165–166, 168–169, 190, 193, 457, 460

H
hospitality, 39, 51–52, 59, 152–153, 158, 201–205, 207, 209–212, 276, 285, 289, 307–308, 311, 373, 378, 380–381, 391, 398, 447–448, 459
humankind, 213–215, 217–218, 225, 331, 356
hygiene, 75, 79, 90, 94, 108, 204, 208, 316–317, 330, 370, 378, 380, 390–391, 452

L
lifestyle, 57, 67–68, 72, 74, 87–89, 93, 95, 111, 123, 188, 190, 192–194, 316–317, 331, 452, 459, 470
loyalty, 38, 73–76, 207, 283, 351, 416
luxury, 18, 74, 76, 100, 102–103, 109–110, 354

M
manufacturing, 143, 225, 263, 288, 350, 455–456, 474
mapping, 84, 127, 141, 143, 196, 255, 306–308, 310, 314, 466
marketers, 27, 43, 49, 53, 63–64, 70, 75, 164–166, 168–169, 171, 213, 269–270, 430
migration, 27, 43, 49, 53, 63–64, 70, 75, 164–166, 168–169, 171, 213, 269–270, 430
mindfulness, 97–99, 101–105, 107, 109–111, 468
motivation, 6, 26, 50–52, 55, 57, 243, 335, 357, 406, 429, 432–433, 436

N
neobanking, 425–435, 437, 439–445, 447, 449

P
pandemic, 1–6, 8–9, 15–20, 23–26, 33, 37, 41–45, 48–49, 55–56, 58, 61, 64, 68–85, 87–89, 92, 95–99, 101–103, 106, 108, 110–111, 114, 117, 119, 123–124, 129–134, 136–137, 139–142, 144–146, 148–150, 152–154, 157, 160–163, 169, 181, 188, 194, 199, 201, 205–206, 209, 227–228, 239–244, 249–250, 252–256, 277, 287–290, 300–302, 304, 306–316, 318–345,

Index 481

354, 357, 359, 364, 371–372, 366–368, 411–414, 416–417, 421–422, 451–460, 462–463, 468, 475, 477
panic, 1–21, 38, 58, 72, 75–77, 134, 253–254, 289, 398
perceptions, 18, 35, 39, 47, 51–52, 73, 75–76, 87, 89–90, 124, 201, 205–206, 211, 229, 237, 364, 378, 391, 443
psychology, 17–21, 48, 50–51, 75, 77, 94, 111, 137–138, 236–237, 280–281, 285, 311, 348–350, 357, 359, 448

R

reliable, 24, 48, 107, 115, 167, 246, 279, 311, 416, 430, 443
resilience, 18, 73–74, 76, 95, 113, 139–141, 143, 145, 147, 149, 151, 153, 155–157, 159, 161, 210, 253, 254, 275–287, 290, 315–317, 319, 321, 323, 325, 327, 329, 344, 459, 478
resilient, 141, 151, 156, 255, 276, 331, 416, 420, 465
retail, 4, 16–17, 21, 24–25, 29, 31, 34–39, 52, 70, 72, 77, 97–101, 104, 106, 108–110, 148, 152, 172–174, 186, 211, 216, 223, 239–253, 255–257, 449, 454, 468
rick, 1, 3, 6–7, 9–10, 12, 15, 18–20, 80, 186, 194, 243, 251, 256, 340, 350, 359, 426, 478
rural, 10, 13, 30, 64, 81, 113–115, 117–119, 121–123, 125, 127, 302, 315–317, 330, 369, 373, 396, 463–464, 468, 472

S

sanitization, 35, 56, 63, 202, 204, 207–210
school, 1, 18, 23, 36, 41, 73, 84, 87, 139, 154, 163, 184, 192, 194, 213, 227, 239, 259, 287, 302, 309, 315, 331–332, 354–355, 359, 363, 425, 437, 459
selling, 100, 121, 146, 164, 184, 223, 241, 270–272, 367, 372, 378, 391
shopping, 5–6, 16–18, 25–26, 28, 34, 37, 55, 58, 67–72, 75, 79–80, 82–84, 98–99, 102, 104, 109, 139, 164–165, 171, 183–186, 188–194, 196–199, 211, 231, 254–255, 289, 332, 355, 428–429, 447, 454
spending, 2–4, 7–9, 16–17, 19–20, 25, 42, 56–57, 62, 64–65, 69, 71, 80, 83, 98, 173, 175, 183, 186, 188, 193, 196, 273, 366, 422, 473
spendthrift, 2–4, 7–10, 12, 14–15, 19
stakeholders, 122–123, 202, 210, 220, 287, 354, 374, 384, 394, 454, 473
sustainability, 65, 72, 84, 101, 106, 110, 124, 141, 151, 202, 220, 225, 254, 256, 276, 312, 359, 463, 469, 475–476
sustainable, 51, 90, 99, 108, 110, 213–219, 221, 223–225, 253, 255, 285, 371–372, 379, 449, 457, 461, 464, 469–470, 477

T

teachers, 155, 314, 353–360, 437, 458
teaching, 154, 160, 353–356, 358–359
teenagers, 183–189, 192, 194, 198–199
telemedicine, 114, 116, 118–127, 143, 146, 149, 158
tourism, 39, 42–44, 46–53, 108, 201–205, 207, 209, 211–212, 253, 276, 278, 282, 285–286, 288–289, 299–301, 307, 309, 311–313, 447–448, 459, 468

trade, 6, 80, 150, 152, 194, 215, 218, 242, 288–289, 299, 301, 309–310, 312–314, 333, 381, 394, 409, 419, 433, 464
transportation, 141, 223, 242, 253–254, 309–310, 381, 383, 474
travellers, 47, 50–51, 142, 146, 207–209, 320, 328–329

U
unconflicted, 2–4, 7–10, 12, 14–15
university, 1, 36, 41, 51, 67, 73, 79, 87, 96, 110, 129, 140, 163, 181, 213, 227, 239, 255–256, 259, 287, 302, 311, 315, 331, 349, 353, 361, 437, 446, 461, 471
utility, 27, 129, 132–133, 135–136, 288, 429

V
virtual, 75, 103, 114, 131–132, 148, 190, 207–208, 241, 301, 414, 417, 452, 456, 458–460, 465
virus, 2, 9, 15, 17, 19–21, 38–39, 42, 53, 67, 68, 74, 77, 81, 87, 91–94, 96, 99, 104, 109, 130–131, 137–142, 151, 155, 157–161, 204, 208, 210, 212, 236, 240, 254, 256, 288–289, 301, 307–312, 314, 330, 451
vital, 42, 45, 49, 56, 59, 101, 106, 123, 203, 244, 261, 263, 339, 378, 381, 395, 435, 448, 476

W
willingness, 227–231, 233, 235–237